Whose Detroit?

Whose Detroit?

Politics,

Labor,

and

Race in

a Modern

American

City

Heather Ann Thompson

CORNELL UNIVERSITY PRESS

Ithaca and London

First published 2001 by Cornell University Press
First printing Cornell Paperbacks 2004

Printed in the United States of America

Library of Congress Cataloging-in-Publication Data

Thompson, Heather Ann, 1963–
  Whose Detroit? : politics, labor, and race in a modern American city
/ Heather Ann Thompson.
   p. cm.
  Includes bibliographical references and index.
  ISBN 0-8014-3520-X (cloth : alk. paper)
  ISBN 0-8014-8884-2 (pbk.)
  1. Detroit (Mich.)—Politics and government—20th century.   2. Detroit (Mich.)—
Race relations.   3. Detroit (Mich.)—Economic conditions—20th century.   4. African
Americans—Michigan—Detroit—Social conditions—20th century.   5. African Americans—
Michigan—Detroit—Economic conditions—20th century.   6. Urban poor—Michigan—
Detroit—History—20th century.   7. Labor movement—Michigan—Detroit—History—20th
century.   8. African Americans—Migrations—History—20th century.   9. Rural-urban
migration—United States—History—20th century.   I. Title.
  F574.D457 T48 2001
  306'.09774'34—dc21
                                              2001003940

Cornell University Press strives to use environmentally responsible suppliers and materials to the fullest extent possible in the publishing of its books. Such materials include vegetable-based, low-VOC inks and acid-free papers that are recycled, totally chlorine-free, or partly composed of nonwood fibers. For further information, visit our website at www.cornell press. cornell.edu.

Cloth printing   10 9 8 7 6 5 4 3 2 1
Paperback printing   10 9 8 7 6 5 4 3 2 1

Contents

For Dillon, Wilder, and baby Ava,
my light, my warmth, my joy;
for Jon, my center;
and finally for Isabel, Keir, Logan,
and Zane, Detroit's future

Abbreviations

BEDC	Black Economic Development Conference
BSUF	Black Student United Front
CAP	Community Action Program
CCB	Citizen Complaint Bureau
CCR	Detroit Commission on Community Relations
CFP	Center for Forensic Psychiatry
DPD	Detroit Police Department
DPOA	Detroit Police Officers Association
DRUM	Dodge Revolutionary Union Movement
ELRUM	Eldon Revolutionary Union Movement
FAA	Foreman's Association of America
FORUM	Forge Revolutionary Union Movement
IEB	International Executive Board UAW
IS	International Socialists
JLC	Jewish Labor Committee
The League	The League of Revolutionary Black Workers
MAD	Mothers Alert Detroit
MCRC	Michigan Civil Rights Commission
MDT	Mayors Development Team
NAACP	National Association for the Advancement of Colored People
NALC	Negro American Labor Council
NCFDA	National Committee for Democratic Action
NCO	Northwest Community Organization
NEMA	North East Mothers Alert
NNLC	National Negro Labor Council
PASCC	Parents and Students for Community Control
RNA	Republic of New Africa
RUM	Revolutionary Union Movement
SEC	State of Emergency Committee
STRESS	Stop the Robberies Enjoy Safe Streets
TAP	Total Action against Poverty

Abbreviations

TULC	Trade Union Leadership Council
UAW	United Automobile Workers
UJC	United Justice Caucus
UNC	United National Caucus
WSU	Wayne State University
WAM	Workers Action Movement
WCO	West Central Organization

Abbreviations for Collections of the Walter P. Reuther Library of Labor and Urban Affairs, Detroit

AFTPC	American Federation of Teachers President's Collection
AHC	Arthur Hughes Collection
CCRC	Commission on Community Relations Collections
CMC	Kenneth Cockrel and Sheila Murphy Collection
DGC	Dan Georgakas Collection
DRUM	Detroit Revolutionary Union Movements Collection
EEC	Enid Eckstein Collection
EDC	Ernest Dillard Collection
IEB	UAW International Executive Board Collection
JLCC	Jewish Labor Committee Collection
JPCC	Jerome P. Cavanagh Collection
LWC	Leonard Woodcock Collection
NDC	New Detroit Collection
OPVPC	Wayne County AFL-CIO Office of the President and Vice President Collection
PSCCRDC	Public Schools Commission on Community Relations Division Collection
RAC	Richard Austin Collection
RGC	Ronald Glotta Collection
SAC	Simon Alpert Collection
STC	Shelton Tappes Collection
UAWFPC	United Auto Workers Fair Practices Collection
UCSPDC	United Community Services Planning Department Collection
UCSSRC	United Community Services Studies and Reports Collection
WPRC	Walter P. Reuther Collection
YBF	Young Biographical File

Introduction

Reassessing the Fate of Postwar

Cities, Politics, and Labor

He was arbitrarily fired. He couldn't believe it. He didn't beg The Man but he asked him rather specifically, "What do you mean fired? Just for asking about my job?" And The Man said, "That's right. You don't ask you do what you're told. You're fired!" The brother went out and he got his gun and he did some firing. Many people thought this was a deplorable situation. I don't; I think it practical, because we have forewarned that corporation.[1]

In the wee hours of July 23, 1967, urbanites took to the streets of Detroit in an uprising that stunned the nation. For days, Detroit's poorest neighborhoods burned, and virtually overnight the city came to symbolize America's inability to solve vexing problems of race and poverty. Almost exactly three years later, a thirty-five-year-old African American autoworker named James Johnson Jr. walked into the Detroit auto plant where he worked and proceeded to shoot and kill two foremen and one die setter in retaliation for numerous racially based offenses that he believed he had long endured. These murders brought the Motor City into the national spotlight once again.[2]

Johnson's actions on July 15, 1970, might have been quickly forgotten after a brief spate of media attention; on the surface they were no different from other violent acts committed before and after in Detroit. But these particular killings touched a nerve in the city as few others had. Even though the fires of the 1967 rebellion had long been extinguished, to civic and labor leaders seeking to rebuild Lyndon B. Johnson's Great Society in Detroit, James Johnson's sensational act signified that black Detroiters had regained little confidence in liberal programs for eradicating racial discrimination in *the city or the plants. Indeed, to much of the city's black community, John-son's act seemed one of intense frustration. It was a clear warning to city and labor leaders that, as long as conditions for Detroit's African Americans re-mained intolerable, violence was inevitable. To many in the city's white neighborhoods, on the other hand, Johnson's violence seemed simply to sub-stantiate a long-held suspicion that urban blacks were determined to destroy the city and its workplaces. And to still other Motor City residents—both black and white revolutionaries seeking a fundamental overhaul of civic and labor relations—Johnson's act was politically symbolic and worthy of Che Guevara or Mao Tse-tung.*

That a desperate figure like Johnson should be so familiar by the early 1970s illustrates how extraordinarily complex both race relations and poli-tics had become in Detroit since World War II. The bitter disagreement about what lessons might be learned from Johnson's killing spree signifies that the Motor City and its auto plants remained in the grips of a severe racial and political crisis long after the bloody days of July 1967. Detroit's future was still uncertain.

While Johnson is clearly not an Everyman, his participation in the Second Great Migration to Detroit during the 1950s, as well as his experiences in Detroit's auto plants, courtrooms, and city streets during the 1960s and 1970s, were certainly understood by many Motor City residents and plant workers. Johnson's story is emblematic of the complexity that was Detroit and the urban North writ large between 1945 and 1985. As such, it is wo-ven throughout this book.[3]

By 1970, the soulful sounds of Marvin Gaye's "Heard It through the Grapevine" and Diana Ross's "Ain't No Mountain High Enough" filtered from the radios of cars and homes across the United States. But while many Americans might have related to the tales of heartbreak and romance told in these Motown tunes, such popular ballads struck an even deeper chord with Detroit's listeners. Indeed, by 1970, the Motor City grapevine was buzzing with ideas for creating a completely new and different urban center, one in which the seemingly insurmountable mountain of problems faced by Detroit since World War II might finally be scaled. Out of the tumultuous 1960s, De-troit had generated powerful hopes for an urban transformation. Still, there was by no means a consensus about the future.

By 1970, African American Detroiters were more determined than ever to make their city a metropolis in which they at last could enjoy the promised, but long delayed, equality of opportunity. Simultaneously, many white city residents were just as determined to return to the "halcyon days" preceding World War II, when their position of dominance seemed far more secure. Significantly, however, these visions of a different Detroit were fragmented along political as well as racial lines. In 1970, even as liberalism was declin-ing as a force in national politics, many Detroiters, both black and white,

James Johnson Jr. at his arraignment for murder, July 16, 1970. *Corbis*.

yearned for the Great Society to triumph in the Motor City. There were yet others, also both black and white, who shared a far more revolutionary dream. With still other residents, overwhelmingly white, advocating conservative law-and-order policy for the future city, Detroit in the early 1970s reflected how extraordinarily complex both race and politics had become in the United States since 1945.

Because these contradictory visions had emerged with such force by the late 1960s, for many years the long-term fate of this major American city remained unpredictable. In fact, well into the early 1970s it was far from clear whether this city would exist as a white-dominated center of racial segregation and political conservatism, a place where Great Society liberals had finally achieved both integration and prosperity, an island of black nationalist and white leftist revolution, or an oasis of opportunity for the black middle class. Because each side of Detroit's multifaceted political constituency believed so firmly in its vision of the future, the Motor City as well as its motor plants became virtual war zones between 1967 and 1973.

This book chronicles the social, economic, and political origins and conditions of this crisis-ridden period, during which Detroit's self-appointed architects drew their detailed blueprints for the future city and its workplaces and fought tirelessly to implement their ideas. In light of the complex political and racial alliances that fueled this urban and labor war at home—and

3

the mixed outcomes of its bitterly fought battles—this book argues more broadly for rethinking our received wisdom about the fate of postwar American cities, liberal politics, and the U.S. labor movement.

* * * *

Because America's inner cities and its national political climate have undergone such a dramatic transformation since World War II, and because the American labor movement as well has changed, scholars have recently questioned exactly how the past became such a different present. What had occurred in previous decades to cause America's inner cities to degenerate from centers of prosperity, growth, and vibrancy into impoverished, shrinking, and decaying postindustrial wastelands by the 1980s? What had happened to the heady days of the Great Society, in which politicians and their constituents could imagine, and thus were willing to fund, a better world—a world in which poverty and discrimination would be unknown? Indeed, how had Americans become so hostile to the progressive dreams that they had once held dear, and so willing to embrace the moral, racial, and fiscal conservatism of the Reagan Right? And, finally, how did the great industrial labor movement of the 1930s, which had played such a pivotal role in shaping the economic and social order during World War II, become such a pale reflection of its former self by the 1980s?

The scholarly attempts to make sense of cities, politics, and labor after 1980 have clearly provided much valuable insight into earlier postwar decades. A literature exists, for example, that delves into the state of urban centers during the 1960s, and it allows one to appreciate just how disenchanted many urban whites had in fact become with a civil rights and War on Poverty–informed liberalism. It demonstrates as well that the black militants of the decade, far from being irrelevant, were key players in the production of postwar politics.[4] Another body of work traces the roots of urban and political crisis back to the 1950s, and it is more valuable still. By highlighting the contentious racial politics that antedated the Great Society, it goes further toward explaining why many urban whites became so hostile to civil rights a decade later, and also why poor inner-city residents engaged in civic uprisings.[5] And by showing that the ongoing process of deindustrialization actually began in the 1950s, this scholarship has provided a more nuanced interpretation of such important postwar phenomena as white flight and union decline than has the scholarship that focuses exclusively on the tumultuous years of the Great Society. Finally, labor scholars have also shed much-needed light on the tremendous odds that the American working class has faced in its battle to be heard, and stay unionized, in every decade after World War II.

But significantly, the very questions that initiated new scholarly examinations of America's recent past are themselves heavily laden with certain problematic assumptions about the character of cities, politics, and labor circa 1980. One key assumption is that the most startling and important fact about American inner cities by the 1980s was that whites had completely abandoned them. Further, when urban centers lost their white residents, they became largely irrelevant social and political entities. Another key premise underlying many new examinations of the postwar period is that the liberal agenda of the Great Society had been fully repudiated in the United States by the 1980s. With so many Americans joining the ranks of the Republican party by that decade, liberalism was surely dead. And finally, a powerful assumption flourishes that the American labor movement's desperate situation by 1980, while notable, was largely unavoidable.

In fact, the 1980s was a far more complex decade than scholars have assumed. It is undeniable that when whites left America's inner cities, many of them became centers of vast poverty and social malaise. It is also the case, however, that by that decade a great many cities had become places where African Americans, and more specifically the black middle class, finally could experience real social, economic, and political opportunity. Similarly, while American liberalism appears to have collapsed by 1980, this was only partially so. Scores of white urbanites did abandon the tenets of Kennedy-Johnson liberalism during the mid-to-late 1970s. This same decade, however, also saw the most dramatic rise of black liberal political power that has occurred in the entire twentieth century. Indeed, the principles as well as practices of 1960s-style liberalism were embraced, championed, and even expanded on in numerous major U.S. cities that came under African American political control in the 1970s.[6] And finally, while the American labor movement was clearly in serious trouble by 1980, its dramatic decline was not inevitable. Labor's fate was not decided, as some have suggested, by its move toward greater bureaucratization during the 1930s, nor by its anticommunism and racial conservatism during the 1940s and 1950s. Neither was labor merely a passive victim of economic circumstance in the decades that followed.[7] Key choices that union leaders themselves made, long after the 1950s had passed, played a pivotal role in undermining their own power by the time that corporations initiated their most vicious anti-labor initiatives during the Reagan Era.[8]

The failure to recognize the full complexity of American urban centers and politics during the 1980s, as well as the internal genesis of labor movement decline by that decade, has vast implications for the story told and not told by recent scholars of the postwar period. Efforts to explain the dramatic white exodus from inner cities, and their simultaneous rejection of postwar liberalism, for example, have led to an overemphasis on the American whites hostile to both African Americans and liberalism in preceding decades. Of course, not every white urbanite in the 1950s, the 1960s, or the 1970s and 1980s opposed racial equality or rejected the premises of liberalism. Likewise, while urban blacks were too often victimized by racist whites, they of course fought back. Indeed, the determined efforts of urban blacks to achieve greater racial equality, political representation, and economic op-

portunity from 1945 onward, in combination with the effective activism of
urban whites sympathetic to civil rights and hostile to political conservatism,
suggests that when white racial conservatives eventually abandoned inner
cities, they did so as losers—not victors—of the intense war for urban control that had raged since World War II. Indeed it was the African American
middle class, supported by hopeful poor and working class blacks as well as
by more than a few white progressives that had triumphed in this drawn out
civic conflict. Having taken electoral control of numerous urban centers in
the 1970s, this black middle class not only sought to rebuild many conflict-
weary cities, it sought to resurrect them along self-consciously liberal lines.
By the 1980s, America's inner cities still were very much alive, and many remained islands of liberal vision, perhaps dampened but hardly washed away
by the vast sea of conservatism swirling around them.

If sounding the death knell for American inner cities and liberalism too
precipitously has obscured much about the postwar period, so have popular
assumptions about why the American labor movement suffered such losses
by the 1980s. To be sure, once unions traded in community-based activism
for more hierarchical modes for conducting labor relations in the 1930s,
worker militancy was constrained. And clearly the internal union purges of
the 1940s and 1950s sapped union strength as well. It is also undeniably the
case that American workers and the unions that represented them were buf-
feted by corporate and market forces beyond their control throughout the
postwar period. Yet during key battles that took place between unions and
companies, and internally, during the 1960s and 1970s—over shop floor
racism, working conditions, and worker representation—union leaders
themselves eliminated still-viable prospects for shaping workers' destiny.
The proposition that labor's future was doomed virtually from the moment
that it gained legal standing, or that its fate at the hands of corporate America in the 1980s was essentially inevitable, has too easily absolved the movement and its officers of very real responsibility for their own plight.

And if the state of cities and politics, as well as the fate of the labor movement, by the 1980s was more complicated than some have assumed it to be,
so was the postwar period as a whole. American history has never been simply black versus white, mainly because for every racial divide, there have always been political bridges linking whites to African Americans. In every
postwar decade, black and white Americans gravitated not just to the middle and the right of the ideological spectrum but also to the left. And, as the
story of cities such as Detroit demonstrate, the Left, Right, and Center
equally shaped the contours of what cities, politics, and the labor movement
became by the 1980s.

In fact Detroit is a fine place to test such abstract claims about the com-
plexities of postwar cities, politics, and labor. Not only is Detroit one of
America's largest cities; it is also home to the American auto industry and a
major industrial union, the United Automobile Workers (UAW). Through-

out the postwar period, Detroit's auto industry set trends for management strategy across the nation, just as the UAW set the bargaining agenda for scores of other American unions. The massive wartime and postwar Second Great Migration and the dramatic transformation of civic and workplace life that it touched off was as important in Detroit as in any other northern city. Like the rest of the urban North, Detroit attempted to come to terms with its new biracial character during the 1950s and, as a result of failing to do this, became a hotbed of political activism in the 1960s for George Wallace supporters, Great Society liberals, black nationalists, and black and white revolutionaries alike. Detroit—arguably more than cities usually thought to epitomize the radical 1960s, such as Berkeley—witnessed militant left-wing activism in virtually every realm of civic and labor life. Detroit experienced the same intense conflicts over housing, education, and law and order as those that raged nationally during this decade, but it also exploded in countless battles at the point of production. And like most northern urban centers in the postwar period, Detroit endured the deleterious effects of both white flight and deindustrialization.

It is fair to say that Detroit has held symbolic meaning for America in every decade since World War II. In the 1940s, this city represented America's vision of itself as an "arsenal of democracy." In the 1950s, it exemplified the best of postwar American consumerism and productivity; in the 1960s, it was deemed a "model" Great Society city; in the 1970s, it was called the "murder capital" of the then-troubled country; and by the 1980s, it represented the worst of what America had become after decades of social and political turmoil.

The Motor City has also been time and again connected to America's northern urban and labor experience by the historic figures that passed through it, and the many famous and infamous events that it experienced. The nation witnessed one of its most brutal cases of hostility to neighborhood integration when Detroit residents attempted to prevent Dr. Ossian Sweet from moving into a white neighborhood in 1925. Dr. Sweet found a potent defender in famed attorney Clarence Darrow. In the 1930s, Detroit saw the founding of the Nation of Islam as well as America's leading industrial union, the UAW. In 1943, Detroit experienced the nation's worst race riot to date, but it also made national headlines as home to the world's most famous black boxer, Joe Louis. During World War II, renowned black Marxist C. L. R. James made Detroit a base for his intellectual and political activities, while Detroit's auto industry bolstered America's military efforts abroad. In the 1950s, such nationally known figures as Paul Robeson, W. E. B. Du Bois, Martin Luther King Jr., Malcolm X, Diana Ross, Stevie Wonder, Marvin Gaye, and Berry Gordy either came from or lived for a time in the Motor City; some worked for a time in Detroit's auto plants as well. By the 1960s, Detroit became known around the world as "Motown," after the recording label, and Detroit's sound became the "Sound of Young America."

When Dr. King led a civil rights procession down Detroit's Woodward Avenue in June 1963, America got a preview of the historic March on Washington. During the 1970s, when the international oil crisis began, the gas-guzzling, hulking automobiles of Detroit were routinely featured in national news footage, either as they rolled off of local assembly lines or sat idling in gas station lines across the country. In 1980, Detroit held the dubious distinction of being the city chosen by the Republican party to hold its national convention that nominated presidential candidate Ronald Reagan.

The postwar history of Detroit—both as "Every City" and as a fascinating urban center in its own right—is clearly a tale worth telling.[9] By excavating the history of inner-city Detroit and its labor movement, and by reexamining their respective fates as the twentieth century neared its close, this book demonstrates the following central claims: America's urban centers did not merely waste away by the 1980s; political tensions among radicals, conservatives, and liberals after World War II shaped urban America as surely as did racial clashes; and finally the U.S. labor movement always had more power over its destiny than its leaders imagined.

Even more broadly, this study calls attention to the fact that when the urban North became a biracial society after the Second World War, it quickly became embroiled in the same political tensions and battles that the South had experienced for generations in labor and civic relations. And just as social and political crisis in the South had always been the product of vision rather than stagnation, so was the crisis-filled period in the North between 1967 and 1973 indicative of promise, not inevitable collapse. Given their brutality and high body counts, the battles to create a more just and equitable biracial South often yielded victories that were most costly to African Americans. The urban North's struggle to come to terms with its biracial character proved to be equally vicious, and its African American victories as qualified and high-priced. But we do not see the major defeats suffered by white racial conservatives in the South as signaling that region's demise. Neither should we view the ability of northern blacks to beat back the forces of white racial conservatism where they lived or their successful appropriation of the political agenda of white racial progressives as an unmitigated disaster heralding urban decay. By taking more seriously the possibilities embedded in postwar urban turmoil, we find that determination—not decline or decay—best characterizes our nation's cities.

1: Beyond Racial Polarization

Political Complexity in the City and Labor

Movement of the 1950s

I came looking to see if I could better my living conditions. I wanted to get schooling in a better system than Mississippi. . . . I wanted just to be able to make a decent living. Earn a decent wage which you could not do in Mississippi.

—Testimony of James Johnson Jr., May 11, 1971[1]

James Johnson Jr. was born on May 28, 1934, in Starkville, Mississippi, to twenty-year-old James Johnson Sr. and fifteen-year-old Eleanor "Edna" Hudson.[2] For these young parents, the grinding poverty that had come as such a shock to many northerners in the 1930s was nothing new. From the moment that each was physically able, they had labored as sharecroppers on an 1,800-acre estate owned by the family of ex-Confederate officer Hubbard Turner Saunders. And although they were delighted by the birth of James Junior, trying to provide for the new family unit only made James and Edna's lives more difficult.[3]

Despite their economic hardships, the Johnsons enjoyed an active social life that revolved around the Josey Creek School and the Josey Creek Missionary Baptist Church. Both school and church were located about a mile away on Highway 82 leading into Starkville. In 1944, the army drafted James Senior. While he was stationed in Missouri and in North Carolina, James Senior sent a monthly military paycheck of $140 to Edna. Her goal, in turn, was to save enough to buy a home for the family far from the property where they labored. About a year after James Senior came home, and right after the birth of daughter Marva,[4] Edna and James Senior finally bought an $800 house with the army checks that Edna had saved.[5] Edna

9

and James Senior's new home was a little wooden "shotgun shack." The house was not sealed, but Edna and James Senior put up weather-stripping to make it warmer. They had a kitchen and two bedrooms now, and although they had no running water, at least there was a well in the backyard.[6]

James Junior was eleven when his parents became homeowners, and yet this move had not made his life much better. James Junior's childhood experiences of working in the fields, attending school, and participating in religious revivals may have been typical, he was by no means a typical child. By the age of twelve, he was unusually terrified of violence, experienced blackouts, suffered hallucinations, and felt intense insecurity around white people. When James was only nine, he had witnessed the gruesome lynching of his cousin Maggie Foster Taylor's brother, Henry, on Highway 82. On June 13, 1943, a mob of whites killed Henry, allegedly for being in love with a white girl. It was after this brutal attack that James went into "a nervous rage" and "heard voices," and this is when his nightmares began.[7] By the time he was thirteen, James had such a hard time sleeping and such a nervous stomach that his mother took him to see Dr. Hunter Ledbetter Scales. The doctor gave him a "Pepto-Bismol-like" medication, and James continued to see him about twice a month. James still woke up screaming and sweating at night, however, and he was still terrified of whites.[8]

James Junior's emotional troubles were further exacerbated by the fact that, throughout his childhood, his father was often verbally and physically abusive to his mother.[9] Indeed, even though they went on to have three more children, over time tensions between Edna and James Senior escalated. Seeking a better life for the family, James Senior decided to go to Michigan to search for a job.[10] When a better position never materialized, James Senior eventually came back to Mississippi, where he got a job as a janitor at Mississippi State University.[11] Because of the strain of uneven employment and the already rocky nature of their relationship, James Senior and Edna divorced soon after his return.

After the divorce, Edna began a new life for herself and her children by taking a job cleaning the house of a white woman, Obera Powell.[12] Edna walked five miles to her job, and the fact that she had to work so far away from home placed a new strain on the family.[13] Although James managed to keep up his attendance first at the Oktibbeha County Training School and then Maben High School, he continued to have terrible nightmares. Clearly, the years of severe economic deprivation, as well as the violence at home and the lynching of Henry Foster in 1943, had scarred James deeply. Shortly after James began high school, he began to think about moving north to find a good job, to flee the poverty and racism of the South, and, he hoped, to escape his own personal demons. He finished one term at Maben High School and then decided to move to Detroit in April of 1953.[14]

When Johnson arrived in the Motor City, housing was difficult to come by, so he went to live with his aunt and uncle, Ora and Charlie Johnson, who *had migrated there in 1942.*[15] *After moving in, James joined the Calvary Baptist Church, decided to finish high school, and got two jobs so that he could pay rent to his relatives and send some money home. Almost immediately, however, he was drafted into the army. When James left Detroit in December 1956, he arranged for his brother L.A. to take one of his jobs as a kitchen helper at St. Joseph's Hospital.*

James was stationed in Fort Jackson, South Carolina, until 1957, and during this time his nervous condition worsened dramatically. His deep-seated fear of whites was only exacerbated in the army, where almost all of the authority figures were white Eventually, recurring emotional problems caused army doctors to recommend his early release. After his discharge, James returned to Detroit and went back to work at the Selfridge Air Force Base, this time as a stock helper. After a few years, James quit the job at the base and remained unemployed for about six months.[16] *Eventually, he began working with his aunt for a white family in the wealthy suburb of Bloomfield Hills. He did yard work and window-washing for several months, but then he quit this seasonal job to take a full-time position as a janitor in a local restaurant, the Scotch and Sirloin.*[17] *With a higher-paying job, Johnson's faith in his decision to move to the North was renewed. Like many recent migrants to the Motor City, he optimistically believed that life in Detroit in the coming years was indeed going to be better than it ever could have been in the South.*

James Johnson Jr. was a constituent of one of the United States' largest demographic transformations of the twentieth century—the Second Great Migration. The disappointments that Johnson faced after he arrived in Detroit mirrored those of many other recent migrants to the Motor City. But Johnson's abiding faith that, despite adversity and disappointment, he one day would find greater opportunity in the North was also held by scores of African Americans new to Detroit after World War II.

The sheer magnitude of the Second Migration certainly unsettled many northern white urbanites. But to the utter dismay of Detroit's hopeful migrant black community, such white unease often translated into vicious violence against them, just as it had in the South. And yet, while brutal and daily white-perpetrated racial violence was certainly one hallmark of Detroit in the 1950s, white racial conservatives were neither the only nor most powerful group trying to determine Detroit's postwar character. First, very real political differences among whites routinely thwarted every white attempt to unify along racial lines. Indeed, for every group of white racial and political conservatives in Detroit, there were other whites who championed civil rights as well as a liberal, if not a leftist, political agenda for the city. Second, but of no less importance, despite the ugly and relentless white-on-black violence that took place in the Motor City, Detroit's African Americans were never passive victims. They, too, became politicized in complex ways during the 1950s and actively sought to shape their urban destiny. In short, because every racial tension visited upon Detroit was immeasurably complicated by contending political visions of how the new biracial metropolis should evolve, and because Detroit's African Americans and progressive whites actually began to unite against racial injustice and political conservatism as the 1950s progressed, this decade would leave a legacy of possibility, not merely polarization, for the Detroiters of the 1960s to reckon with.

* * * *

Between 1910 and 1966, the number of African Americans living outside the South rose from 800,800 to 9.7 million—an eleven-fold increase.[18] The most concentrated movement occurred during World Wars I and II, as the labor markets of the northern cities opened up to blacks.[19] Of the 6.5 million African Americans who moved from the rural South to the urban North between 1910 and 1970, 5.5 million migrated after 1940.[20]

Wartime jobs are what lured southern African Americans like James Johnson's father to the North. Changes in the southern labor market soon became an equally important incentive to move. The introduction of cotton-picking machinery, for example, signaled the demise of the labor-intensive sharecropping system.[21] A new reliance on chemical herbicides also contributed to what has been called a general "black disengagement from southern agriculture," as did landowners' resistance to paying farm laborers a minimum wage.[22] As a result of all these factors, 1,597,000 southern African Americans migrated to the North between 1940 and 1950, and another 1,457,000 migrated between 1950 and 1960.[23] By 1966, the proportion of American blacks living in the South had dropped to 55 percent.[24] In Johnson's home state of Mississippi alone, the percentage dropped well below that.[25]

African Americans who left the South during the 1940s and 1950s headed for a number of major northern cities, including Chicago, St. Louis, Cleveland, New York, and also Detroit.[26] Detroit in particular attracted thousands of men and women hungry for a decent wage, since auto magnate Henry Ford enjoyed a national reputation as the black man's friend, willing to employ him when others would not.[27] As testimony to the magnitude of postwar southern migration to the Motor City, by 1970, most black Detroiters had direct family ties to Arkansas, Mississippi, Louisiana, Georgia, and the Carolinas.[28] And, as a result of this massive migration, African Americans fundamentally altered the city's geography, dramatically recomposed its working class, and unwittingly unsettled both the civic and labor order.

African Americans, of course, had not migrated to an empty city. Since the late 1800s, Detroit had been a magnet for the world's immigrants, who found the promise of an auto industry job, and eventually a decent union wage, a powerful enticement. Postwar Detroit was as ethnically diverse as any major northern city, with 81,383 migrants from Canada, 59,343 from

Poland, 29,908 from Italy, 22,868 from Germany, 26,102 from England and Wales, and 21,976 from Russia.[29] These and immigrants from other countries greatly cherished their ethnic individuality. Despite their ethnic differences and the fact that political differences had also divided them during the not-so-distant 1930s, Detroit's ethnic whites came out of World War II optimistic that the postwar period would be characterized by political unity that, in turn, would facilitate social stability and economic security. The moment that hostilities ceased abroad, however, political tensions at home reerupted with a vengeance.

Detroiters were not likely to forget the political clashes in their city before World War II. During the depression, and especially during Franklin D. Roosevelt's First New Deal, Detroit had experienced some of the nation's most severe political fragmentation and worst social upheaval. The depression hit the Motor City hard, and in its wake, communists, socialists, right-wing populists, and left- as well as right-leaning liberals vied for political control.[30] But though Detroiters appeared irreparably divided during this period, in fact a cross-fertilization of their seemingly incompatible agendas was taking place. For example, the UAW, which became a key supporter of the New Deal, largely succeeded in its battle for industrywide recognition because of the agitation and activism of communists and socialists in its midst. Likewise, liberal Democratic party support of union recognition made FDR the electoral choice of many Motor City residents who had previously been suspicious of him. And, of course, during FDR's first term in office the threat posed by both conservative demagogues and Communist party organizers in cities like Detroit led the president to adopt far more aggressive measures for improving life in America during his second term.[31]

Out of this heady political mix that was the 1930s came the Second New Deal. Not surprisingly, FDR's affirmation of a worker's right to join a union, as well as his popular welfare and work initiatives, went a long way toward dissipating political discord in Detroit. And because Detroiters seemed so willing to put aside their political differences for the war effort thereafter, a New Deal consensus appeared to reign. Certainly, political consensus, even during wartime, only ran so deep. Each of FDR's Second New Deal initiatives generated much political controversy, and, of course, labor conflict surfaced repeatedly in countless wartime work stoppages despite the labor movement's "No Strike Pledge" to industry and government alike. Compared with the political front of the pre–Second New Deal period, however, that of the war years was remarkably calm.

As soon as Detroiters came home from the battlefronts of Europe and the Pacific and began converting their auto plants to peacetime production, it became clear that any wartime political unity had in fact been fleeting. Political fragmentation once again became a Detroit hallmark. Certainly the political debate had shifted markedly from what it was in the 1930s, primarily because the Communist party's erratic positions on the war had undermined much of the Left's support base, and also because the programs of the Second New Deal had stolen the thunder of the city's right-wing populists. With the power of both the far Right and the far Left in Detroit on the wane during the war, immediately thereafter political debates largely took place within the framework of New Deal liberalism. This fact, however, did not ensure greater civic harmony. Indeed, from 1945 to 1959, those in the New Deal coalition who saw themselves as more conservative regarding fiscal as well as domestic and foreign policy continually fought those New Dealers more progressive vis-à-vis these same policies for the right to shape the new postwar city and labor movement in their image.

Detroit's postwar political discord is clearly reflected in the mayoral elections of 1945 and 1949, as well as in the bitter factional fighting that came to polarize the city's largest labor union, the UAW, between 1946 and 1947. In 1945, mayoral candidate Richard Frankensteen, a left-of-center liberal who supported racial equality as well as a militant posture for the labor movement, faced off against a politician noticeably to his right named Edward Jefferies. Indicating that a quite conservative pall had fallen over Detroit immediately after the war, it was Jefferies who won that year. But indicative as well of how politically fractured white voters had become in this same period, the bitter 1945 election had been close.

Encouraged by the closeness of the race, Frankensteen decided to run against Jefferies once again in 1949. This time, however, an even more conservative candidate, Albert Cobo, as well as another left-liberal contender, George Edwards, entered the race. The candidates in the 1949 mayoral election spanned the political spectrum and yet once again it was the most right-leaning candidate, Cobo, who emerged victorious. Both Jefferies and Cobo won their offices after embracing the anti-Communist rhetoric of the cold war.[32] Given both Frankensteen's and Edwards's left-of-center position in the New Deal coalition, as well as the fact that Frankensteen openly had opposed anti-Communist purging in the UAW and Edwards had once been a member of the Socialist party, their opponents had much fuel to fire up voter suspicions that these men were "subversive." Campaign literature from both the Jefferies and Cobo camps accused Frankensteen and Edwards, respectively, of being too "Pro-Negro."[33] Considering that blacks were becoming a larger percentage of the Detroit population, this accusation struck a particular chord among those hostile to this demographic transformation. During the 1945 election, white neighborhoods were mysteriously flooded with cards claiming that a vote for Frankensteen was "a blow to White Exclusive neighborhoods."[34] And the discrediting of Edwards's racial progressivism in the 1949 election was even more explicit.[35] But while left-of-center liberals had clearly suffered a major defeat in the 1945 and 1949 elections, their narrow losses indicate that numerous Detroiters still held a progressive vision for the city and thus that urban conservatives were unlikely to rule indefinitely.

A similar conflict plagued Detroit's labor movement during this period. Given its genesis, the political spectrum of the UAW was far to the left of that in the city proper, but, nevertheless, ideological battles in the labor arena were intense.[36] Before World War II, communists and militant socialists had enjoyed enormous power in the UAW, particularly because their often aggressive and uncompromising efforts had secured union recognition. And even though the Communist party's earlier ideological and strategic waffling vis-à-vis the war effort had cost it credibility in the labor movement just as it had in the city, during and after the war there was still a left-of-center force to be reckoned with in the UAW. Indeed, in 1942, left-leaning UAW leaders openly supported blacks' efforts to move, amidst much controversy, into a new housing project in the city. And when whites openly attacked blacks during an infamous riot in 1943, the UAW's left-of-center president, R. J. Thomas, "mercilessly criticized the conduct of the mayor and police . . . and mobilized union stewards to end the violence."[37]

But the left-of-center voices in Detroit's biggest union met with serious internal resistance during these years. Take, for example, the motion introduced by black union member Shelton Tappes to get a black man on the International Executive Board of the UAW during the union's 1943 convention. Whereas Tappes's effort was supported by UAW leaders George Addes and Richard Frankensteen, his motion failed after other key UAW figures, most notably Walter Reuther, opposed it.[38] Thus, when the war came to an end, the question of whether the UAW's more progressive or more conservative forces would guide this union into the 1950s was uncertain.

During a bitter factional fight for control of the UAW in 1946–47, this question was decided, at least on the surface. The left wing of the UAW suffered as major a setback in this struggle, as had the city's left-of-center political forces. Indeed, in 1946–47, a left-center caucus comprised of communists, non-communist leftists, and progressive New Dealers and led by Thomas and Addes engaged in numerous bitter battles with a right-center caucus comprised of former socialists, New Deal stalwarts, and conservative Catholic trade unionists.[39] And in 1947, the head of the right-center group, Reuther, successfully took control of the 800,000-member UAW. Just as the city's mayoral victors had tarred their opponents with the brush of "communism," so had the right-center caucus in the UAW used unsavory red-baiting tactics to ensure its triumph. Also as in the city, however, the defeat of left-center forces in the UAW did not mean that political consensus was now on the horizon.[40] Significantly, while Reuther had defeated Thomas for the UAW presidency in 1946, his "margin of victory consisted of only 124 votes of over 8700 cast," indicating that not everyone in the UAW saw the future of the union as he did.[41] Indeed worker actions in the 1950s and thereafter would prove that a left vision of postwar labor relations was not abandoned when the Reuther caucus took over.

Within this context of a politically fragmented white community and the cold war–fueled ascendancy of the white racial and political conservatives in both the Motor City and its motor plants, the Second Great Migration of southern blacks took place. As the brutal attacks by working-class whites on poor blacks attempting to move into the Sojourner Truth housing development in 1942 and the grisly riot of 1943 make clear, white racial conservatism played a visible role in postmigration Detroit.[42] As blacks came to comprise an ever-greater percentage of Detroit's population, and as they grew increasingly insistent on equal treatment and access to civic resources, conservative whites worried greatly about their future. Believing that all Detroiters were feeling the pinch of a tight postwar housing market and the uncertainty of the postwar economy to an equal degree, such whites were not sympathetic to the plight of city blacks.[43] Thus, as the numbers of blacks in Detroit increased, racial conflict escalated.

As historian Thomas Sugrue has shown, the issue of access to housing most split city residents along racial lines after the war and into the 1950s.[44] Between 1950 and 1960, Detroit had gained 183,183 African Americans, and this group primarily resided in areas known as the Black Bottom and Paradise Valley—a thirty-block district that originally had been home to the city's Jewish population. Life for these transplanted southerners was both exhilarating and exceedingly difficult. On the one hand, they made Paradise Valley a cultural Mecca of music, dance, poetry, and painting. There, blacks socialized in the Chesterfield Lounge, the Flame Bar, and the Forest Club, each of which hosted some of the country's finest African American entertainers, such as Josephine Baker, Lionel Hampton, Sarah Vaughn, and Nat King Cole.[45] On the other hand, the average lifespan for African Americans living in Paradise Valley fell far below that of Detroit's whites, partly because their death rate from pneumonia was three times higher and the percentage of blacks with tuberculosis was 71.5 percent higher as well.[46] From the earliest days of the migration, the health statistics in Detroit's black neighborhoods were so dire that city officials could not help but notice.[47] Yet because city officials did so little to change the situation, conditions only worsened with time. In 1950, the United Community Services found that in the all-black subcommunities of Cadillac, John R., Mt. Elliot, Fort, Michigan, and Cass, most dwellings were still in extremely poor condition, severe overcrowding still existed, and there was still much death from disease.[48]

Of course, not every migrant endured such onerous conditions, and not every African American new to Detroit experienced deprivation or difficulty to an equal degree. Some, such as the migrant father of Detroiter Bernard Odell, owned small businesses.[49] Others, such as Charles Diggs Sr., became politicians, and still others, like Shelton Tappes and Hodges Mason, became important figures in the UAW.[50] Clearly, the Black Bottom was as diverse in terms of class as it was isolated by race. No matter what their class background, however, it was extremely difficult for African Americans of any status or means to move out of unhealthy and impoverished neighborhoods, particularly since the Detroit Housing Commission had formally adopted a policy of residential segregation in the riot year of 1943.[51]

Despite both the legal and social mandates for segregated housing, however, Detroit's African American population eventually began to seek housing outside of the lower East Side. According to scholar June Manning Thomas, in 1952 the black poor's need for shelter meant that there were 5,226 black families on the city's waiting list for public housing, and these African Americans had to find a place to live with or without the help of government officials or the goodwill of white Detroiters.[52] Indeed, the city's racially conservative whites had no intention of sharing Detroit's notoriously limited housing stock. Too often they greeted black attempts to move out of the Black Bottom with brutal violence. In 1955, Detroit's Commission on Community Relations (CCR) noted that the most vicious housing violence was erupting in city neighborhoods that were "on the periphery of the area most heavily populated by Negroes," because "there is a strong feeling in this 'border' area that it is being 'invaded' by colored people."[53] The CCR remarked further that "the one outstanding fact here is that mass intimidation is an important part of these cases." In one such case cited by the CCR, whites held two mass organizing meetings; one was attended by 600–800 people, the other by about 1500 people.[54]

Such white opposition to black residential mobility was expressed politically as well as physically. For example, whites' demand that the city build more white housing set in motion urban renewal projects that quickly raised the specter of housing blacks in ways that these very whites strongly opposed. At the behest of his white constituents, for example, Mayor Jefferies condemned 129 acres of inhabited land on Detroit's all-black lower East Side in November 1946 to construct new housing. While his white constituents were delighted, they also felt it necessary to clarify their solid opposition to erecting any public housing in this area. Quite unexpectedly Jefferies's major slum-clearance initiative, called the "Detroit Plan," had become politically dicey. To appease his conservative support base, Jefferies quickly denounced any plan for erecting public housing on the cleared land. His constituents, such as those who read the Polish edition of a local newspaper called the *Home Gazette,* believed firmly that "American citizens have the right to demand that their children have a right to be brought up in an area of their choosing without being forced to associate with an element which breeds crime, immorality, and rowdyism."[55] And when the conservative Cobo became mayor in 1949, he was equally determined not to disappoint such electors. Cobo repeatedly assured white Detroiters that urban renewal and public housing would never be synonymous.[56]

City conservatives' success in preventing the construction of sufficient housing for city blacks during the late 1940s meant that urban renewal cost more than 6,000 black Detroiters their homes. Ironically, this in itself only fueled white conservatives' fears. Such severe African American displacement virtually ensured that blacks would be forced to seek housing in all-white neighborhoods. As attorney and professor Harold Norris noted in 1952, "The city is creating refugees . . . [and] there will be a price to pay for this inhumane eviction policy."[57] Indeed, racially conservative whites may have temporarily prevented African Americans from leaving the Black Bottom for new public housing developments, but they failed in their larger effort to keep the city fully segregated. As Detroit scholar Steve Babson points out, "The very color line that whites hoped Cobo would preserve with his anti–public housing policies, was breached by the Mayor's demolition crews. As Cobo's bulldozers pushed poorer blacks into surrounding black neighborhoods, higher income blacks, in turn, pushed into nearby white areas."[58] And, according to social geographers Bryan Thompson and Robert Sinclair, between 1950 and 1960 "no fewer than 83 additional census tracts became 50 percent black compared to 24 in the previous decade."[59] Thus, Detroit's housing issue only became more contentious as many whites refused to accede to neighborhood integration gracefully, while many blacks had little choice but to move into neighborhoods occupied by these very whites.

Housing was not the only issue that divided Detroit racially during the 1950s. Equal access to education soon paralleled housing integration in its rancor. Because many of Detroit's southern black migrants either brought children or had children within ten years of their arrival, the Detroit public school system was as demographically disrupted as the housing market. Writing in 1967, experts appointed by the federal government noted that, over the previous decade, "the [Detroit] school system had gained 50,000 to 60,000 children. Fifty-one percent of the elementary school classes were overcrowded. Simply to achieve a statewide average, the system needed an additional 1,651 teachers and 1,000 classrooms."[60] As black children flooded into certain city schools, white children exited them due to parental fears about race-mixing and declining standards. As one such white parent put it, city officials should "separate the whites and the Negroes, especially in the schools."[61]

That African American residents needed decent places to live and decent schools for their children clearly heightened racial tensions in the postwar Motor City. Not surprisingly, African Americans' need for secure and decent-paying jobs also generated noticeable racial conflict in the city's motor plants. It was logical that black migrants would gravitate most to jobs in the auto industry. By 1930, 14 percent of all autoworkers were African American because auto employers had made a push to bring blacks north to work in their factories during World War I. As scholar Joyce Peterson Shaw notes, during the Great War, "employment agencies distributed advertisements with glowing accounts of conditions and wages in northern factories. Bus companies helped distribute leaflets urging blacks to use their services to take them to a better life."[62]

During and after World War II, however, northern industrial employers became far more circumspect about hiring "too many" blacks and they often specifically requested white workers when they contacted the U.S. Employment Service. According to Detroit's African American newspaper, the *Michigan Chronicle,* on 31 August 1946, General Motors went directly to the U.S. Employment Service in Washington, asking that it send "white workers" to Detroit.[63] Auto employers' preference for white over black hires in their facilities may well have stemmed from a suspicion that black workers would be political troublemakers on the shop floor. As scholar Roger Keeran points out, "the intense activity of the communists in support of Black rights during the war naturally resulted in increased Party membership and influence among black autoworkers."[64] Indeed, by 1942, the Communist party's recruitment in Michigan was averaging 39 African American members a month, which was "more than double the monthly average of 19 in 1941."[65]

Regardless of their prejudices, however, auto employers were forced by the tremendous wartime and postwar demand for their products to hire thousands of African Americans. Yet, as with housing and schools, the jobs available to blacks were noticeably the worst. Auto companies not only routinely relegated their new African Americans hires to the least desirable jobs, but they also forced them to labor disproportionately in the industry's dangerous foundry and stamping operations. While virtually every white-owned company in Detroit placed blacks in the most inferior and most hazardous jobs, auto companies also sent them to extremely hostile all-white plants that in turn precipitated numerous ugly "hate strikes." In 1941 alone, whites shut down Curtis Aircraft, Hudson Motors, and Packard Motors in protest of the influx of black workers. In 1943, Packard Motors experienced another particularly vicious strike that dramatically escalated racial tensions throughout the industry.[66]

This sentiment did not disappear during the 1950s. Despite white Detroiters' deep commitment to trade unionism, particularly to the industrial unionism of the CIO, they were not always persuaded that the New Deal's promise of workingmen's rights necessarily extended to black citizens. Indeed, according to survey results in 1951, "the [Detroit] CIO has slightly larger numbers opposed to equal treatment of Negroes than do other unions."[67] Notably, 65 percent of CIO members surveyed in the Motor City opposed such equality.[68] Far fewer whites advocated formal segregation in the workplace than they did in housing (2 percent compared with 56 percent). Integration in the workplace, however, was far less of a potential threat than it was in the neighborhood, as employers made sure to lock blacks away in the least-skilled and most dangerous areas of a given plant.

Although black Detroiters' overwhelming need to draw on civic resources such as housing, education, and jobs clearly fueled tremendous white racial hostility, it is nevertheless a mistake to see racial polarization as the dominating force in postwar Detroit. While white racial brutality clearly flourished after the Second Great Migration, that was not the only, nor even the most important, result of this demographic transformation. This dramatic migration also fueled African Americans' determination to achieve equal opportunity in both the city and its workplaces, and, significantly, numerous whites not only sympathized with these efforts but also actively promoted them. Indeed, the most notable fact about the mass movement of African Americans to Detroit was that it brought greater political complexity than already existed to both the urban center and its labor movement. During the 1950s, Detroit was as politically fragmented as it was racially divided.

While blacks were certainly marginalized and intensely discriminated against in postwar Detroit, they were never passive victims.[69] Between 1945 and 1960, a full-fledged civil rights movement was being born in northern cities just as it was in the South. And because of Detroit migrants' southern roots and their long history of resisting discrimination in that region, they arrived in the Motor City well versed in the necessity of fighting racism where they lived and worked simultaneously. Armed with such a broad-based activist tradition, Detroit's black community was well equipped during the 1950s to challenge every racially exclusive and discriminatory practice of the city and the auto industry at once.

Because class divisions within the black community were even more palpable in the North than they had been in the South, such fault lines always had the potential to compromise mass action. While Detroit's blacks fully recognized the class divisions in their midst, however, they were united by the shared experiences of being forced into the least desirable housing and jobs, barred from most positions of both civic and labor authority, and singled out for punishment by the keepers of law and order.[70] Indeed, during the 1950s, racial and political consciousness, not class consciousness, led Detroit's African Americans to form a formidable civil rights movement.[71]

The prevalence of residential discrimination first led scores of black Detroiters to join local civil rights groups and to encourage these organizations to use both direct action and legal activism to make Detroit a better place to live. Formed in 1911, the Detroit Branch NAACP was one of the oldest chapters in the country and became one of the largest as the 1950s progressed. When the NAACP successfully waged a dramatic legal battle against discrimination in public housing between 1950 and 1954, it won great favor among city blacks from every walk of life. In 1958, once again the NAACP and other civil rights groups enjoyed a key victory when they forced city officials, who were planning to raze a black neighborhood of 3,000 to 3,400 families to make room for a new medical center, to build low-income housing on that site as well as three black churches.[72] Through actions such as these, the Detroit civil rights movement made it clear to local whites that the desegregation of city neighborhoods was a top priority, but it was by no means the only priority. City blacks were also determined to target the rampant segregation that plagued city schools.

Thanks to the activism of lawyers for the NAACP nationally, in 1954, the U.S. Supreme Court finally outlawed school segregation, and Detroit blacks ran with this ruling to the same extent that blacks living in Little Rock did. Even before the famed *Brown v. the Board of Education* mandate, however, blacks had already pressured city leaders to adopt an "intercultural policy" for Detroit's school system in 1945. After *Brown*, blacks pushed city officials even harder and forced them to adopt a Fair Employment Practices provision for the city's educational facilities in 1955, to endorse a Fair Employment Practices Act in 1956, to support the goal of Equal Educational Opportunity in 1957, and to pass a nondiscrimination bylaw for all city schools in 1959.[73] The NAACP was particularly gratified to see that it had succeeded in pressuring the city also to appoint the first African American to Detroit's Board of Education in 1955, because this indicated clearly that blacks might play an important role in shaping school policy.[74]

The Detroit civil rights movement also attempted to desegregate city restaurants and end hiring discrimination in major urban department stores. In 1951 and 1952, NAACP volunteers on a "Restaurant Discrimination Committee" conducted sit-ins because, as Detroiter Clyde Cleveland recalls, "the North was just as segregated as the South when I was growing up, particularly in terms of housing, [and] the experiences that I had of not being served at a restaurant were not in Georgia or Alabama or Mississippi—they were right here in the city of Detroit."[75] Many black residents became optimistic as the Detroit civil rights movement actively fought all aspects of urban exclusion. As all city blacks knew, however, two key barriers to securing a better life still had to be eliminated: police brutality and the rampant discrimination that African Americans faced on Detroit's shop floors and within its largest union.

Between 1950 and 1960, the abominable state of police-community relations is what most encouraged Detroiters to participate in the civil rights movement. After the Second Great Migration, whenever conflicts about housing or education erupted, city leaders charged the Detroit Police Department (DPD) with restoring law and order. Yet, between 1950 and 1960, increasing numbers of black citizens began to feel that the police did not serve and protect all Detroiters equally. In 1951, 21 percent of the Detroit blacks surveyed, as compared with only 4 percent of the whites, "included the Police Department as one of the three most important matters that needs attention in the city."[76] One black respondent noted that the police "are too prejudiced. All Negroes look alike to them; they can't tell a good Negro from a bad one."[77] Another suggested that "the police shouldn't be so quick to shoot and go into homes and wreck them as they do some Negro homes."[78] According to longtime Detroiter Arthur Johnson, "the ugliest part of the problem in the '50s was police brutality against Black people."[79]

Before World War II, the majority (65 percent) of Detroit's white police officers came from the Midwest, and almost half of all officers grew up in small rural towns. In the early 1940s, almost one-quarter of the DPD consisted of men whose previous job had been as a foreman or a skilled craftsman,[80] although the work backgrounds of police officers became a bit more diverse by 1945, with the entrance of hundreds of returning veterans. During the 1950s, more police recruits began to come from the South, although most still came from Detroit's virtually all-white pool of tool and die workers, pipe-fitters, grinders, drill press operators, postal clerks, and mail carriers; this pool also included former foremen, inspectors, and security personnel from the auto industry.[81] Because the Second Great Migration had no impact whatsoever on the DPD's hiring practices, it remained remarkably homogeneous throughout the 1950s.[82] The few blacks who were hired endured much white hostility. In 1957, for example, "white police officers revolted against the Commissioner's orders to integrate scout cars."[83] Clearly, the DPD's all-white character did not bode well for black efforts to improve civic race relations as the 1960s dawned.

But city blacks were undaunted. In response to escalating acts of racial brutality, in 1957 the NAACP conducted "an analysis of police brutality complaints reported to the Detroit Branch NAACP in the period from January 1, 1956 to July 30, 1957."[84] With this report, the NAACP intended to bring the DPD's rampant racism to the attention of city officials and also to suggest ways for them to resolve the problem. The organization noted in its report that it had received 103 complaints and that the most frequent type stemmed from "physical assault followed by racial epithets."[85] Of the 103 complaints, 33 involved physical assault and 23 involved both physical and verbal assault; 12 complaints arose from racial epithets on the part of police officers and 4 from false arrests. Eighteen complaints were filed by black women, and one complaint came from a 16-year-old black boy.[86] The NAACP pointed out as well that "90 percent of the complainants are working people without a previous record who believe they are subjected to unwarranted abuse because of their race."[87] Seeking to correct this situation, the NAACP suggested "organizing a representative biracial citizens group to make a survey of the police department and recommend improvements based on their findings."[88]

Just as a civil rights movement began to tackle the city's ever-present injustices in the 1950s, so did a civil rights movement come of age in Detroit's auto plants. The labor civil rights movement shared much, including leadership personnel and tactics, with its urban counterpart. In the 1940s, for example, city civil rights activist George Crockett Jr., who was also a senior attorney for the U.S. Department of Labor and one of the first hearings officers in FDR's Fair Employment Practices Commission, turned his attention to Detroit's auto industry, where he pushed for a UAW Fair Practices Department to achieve greater racial equity in the union's ranks, as well as to get "no discrimination" clauses placed in all UAW contracts with the major auto employers. Crockett sometimes found himself at odds with UAW officials over such intra-union civil rights efforts, but he was undeterred. Throughout the 1950s, Crockett continued to promote civil rights in the labor arena

Civil rights demonstration outside of Kresge Department Store, 1961. *Walter P. Reuther Library, Wayne State University.*

by fighting to integrate UAW bowling leagues as well as the leadership of various UAW locals. Because the UAW supported at least the principle of civil rights, the black middle-class leadership of Detroit's civil rights movement largely supported its white leaders, just as it stood by white progressives in the city. As historian Philip Foner points out, "in the eyes of the

23

NAACP's Labor Department, the UAW was 'the best of the industrial unions on the issue of race.'"[89]

Nevertheless, Detroit's civil rights activists were always outspoken about the need for this union, and all city whites, to take a far more active role in eradicating racial inequality. As they well realized, there was a widespread feeling among working-class blacks that white labor leaders needed to be pushed in that direction. To African Americans on the line, "the disparity between UAW rhetoric and conditions in the union and on the job was really what mattered."[90] As a result of this sentiment, in 1957, thirteen black union members came together to form a civil rights organization for workers in the UAW called the Trade Union Leadership Conference (TULC). Although the TULC only had 500 members when it started, by the mid-1960s it had 13,000 registered members, with many more nonmember workers supporting its goals.[91] As in the city, whites in the auto plants were put on notice that their discriminatory desires would not be allowed to dominate postwar Detroit.

If it were the case that blacks alone were agitating against racial discrimination in the Motor City and the motor plants then, indeed, racial polarization (albeit with blacks and whites more evenly matched in their efforts) would appear to have dominated Detroit's postwar landscape. Significantly, however, many city whites joined black efforts to end civic and labor discrimination, and thus white racial solidarity was always being undermined. The existence and importance of white opposition to prejudice and white privilege in postwar Detroit became clear in 1947, when a group of white families joined with several black families to form a nonprofit organization called the Schoolcraft Gardens Cooperative Association in order to build a new 400-unit housing development. The association bought a seventy-acre tract of land and drew up plans for its new biracial neighborhood that, in addition to housing, would offer playgrounds, community facilities, and even a shopping center.[92]

By 1949, the proposed Schoolcraft development had generated much political tension within Detroit's white community. Both reflecting and fueling this tension, a story appearing in the conservative *Brightmoor Journal* on the eve of Cobo's election intimated that the Schoolcraft Association had chosen the particular plot that it did because "it was on route to the new race track."[93] The article then suggested that white Detroiters should worry greatly about the "race-mixing, sex, and gambling" that were sure to take place if the cooperative was built.[94] By December 1949, and for months thereafter, a series of articles appeared in several other conservative white community newspapers, such as the *Redford Record*, "in which various appeals to racial prejudice were made under such banner headlines as 'Co op Seeking Conflict? Move to Bring Racial Housing into Area' and 'Biracial Group Seeks Tax-payers Cash.'"[95] In addition, racially conservative white homeowners had formed their own organization called the Tel-Craft Association and began to petition the city's Common Council to change the local zoning ordinances so that Schoolcraft Gardens could not be built. In the weeks that it took council to decide this issue, both black and white members of the Schoolcraft Association wondered openly whether "the responsible elected officials of the city government [would] bow to the demands of a small group of bigoted citizens who have stooped to a campaign of lies, misrepresentations, and appeals to religious and racial prejudice."[96] Their answer came in March 1950, when the Cobo-sympathetic council decided in favor of the Tel-Craft Association and rezoned the proposed Schoolcraft Gardens plot.

The significance of the political battle over Schoolcraft Gardens cannot be overestimated. The fact that city whites were actively supporting biracial neighborhoods indicates clearly that differing political perspectives on how best to deal with Detroit's postmigration demography directly served to undermine white racial solidarity. And although biracial political solutions to the city's racial problems had not yet, in 1950, found a following that was strong enough to shape the contours of the postwar city, numerous city whites were determined to change this situation. Indeed, after supporting biracial initiatives such as Schoolcraft Gardens, progressive whites in Detroit stepped up their efforts to create a more racially just city by working hard to implement *Brown* in city schools, by joining black Detroiters during restaurant sit-ins, and by helping to set up important checks on the DPD, such as a city department to hear citizen complaints.

Having worked collectively to try to elect left-liberals such as George Edwards in the early postwar years and then having worked individually in the legal arena or within city agencies to promote equal opportunity, many white Detroiters clearly rejected the premises of white solidarity. Take, for instance, two key figures in Detroit who repeatedly and publicly rejected any appeal to white privilege and who worked actively to end it: white attorney Maurice Sugar and white sociologist-turned-city-official Mel Ravitz. Not only did Sugar personally recoil from the idea of white dominance, in legal battle after legal battle he represented blacks as well as whites and fought directly against segregation initiatives in the city and the labor movement.[97] Likewise, Ravitz worked tirelessly in the 1950s to eliminate segregation in Detroit by creating neighborhood block clubs and also by supporting various civil rights initiatives as a member of the Detroit City Planning Commission.

Civil rights activism by both blacks and whites only cemented the view of Detroit's racially conservative whites that ridding Detroit of all African Americans, or at least keeping them segregated from whites, was the best way to achieve civic harmony. As one white Detroiter suggested, "send them to Africa. Make a community of their own. Send them back South. Send them."[98] And, when they were asked what should be done about "Negro-White Relations," a full 68 percent advocated some form of city segregation.[99] According to one of these whites, "I'd like to see the city sectioned off and have different races sectioned off and each live in their own area. I hate to see a territory invaded, like by colored."[100] With 54 percent of Detroit's whites feeling "unfavorable toward full acceptance" of the city's African Americans and with these same whites feeling under siege from the many "Pro-Black" whites there, white out-migration to nearby suburbs, in addition to racial violence and political divisiveness, characterized the city in the 1950s.[101] Of course, a distaste for living near blacks and a disgust with the political agenda of racially progressive whites were not the only things fueling suburbanization in this decade.[102] Many whites left after having witnessed or participated in "more than 200 racial incidents . . . when blacks broke through the city's invisible racial lines."[103] Others left because they were tired of Detroit's ugly political factionalism in every civic election since 1946. But as Sugrue points out, many also left because "between 1954 and 1960, Detroit lost nearly 90,000 jobs, many of which evaporated during a severe recession in 1957 and 1958."[104] And, just as important, a new matrix of federally funded freeways and the more affordable automobile made white mobility away from any city problem both possible and highly attractive.

But while white flight in the 1950s was dramatic and indicative of the degree of postwar instability, it was not itself a decisive factor in Detroit's long-term social or economic viability. Such outmigration was certainly a drain on city resources, but it by no means dealt the city a death blow. Most white urbanites did not pursue the dream of less contentious, more affluent, more homogeneous living on the open suburban frontier. Most stayed in Detroit—sometimes because of economic barriers to their own mobility but just as often because they still laid major claim to the city. For every white Detroiter who left the urban center because he or she hated its new racial composition or felt that "everything seems too crowded here in the city to raise a family," there were many others who remained committed to inner-city living and decided to stay put.[105] Despite white conservatives' hostility to what Detroit had become since World War II, most of them were nevertheless unwilling to surrender the city to blacks. And despite progressive whites' dismay at Detroit's racial injustices, they were equally unwilling to give up on the dream of biracial civic coexistence. Instead, each white group still sought political solutions to the thorny racial problems introduced to Detroit after 1945.

Of course, the suburbs' racially exclusive nature made out-migration an impossibility for African American Detroiters. But rather than lament such unjust barriers, they took pleasure in the fact that their efforts to achieve equitable biracial living in their city over the course of the 1950s seemed to be gaining momentum. Granted, Detroit and its auto plants had become more politically and racially fractured than ever during that decade, and, on the surface, this did not bode well for the future. Nevertheless, by 1959, at least the city's African American community and its civil-rights-sympathetic whites had reason to be optimistic. In that year, city blacks, in deliberate alliance with racially progressive white Detroiters, began to mobilize very effectively to take control of the city. Because these Motor City residents worked collectively and tirelessly as the 1950s came to a close to bring their social, economic, and political agenda for a different Detroit to the electoral arena, in 1961 white racial conservatism would suffer a major defeat.

2: Optimism and Crisis in the

New Liberal Metropolis

It is not without significance also that Detroit is the only city with a population of over one million people that has not experienced a large-scaled, racial
explosion in the past few years. . . . I believe this indicates how far we have
come in Detroit since the infamous period of the Summer of 1943, when
racial hostilities turned our city into an armed camp.[1]

By 1960, James Johnson Jr. had been in Detroit for seven years, but he still
made too little money to live on his own. One of the perks of his new job at
the Scotch and Sirloin, however, was that it enabled him to take cooking
classes at Chadsey High School. The six-month course cost over $150, and
the restaurant deducted the money from Johnson's paychecks. After completing the course and getting his cooking certificate, Johnson stayed at the
restaurant making $80 a week until December 1964, when he had a fight
with a waiter named Horace Hunter over a customer's order. In this altercation, James was convinced that his fellow employee was acting on behalf
of the management, which he believed wanted to fire him because he now
made more than minimum wage. Johnson felt that he had "been there over
four years, [was] always underpaid and was like a worn out shoe."[2] In the
heat of the fight with Hunter, Johnson stabbed him in the side with a ten-
inch butcher knife—lashing out for the first time with violence at what he
felt was managerial harassment.

Fearing prosecution and feeling generally discouraged with the job
prospects in Detroit, Johnson went to Chicago to live with his sister Nancy,
who had migrated there instead of to Detroit. When he arrived in Chicago,
Johnson got a job in the assembly division of the Jefferson Electric Company, where he made $60 a week.[3] In time, he worked his way up to a po-
sition as a coil cutter, making $2.60 an hour, but after seven weeks the man
who had vacated that better job returned, and Johnson had to return to as-

sembly. Hating the job in assembly, missing Detroit, and hoping that op-
portunities there had improved, Johnson went back to the Motor City.

Johnson's ever-present hope that he would find a better life in Detroit
reflected that of many black motor city residents during this period. Even
though the North turned out to be distressingly similar to a South that
blacks had fled in droves, the migration process, as well as the growing civil
rights activism during the 1950s, fueled a powerful conviction among them
that if the North was not the "Promised Land" that African Americans had
believed it to be, they now had the political means to make it so.

In 1960, Detroit's progressive forces began to mobilize across racial and
class lines to rid the city of its segregation, poverty, and right-leaning civic
leadership. Almost overnight, a powerful biracial coalition managed to
transform Detroit into a city where pro–civil rights liberals enjoyed enormous and nationally envied power. After a pivotal mayoral election in 1961,
a very different Detroit not only seemed possible; it also seemed probable.
As a close look at 1961–67, particularly 1964–67, reveals, however, despite
their many dramatic initiatives, Detroit's new liberal leadership was never
able to transform the city to the extent that it had promised its constituents.
Racial discrimination and inequality still plagued Detroit, and, not surprisingly, this fact soon generated much citizen disappointment. Even though
both black and white liberal leaders valiantly attempted to respond to this
disappointment by stepping up their efforts to deal with issues such as deteriorating police-community relations, they made little tangible progress. In
time, they faced criticism from every camp. Some Detroiters believed that
conservatives should have remained in charge. Others felt that liberals could
still succeed if they became more forceful. In July 1967, however, the citizens
most deeply disillusioned with their city and the political process spoke the
loudest when they set Detroit ablaze. As the Motor City burned in the fires
of the 1967 rebellion, the heady optimism that Detroit liberals had felt in
1961 seemed all but impossible to recapture. The city was experiencing its
most severe social and political crisis to date.

* * * *

As we have seen, black Detroiters had questioned the motives and the policies of civic leaders throughout the 1950s. In 1957, Louis Miriani, a politician even more unsympathetic to the black community than Albert Cobo,
became mayor after Cobo's death, and local African Americans were deeply
distressed. City blacks feared that Miriani's aggressive law-and-order initiatives would soon make their lives even more unpleasant. Indeed, the mayor
succeeded in upsetting them from his first days in office. His decision to in-
tensify the police's presence in the city's poorest areas in particular, dramatically exacerbated tensions between the DPD and Detroit's black community. According to the *Detroit Free Press,* there existed "a profound feeling

Mayor Jerome Cavanagh. *Walter P. Reuther, Wayne State University.*

of dissatisfaction among the Negroes of the community in Detroit which rested on the fact that Miriani's Police Commissioner had ordered a crackdown against crime. . . . Negroes felt this was aimed directly at them. . . . [T]hey could not communicate with Miriani."[4] By 1961, when Miriani sought reelection, black Detroiters were determined to beat back the racial conservatives who had ruled their city for so long. When Jerome Cavanagh, a political newcomer who not only announced his intention to defeat Miriani but also made his civil rights sympathies clear, entered the race, blacks and white progressives were elated.

Cavanagh, a thirty-three-year-old father of six, was the former chairman of the Wayne County Young Democrats and a practicing attorney.[5] He immediately captured the attention of many young Detroiters because they perceived his proposed city initiatives to be "an extension of the 'New Frontier' youth movement started by President Kennedy."[6] But his appeal went beyond the city's youth. Older whites who long had been pushing for a more progressive political agenda in Detroit gravitated toward Cavanagh as a social visionary. Older blacks also seeking a political overhaul were additionally attracted to Cavanagh's vocal support of civil rights. They had taken particular note of the fact that Cavanagh had unequivocally supported a civil rights amendment intended to give the City Council advise-and-consent powers over the mayor's appointment to the Commission on Community Relations (CCR). And even when this amendment, crafted by Detroit's lone black councilman, William Patrick, officially died in a council vote on October 3, 1961, Cavanagh still advocated its adoption.

Black and progressive white Detroiters worked hard together to elect Cavanagh. As both groups well knew, however, the black vote would be the most vital. By 1961, blacks comprised more than one-third of the city's population and were thus central to Cavanagh's hopes of capturing the mayoralty. Inspired by Cavanagh's campaign declaration that "he would clearly define to all his department heads his racial policies,"[7] as well as by his oft-stated opinion that "it was time for a new and vigorous administration,"[8] Detroit's black middle class organized a massive get-out-the-vote drive. Black organizations ranging from the TULC to the NAACP to the Cotillion Club to the Wolverine Bar Association of Michigan to the Detroit Interdenomination Ministerial Alliance gave their time and money to this voter registration effort.[9] Although several key figures in the black middle class had activist roots to the left of the Democratic party—indeed, some had been members or at least defenders of the Communist Party—the civil rights imperative of defeating Miriani led them to support Cavanagh's platform. By 1961, it appeared that electing Cavanagh was the most logical way to secure the long-sought goal of attaining greater social, racial, and economic equality in Detroit.

The 1961 mayoral election made it clear that not only was the black vote instrumental in reshaping Detroit politics, but also that a new coalition of the city's politically liberal black and white residents had become a real force to contend with. In what the *Detroit News* described as "the biggest political upset here in 32 years," Cavanagh received 200,413 votes to Miriani's 158,778.[10] Cavanagh had won by a five-to-one margin in "precincts that are heavily Negro."[11] Voting returns revealed as well that many in Detroit's white working class had also voted for Cavanagh. As the *Detroit Free Press* put it, "while Cavanagh did well among the large Negro segment of the community, he also did well across the board in many workingmen's areas of the city."[12] Clearly, Cavanagh had successfully wooed Detroit's black, as well as a significant portion of its white, electorate into a revitalized liberal coalition. This new liberal alliance made the future of the city look bright for the first time since the Second Great Migration had begun.

During his first term in office, Mayor Cavanagh rode the wave of this new optimism and began seeking concrete ways to improve the city and its ever-tense race relations. Well aware that his success depended on his heeding the needs of all his constituents, Cavanagh encouraged the public's involvement in shaping civic policy by, among other things, deliberately drawing from many facets of the Detroit community when appointing new leaders to various city agencies.

The mayor's ability to address such dicey social issues as police-community relations and demographic disruption in the schools without alienating his racially and economically diverse constituents earned Cavanagh a second term in 1965. Cavanagh was most encouraged by the tremendous vote of confidence he received from city residents that year, but he was even more excited by the possibilities for Detroit that he saw in the Economic Opportunity Act of 1964 and President Lyndon B. Johnson's ambitious War on Poverty. In such national initiatives, the mayor could see the chance for lasting civic peace—a peace based on unprecedented economic security and equality. The Detroiters who had elected Cavanagh, as well as growing numbers of whites who had not, also were optimistic that the War on Poverty could end city troubles and move their metropolis forward.

From the moment that the Great Society began, it was clear that Cavanagh fully shared LBJ's conviction that the life of every American citizen would be improved if politicians succeeded in bringing the nation's poor into the economic and social mainstream. In key respects, however, the mayor was a step ahead of the Democrats in Washington when it came to tackling the vexing problem of urban inequality. According to the United Community Services, "planning for Detroit's part in the nationwide War on Poverty began with a meeting called by Mayor Cavanagh in April, 1964, six months before Congress was to pass the Economic Opportunity Act (EOA)."[13] And as soon as Congress did enact the EOA, liberal leaders in Detroit pushed hard for such projects as Head Start and the Model Cities/Model Neighborhood Project and for a local extension of the Community Action Program (CAP).[14] In Detroit, CAP took the form of the City of Detroit Mayor's Committee, Total Action against Poverty, or TAP. Between November 23, 1964, and August 31, 1966, the Cavanagh administration used its $3,913,298 budget to set up four Neighborhood Community Action Centers and twenty subcenters. Each was intended to be "the points of contact between TAP component projects and the people they are designed to serve."[15] It is significant that the Cavanagh administration was fully committed as well to the "maximum feasible participation" of the community that it served. According to civic leaders, "the poor, themselves, will be hired to help formulate and carry out much of the program."[16]

The War on Poverty in Detroit was comprehensive indeed. TAP's component projects ultimately included "program development, medical, dental and health clinics, home management instruction, homemaker services, cultural enrichment field trips, school community projects, pre-school education, assistant attendance officers, intramural physical education, extended school projects, school retention programs, school preparation programs, educational stimulus centers, and a reading materials distribution component."[17] In addition to these services, TAP centers offered marriage and family counseling, classes for expectant parents, school health examinations, child immunizations, advice on food purchasing and credit buying, and even legal services for the poor.[18]

Detroiters in need enthusiastically embraced such programs. Between June 28, 1965, and August 27, 1965, more than 24,000 mothers and their children participated in TAP's education and recreation services. During the same period, 6,000 poor children were enrolled in Head Start programs. And between June 4, 1965, and December 4, 1966, 600 Detroiters completed "on-the-job training" programs.[19] In total, between January 1, 1965, and April 1966, more than 93,000 Detroiters had made contact with TAP centers around the city, and these centers had made 113,000 job referrals as well as filed 44,000 requests for medical and dental care.[20] Detroiters not only used the TAP centers, but they also received aid in less direct ways through OEO-funded work training services, public school programs, and even programs for the city's parochial schools.[21]

Detroit's Great Society initiatives were more far reaching than anything city leaders had previously undertaken. But what most set these liberal programs apart from previous political and economic initiatives was the degree to which the black middle-class influenced the types of services offered to the urban poor and the extent to which this group was involved in implementing the various poverty programs.

The cooperative relationship between white liberal leaders and Detroit's black middle class was relatively easy to forge, partly because the city's newly powerful core of black middle-class liberals understood the "problems" facing poor urban blacks in much the same way that the white liberals of the Cavanagh and Johnson administrations did. While the Detroit Urban League maintain that "Negro families cannot be put together under one label," as the deeply scarring and degenerative social and economic problems of some blacks "are not the problems of middle-class Negroes or even all lower status Negroes, but they are problems faced everyday by [a] group of disadvantaged Negroes,"[22] this organization nevertheless agreed that one of the major problems facing poor urban blacks was that of status and manhood deprivation. As the Urban League officals put it "The low-income Negro family tends to be wife-dominated, the male loses a great deal of i is self-respect, and the family loses respect for him."[23] As much of the black middle class saw it, this lack of self-respect in turn generated other serious problems such as the inability to advance in jobs and chronic unemployment. In cyclical fashion, these economic difficulties "gnaw[ed] away at [black] manhood."[24] When the Detroit Urban League published its detailed report on the city's social ills in 1966, not surprisingly it met with high praise from important white liberals such as Daniel Patrick Moynihan.[25]

In addition to sharing much of the ideology upon which the Great Society was founded, Detroit's black middle-class leaders also became actively involved in virtually every War on Poverty initiative. The NAACP and the Urban League were vocal participants in TAP along with the Board of Commerce, city churches, the Department of Education, and the UAW.[26] Although the NAACP did not actually sit on TAP's Policy-Advisory Committee, as did the Urban League, it participated in virtually every TAP program. Detroit's civil rights leaders were particularly committed to TAP's various community uplift programs. In TAP's Operation Bootstrap, for example, two of the four key financial sponsors were Robert Tindal of the NAACP and William Raymond of the Detroit Urban League.[27]

Although the leaders of Detroit's black middle class gave almost un-qualified support to Cavanagh's War on Poverty, they nevertheless cautioned the mayor to remember that the city's problems were as much a product of racial discrimination as economic deprivation. Whereas TAP officials tended to lump all "low-income families" together and tried repeatedly to address the fact that such poor families "spend most of their resources on the bare necessities of survival [with] little left over for clothes, diet and health, bus fare, insurance, toys, and other things which are an everyday part of the lives of most of us,"[28] black leaders pointed out that African Americans fell dis-proportionately into this group. Thus, according to civil rights leaders, ad-ministration liberals should insist on certain non-TAP efforts, such as deseg-regating housing and schools, if they were serious about eradicating inequality. Civil rights leaders were not surprised when the Detroit Com-mission on Community Relations (CCR) found that the "the median income of nonwhites during 1959 was $4,400, while median income among whites was $7,300 or 66% higher"[29] and concluded in 1963 that "the differences between whites and nonwhites [are] much too significant and disturbing to be minimized or ignored."[30]

The black middle class was right to call attention to the race-based nature of deprivation in the Motor City. Not only did African Americans remain more disadvantaged economically by the mid-1960s, but in key respects they were also more socially and residentially segregated from whites than ever. According to scholars Albert J. Mayer and Thomas F. Hoult, "In 1930, 51 percent of all Negro residents lived in white or predominantly white areas [but] by 1960, only 15 percent of Negro residents lived in so-called white ar-eas."[31] And whereas Detroit had sixteen all-black census tracts in 1940 and forty in 1950, it had eighty-nine in 1960.[32] Unsurprisingly, the all-black cen-sus tracts were in need of public assistance to a far greater extent than were the all-white tracts.[33]

But while the city's white liberal leaders were well aware that race was a poverty factor and had supported equality measures such as Open Occu-pancy,[34] most felt that their programs in Detroit were sufficiently compre-hensive, if not something to be proud of. Such confidence was continually bolstered by positive feedback from outside the city. In January 1965, for ex-ample, the U.S. Chamber of Commerce chose Detroit as the site of its up-coming meeting of the Task Force on Economic Growth and Opportunity "because it is representative of a major urban community [that] has taken steps to help solve its problems."[35] After visiting Detroit's TAP centers in February 1965, Morton Engleberg, OEO director of public affairs, wrote to Robert E. Toohey, Cavanagh's special assistant, to say that he was convinced "if every city follows Detroit's example, the War on Poverty will soon be won."[36] Daniel Patrick Moynihan went even further in his praise of the liberal experiment in Detroit when he noted the same year that "Detroit had everything the Great Society could wish for in a municipality," including two black congressmen as well as "a splendid mayor and a fine governor."[37] According to Moynihan, Detroit had actually "found the road to racial peace in the programs and policies instituted by Cavanagh, with assistance from the Democratic administrations in Washington."[38]

But just as the Cavanagh administration was basking in the glow of national praise, it began to appear that trouble was brewing in paradise. In fact, just when civic liberals felt most confident that their programs were thriving, the city's historic but theretofore successfully contained racial tensions and political divisiveness again began threatening to upset Detroit's civic stability. Indeed just as civic liberals grew more committed to their various Great Society and War on Poverty initiatives, many black Detroiters began to question both the pace and parameters of the liberal agenda itself. The fact that the city was still governed, managed, taught, and represented almost exclusively by whites, despite the efforts of the civil rights leadership and the promises of the Cavanagh administration to rectify such imbalances, began to generate much discontent. The political alliance between white progressives and the black community that had put Cavanagh in office itself was fracturing with dire implications for civic peace.[39]

Not only had many black residents begun to doubt their liberal leaders' progress, but just as seriously, they had begun to question the wisdom of their own civil rights leadership. As the city's black civil rights leaders became more wedded to and excited by the Cavanagh administration's antipoverty efforts, many of their poor and working-class black constituents grew more critical of their involvement in these initiatives. It had not escaped Detroit's African Americans that even though middle-class black civil rights leaders became involved in every Great Society program and had developed a good relationship with the Cavanagh leadership, brutal discrimination continued to flourish in the city.

But because most poor and working-class black Detroiters still considered the black middle class their voice in city politics, at least initially they expressed their mounting discontent by flooding the offices of civil rights organizations with growing numbers of formal complaints about the inequality that still raged in the Motor City. Indeed, as the 1960s wore on, the NAACP began receiving hundreds of complaints from community blacks like Mr. and Mrs. Herbert Wilson, whose son, Harvey, had been harassed repeatedly by a white girl at his school. This girl kept calling Harvey "a black nigger," and when he had enough and finally kicked her, his white teacher, Mrs. Truaell, slapped him.[40] There were also complaints like that of Mrs. Thomasyne Faulkner, who tried to rent an apartment and was told by the owner that "they did not rent to colored."[41]

Civil rights leaders handled these complaints expeditiously and aggressively.[42] Yet despite escalating black dissatisfaction with Cavanagh's Great

Society initiatives, they did not challenge the pace or perameters of the administration's plans for combating Detroit's economic and social ills. No matter how many horror stories they heard from their constituents, these black leaders rarely questioned that the solution to urban inequality could be found within the liberal agenda. Indeed, they had fought too hard and too long for a real political voice in Detroit to relinquish it when the going got tough. Robert Tindal, the NAACP's executive secretary, spoke for most of the city's middle-class black leadership when he said that he found "very little solution to the problems other than the ballot box."[43] Even though intimidation still was the modus operandi of many of the city's most racially conservative whites, black leaders believed that it was morally and strategically important to continue to work closely with the city's liberal whites.[44]

Although they continued to hope that Detroit eventually would become an equitable biracial center, Detroit's middle-class civil rights leaders were not blind to the fact that so little change had taken place after 1964. According to complaints filed with both the NAACP and the Michigan Civil Rights Commission (MCRC), not only were white merchants in the black community still charging exorbitant prices for food and clothing, but white landlords also were continuing to overcharge for housing while white realtors still attempted to relegate blacks to the city's least-developed and most impoverished neighborhoods. Particularly disturbing was evidence that housing inequities were still one of the most serious problems facing Detroit's black citizens. Indeed, in certain black neighborhoods where over 44 percent of the residents had migrated from the South, only 14 percent could afford to own their own homes, leaving over 85 percent of them to pay exorbitant rents to discriminatory landlords and real estate firms.[45] As the CCR noted in 1966, "houses in changing neighborhoods are marketed exclusively to Negroes," and "white buyers are diverted from these areas."[46]

By the mid-1960s, it also became abundantly clear to the black middle class that little had changed for African Americans in the educational arena. When the U.S. Supreme Court declared segregated education unconstitutional in 1954, Detroit civil rights leaders were optimistic that the city's public school system would eventually be desegregated. To their dismay, however, every year after *Brown v. the Board of Education,* Detroit schools had actually become more, not less, segregated. In 1964, when the Cavanagh administration committed the city to the Detroit Program for an Integrated School System,[47] black civil rights leaders regained much of their optimism, but by 1966, even they could see that Detroit's schools remained extremely segregated.[48]

Black community leaders also could not miss that economic opportunity for city African Americans remained equally elusive despite a booming economy and the numerous War on Poverty programs. Although African Americans had successfully penetrated the unionized labor market (25 percent of the UAW membership was black in the late 1960s, as compared with 14 percent in 1930), they still were not fully sharing the great prosperity to be had in Detroit.[49] Throughout Detroit, whites had managed to keep the majority of higher-paying and more prestigious jobs. Indeed citywide, 23 percent of whites were managers, proprietors, officials, semi-professionals, or professionals, as compared with only 9 percent of blacks. Conversely, 40 percent of blacks were categorized as machine "operators," as compared with 27 percent of whites. Just as significant, 22 percent of blacks, as compared with 10 percent of whites, worked in private households and service positions.[50]

While many black Detroiters were employed in the least lucrative and desirable jobs throughout the 1960s, many found it exceedingly difficult to get any job at all. According to a Detroit Planning Commission report, by the late 1960s, in one city neighborhood, over 90 percent of the total number of applicants for what residents viewed as "decent jobs" were black, and 96 percent of those applicants were unemployed.[51] This staggering black unemployment existed in a city whose overall unemployment rate bottomed out at a 15-year low of 3.8 percent in 1968.[52] Barriers to black employment ranged from the outright refusal of local white businesses to hire blacks to the more indirect but equally devastating barriers like the lack of "bus tickets, lunch money, safety shoes, hair cuts, [and] dental work."[53]

The cost of this economic deprivation was enormous. Throughout the 1960s, increased numbers of Detroit's black unemployed were forced onto the welfare rolls. But while the effects of job and housing discrimination had frayed the economic fabric of many black families, the fact that they had been forced to apply for government assistance at the very historical moment when they were most optimistic about breaking free of social and economic oppression was particularly devastating. And, of course, with Detroiters on welfare only receiving $44 per month to cover "food, clothing, school expenses, entertainment, bus fare, personal care, everything," government aid did not alleviate want.[54] As the United Community Services noted, "the use of 'ceilings' to limit the amount of assistance obviously prevents numerous families from having their 'basic' needs met, under this program. These families may number as high as 50 percent of the total of all ADC families."[55]

The city's black middle class was distressed by the fact that African Americans' equal access to housing, education, and employment had not improved since the late 1940s. Their expectations of white liberals and the Great Society were not being realized as quickly as predicted. But what quickly turned black leaders' discomfort with the pace of liberal progress into alarm, was the realization that police-community relations in particular had deteriorated during the 1960s. In fact, it was the actions of the Detroit Police Department (DPD) that would plunge Detroit, which had for years just simmered with discontent, into a full-blown urban crisis.

While many city departments had remained largely white since Cavanagh took office, the DPD remained the whitest of them all. Even though police officers were placed in charge of the safety and stability of the entire community, which was almost 50 percent African American by 1965, only 2.8 percent of the police force was black.[56] And in the 1960s, as in the previous decade, even when city blacks did manage to penetrate the ranks of the DPD, white officers routinely made their work lives most difficult. Indeed, harassment of black officers by white had increased noticeably since the 1950s as a marginally higher number of African Americans joined the force. For example, in 1966 the NAACP received a letter from a Mrs. Jessie Wallace in which she expressed her concern "over the mistreatment of patrolman Kenneth Johnson at the hands of his white fellow officers because of his testimony revealing the brutal beating of a 15 year old Negro youth in the Vernor Station Garage."[57] Indicating the prevalence of racial discrimination within the DPD, black policemen on the force felt compelled to form an organization called Concerned Officers for Equal Justice in order to call attention to their plight.

Even more troubling than the DPD's hiring and personnel practices was its blatant support of white interests over black in the city and its barely concealed animosity toward black citizens. As a political scientist from Wayne State University pointed out, "recruits came into the police department with all of the prejudices, hatreds and hang ups contained in the general population."[58] Cavanagh had attempted to improve police-community relations by appointing a liberal police commissioner, George Edwards, but overall, even his well-meaning efforts failed in the face of officer recalcitrance. According to Edwards, "90 percent of the 4,767-man Detroit Police Department are bigoted, and [a] dislike for Negroes is reflected constantly in their language and often in physical abuse."[59]

There were, of course, police officers who did not let personal biases prevent them from fairly and effectively carrying out their duties. However other officers felt very strongly that blacks greatly exaggerated racism in the city as well as within the force.[60] A 1969 survey of police officers indicated that as many as 37 percent of white officers believed that blacks were treated the same as whites in terms of housing, 59 percent thought blacks received the same educational advantages as whites, 43 percent thought job opportunities for blacks and whites were equal, and 57 percent believed law enforcement treated blacks no differently from whites. Black officers surveyed did not see things this way at all. Three percent of black policemen thought blacks got the same access to housing as whites, 3 percent thought blacks had the same educational opportunities, 8 percent thought blacks enjoyed the same job opportunities, and 6 percent thought blacks and whites were treated the same way by law enforcement.[61]

City blacks had much reason to believe that the DPD was a racist organization.[62] Indeed leaders of the NAACP felt compelled to note that the police "operate under the bigoted misapprehension that most Negroes are criminals." Because this organization had "personally investigated and protested numerous episodes of police brutality or Negro citizens which, even when verified by the courts or the Civil Rights Commission, has never resulted in any effective action against the guilty police officer," it felt more than qualified to speak out on this issue.[63] A particularly egregious incident brought to the NAACP's attention occurred on September 12, 1965, when four African American boys who were playing football in the street were questioned by the DPD, who demanded identification and told the youths to leave the area. When the boys protested, they were arrested and subsequently beaten, kicked, and stomped by at least five white officers in the precinct where they were being detained.[64]

Despite the Cavanagh administration's public commitment to reforming the DPD and the valiant efforts of liberal Police Commissioner Edwards to that end, by the late 1960s, Detroit's blacks had heard one too many tales of friends and relatives being mistreated by the DPD to have much faith in their civic leaders. They knew all too well about incidents like the one that befell two black couples, Mr. and Mrs. James Gray and Mr. and Mrs. George Brezell. The Grays and the Brezells mistakenly had driven down a dead-end street and, as they came to a stop, they were accosted by heavily armed white men who shot at them, saying, "there are no niggers living on this street." Despite the couples' report to the police, no arrests were made.[65] Many city blacks also had heard about an African American woman named Barbara

Picketers at Detroit Police Headquarters protesting the fatal shooting of a black woman, July 13, 1963. *Walter P. Reuther Library, Wayne State University.*

Jackson who was badly injured when the police decided to arrest her. Regarding Ms. Jackson's injuries in this arrest, the DPD claimed that she "fell attempting to escape." Ms. Jackson, however, reported to the NAACP that "the officer picked her up and slammed her to the ground [and] then another officer pulled off her wig and kicked her with the comment 'now you're really going to the hospital.'"[66] Based on their experiences of the past decade, black Detroiters had every reason to believe that Jackson was telling the truth.

Even the wealthiest of Detroit's African Americans came to speak out against police excess as the 1960s unfolded. In 1965, members of the Cotillion Club, an elite black social organization, noted in a letter to Cavanagh that police-community relations had deteriorated dramatically since 1963, when, in that year alone, "there were almost 500 cases of police-inflicted injuries; and 300 of these were in the five predominantly Negro Precinct areas."[67] Indeed, according to city records, between May 1961 and February 1964, there had been 1,507 "altercations" between the police and Detroit citizens resulting in the injury of 1,041 citizens, most of them black. Of those citizen injuries, 690 were head injuries. In those same altercations, 580 police officers were also injured and, significantly, 303 of those injuries were to the officers' hands, knuckles, and fingers.[68] Despite such alarming statistics, Commissioner Edwards's successor, Ray Girardin, maintained that "while Detroit's citizens can be divided into many categories—racial, religious, political, economic—the police will divide them into only two: those who obey the law and those who don't."[69]

The problem for blacks in Detroit was that the police too often equated them with lawlessness. Well aware of this, white liberal leaders took great pains to denounce such an association. As Richard V. Marks, a white liberal in the CCR, wrote, "the 'crime in the streets' issue is more than a 'fact' stated about white or black criminality. . . . [I]t is in reality a euphemism for hold-the-line government and community policy regarding the Negro struggle for Civil Rights, jobs, etc."[70] Marks went on to state emphatically that black Detroiters were as opposed to crime as were city whites and that they were just "as desperately concerned that there will be proper policing in their communities as any other citizen in our city."[71] Bolstering Marks's claims, one black Detroiter, Leigins S. Moore, wrote to his local clergyman, Reverend Charles Williams, "we, too, believe in law and order. . . . [W]e do not wish to give any comfort to the hoodlum and law violators."[72] Despite the care that both white liberal leaders and ordinary black citizens took to distinguish between the need to fight crime and the criminal actions of the DPD, the force itself took little notice.

The fact that the DPD was impervious to change only escalated black anger in Detroit. As one black doctor, Thomas Green, wrote to Cavanagh, "as a city physician I have been stopped and questioned any number of times. . . . [S]ome of my colleagues have had a similar experience. [The police] don't need any more help or encouragement in that regard."[73] Another black Detroiter questioned city officials this way: "How could you possibly ignore what is common knowledge to every citizen group in the community, and give your unqualified support of an obvious evil that exists in our city?"[74] And, as Detroiter Mattie Barrow wrote to Cavanagh in 1965, "Yes, Mr. Mayor, if you can not use your power to stop this unjust brutality against Negro citizens we will have to elect someone who will."[75]

From the moment Cavanagh embarked on implementing LBJ's Great Society, much of his black constituency was losing faith in such an initiative. But the possibilities for the city's long-term social peace and political stability were compromised not only by black disaffection with liberal programmatic initiatives but also by the fact that the city's white racial conservatives had become openly hostile to them. Even as poor, working-class, middle-class, and wealthy blacks began to have serious doubts about whether any substantive change was occurring in their city, many white Detroiters, also from every class background, were becoming convinced that too much change had already taken place.

In 1965, an editorial on television station WJBK reflected the growing sentiments of these whites when it addressed civic liberals' attempts to reform the DPD: "We don't like the sound of it. The city must be protected, and the police must have the full backing in doing their job, or the community one day might have to go back to the law of the jungle."[76] Just as the Cavanagh administration's attempt to deal with the police generated the most vocal black criticism of its agenda, so did it raise a flag for racially conservative whites in the city who had either never supported the mayor or had voted for him with a great deal of trepidation given his civil rights sympathies. At the very moment city officials were becoming more critical of the DPD's actions, many white Detroiters began calling for greater police strength in the face of alleged black criminality. Because the local media routinely presented crime news in a way that emphasized black participation, white conservatives saw any censuring of the police as giving the green light to black hoodlums.[77] Indeed, these whites came openly to question the motivations of the city's liberal leadership when it took on the DPD, suspecting that it was actually encouraging lawlessness.

By the mid-1960s, as city blacks began filing complaints against the police, Detroit's racially conservative element began openly criticizing Cavanagh's reform efforts. As one particularly passionate critic A. Rahrig wrote to the mayor, "we whites are getting sick! Sick! Of the crying do gooders, NAACP-etc. That are always on the side of the person who robs, kills, or beats a person to death just for kicks."[78] George Gerhold opined in his letter to the mayor, "believe me, without police protection our civilization will go back to jungle law and cannibalism in a very short time."[79] And E. Vick complained that "I don't hear much about improving the morals and behavior of the young Negroes on the part of the so-called Civil Rights groups who are constantly complaining about the police."[80] A letter to Cavanagh from a policeman's wife in 1965 best sums up the growing conservative suspicion that the mayor was chipping away at needed police strength. She specifically cautioned Cavanagh not to "further weaken the protection of Detroit's citizens against the daily rapes, robberies, knifings and murders by lawless members of the Negro community. . . . With the black man's switchblade at their throats, the white community wants a strong, resolute force of well-trained police officers."[81]

Just as the liberal administration's stand against police brutality generated quite virulent attacks from Detroit's conservative white community, its other War on Poverty initiatives soon fueled serious discontent as well. As Elma N. French wrote to Cavanagh regarding the city's "poverty program and the government training programs," blacks "are staying on government aid for generations. . . . [T]hey can see all the movies they wish, buy all the booze they can consume and most of them have a car." She went on to warn the mayor that "tomorrow they will make similar demands on the school board, then the various city, county, state and national offices—until they have the balance of power locally and nationally. . . . God help the white man when the Negro gets control."[82] Another white woman, Pauline Ford, shared French's fears that blacks wanted to take over the Motor City and that the mayor was facilitating their goal. As she wrote to Cavanagh, "surely you know by now that it is impossible to please the Negroes. . . . [I]f you bow to the Negroes, no self-respecting person could vote for you."[83] Another anonymous letter to Cavanagh was even harsher about his policies: "well, have you found you have let the Nigro Situation get out of hand, and what you gona do about it—Bear down or GIVE UP and let them take over. . . [W]e are promised a GHOST city by 1975."[84]

As conservative white Detroiters began speaking out against the Cavanagh administration, so did certain white politicians such as Councilwoman Mary V. Beck. Beck had been popular with many city whites since her initial election to council in 1953, and she, like her electors, became increasingly critical of the mayor as the 1960s progressed. In 1967, Beck took the audacious step of trying to recall Cavanagh hoping to oust him from office or at least get him to alter his political course. To Cavanagh's tremendous relief, however, black and white liberals in his administration and within the very-powerful UAW stood by him. In Cavanagh's defense, union leaders stated that "the UAW, therefore, strongly urges that the citizens of Detroit not permit themselves to be diverted by the few who resort to abuse . . . to solve problems [and] . . . sow the seeds of hate and prejudice at the expense of the total community."[85] But while the mayor thwarted Beck's offensive, he did not quell conservative whites' seething criticism of his police and welfare policies.

Overall, Cavanagh chose largely to ignore critical whites.[86] The mayor was far more concerned with the escalating discontent of those poor and working-class black Detroiters whose votes had cemented his electoral win.

Therefore, between 1965 and 1967, he decided to step up his efforts to implement the Great Society and, most pressingly, to reform the DPD. Cavanagh was determined to address the troubling fact that, although the city had received its "first application for a complaint alleging denial of equal protection of the laws because of race" in February 1964,[87] between 1964 and 1966, it had received an additional 174 complaints against law enforcement agencies specifically.[88] But when the mayor decided to accelerate his reform efforts, he never adequately analyzed why his administration's previous efforts had failed.

The Cavanagh administration initially had addressed the police problem by calling for equal employment opportunities within the force, by ordering greater training and discipline for its officers, and by increasing the communication both within the DPD and between the DPD and the community.[89] On September 16, 1964, for example, the CCR had written to Commissioner Girardin to strongly suggest he invite "representatives of such groups as the NAACP . . . to participate in regularly scheduled meetings with the Commission and the DPD."[90] Girardin agreed to do this and also agreed to "investigate all citizen complaints alleging: misconduct, mistreatment or discrimination by any police officer, police departmental actions resulting in the denial of civil rights or civil liberties" through the Citizen Complaint Bureau (CCB).[91] These proposed meetings between the CCR, the DPD, and the NAACP were well under way by December 1964, and correspondence regarding the various issues on the table that year went to all of these parties.[92] The CCB was also very busy. According to the police department, "As of November 22, 1965 the Bureau has received 89 complaints."[93]

But these early reform efforts had failed largely because the Cavanagh administration accepted the premise that the DPD should play a role in its own reform, rather than be subjected to a civilian review board. As letters from Commissioner Girardin to the Reverend James Wadsworth of the NAACP make clear, the meetings on citizen grievances had accomplished virtually nothing. Regarding black Detroiters Leonard Joseph, Eugene Tyson, Ruth Rembert, and Donna Tyson, Girardin wrote, "your complainants' allegations that they were discriminated against because of their race is not sustained by this investigation."[94] Regarding complainant Eugene Dowdell, Girardin concluded, "the allegation based upon race is not sustained by our investigation."[95] And for Leo Smith and Leroy Smith, "Investigation of the . . . case . . . [also] failed to produce sufficient evidence to sustain any action regarding racial overtones."[96] Clearly, Commissioner Girardin did not believe that his officers discriminated against black Detroiters, and he assured Wadsworth, "you know you and the other officers of the NAACP have my very best wishes for success in the coming years."[97] But the NAACP was no more encouraged by Girardin's sentiments than was the black community at large. Of the 89 complaints filed with the CCB, only 52 were investigated as of November 22, 1965, and of those, "38 complaints were not sustained."[98]

Even when the mayor escalated police reform efforts after 1965, little progress was made because, once again, the police retained too much control over the reform process. In 1966, Cavanagh called on the MCRC to intercede with the DPD to improve police procedure. In a seemingly cooperative gesture, that April, Commissioner Girardin signed a document with Burton Gordin, executive director of the MCRC, which included a fourteen-point "memorandum of agreement between the Michigan Civil Rights Commission and the DPD on the procedural steps in the investigations of civil rights complaints." Almost immediately, however, there was a "breakdown of the Girardin-Gordin agreement" because the DPD would not produce documents (such as officer arrest notes) in good faith.[99]

Despite the continuing dismal results of police reform efforts, well into 1967 citizens nevertheless filed official complaints against the police, naively hoping the more evidence of police abuse that civic leaders had before them, the more aggressively they would act against renegade members of law enforcement. Where there had been 105 citizen complaints filed against the DPD in 1965, for example, in 1967 there were 278.[100] And as the black middle class well knew, this dramatic escalation of citizen complaints was a very ominous sign. Without significant and immediate reform, these middle-class leaders feared that real trouble was on the horizon.

By 1967, black leaders began trying desperately to let the white liberal leadership know just how serious city blacks' frustration was. As Dr. Albert Wheeler, president of the Michigan Conference of NAACP Branches, put it bluntly when he spoke before the MCRC's Conference for Municipal Officials on January 16, 1967, "part of my mixed emotions here today is hopelessness and frustration—we have spent endless hours in meetings and negotiations only to reap ineffective token remedies. Even reasonable, honest, long-suffering Negroes like me are beginning to lose patience and hope in meetings such as this."[101] But while black leaders willingly expressed their dismay with the Cavanagh administration's inability to effect real change, they nevertheless stuck by their white liberal friends and did not consider joining forces with discontented blacks to demand more aggressive action.[102] Indeed, the increasingly anti-liberal grassroots discontent surfacing around them greatly alarmed the black middle class and it warned white civic leaders of the serious threat that they both faced if substantive change did not soon occur. Again, as Wheeler put it, there is a "large mass of human beings [which] has been on the side lines hoping against hope that NAACP, the Urban League, CORE, ACLU, and Federal, State, and Local Civil Rights Commissions were going to open new doors for training, for opportunity, for family life, and for human dignity. But day-by-day and year-by-year, defeats which these groups experience only add to the bitterness of the human beings in the ghetto and drives younger people into the camps of the militants and the black nationalists."[103]

Although black nationalism was not a significant political force in Detroit until the late 1960s, middle-class blacks clearly considered it a potential

44

problem. They had taken notice when Malcolm X helped to organize the Northern Grassroots Conference at Mr. Kelley's Lounge and Recreation Center in Detroit in 1963. Even though there were only about 700 people in attendance, liberal observers were alarmed that this group represented eleven states. Even more unsettling was the fact that Malcolm X's highly inflammatory "Message to the Grass Roots" speech at this gathering had been recorded so that every disillusioned Detroiter would have the opportunity to consider its message.[104] As Dr. Wheeler noted with trepidation, "This is a relatively small group whose future and destiny depend upon whether you as public officials continue to bury your heads in the sands of unreality or whether you face the racial issue honestly and courageously."[105]

Thanks to the numerous warnings of the black middle class, by 1967, Detroit's white liberal leaders were certainly aware that "even though there has been improvement, mutual distrust, suspicion and hostility continues to exist between police officers and members of the Negro community."[106] And just as important, they recognized that "the 'alienated cores' of a Negro poor are potential powder kegs in Detroit (as elsewhere) and a systematic effort is being made to ignite, exploit and direct a chain explosion within them. The effort is being made by black nationalists, Maoists, terrorist, and other minuscule groups."[107] But white liberal leaders still focused primarily on the fact that the all-powerful NAACP stood by them and thus believed that they could still shape the city as planned. Indeed, while some black leaders had become openly critical of Cavanagh, it is significant that the city's biggest civil rights organization dutifully supported him. On January 25, 1965, when black representatives from Northern High School, the Cotillion Club, and the Urban League met at black attorney George Crockett's office to write a letter to the mayor saying that he had not fulfilled his commitments to the black community,[108] the NAACP did not send a representative and later refused to sign the letter.[109]

The fact that black leaders such as Crockett were willing to censure the Cavanagh administration undoubtedly heartened many in the black community. Others, however, were outraged by the willingness of black middle-class liberals to stick by white political allies even after their complaints and warnings went unheeded. These citizens knew well that black leaders had been expressing their discontent and had been warning the city's white administration with no satisfaction for years. In 1961, for example, Whitney Young, director of the National Urban League, had spoken publicly on black leaders' dismay that "the continuing segregation in schools and other places of public service and accommodation . . . stifles the community and perpetuates suspicion, fears and hatreds all which serve to keep the Negro citizen out of the mainstream life."[110] Then, in the spring of 1965, the executive director of the Detroit Urban League, Francis Kornegay, had written to Cavanagh suggesting that, together, they set up a "broad and representative forum [before the summer] to . . . help reduce the possibilities of racial conflict, tension, and incidents which could transpose us from the asset side to the liability side of the human ledger."[111] Because so little had changed since 1961, or even after 1964, however, in the summer of 1967, a segment of Detroit finally did what civic leaders had feared most—it set city neighborhoods ablaze. In doing so, these Detroiters fully shattered the 1961 dream that the Motor City soon would be economically secure, socially peaceful, and politically stable.

In the wee hours of July 23, 1967, Detroit police officers engaged in a routine raid on a "blind pig" in the city where a party was taking place to celebrate the return of a black veteran from Vietnam. But when these officers arrested 82 people, they touched a nerve in the black community. In the one hour that it took to make its arrests, the DPD attracted the attention of more than 200 local residents. According to an eyewitness, "Negroes coming out Sunday morning were first dismayed by the presence of the police. As onlookers grew, the police increased their force. Dismay turned to anger at the show of force."[112] By 8:25 that morning, the crowd assembled had grown noticeably agitated and unruly. Specifically, the residents of this poor neighborhood began throwing bottles into the windows of police cars and setting fires. By 8:30 a.m., Michigan's governor, George Romney, felt it necessary to fly over the area in a helicopter. By the time Romney was circling above, police in full riot gear had blocked off one square mile of the city, and, at that point, "several Negroes in a green paneled truck drove through the area minutes later with sound equipment repeating 'This is Black Power. Fight for your rights!'"[113] Romney and Cavanagh then decided to call in 9,200 National Guardsmen and 800 State Police officers.

By 2:15 a.m. on July 24, 1967, Cavanagh and Romney agreed to call in federal help, and by 9 a.m., President Johnson sent in 4,700 paratroopers from the 3d Brigade 82d Airborne Division and the 2d Brigade 101st Airborne Division which had recently returned from Vietnam. As members of the military attempted to restore order, the violence taking place around them was staggering. During this melee, the age-old hostilities between black urbanites and the DPD boiled over in shocking ways. Rumors flew through city streets that black Detroiters in the riot zone were taking every opportunity to attack police cars and to snipe at officers from behind windows. Before confirming the truth of these rumors, local police officers unleashed their fury on city blacks.[114] Journalists from the *Washington Post* reported two such incidents of extraordinary police violence. In one case, a black man came into the emergency room of a Detroit hospital with his hands cuffed behind his back and his face was covered in blood. As journalists wrote, "'Somebody help me, somebody help me,' the Negro pleaded. A blue helmeted policeman stepped up to the handcuffed prisoner and kicked him in the groin. 'You should have thought of that before you started this, Nigger' the policeman said."[115] In another case, a drunken black man whom the police recently had arrested was shouting curses from the back of a squad car when a short, thick-necked white city policeman in a riot helmet yelled back at the drunk to "Shut Up." Apparently the prisoner made some obscene reference to the policeman's ancestry. "You can't call my mother that you Black bastard. I won't kill you in front of the newspaper reporters"—the latter remark with an angry glance in our direction—"But I'll shut your mouth." With that he thrust the butt of his rifle into the car and smashed the handcuffed prisoner in the face again and again and again. The prisoner collapsed and rolled onto the floor of the car.[116]

As a result of such extreme violence, when the military finally was able to restore order in the Motor City, thirty-three black and ten white Detroiters were dead.[117]

The magnitude of destruction and violence in Detroit's July insurrection shocked not only the Motor City but the whole of America. Although there had been other urban uprisings in recent years, most notably in Watts and in Newark, it was Detroit's upheaval that caused President Johnson to appoint a special commission to determine why such conflict was erupting at the very height of his ambitious plans to improve life for America's poor. Johnson suspected that black nationalist troublemakers were sparking the nation's urban uprisings. However the experts that Johnson had appointed to the Kerner Commission, to determine the cause of the nations rash of urban uprisings after 1964, disagreed. According to the commission, urban uprisings were in fact the expression of pent-up (and largely legitimate) frustration with the persistence of de facto segregation, the ever-present reality of racial discrimination, and the overwhelming evidence of police brutality in African American areas of the nation's cities.

Because 1967 witnessed a total of 164 eruptions in 128 cities across the United States, much recent scholarship has suggested that it was precisely this sort of urban upheaval that sounded the death knell for America's inner cities. But this perspective ignores the fact that, just as the catastrophic Great Depression generated new political options for how America might be ordered, the polarizing urban rebellions of the 1960s generated new political possibilities for America's inner cities. In this case, racial inequalities and tensions, not economics alone, would lead to a new moment of extraordinary political uncertainty as the 1960s ended and the 1970s began.

3: Driving Desperation on the

Auto Shop Floor

I realize that the UAW is not a perfect organization, however, in the field of civil rights we have come a long way together and it has always been in the forefront for equal justice for all. It is now more than ever very much needed for us to close ranks and fight together for equal rights for all.[1]

After moving back to Detroit on March 7, 1965, James Johnson Jr. got a job at Michigan Drum, a small company owned by a man named Harold Hoffman. Johnson made $80 a week working in pit burn drums with rubber cement that he scooped up with a shovel. This job was physically grueling because the pit was extremely hot, and the shoveling required in it was very strenuous. All but two of the workers at this low-paying and dirty facility were black, and the supervisor was white. This supervisor did not get along with the black workers at all, and he made Johnson in particular feel uncomfortable. Nevertheless, Johnson tried not to cause trouble on the job. Even though Michigan Drum was a Teamster shop, Johnson never took the issue of his inhumane working conditions to the union. Instead, he began politely asking his supervisor to take him out of the pit because of the terribly hot temperature. But Johnson never got a transfer. When he finally decided that the supervisor was determined to keep him in the pit, Johnson quit this job and began looking for a new one.

In January 1966, Johnson finally landed another job that was less physically demanding and seemed to offer more security, although it did not pay nearly as much as he had hoped. Working as a janitor for the City of Detroit in both the Bureau of Weights and Measures and the Bureau of Markets, Johnson made about $2.90 an hour. It bothered him that he was earning far less than he might have in the auto industry. But as the scores of black workers who did get hired in that industry soon realized, life on the assembly line, while more lucrative, was far from the ideal that Johnson imagined it to be.

In 1967, the optimism that had inspired liberal city leaders to action in 1961 had gone up in smoke. A similar fate befell the early-1960s hopefulness of Detroit's labor liberals. In fact, the liberal leaders of Detroit's UAW had a great deal in common with their civic counterparts. This contingent not only came to work closely with the Cavanagh administration to implement various civil rights and Great Society initiatives in Detroit, but it had also promised its constituency a similarly daunting array of reforms during the 1960s. Specifically, UAW leaders had promised workers that they would make inroads in eliminating the racial discrimination that had flourished on shop floors ever since the Second Great Migration. They also committed themselves to reining in the foremen abuses that their workers routinely endured.

But just as civic liberals had largely failed to end discrimination or eradicate police brutality in the city, so did labor leaders fail in their efforts to bring similar reforms to the shop floor. In time, liberal labor leaders were also faced with a deeply disenchanted constituency. Some workers channeled their frustration into filing more workplace grievances. Some joined groups that urged the union to become more aggressive with the company. Others simply stayed home from work. And mirroring the situation simultaneously unfolding in the city, the plants' most disillusioned workers chose to lash out. By 1967, Detroit's shop floors became the site of many violent confrontations between frustrated laborers and their foremen, and thus, by that year, the social and political crisis that had befallen the city had come to encompass its workplaces as well.

* * * *

As we have seen, Detroit's African American residents had greeted the 1960s with much optimism. And as workers in Detroit's auto plants, African Americans felt similarly positive about the future. In 1957, Detroit's black autoworkers also began to mobilize against the racial discrimination that persisted in their own union by forming the Trade Union Leadership Council (TULC). With the TULC, they hoped "to demand Black entrance into the skilled trades and into the leadership of the UAW."[2]

The TULC was a formidable group, and workers greatly respected its top officers. Many had been UAW activists for years, both aiding the union in its early battles for recognition and helping it in many dangerous confrontations with management.[3] TULC activists Robert Battle III, Horrace Sheffield, Shelton Tappes, and Marc Stepp were particularly known for their work on behalf of the early UAW, but other TULC members also enjoyed a positive reputation on the shop floor. It greatly heartened black workers that the TULC was willing to express to both the union and management what they had long felt about their position in the plants. As Sheffield said publicly, "there is no denying the plain fact that most Negroes in and out of labor are not satisfied with the movement towards eliminating racial discrimination that still exists."[4] To eradicate such discrimination, the TULC leaders first conducted "accurate surveys of each union . . . to find where the problem exists,"[5] and then they began to push for the placement of a black man on the International Executive Board (IEB) of the UAW.

Simultaneous to engaging in these union reform efforts, the TULC also was actively involving itself in efforts to bring about racial equality in the city of Detroit. To TULC activists, the labor and civic arenas were inexorably linked. In fact, the TULC put as much effort into civic activism as it did into the labor activism for which it is known. Seeking to fill the void that "the organization believes to exist between labor and the general public,"[6] the TULC's community activism centered on the A. Philip Randolph Freedom House, which it established in a renovated hardware store.[7] In the Freedom House, the TULC held educational events and debates as well as sponsored classes in art and music; typing and shorthand courses; leadership development classes; reading efficiency classes; sewing, modeling, and fashion designing classes. It also provided job-training services.[8]

Like their fellow activists in the NAACP, the TULC believed that one of the best ways to improve the city was to work with progressive whites to oust conservatives wherever they held power. According to TULC leaders, they had "developed a genuine rapport with all facets of the Negro Community and a spirit of fellowship and cooperation with the white liberal community."[9] In that spirit, on August 24, 1960, Battle issued a press release on behalf of the TULC endorsing the "national Democratic Party ticket of Senators John Kennedy and Lyndon Johnson in the November election." Battle stated that the TULC "earnestly believes that the chances of the Negro people for greater progress in achieving first-class citizenship everywhere in this country will be greater if we stick to our historic allies, [and] support the political party that is more responsive to the people's needs which is now represented by the Kennedy-Johnson ticket."[10]

The TULC's commitment to Detroit's white racial progressives was as firm as its loyalty to the Kennedy liberals in Washington. The TULC shared the belief of local white progressives that the ballot box was the key to social change,[11] and it came to support the efforts of any racial reformer seeking power in Detroit. As Sheffield saw it, "the coalition between the labor movement, the Negro community, the Democratic party, liberal white forces, and other ethnic groups has really made for some progressive changes."[12]

When the opportunity to elect a civil rights–supporting mayor finally arose in 1961, not surprisingly TULC leaders were optimistic that their work with Detroit's progressive whites and their growing presence within the liberally led UAW would spell the end for the oppressive racial conditions that flourished under Mayor Louis Miriani. As the 1961 election neared, however, TULC leaders had a rude awakening. The UAW chose to endorse Miriani, not Cavanagh, for the mayoralty. Officially, the UAW did not make independent endorsements for mayor, but, rather, it accepted the candidate chosen by the Wayne County AFL-CIO. This, however, did not make TULC leaders feel any better. The UAW's support of Miriani not only disappointed TULC officials; it also surprised them.

It was not as if the TULC believed that its desires and those of the UAW hierarchy were necessarily one and the same. In fact, when black reformers created the TULC, the UAW leadership made it clear that it viewed this new organization with much suspicion. The TULC's vocal position that it was not going to "wait any longer" to end discrimination in the labor movement, combined with the fact that some TULC leaders hailed from the historically combative and left-wing Local 600, had made the UAW's top brass very uneasy. The reality was that TULC leaders had always attempted to persuade the UAW that their group's primary target was not the UAW. In fact, the TULC reserved most of its venom for labor groups other than the UAW (particularly the national AFL-CIO), and its leadership had made the conscious decision to work with the UAW toward a better future for black workers. As Sheffield put it, "we are going to fight with everything in our power, in a constructive way, along with other liberals within the UAW—and there are a lot of them—who feel this question [discrimination] must be met."[13]

But while UAW officials promoted themselves as racial progressives, given the many racially conservative whites in the union, they nevertheless sought to distance themselves from the TULC whenever it advocated a more accelerated pace of integrating the labor movement.[14] Sensing this UAW wariness, TULC leaders consistently tried to assuage union fears by pointing to the cooperative future that they envisioned. TULC leaders began circulating the TULC Constitution among top UAW leaders, but when even this did not alleviate UAW concern, they did tend to go on the offensive.[15] In a letter to UAW leader Bill Beckham, for example, the TULC's Executive Committee countered his assertion that the TULC "is harmful because its presence tends to interfere with the evolutionary process that is doing so much to bring the Negro to full equality" by reiterating the necessity of their program for more accelerated change and then chiding him for painting the TULC as a group of troublemakers.[16] As TULC leaders wrote, "it has come to our attention that you have continued your misrepresentations of the TULC notwithstanding the fact that you have been amply informed, on several occasions, of precisely what the activities and objective of the TULC were."[17] They then went on to say that "it is most apparent that either you do not read too well or else you are incapable of understanding what you read."[18]

Such caustic responses did not sit well with UAW leaders. Many felt strongly that the white hostility to blacks that erupted routinely in the city might also erupt in the plants if provoked by such racially charged TULC rhetoric. Notably, however, these leaders did not simply ignore TULC desires. Indeed, top union officials privately assured the TULC that greater black representation soon would become a reality. Because UAW leaders at least theoretically supported TULC goals, and because they did not exhibit overt hostility when the TULC repeatedly took the issue of greater black representation up at the union's annual conventions, the two organizations had seemed to settle into a fairly good working relationship by 1961. Of course, this was yet another reason why the TULC had assumed that the UAW would be at the forefront of electoral efforts to roll back racial conservatism in city politics.

From the UAW's perspective, however, the question of whom to support in the mayoral election of 1961 was not at an easy one. Not only did the UAW believe that its overwhelming white constituency would insist on an endorsement of Miriani, but Miriani was also a friend, not a foe, to the UAW leadership. While many black workers and citizens recoiled from the idea that Miriani might win the mayoralty again, UAW leaders believed that the mayor had done the best job of leading the city that anyone could have, given how tense civic relations had become since World War II. As Alex Roche, the Committee on Political Education (COPE) director at UAW Local 223, put it, "while conditions in the city of Detroit have not exactly been rosy over the past few years . . . in view of all these demands upon our city government, it is evident that Mayor Miriani has done an excellent job of running our affairs despite the fact that many of us are frequently unhappy about one thing or another. We had better stick with those whose leadership we can depend on."[19]

The UAW's certainty that its constituents would want it to back Miriani is supported by the fact that the union endorsed him even before every candidate had declared his attention to run. And even before the AFL-CIO officially announced its endorsement on June 20, 1961, the UAW already had invited the mayor to speak at two rallies against unemployment and also to be a featured guest at its most recent annual convention. These moves greatly alarmed the TULC, which saw the convention invitation in particular as a most ominous sign for the upcoming election. The TULC also found it ironic that the UAW had placed civil rights luminary Martin Luther King Jr. on the same featured speaker's roster.[20] The UAW, however, saw no inconsistency in its lineup of honored guests. Indeed, union leaders believed not only that their own commitment to civil rights was beyond reproach, but also that Detroit's labor movement was fully of one mind about who should be elected in 1961. As Al Barbour of the Wayne County AFL-CIO wrote to UAW leader Roy Reuther, Walter Reuther's brother, "we really appreciate the excellent letter you sent out to the affiliated UAW local unions for the upcoming election of Tuesday, November 7th . . . [because] the trade union movement is going in one direction; I am real optimistic for the endorsed candidates."[21]

Had UAW and AFL-CIO leaders paid closer attention to the TULC and its black constituents, however, they would have quickly realized that the trade union movement was not going in the same direction at all. When asked his thoughts on Miriani, TULC Vice President Horace Sheffield forcefully maintained that "the Mayor had been an obstinate person—you go down to try and see him on any problem pertaining to the Negro community, or pertaining to labor ... [and he] was never around."[22] In the *Michigan Chronicle,* Sheffield lashed out specifically at Miriani's reelection bid when he noted that "in Detroit, where 39 percent of the Negro labor force is unemployed as of March 1961—and that's over 12,000 Negroes—in this context, talk of the past, or promises for the future just don't catch on, for all of us live in the present, we have to feed out children and pay our bills daily."[23]

Horace Sheffield of the Trade Union Leadership Council, January 7, 1972. *Walter P. Reuther, Wayne State University.*

But while TULC leaders were greatly taken aback by the UAW's support of Miriani, and while they still greatly valued their relationship with top union leaders, these civil rights activists did not waver in their determination to beat back racial conservatism in the city as the election of 1961 approached. Despite the UAW's endorsement of Miriani, and with the Wayne County AFL-CIO and UAW staffers across the city mobilizing on a massive scale for his reelection, the TULC did everything it could to elect Cavanagh. As a result of the TULC's combined efforts with the city's civil rights forces, black and white Detroiters together, to the UAW's amazement, had thwarted the electoral desires of its racially conservative white constituents.[24]

Sheffield's role in securing this dramatic political upset did not sit well with the Detroit labor movement's leadership. By 1961, Sheffield was a spokesman for and leader of the TULC, as well as the coordinator of the Fifteenth Congressional District of the Wayne County AFL-CIO's COPE program, which had handed down the directive that union members should support Miriani. One of the key jobs of COPE coordinators was to get the vote out, and, as the campaign of 1961 unfolded, labor leaders had warned Sheffield not to forget his loyalties. On October 23, 1961, Al Barbour of the AFL-CIO wrote directly to Sheffield to remind him that "*all* of us are expected to abide by and support those decisions [to support Miriani]. This is particularly true of trade union leadership."[25] Barbour had sent copies of this letter to UAW leaders Walter Reuther, Emil Mazey, Leonard Woodcock, Douglas Fraser, Joseph McCusker, George Merrelli, Ken Morris, and Roy Reuther, indicating that these men were equally concerned about Sheffield's vocal criticism of Miriani. In response to Barbour, Sheffield defended his anti-Miriani views but eventually went on to assure him that he was "well aware of the responsibility I have to the political program of the Wayne County AFL-CIO."[26] Yet, while Sheffield did dutifully spread the word that the AFL-CIO and UAW each were asking workers to support Miriani in his capacity as COPE coordinator, at various other public functions he still used his personal time to campaign vigorously for Cavanagh.

Not surprisingly, it took some time for relations between labor's top brass and Sheffield to warm. Even though leaders of the UAW and TULC improved their relationship after 1961, in part because Cavanagh's many civic initiatives required that they work together, mutual suspicion abounded. In 1966, when Walter Reuther attempted to send Sheffield to a post in Washington, D.C., for example, black trade unionists were fully persuaded that the UAW still harbored ill feelings toward the TULC and was retaliating against Sheffield for his renegade campaigning during the 1961 election. At a public event in 1966, the TULC's Battle accused Emil Mazey, Al Barbour, and even black UAW leader Nelson "Jack" Edwards of engaging in a "conspiracy" to remove Sheffield from Detroit for his earlier support of Cavanagh against UAW protocol.[27] As the *Detroit News* reported, at this "raucous biracial gathering," not just Battle but more than "250 persons shouted and hissed their protests Saturday night against the reassignment to Washington of Horace Sheffield."[28] Clearly, many civic liberals, both black and white, took exception to the suspected political overtones behind Reuther's directive to Sheffield. Jack Casper of the Jewish Labor Committee, for example, wrote to colleague Irwin Small of his relief that, at least, Sheffield was not backing down by capitulating to Reuther's desires.[29] As Casper put it, "as of the moment he [Sheffield] refused to go and, in response to an ultimatum to go or get out delivered at a meeting with Walter, Roy and Bluestone, [Sheffield] is planning to return to the shops."[30]

The fact that vocal liberal activists like Casper supported Sheffield (indeed he wrote, "every feeling of loyalty I have is with Horace")[31] and the fact that Mayor Cavanagh himself was one of those attending the "raucous" gathering in support of Sheffield, certainly reflected tensions between city liberals and the UAW's leadership long after the 1961 election.[32] But between 1961 and 1964, the UAW actually had come to enjoy a most cooperative working relationship with the Cavanagh administration and, in turn, mended its fences with TULC leaders. Indicating an easing of UAW/TULC tensions on May 8, 1962, 2,400 delegates at the UAW's Constitutional Convention voted unanimously to elect African American UAW member Nelson "Jack" Edwards to the union's twenty-seven-man IEB.[33] And, in 1964, when Cavanagh began trying to sell fellow Detroit liberals on the merits of bringing LBJ's Great Society initiatives to the city, the leadership of the UAW, along with the leadership of the TULC, stood firmly behind him.

The UAW-Cavanagh détente was facilitated to a large extent by the fact that the UAW's top leadership had an independent and close relationship with the Johnson administration. When UAW leaders heard Washington Democrats speak of the imperative to push for the Great Society, they went on record that their union is "is vitally interested in the War on Poverty" and began actively to discuss concrete ways in which it could help the program along.[34] As the UAW's Bluestone wrote to Brendan Sexton, acting director of program support in the Office of Economic Opportunity, "within the next couple of weeks, the UAW officers will be discussing ways and means to involve staff and local union leadership in the anti-poverty program. . . . I would appreciate any ideas you may have on this subject which may form the basis of an activity program for the UAW to undertake."[35] In regard to national liberal efforts to train field workers in community development, Walter Reuther himself wrote to Sexton that "I share your view that this is a worthwhile project and we ought to move ahead without further delay."[36]

In seeking out its own role to play in the War on Poverty and Great Society programs emanating from Washington, and hoping to shape these initiatives as well, the UAW's leadership necessarily found itself working with Cavanagh and, thus, endorsing his administration.[37] In 1966, Walter Reuther wrote Mayor Cavanagh a passionate letter expressing his belief that "Detroit can become an exciting and shining model of a 20th century city in the Great Society." He pledged "on behalf of the officers and members of the UAW, our fullest cooperation, including moral commitment and financial support" for, in this case, their joint plan to create a civic organization called the Detroit Citizens Development Authority.[38]

At the height of the Cavanagh administration's efforts to bring the Great Society to Detroit, virtually every top UAW leader worked closely with civic liberals and TULC leaders alike to wage a real War on Poverty. Top UAW officials such as Doug Fraser and TULC leaders such as Marc Stepp each were pivotal figures on Detroit's Total Action against Poverty Policy-Advisory Committee. Additionally, when City Councilman Mel Ravitz initiated a series of meetings on the city's poverty program that would in turn forward suggestions to the mayor, UAW leaders Ken Bannon, Irving Bluestone, Anthony Canole, Marcellius Ivory, Olga Magdar, and William H. Oliver, along with TULC leader Battle, actively participated.[39] That the UAW eventually came to support not just Cavanagh's Great Society initiatives but also Cavanagh "the man" became clear in 1967, when Councilwoman Mary Beck attempted to unseat the mayor with her recall campaign. Despite the fact that the *Detroit News* had suggested in 1953 that "members of organized labor and their friends never had a more true friend . . . than Mary Beck,"[40] UAW officials including Bluestone and Millie Jefferies drafted public statements indicating that the UAW's support of Cavanagh was unwavering.[41] And, in response to such UAW support, Cavanagh personally wrote to Walter Reuther, "I greatly appreciate the expression of your opinions in this matter. . . . I think that your statement will be extremely influential in stabilizing attitudes within our community."[42]

The UAW leadership's support of the Cavanagh administration only grew as the Johnson administration came to endorse greater racial equality initiatives for America. Cavanagh had always been vocal about his support of civil rights, but after Congress passed federal civil rights measures and LBJ began to speak out on their behalf, the UAW and Cavanagh really came to share a public commitment to making civil rights a cornerstone of the city's political agenda. True, the UAW had been a vital presence in the 1963 March on Washington, but it was not until the OEO in Washington came to address the economics of racial discrimination more explicitly that the UAW followed suit. By 1966, UAW leaders such as Bluestone were sharing thoughts with officials in the Equal Opportunity Commission about "the dismal figures concerning the unemployment of minority groups in a period when national unemployment is at its lowest point in many, many years," and about "the great moral problem of equal opportunity for all."[43] And just as Washington politicians came to involve themselves more actively in the civil rights dramas being played out in the South, so did the UAW. Walter Reuther, for example, personally wrote to Myrlie Evers after her husband's brutal murder: "in your hour of grief and profound sorrow, we tender you our sincere condolences. While we can never replace your immeasurable loss, those of us who remain solemnly pledge that your husband, Medger Evers, soldier in the fight for freedom and dignity, shall not have died in vain."[44] In concert with various Washington liberals, by 1966 the UAW was helping to better the lives of both Mexican farm workers in the West and African American sharecroppers in the South.

Simultaneously, UAW leaders came to speak out more aggressively against the racial discrimination that obviously still plagued Detroit and its auto plants. On June 23, 1963, Walter Reuther, Joseph McCusker, and George Merrelli walked with Cavanagh and Martin Luther King Jr. in a massive march for civil rights down Detroit's Woodward Avenue. The presence of these union leaders at this civil rights event, like their activism in TAP, not only placed the UAW firmly within the Cavanagh fold, but also served further to mend fences between the UAW and the TULC. UAW participation in that march, for example, prompted the president of Local 835, Eugene Martin, to write to the TULC asking its leaders to recognize the real strides that the UAW had been making in furthering the cause of black equality.[45] Although initially dubious, the TULC came to agree with Martin's assessment: On October 23, 1965, it awarded Reuther the TULC's A. Philip Randolph Freedom Award at the organization's annual Freedom Ball. By 1965, Reuther had also received the National Urban League's Equal Opportunity Day Award,[46] as well as a civil rights award from the U.S. Department of Labor for his efforts to tackle discrimination in the workplace. When Hugh Murphy from the U.S. Department of Labor presented Reuther with this honor for opening the skilled trades to more African Americans, he claimed that "few Americans have distinguished themselves in the field of civil rights as the President of the United Autoworkers, Walter P. Reuther."[47]

Clearly it helped the UAW's top leadership to warm to the Cavanagh administration when the Johnson administration came to see him as its poster boy for the Great Society. Likewise, the UAW's support of Cavanagh persuaded many initially suspicious white workers that the mayor's liberal initiatives might have some merit. Indeed the UAW's strong support for Cavanagh clearly facilitated his landslide second term election victory. But just as the city's most conservative white residents and workers remained unnerved by the mayor's civil rights sympathies, so did they remain leery of the UAW's involvement in anti-discrimination measures. While many of these workers supported other Great Society efforts (such as those to secure full employment and more humane workplaces), a fair number of them actively discouraged the UAW from putting too much effort into addressing the needs of African Americans. As one woman, Ethel Schlacht, wrote to Walter Reuther, "how can you be so blind, as to suggest and justify Negro riots, and bloodshed?"[48] Worker Wallace H. Brown wrote to Reuther, "since you have an affinity for joining off-color organizations, you should resign your position and take up full time job marching for civil rights."[49]

Composite image of the march down Woodward Avenue, June 1963, showing Walter P. Reuther, Benjamin McFall, Dr. Martin Luther King Jr., and the Reverend C. L. Franklin. *Walter P. Reuther Library, Wayne State University.*

But while the UAW's more deliberate support of civil rights made its conservative white workers uneasy, its new public commitment to fighting for the oppressed thrilled other whites and blacks in the plants. Indeed, the UAW's new identity as both War on Poverty warrior and civil rights champion inspired many laborers—particularly African Americans—to see the future of labor relations more optimistically than they had been able to for decades.

By the mid-1960s, blacks had come to comprise 65 percent to 70 percent of UAW units such as UAW Local 7, 60 percent of UAW Local 3, and 65 percent of plants such as Eldon Avenue gear and axle. That the now-numerous black autoworkers seemed hopeful about the future certainly gladdened union officials.[50] But though their heart was in the right place, these leaders never really grasped how desperately their black constituents needed change on the shop floor. And for the blacks who labored in Detroit's auto plants and in the facilities of the Chrysler Corporation, this need was particularly acute.

Although the Ford Motor Company had hired more African American autoworkers than any other Detroit firm before World War II, thereafter it was Chrysler that took the lead in black hiring. By the 1960s, Chrysler's four huge plants in Detroit made it not only a "major inner-city employer" but also *the* major employer of the city's African Americans.[51] But Chrysler most often hired blacks without giving them either sufficient job security or upward mobility, and it also tended to relegate them to the most hazardous jobs. In addition, African Americans worked in the most labor-intensive, most extraordinarily dirty, and most unsafe operations within Chrysler's decrepit foundry, stamping, and paint facilities.[52] They particularly suffered from the fact Chrysler had invested very little in its inner-city plants and automotive machinery during the 1960s, while running its old equipment at and above full productive capacity.

And while blacks worked in Chrysler's most decayed plants and dangerous jobs, the company they worked for was turning out more and more cars to meet growing consumer demand. In fact, by the 1960s, Chrysler was routinely putting all of its Detroit workers on six- to seven-day schedules and was working them twelve-hour shifts. The effect of this speed-up and forced overtime was that Chrysler's workers, particularly its black workers in the worst jobs, were strained both physically and emotionally. The faster the line ran, the more tired the workers became. The older and more decrepit the machinery, the more auto jobs became a health and safety hazard. In combination, Chrysler's inadequate internal investment and managerial aggressiveness, along with its inhumane overtime demands, contributed to the hazardous conditions that increasingly made the life of black workers in particular, but all workers to a great extent, hard to bear.

In the early 1960s, right when UAW and TULC leaders were wrangling over who should rule Detroit, Chrysler's black and white line workers were really feeling squeezed. Daily they were enduring the effects of management's attempt to wring as much production out of them as it could with as little attention to shop-floor conditions as possible. In 1960, for example, managers penalized Jefferson Avenue assembly worker Charles Stein for slacking off even though they had assigned him to two different jobs simultaneously. Outraged, Stein maintained that "he could not perform [these tasks] because of the speed of the line," and even his union steward, J. Jesse, felt compelled to note that "the employees who have always worked in this department are doing their work under duress and strain beyond the ordinary capacity of an average able-bodied man and are constantly complaining [of] backaches, muscle-strain, tension and fatigue."[53] Likewise, when Chrysler management gave worker W. Eichrecht a time-off penalty "because he could not uphold his new workload," Eichrecht's union steward argued that there had been "speed up on this operation. Therefore the penalty given . . . is unjust."[54]

In addition to the speed-up, workers also endured numerous safety hazards and injuries as a result. In 1962, workers were furious that Department 9174 was still a "health hazard [even though] this condition [had] been brought to the attention of management on numerous occasions [but] no corrective measures have been taken."[55] Likewise, "for many months," the employees of Department 9171 at Jefferson assembly had been "suffering from the exhaust fumes that are caused by the worn out jitneys that are being used to supply the production line with material. These jitneys are so bad at times that the operators on the line have to walk away from their operations while the jitney driver is dropping or picking up a load because the fumes are so bad they can't breathe."[56] Workers in this department were alarmed that "all that management has given is a lot of lip service and no action."[57] With such management disregard for health and safety, many workers were also eventually injured. H. Thompson at Chrysler's Eight Mile Road stamping plant was hurt "while transporting material on Hi-Lo #20858 . . . [after] the lift chain broke, which was temporarily welded when broken previously."[58] And another worker at that plant "was hit on the head by a 1 × 6 Hex bolt which became loose from the top of the press that she was working on and as a result was injured causing her to lose time from work."[59]

While it was certainly bad enough that workers had to work faster than they were physically able in order to keep their jobs, and also that they had to risk life and limb as they labored, what made line life particularly intolerable was the fact that line supervisors and foremen wielded their power most capriciously. On June 13, 1962, for example, workers in Department 9890 of Chrysler's Eight Mile stamping plant facility complained to their chief steward, T. Brooks, about "Supervisor H. Goscinski's attitude [because] he has constantly used abusive language . . . [and] he also uses threats."[60] At Jefferson Avenue assembly, workers noted "management's procedure of interviewing employees at home, when they are absent from work,"[61] and workers in Department 9150 of that plant charged that Foreman E. Grant and General Foreman H. Gallo had made "threats against these employees . . . [who] had reason to believe they were working above normal [speed]."[62] Likewise, workers C. England, B. Susylo, O. Pearson, and R. Webster in Department 9150 accused Foreman C. Hunt and General Foreman H. Gallo of "making threats against these employers."[63] Indeed, just as many Detroiters were coming to see police brutality as their biggest city concern as the 1960s progressed, in the plants, the issue of foreman abuse came to take center stage.

Like city policemen, auto plant foremen were overwhelmingly white and came largely from the ranks of the older, premigration workforce. In the early days of the auto industry, foremen typically were drafted right off of the shop floor after many years of reliable service to the company. Although these early foremen most often came from the skilled trades, as opposed to the assembly line,[64] for a time their cultural roots were firmly within the working class. When a worker became a foreman, he usually stayed in his original department, oversaw the output of men whom he had known for years, and was usually still paid an hourly wage.[65] Because foremen often managed employees in the same trades as their own, they would assist in the production setups, laboring side by side with the workers.[66] Certainly, the move into management often placed foremen at serious odds with workers, but in many respects reciprocal relations between foremen and workers had been preserved.[67] This reciprocal relationship was rooted in the fact that, as scholar Steve Jefferys points out, "often the supervisor had the personal authority to recruit family or friends or workers from a similar ethnic background"[68] into the always-sought-after auto jobs. Even in the plants where foremen had little to do with hiring, they almost always had an important degree of discretion when it came to firing.

As the work process altered dramatically during the 1920s and 1930s, foremen began to earn a reputation as seasoned disciplinarians. But several events during the late 1930s and early 1940s indicate that foremen were still culturally and ideologically identified with the working class, despite their more extensive managerial responsibilities. This became particularly evident after the passage of the Wagner Act. For years after the law went into effect, debates raged over whether a foreman was an "employer" or an "employee."[69] For the foremen who felt squeezed by top management during the productivity pushes of the war years and who then felt the intense job insecurity of the immediate postwar years firsthand, it was never that obvious that they were now a part of the managerial, not the working, class.

In 1938, foremen at Detroit's Kelsey-Hayes Wheel Company were so concerned about the familiar labor issues of better wages, working conditions, working hours, and job security that they tried to affiliate with the UAW. And even when the UAW rejected an outright affiliation, the men organized the United Foremen and Supervisors, Local Industrial Union 918, and became a CIO affiliate.[70] In 1941, when foremen at the Ford Motor Company found their wage and job security situation to be little better than that of the UAW members whom they supervised, many of them tried to affiliate with the UAW Local 600. When this was unsuccessful, they organized the Foremen's Association of America (FAA). By 1945, the FAA union had 33,000 members and 152 chapters.[71] As historian Nelson Lichtenstein noted, "foremen began to explore and expand the definition of what constituted a self-conscious working-class identity at mid-century."[72]

Any institutional, cultural, or ideological ties that had bound the auto foremen to the autoworkers, however, were completely severed by the early 1960s. As early as 1939, the National Labor Relations Board pressured the CIO to disband all of the UFS 918 locals. In 1947, a decisive labor dispute at Ford (in combination with the rigorous enforcement of the new Taft-Hartley Act) dealt the death blow to the FAA. Then, throughout the 1950s, top auto management called on foremen to tighten the reins of shop-floor control and to repudiate unionism in any form. In the early 1960s, Chrysler sought to achieve greater shop-floor control by "increas[ing] the number of foremen from a ratio of one to every seventy-five to eighty workers in the 1950s to one for every twenty or twenty-five workers."[73] Ironically, by bolstering the numerical strength of foremen, Chrysler had actually weakened an individual foreman's power to make decisions and to solve problems on the shop floor.

During this same period, Chrysler had also strengthened its corporate labor relations staff in order to centralize all personnel decision-making power to bring the company in line with the other auto companies. This had two significant consequences. First, Chrysler had seriously tampered with the foremen's traditional relationship with the workers when it removed any discretionary bargaining from the front line. Without the foremen's ability to work things out with employees, workers saw less and less that was worthy about these bosses. Whether a worker got along with his particular foreman was much less important when ethnic and friendship connections were no longer avenues for future jobs or insurance against job loss. As Jefferys points out, the control that labor-relations personnel had over the situation on the shop floor "reduced the status of both steward and the foreman and undermined any mutual respect."[74] Equally significant, however, was that Chrysler's elimination of foremen's shop-floor bargaining and negotiating prerogatives had left them with only one role—that of rigid disciplinarians. With little power to resolve problems or incentive to cajole workers into a mutually beneficial resolution of a dispute remaining, foremen increasingly resorted to harassment and intimidation.

Foremen's willingness to police the workforce was also inexorably linked to the rapidly changing racial profile of the workers whom they were supervising. As older white foremen found themselves in charge of younger black workers, the cultural and ideological ties that previously were an incentive for problem-solving had virtually disappeared. Any respect foremen had felt for their workers based on shared friendships, neighborhoods, religion, ethnic traditions, or family backgrounds gave way to distrust, dislike, and disrespect of the newer black workers. Foremen not only were hostile to black workers whom they considered foreign, but they also reviled the youth culture's newly adopted styles of dress, language, and music shared by black and white workers alike. They perceived younger workers to be lacking any respect for authority.

Regardless of their age, however, Detroit's black workers endured foreman aggression the most consistently. For Chrysler's black workers, management's insensitivity to employee grievances was exacerbated by its racially discriminatory practices. Take the case of black worker H. Lewis at Chrysler's Jefferson assembly plant. His foreman, G. Narrod, singled him out for "loafing" on the job. Apparently, Lewis was not the only black worker targeted for penalties by this foreman, because the union noted that "the inhuman impositions that are being experienced [there] must come to an end ... [and] if top management knowingly permits the metal shop regime to commit wrongful acts such as the ones imposed on employee H. Lewis 910–6658, then perhaps someone should contact the Fair Employment Practices Commission or the NAACP."[75] Interestingly, plenty of black workers did begin to contact the NAACP regarding the abuses they endured on the line in this period. This organization had received hundreds of complaints from black workers similar to that of James Lee Cowans, whose foreman at Chrysler continually harassed and tried to fire him, and Robert Washington, who was demoted to a dangerous, heavy, and unskilled job at a General Motors plant where he was seriously injured.[76]

Not only did line management disrespect black workers on their jobs, but it also ignored black seniority when offering promotions. Black workers with seniority ranging from 1935 to 1945 at Chrysler's Jefferson plant, for example, had not been canvassed when skilled trades jobs opened up in the machine repair–welding gun repair department; and because management had been handpicking white workers from the same department for these positions, the local union had "no alternative but to charge racial discrimination."[77] According to the black workers at Jefferson, "in view of the fact that we pay as much as any other race or group for the company built cars that we buy, we feel that discrimination has no place within the walls of our livelihood."[78]

Increasingly, however, virtually every worker, not just black workers, complained bitterly about foremen mistreatment. At Jefferson Avenue assembly, for instance, several workers noted "the arrogant attitude and deliberate action of Foreman Narrod,"[79] while others pointed out that Foreman William Rinke "on numerous occasions" has "threatened both probationary and seniority workers."[80] Workers not only called attention to the ever-present belligerent attitudes and aggressive demeanor of their line foremen, but they also said that management sensitivity to worker needs was reaching an all-time low. Consider the case of worker Ed Krupkinski at Chrysler's Hamtramck facility; he "complained about a severe pain in back of his neck, he could feel bumps all over his neck."[81] Management would "not send him home because he did not have a fever [and when] Ed told the people in medical that he could not stand the pain . . . they still refused him a pass to go home."[82] Likewise, when worker H. Dore had been injured at the Jefferson Avenue assembly plant and "was on this table suffering from immeasurable agony," Dore claimed that the foreman, E. Piwonski, was "more concerned about getting the line moving than getting Dore to medical."[83] Similarly, when worker T. Browner told his foreman, L. Lacroix, that "he had a headache and a pain in his chest," this supervisor delayed his "pass to first aid" and then the general foreman, Mike Melasic, allegedly said, "this is not an emergency; I'll send him as soon as I can get squared off."[84]

Between 1960 and 1964, because so many workers had become disillusioned with shop-floor relations and their union's inability to improve them, dissident groups began to spring up in Detroit's auto plants. While many black workers gravitated to the TULC during this period, some disaffected white workers also began to dissent in an organization called the National

Committee for Democratic Action in UAW (NCFDA). The NCFDA, which in the early 1960s claimed a presence in UAW Locals 3, 15, 22, 140, 155, 163, 212, 306, 599, 600, and 659, stated publicly that "there is an urgent need in the UAW for a return to the militant and united action which was the strength of the rank and file in the 1930s."[85] Workers in the NCFDA "felt that they had enough abuses from the management over speed up and intimidation," and complained that "speed up still resembles sweatshop conditions of old." They wanted, therefore, "to promote growth and progress of the UAW on a democratic basis."[86]

Historically, the UAW did not take kindly to dissidents within its ranks, and the dissent that erupted on its shop floors during the early 1960s was no exception. In addition to viewing the TULC with suspicion for years, some in the UAW actually kept the NCFDA under surveillance. When the NCFDA organized a picnic on Detroit's Belle Isle, for example, to discuss "many problems of seniority, classification and working conditions when the 1961 models get under way,"[87] anonymous individuals surreptitiously attended this event and then reported back to the UAW. According to the author of the report, "arrived about 10:00 a.m.—practically nobody there, so I drove around and for a little while . . . parked on opposite road . . . we sat on a bench about 40 feet from where women were congregating . . . there was nobody there at that time that I recognized."[88] The report went on to recount various speeches given that day and then noted with regret that, "due to traffic and other noises, there was considerable other parts of the speech that I missed."[89] After the UAW received this report, someone typed a document with the initials "A.H." at the bottom, which called attention to the criticisms of the UAW voiced by individual speakers at the Belle Isle event. Particularly noted were the criticisms heard from an outspoken NCFDA member named Andy Kranson, who "spoke for 40 minutes."[90] The author of this document then went on to mention that "Ted Morgan, Recording Secretary, UAW Local 7, called and said the Local cannot tolerate statement of Kranson," and that "UAW Local 7 is scheduling a special meeting of Board next Wednesday and would like direction."[91]

UAW leaders saw the NCFDA's actions as an assault largely because they *had* been trying hard to improve conditions for their constituents on the shop floor during these years. Between 1960 and 1964, the union had not sat idly by as auto companies sped up the line, ignored health and safety hazards, and allowed foremen to abuse line workers. While top UAW officials were preoccupied with civic election efforts and establishing a good working relationship with the Cavanagh administration, local union officials were filing numerous grievances on behalf of workers in many Chrysler plants and were demanding that the company alter its inhumane course.

Union leaders at the Jefferson Avenue assembly plant, for example, more than willingly brought management's attention, once again, to the fact that "there is a health hazard at bays S-22 to S-25 at the front of the glass lines in Department 9172 [in which workers] are inhaling the [paint and thinner] fumes and it is making them sick,"[92] while numerous presidents of UAW locals also put Chrysler on strike notice for issues such as "health and safety" as well as "harassment and coercion" many times between 1960 and 1964.[93] Local union officers were also extremely aggressive in filing grievances against abusive line supervisors and foremen during this period. When Chrysler's safety engineer had approached the workers of Department 3505 at the Eight Mile Road plant with "his Hitleristic demands for immediate obedience" in 1962, for instance, the UAW in turn demanded "an apology" and it told the plant manager to give this man "special instructions on how to conduct himself while being in a supervisory capacity."[94] Likewise, the union demanded that the management at this plant also "immediately penalize Supervisor Marrizio for his retaliatory tactics," that it instruct Supervisor E. Wasser "in regards to the grievance procedure and how it functions," and that E. Wassser give worker E. Chiciuk "an immediate apology for the derogatory remarks."[95]

Regardless of how many grievances were filed, how many union demands were levied, and how many dissident organizations were in existence, Chrysler continued its inhumane treatment of line workers. Indeed, by 1964, tensions between workers and management in Detroit's plants were at an all-time high. But as a result of the UAW, along with the TULC, plunging headlong into various local initiatives of the Great Society that year, workers soon came to believe that their work lives might actually improve. Indeed, after 1964, despite the UAW's previously spotty record of successfully checking management's abuses, its new activist agenda offered workers hope that the established labor-relations mechanisms for dispute resolution might now be more effective. The union had recommitted itself to fighting for the underdog.

True to its word, between 1964 and 1967, the UAW did step up its fight for workers. While UAW officials at the local level filed grievance after grievance on behalf of workers, the UAW International tried to gain more for workers in negotiations with management at the national level.[96] During the 1964 contract negotiations with Chrysler, for example, Walter Reuther signaled his intention to make serious demands on the company when he said, "in 1961 we made substantial concessions to Chrysler [because of the 1958–59 recession]. We helped them survive. We volunteered these concessions. They are now obligated to respond in kind."[97] And as a result of the UAW's determination to stand firm with the company, Chrysler itself reported on September 9, 1964, that it had finally reached "a new three year labor agreement which will give Chrysler employees an unprecedented pension benefits of $4.25 per month per year of service, two additional fully paid holidays, new and improved early retirement benefits, increased protection for widows and families and deceased employees and retirees, Group, Life and Sickness and Accident insurance fully paid by the company, and substantial wage increases over three years of the contract."[98] It soon would prove significant, however, that in its list of shiny new contract provisions, Chrysler did not mention any new language addressing its tendency to speed up the line, run its plants unsafely, or abuse its workers. Nor was there any mention of any new provision to address racial discrimination in the workplace.

Despite the UAW's post-1964 commitment to tackling problems in the auto industry, it was largely up to the TULC to bring the racial equality components of the Great Society to the shop floor. A year before the 1964 contract expired, for example, the TULC's eighty-four-member Executive Board wrote a four-page letter to Reuther indicating its opinion of what the UAW's key bargaining issues should be when it came to the table with the auto companies. Specifically, the board urged Reuther "to shelve his profit-making program and concentrate on a 'work sharing' plan to open Negro employment opportunities."[99] As TULC President Battle went on to say in this letter, "what you have done to date will not do. . . . [O]nly action will bring action. . . . [T]alk alone, good intentions, sterile resolutions and blustering timidity will bring only stagnation."[100]

Between 1964 and 1967, the TULC was also noticeably vocal about the necessity of monitoring foremen's abuse of workers, particularly those offenses with distinctly racial overtones. After 1964, the TULC paid close attention to the actions of foremen like Whitney, whom workers claimed was "a slave driver and has no respect for them as human beings."[101] And, inspired by the TULC's vigilance, black workers became determined not to back down in the face of such affronts either. As black worker Harold Echols reported about his encounter with Chrysler General Foreman Don Volkner, "[he] came on my job site. He told me to get off my ass and go to work. . . . Don said you god dam people, think your so dam smart. I asked him what did he mean. . . . I also asked him if he was race baiting."[102] When he got no answer from Volkner, Echols went to Cal Sarmaras, the supervisor of his department, and angrily informed him that "there were laws that superseded the contract. The Civil Rights Law, The Federal Law, Equal Opportunity of Employment."[103]

That union officials themselves were sometimes discriminatory was a dicey issue for TULC leaders. Take the case of UAW Chief Steward Ed "Frenchy" Manceau, whom black worker William Porter at UAW Local 212 claimed was "placing Negroes in his Department (with seniority) on the worst jobs (not the open jobs)."[104] But while the TULC would have agreed with workers like Porter "that discrimination should not be practiced, especially by union representatives,"[105] it most often decided to stand with the UAW rather than against it. Indeed, as several of its leaders, including Horace Sheffield and Marc Stepp, came to fill leadership positions within the UAW, the TULC increasingly encouraged black workers to have faith in the labor relations system and in their union representative's commitment to bettering conditions on the shop floor. TULC leaders still believed in the International UAW's new public commitment to furthering civil rights. They were encouraged as well that, at the local level, there were union officials such as District Committeeman Robert Giles from the Detroit Diesel plant, Local 163, who were aggressively tackling racism on the shop floor. Giles, for example, had approached the NAACP directly to request "a formal investigation for personal discrimination towards a Negro [for] his race only. I demand immediate action."[106]

Between 1964 and 1967, however, black workers themselves began to doubt that UAW officials were in fact representing them as dutifully as they should. As a result, after 1964, workers began taking their grievances to the Michigan Civil Rights Commission (MCRC), which was fully outside of the industry's labor relations system. Worker William E. Mims, for example, claimed before the MCRC that "the International Union failed to represent him because of his race."[107] Likewise, UAW Local 3 worker Matthew Brown also took his complaint "that because of his race he was denied adequate representation" to the MCRC.[108] But the MCRC many times ruled against black workers who brought cases before it, as it did with both Mims and Brown, and it did not even attempt to address the fact that blacks were still disproportionately barricaded into the least safe and lowest-paying jobs in the plants. Clearly, neither Cavanagh's election nor the TULC's ability to get a black man on the IEB nor the UAW's public commitment to civil rights had meant as much as black workers had hoped when 1964 began. Even though workers like William Echols had felt empowered by liberal federal legislation, and had told his supervisor, Cal Samaras, that he was willing to call on civil rights laws to have his needs addressed, this had gotten him nowhere. According to Echols, Samaras reportedly told him to "take those laws an stick them up my ass."[109]

Between 1964 and 1967, like the period that preceded it, it was not just black workers who were growing disillusioned with their union leadership. Many white workers had also become convinced that labor liberals' new initiatives had amounted to very little. By 1967, the line speed still was inhumane, safety conditions still were abominable, and workers saw little evidence that the union's post-1964 efforts to take management on more aggressively had paid off. Take, for example, the situation still facing production workers in the welders' area at the Jefferson Avenue plant. As union officials noted, this area was so unsafe that "there have been a couple of men hurt in this area already because of the condition that exists," despite the fact that the union had repeatedly notified management about the problem.[110] Even the union had to concede in this particular case that "the way it looks now is that somebody has to get seriously hurt or maybe killed before this problem is solved."[111]

As we have seen, when workers grew discontented with shop-floor conditions between 1960 and 1964, some of them gravitated toward dissident groups within the UAW. But this is not the path that workers tended to take thereafter. It is true that, in 1966, some skilled workers did try to create an in-plant presence of the International Society of Skilled Trades in order to push the UAW to take a more militant posture in fighting for their needs.[112] In addition, a biracial group called Concerned Members for Better Unionism tried to organize workers to reform the union in more radical directions that year.[113] But neither of these groups amounted to much, and even the earlier dissident group that did have a noticeable shop-floor presence, the NCFDA, faded from view after 1964. In fact, most workers initially dealt with the problems still raging on their shop floors after 1964 by simply not coming into work. Between 1964 and 1967, Detroit's auto plants were plagued by such serious worker absenteeism that the minutes of virtually every meeting between labor and management at the local level include some mention of it.[114] At one such "special meeting" called by management at the Jefferson assembly plant, company officials noted "that absenteeism has become a very serious problem at this plant," and they pointed out that such "absenteeism can cause a poor showing [for the foremen] . . . and make it necessary to shut down for relief."[115]

If workers chose to register their growing discontent with plant life only by not showing up, then Detroit's auto plants might have been spared any explosion of violent unrest such as that which came to polarize the Motor City in 1967. But just as police aggression made a civic crisis virtually inevitable, unmitigated foreman aggression sent line workers in equally violent and explosive directions that year as well. Despite the fact that UAW officials had been filing grievances about managerial abuse since 1964, foremen, like their law enforcement counterparts, continued to act with virtual impunity. Union officials at Chrysler's Hamtramck complex, for example, still were complaining on March 28, 1967, that "the foreman in Department 9170, Group #9, is harassing and threatening employees."[116] And at Chrysler's Huber Avenue foundry, where a large percentage of the workforce was African American, the union again had to request in 1967 "that something be done about the foreman on the third shift, Mr. Lazorshak in Department 3330. This man is a 'WILD MAN.' . . . [T]his man is constantly harassing all the employees. . . . [T]his foreman told [one] employee that he 'didn't give a damn about his family'" when that worker needed to attend to a family emergency.[117]

By 1967, workers had become so completely fed up with the union's promises that offensive line foremen would be penalized that some began refusing to obey any foreman's directive. For example, in 1967, Chrysler worker S. Minus was discharged because of "his failure to follow a direct order from his supervisor."[118] Minus's discharge followed that of employee E. Webb, who reportedly was "insubordinate" and also had failed "to follow supervisor's instructions."[119] According to Chrysler management, not only male workers like C. Hickman "refused to follow the instructions of his foreman, even against the advice of his Chief Steward,"[120] but so did female employees such as S. Kiertaniz, whom the company also discharged for being "insubordinate to her superintendent."[121] Such overt disobedience not only alarmed Chrysler, but it also greatly worried the UAW and TULC leadership because it clearly indicated that their best-laid plans for responding more effectively to worker needs after 1964 had not been effective.

But what really served to dash UAW and TULC dreams of more equitable, and thus more peaceful, labor relations was the fact that numerous workers had gone beyond simply disobeying their line foremen, and they now were fighting them physically as well. Physical violence on the shop floors was not unknown at Detroit's auto plants, but, by 1967, these factories had become synonymous with such violence. Take the case of worker D. Britton, who needed to go home to deal with a family emergency. Apparently, when he requested a pass to leave, his foreman "screamed back about having more important things to do."[122] According to the union at UAW Local 7, at this point worker Britton felt "like a prisoner in a jail and being treated like one came close to [General Foreman] W. Lemay, with the intention of making his point clear that he had to go home. When he done this W. Lemay backed up into a coat rack lost balance and fell backward on the floor with D. Britton falling on top of him with hands accidentally landing on W. Lemay's face, W. Lemay then got up claiming that D. Britton deliberately struck him."[123] Worker G. Wolfe at UAW Local 212 also "became involved in an altercation with Foreman Baumgardner which culminated in violence" when he asked for a medical pass and did not get one.[124] When the foreman accused Wolfe of being drunk, Wolfe "punched him in the cheek," and then he "again hit the foreman."[125]

Such acts of violence only escalated between 1964 and 1967. In 1966, workers like UAW Local 3's Johnny Hatcher got so angry with his foreman that he "deliberately struck the supervisor with a car door and then proceeded to profane the supervisor."[126] And on February 16, 1966, another worker, John Jackson, also threatened his supervisor and "used extremely profane and abusive language."[127] In 1967, workers such as L. Jenkins and R. Philson actually lost their jobs because of their verbal and physical responses to shop-floor tensions. According to reports, Jenkins "used abusive, profane and obscene language toward his supervisor and threatened his supervisor with bodily harm," and in a separate incident, Philson had engaged in an ugly fight.[128] Notably, tensions were so high in Detroit's auto plants by 1967 that violence between workers had also escalated. In that year, it was not at all unusual to hear of employees such as William H. Reed, who had become "involved in an assault on another employee within the plant."[129]

Back in 1963, UAW leaders had warned Chrysler that conditions "have reached a peak where immediate action must be taken to correct them or drastic measures will have to be taken."[130] By 1964, galvanized by their Great Society mission and greatly angered that shop-floor abuses, particularly those perpetuated by company foreman, had continued unabated, union officials again approached Chrysler. This time they more forcefully told the company that "mental and physical suffering can't be measured as easily as time and money, and that is why this local union cannot tolerate totalitarianism, which will, without a doubt, end in rebellion."[131] When union leaders spoke these omniscient words, however, they never predicted that worker anger was also escalating toward the UAW itself. Indeed, between 1964 and 1967, liberals in the auto plants, like their civic counterparts, were so confident about their efforts to improve life for the oppressed that they did not appreciate just how disenchanted their constituents had become. And because the TULC's early efforts to push liberal white union leaders in more militant directions had largely failed, as had the NAACP's efforts to push civil liberals, when workers rebelled on the shop floor their ire was directed as much against black leaders as white. By 1967, many workers considered the strategic agendas of both black and white labor liberals equally ineffective.

Although auto plants were as riddled with conflict as was the Motor City in 1967, the plants saw no specific outburst like the civic rebellion against the police on July 23. Rather, the violence associated with worker resistance to foreman aggression punctuated shop-floor life throughout that year. Just as city residents had come to question the efficacy of liberal strategies for bettering civic relations between 1964 and 1967, so had workers come to question the viability of liberal plans to improve conditions on the shop floor during that period. But as had been the case before in this complex and ever-changing metropolis, the crisis that now gripped both the city and its plants would soon generate completely new political possibilities for Detroit.

4: Citizens, Politicians, and the Escalating War for Detroit's Civic Future

> Detroit had a reputation as the revolutionary capital of America. . . . There was a perception that Detroit might be up for grabs. There was a perception that there were enough cracks in the armor that maybe you could wrest control from the elites. . . . Detroit also was the center of all the anti-racism stuff going on in the country.[1]

As the Motor City and its auto plants slowly lurched toward social and political chaos between 1964 and 1967, James Johnson Jr. continued to go to work every day at Michigan Drum. Because he still made too little money to buy his own home, Johnson lived with various family members over the next two and a half years, including his sister Marva and his first cousin Maggie Foster Taylor.[2] Maggie was born in 1927 in Crawford, Mississippi, very near Starksville.[3] She had known Johnson since his birth, and it was her brother's lynching that had such a profoundly disturbing impact on him. Maggie had moved to Michigan in 1953. She managed to buy a home in July 1963, and from 1965 to 1970, James either lived with her or with Marva.

It was only two years after Johnson moved back to Detroit that poor urbanites there exploded in civic rebellion and autoworkers began lashing out at their line foremen. Because he was a loner, and usually came home from work every day to read the Bible or watch television, Johnson did not participate in either the city or workplace unrest of 1967. Like many other Detroiters, however, he knew firsthand what had precipitated such upheaval.

In July 1967, numerous Detroiters had chosen rebellion in the streets as the way to express their dismay with the liberal leadership's inability to establish greater racial equality or reform the Detroit Police Department. Like their counterparts in the auto industry, they had taken the disappointments that followed the optimism of 1964 hard, and they had little patience left for liberal promises. Yet despite the tremendous shock of the civic uprising, between 1967 and 1972, white liberal leaders, along with their allies in the black middle class, still refused to abandon their plans to improve the city. The problem for these liberals was that, in this same period, grassroots discontent was finding expression in increasingly popular radical as well as conservative movements, both of which sought a complete political overhaul of the city. While civic liberals worried about these mounting assaults from both the Left and Right, at least initially they dismissed the right-wing challenge while they sought to appease their left-wing critics by putting new energy into already-discredited programs for change. Not surprisingly, rather than diffuse community discontent, this approach only fueled resentment. And, as civic radicals and conservatives alike began mobilizing to take power in Detroit, and a full-scale war for urban control began, the future of this city was completely up for grabs.

* * * *

From the moment that the residents of Detroit's poorest neighborhoods went on their rampage of looting and arson in the wee hours of July 23, 1967, it was obvious that they were not just lashing out at members of law enforcement, figures against whom they had obvious grievances. They were also raging against the strategies and politics of white administration liberals and the middle-class black leaders of the city's civil rights movement. As one observer of the chaos noted, "none of the so-called leaders [of the black community] were able to control or affect any aspect of the situation," and, when black Congressman John Conyers arrived at the scene, he "was booed and stoned off the streets [and reportedly] his office was burned to the ground." Most importantly, civic rebels were expressing their disappointment with black leaders, specifically in the language of black nationalism and revolution. For example, when black Congressman Charles Diggs arrived, hoping to bring calm to the situation, he was told, "Go home Diggs. . . . [W]e want Stokely Carmichael."[4]

The arrival of this Black Power sentiment certainly caused Detroit's liberal leaders to fear irreparable political divisiveness. And the reaction of racially conservative whites to the 1967 upheaval only confirmed these fears. Not only were such whites horrified by recent civic unrest, but many of them firmly believed that the city's liberal leadership had taken exactly the wrong message from that upheaval. As one white Detroiter put it, "The nigger is being treated with velvet gloves by the politicians. White people are getting sore about all this soft-soaping. They're using this riot idea to get something for nothing."[5] Civic leaders like Cavanagh were deeply alarmed by such white sentiments, because they indicated that restoring urban stability in the near future was unlikely. As Cavanagh wrote to David Brown, a researcher from the University of Massachusetts at Amherst, "Detroit's riot made it quite clear to me that America faces its gravest social crisis since Reconstruction. . . . [T]he problems of generations are residing in these cities."[6] But despite the growing threat of both black radical and white conservative critics in their city, liberal leaders were not yet ready to throw in the towel. They were heartened by the fact that at least some Detroiters were responding to the upheaval of 1967 by trying even harder to achieve racial cooperation and progress in ways familiar to them.

In 1968, Polish and black Detroiters came together, for example, to create the Black Polish Conference; a group of over "4,000 interested persons" that offered a forum for blacks and whites to improve communication.[7] As its members believed, "Blacks and Poles share many of the same problems and that by working together, we can overcome these problems without losing our ethnic identities."[8] The Black Polish Conference was not the only group suggesting that biracial communication was still the answer to the city's current crisis. Numbers of city residents were also in the process of reinvigorating the "block clubs" of the 1950s, hoping to encourage greater racial harmony by providing "a convenient meeting ground for both Negro and white residents who might otherwise have some difficulty relating to each other easily."[9] Other citizens, also both black and white, had come together after the chaos of 1967 to form an organization called Focus Hope, whose mission statement pledged "intelligent and practical activism to overcome racism."[10] When white Detroiter Eleanor Josaitis, along with Father William Cunningham, Father Jerome Fraser, and fifty priests connected with the civil rights movement, created Focus Hope, they "wanted the black and white community to work together."[11] Symbolically Focus Hope's logo was a pair of hands, one white and one black, trying valiantly to reach each other.

Greatly encouraged by these signs of biracial cooperation, the Cavanagh administration created its own committee to deal with both the immediate crisis and long-term urban development issues. The Mayor's Development Team (MDT) was intended to coordinate the actions of all public agencies, to address issues of most concern to city residents, and to create a "blueprint for the social and physical redevelopment of the city."[12] Simultaneously, several civic, business, labor, and civil rights leaders collectively formed the New Detroit Committee (or New Detroit), which brought together a diverse group of local luminaries, including Robert Tindal of the NAACP, Chrysler Chairman Lynne Townsend, and UAW President Walter Reuther. Once formed, New Detroit had a leadership committee comprised of thirty-nine members, nine of whom were black. Out of the hundred-person New Detroit staff, fifteen were black.[13] New Detroit was intended to be a counterpart to the MDT, marshaling private as opposed to public funds to rebuild the city. The sheer size, scope, and budget of New Detroit meant that it would be the backbone of any liberal attempt to improve conditions in the Motor City and regain political legitimacy after 1967.

But New Detroit had a difficult task. The organization could ill afford to alienate the city's growing radical or growing conservative contingents.

The New Detroit Committee, July 1967. Front row, left to right: The Very Reverend Malcolm Carron, James B. Ogden, Walker L. Cisler, Jean Washington, Joseph L. Hudson Jr., Damon Keith, Lorenzo Freeman, and Mrs. Lena Bivens. Second row, left to right: Max M. Fisher, Arthur Johnson, Virgil E. Boyd, John S. Pingel, Paul M. Borman, John W. Armstrong, Jack Wood, and William T. Gossett. Third row, left to right: Delos Hamlin, Emil Lockwood, Robert Tindal, and Ed Carey. Back row, left to right: Curtis Potter, Ralph T. McElvenny, Norvel Harrington, William M. Day, James M. Roche, Allen Merrell, William Ryan, and the Reverend Robert Potts. *Walter P. Reuther Library, Wayne State University.*

To straddle such political fences, New Detroit made sure that its leadership represented business leaders, church leaders, university officials, community organizations, city unions, and even black militants. Indeed, on August 1, 1967, when New Detroit announced who would sit on its leadership committee, department store owner J. L. Hudson proudly proclaimed that he was "determined to include aggressive grassroots Negro leadership"; ultimately, "three of nine Negro members proudly acknowledged the label of militant."[14]

Immediately after forming, New Detroit created five task forces that, by January 1968, had increased to eight: law, communications, community services, youth, recreation and cultural affairs, economic development, employment, education, and housing.[15] Each of these New Detroit subgroups had the potential to embroil the entire organization in community conflict. But, as it outlined which problems each task force would tackle, New Detroit made it clear that it cared little what Detroit's conservative white community thought. New Detroit not only went on record as a strong supporter of open housing, but it even charged that "the current procrastination in enacting adequate legislation in this field is a reflection of the apathy in the white community towards racial justice for all citizens."[16] Like the civil rights liberals who brought the Cavanagh administration to power in 1961, New Detroit leaders also made their intolerance of white racial conservatism clear. According to New Detroit leaders, "fundamental progress on the attack on racism must be made on a regional basis in the white community and from within the white community [because] it is this group—much more than lack of money or of trained personnel or workable processes—that effectively prevents the resolution of this national crisis."[17]

New Detroit publicly censured white racism and openly rewarded those in Detroit who were working in biracial community groups, as well as those in primarily African American neighborhood groups whose politics were far to its left. Of those militant leftist organizations, for example, the Federation for Self-determination received a $100,000 matching-funds grant for a forty-two-month period. Clearly, New Detroit was far more worried about alienating black radicals than white conservatives in its attempts to reconstruct the postrebellion city. The overwhelmingly white liberal leadership of New Detroit still believed that if average poor and working-class African Americans believed that tangible progress was being made by city leaders, they would ultimately reject black nationalism. And because it considered white conservatives only a fringe element, New Detroit believed that if black faith could be restored, peace would return and liberal leadership would be secure.

Although perhaps a bit too optimistic about its agenda, New Detroit certainly was prescient about what lie ahead for the city if its social and economic intervention failed. Just as New Detroit began attempting to restore community faith in the leadership of Cavanagh liberals, new incidents of severe police brutality seriously undermined its efforts to avert even greater crisis. Such an incident of police aggression took place on March 29, 1968, when members of a black group called the Republic of New Africa (RNA) were holding a meeting at a Detroit church. This meeting of 250 adults and numbers of children was in progress when the Detroit Police Department (DPD) raided the building shortly before midnight. According to the janitor of the New Bethel Church, who was not a member of the RNA, a police squad car had "stopped suddenly in front of the church's main entrance. A police officer emerged and as soon as he reached the curb of the sidewalk he fired at the church door with a rifle resembling a pump gun."[18] According to another non-RNA eyewitness, a Miss Keyes, "There were repeated volleys of gunfire discharged by policemen into the church." Keyes and her friend Miss Huey, both of whom lived in apartments across the street, heard police shout repeatedly, "Come out you B-M-F's, come out!"[19]

According to the church janitor, the police then stormed the sanctuary, at which point "occupants of the church lobby, and those still in the nave of the church, scattered in all directions. Some crawled under church pews."[20] While this witness at no time observed shooting by any members of the RNA, he did "observe one white officer deliberately shoot a negro male with hands aloft who had moved too slowly in response to orders."[21] After this shooting, the janitor reported that the police went on a rampage "ripping beads from around the necks of those who wore them and near choking people. One person carrying a green bible was berated, the abuse seemed to center around the bible in some way."[22]

Even though security officers for the RNA had searched everyone for weapons who came to this meeting, as was the organization's policy, in the melee that night one DPD officer was killed and another was severely injured. According to Police Commissioner Johannes Spreen's account, at 11:42 p.m., two police officers from the Tenth Precinct, Richard Worobec and Michael Czapski, drove by the church where they "observed a group of persons, some of whom were armed with rifles." These officers stopped to investigate and called for backup, and when they decided to enter the church, they "met with a hail of gunfire." In the wake of this shooting, police officers corralled 142 men, women, and children in the middle of the night and took them downtown to police headquarters.[23]

This massive roundup, and the numerous arrests that accompanied it, outraged poor as well as working-class blacks, as it did middle-class leaders from both the white and black community. On the night of the arrests, a particularly incensed black civil rights activist, George Crockett Jr., who by the 1960s was a Recorder's Court judge, went down to the city jail and held bond hearings until the early hours of the morning.[24] Not surprisingly, Crockett's judicial activism brought on the wrath of the DPD. Within days, DPD officers began circulating a "petition of impeachment and/or removal of Judge Crockett, Jr. from the Recorder's Court of the City of Detroit."[25] This police response, and the amount of encouragement that officers received from conservative whites who signed the petition, did not surprise Crockett,[26] but it greatly upset white liberals such as Richard Marks, who felt compelled to respond. Marks maintained that "whether willing or not, the Detroit Police Officer's Association [DPOA] approach has pressed our community's political system to the limit, usurping the way in which no responsible leadership would permit."[27]

Indeed, liberal officials in Detroit were so horrified by what had transpired at the New Bethel Church that the Detroit Commission on Community Relations (CCR) immediately drew up and circulated a memo about this event. A CCR official drafted the memo to individual UAW leaders and others, "as one of the persons in this community around which

I believe a 'new partnership' must be built, I hope that you will give this memorandum on the New Bethel incident your close attention."[28] In this memo, the CCR suggested that "the entire episode is a tragedy of individual and monumental social dimension," and that it was "part of the inheritance of the ghetto rebellion in the summer of '67 in which issues of community policy and response were never properly resolved."[29] But while the CCR conceded that "it must be frankly admitted that we have not achieved racial or community change in substance,"[30] it did not advocate substantive policy or strategy changes. Instead the CCR focused on how best to deal with the issue of the DPOA petition to recall Judge Crockett. Ultimately it set up the Committee to Honor Judge Crockett in Support of Law and Justice, which was endorsed by Democratic senators, representatives, UAW leaders, and other civic agencies of the Cavanagh administration. This committee immediately began holding brunches, making bumper stickers, and speaking publicly about the need to keep Crockett on the bench.[31] Feeling vindicated when they eventually thwarted the effort to remove Crockett, with little introspection the Cavanagh liberals in the city continued their existing efforts to rein in the police officers who kept bringing Detroit to the brink of disaster.

Two months after the New Bethel incident, liberals had the perfect opportunity to assess just how effective their efforts with the police were. The Midwest contingent of the Poor People's Movement had decided to come to Motown. Unlike Chicago politicians, the Cavanagh administration welcomed these demonstrators to Detroit.[32] City officials happily granted permits for movement members to hold a rally at downtown Cobo Hall and then called on the DPD to make sure that everything ran smoothly.

On May 13, 1968, civil rights activists from both the black and white community converged on Cobo Hall to hold a massive rally for jobs and racial justice. Before this event, coordinators from the Poor People's Movement had met on May 11 to make sure that marchers would be well-organized and that marshals would be well-trained, so that the event would be peaceful.[33] On the day of the planned march and rally, hundreds of Detroiters were congregating outside of Cobo Hall when, all of the sudden, the mounted police of the DPD charged the crowd, and complete chaos ensued. As Sam J. Dennis, a field representative of the U.S. Department of Justice who was attending this event, reported, "I saw police officers ride horses into a crowd which I judged to be under control. In addition, I saw officers strike individuals in that crowd with their night sticks."[34] Another official observer of the Cobo Hall riot said, "the actions of the horsemen on the crowd were, in my judgment, uncalled for. The crowd was just standing there observing, walking in and walking out. I observed no provocation on the part of the marchers, marshals, or the crowd for officers to behave in that manner. As the crowd of people sought refuge inside Cobo Hall, foot patrolmen quickly seized and manhandled them inside the building."[35]

The numbers of Detroit community residents injured during the Cobo Hall incident once again sent shock waves through the city. The Detroit office of the Southern Christian Leadership Conference wrote to the mayor that "never before to our knowledge has an act of such blatant abuse of police power been witnessed by so many unimpeachable eyewitnesses."[36] White progressive groups also launched a public protest against the events at Cobo Hall. As one organization stated, "we, as concerned white people in the metropolitan area of Detroit; strongly protest the brutality of the Detroit Police Department. It is precisely that kind of unwarranted violence, as evidenced on 13 May 1968 upon the Poor People Campaign, which creates suspicion and hatred of police."[37] Finally, groups of blacks and whites together protested the Cobo Hall police attack by filing a lawsuit against the mayor, the police commissioner, and the Wayne County prosecutor, among others. According to the litigants, once the event at Cobo Hall had faded from the headlines, the named defendants "refused or failed to discipline or remove from office those policemen whose manifest bigotry and brutality make them unfit to serve as preservers of the public peace."[38] But despite this suit, and the other expressions of public anger, liberal leaders still did not alter their strategy for dealing with police-community relations. This lack of a new direction not only stunned many black and white Detroiters, but it also fueled a growing feeling among some of them that more radical strategies were now an imperative.

This sentiment was only exacerbated by the fact that, immediately after the 1967 rebellion, there occurred an extraordinary number of incidents of police brutality in Detroit's school system. From their dealings with schools before 1967, liberal civic leaders knew that "there is a general alienation within the school system between faculty and administration, student body and administration, faculty and community." They also knew that "this alienation is particularly acute in all black and mixed communities."[39] What they did not appreciate, however, was the fact that the DPD would turn an already bad situation in city schools far worse.

Take an event at Cooley High School on September 19, 1969. Arriving at Cooley armed with bricks, beer bottles, and beer cans, numbers of white students began shouting racial epithets at the black students who composed only about 20 percent of the high school population. These students soon felt under siege as white teenagers shouted, "get out of our school Nigger! All you shitty bastards!" and threatened "you're gonna get it Niggers. . . [S]hitty bastards go back to the plantations where you belong. . . . [Y]ou Niggers aint gonna stay in our school."[40] White adults, "seen in three pickup trucks with cardboard KKK signs taped on," were also at Cooley that day, egging the white students on.[41]

In the midst of this racial attack, someone at Cooley called the police to put an end to the white aggression. But no white students were ever arrested, and it was the black students who experienced the DPD's wrath. The following accounts detail the horrors endured by black eleventh and twelfth graders at Cooley High.

Here is Deborah Bailey's account:

> I was proceeding down the second floor corridor stairwell when approximately 45 officers rushed up the stairs holding baseball bats and ax handles. . . . I saw them beating Willie Jones. He was hand cuffed. They drug him out of a car. They beat him outside and they beat him against the wall. They beat him going outside of the building and while inside the building. . . . Then, about 5 or 10 minutes later, they brought Reed Anderson in. He was handcuffed. Blood was coming from everywhere. All around. I couldn't take too much more. I was shaking all over. Blood looked like it was coming from his eyes, his nose, everywhere.

Here is Willie Jones's account:

> There was a problem outside of the school between black students and white students and police officers. . . . White students were around the driveway with their chains and bats screaming "whiteys get those Niggers. . . . The policemen drug me out and threw me into the wall head first. . . . I hit the wall and bounced back and he threw me in again. . . . I hit the wall three times head first. Then I fell. The police officers kicked me and elbowed me and stepped on me. Two officers came and helped me up; one officer hit me a couple more times. . . . I saw Reed complaining about the loss of blood to his hands with wire cuffs. There was this real short officer telling Reed to shut up. He said "we can do better than this, you Niggers." . . . [T]his one officer was walking around with a bat saying, "I got this Nigger's blood all over me." . . . [H]e was smiling and looking real happy about it. I started to take my jacket off so I could press it against Reed's head. The police officer hit me across my stomach and chest with an ax handle. . . . I had a fractured skull, a slight concussion, a broken hip bone and shoulder bones.[42]

These egregious cases of police brutality were not unique. Conflicts between police and students also were reported at both elementary and junior high schools.[43]

Having netted success in their efforts to reform the police department in 1969, civic liberals turned to the electoral arena hoping that activism there would dissipate the deepening crisis in the Motor City. As the 1969 mayoral election neared, the city's white liberal leaders, clearly influenced by the city's black middle-class, pinned their hopes on a political newcomer, Richard Austin, to heal Detroit's wounds. As the *Detroit News* saw it, "this may well be one of the crucial elections in the city's history."[44]

Austin was a migrant from Alabama who had become Michigan's first black certified public accountant as well as the first black auditor of Wayne County. Austin was a well-respected member of the black middle class, but what is more important, he was a moderate liberal whom white administration

liberals hoped would defeat white candidate Roman Gribbs, a former prosecutor and then a leader in law enforcement who played continually on white
fears of black "criminality" and "dependency." Indeed, Gribbs "promised an
all-out fight against crime in the streets," and he also advocated bringing police councilors into public schools.[45] When Gribbs suggested the creation of
"small units of police with crime-fighting responsibility assigned to certain
neighborhoods," city liberals, both black and white, feared that this would
only increase hostility between police and inner-city residents. Allegedly, as an
assistant prosecutor for the city, Gribbs had actually tried to "keep Negroes
off of the jury," which indicated to them that it would most likely be blacks
targeted in any crime crackdown that he proposed.[46]

Adding to the alarm of both white and black liberals, and only confirming their support of Austin, was the entrance of write-in candidate Mary
Beck, whose earlier recall effort against Cavanagh and her promise that as
mayor she would be "getting tough on crime" made her even more threatening than Gribbs. As an ad for Beck's campaign maintained, "only the
Communists can benefit by destroying our society through permissiveness or
lawlessness."[47]

Austin's willingness to tackle the dicey issue of police-community relations, and ultimately his advocacy of "civilian control of police and all other
city departments," indeed made him popular with both discontented city
blacks and white progressives, who still had not come up with any leadership alternatives to the disappointing Democratic party.[48] And yet such
views simultaneously drew the ire of Detroit's conservative whites, who
firmly believed that the new mayor should grant more, not less, power to the
police. If elected, either Gribbs or Beck would do just that. Much to the surprised delight of his supporters, however, Austin won the mayoral primary
on September 9, 1969, with 45,856 votes to Gribbs's 34,650 and Beck's
26,480.

Despite Austin's victory, however, the tremendous voter support for Beck
indicated that many whites in the city were even more conservative than
Gribbs, a potential obstacle to Austin in the upcoming November election.
As the *Detroit News* put it, Beck "apparently still is the darling of conservative homeowners," and she recently "accepted enthusiastically the support
of the right-wing youth group that had backed former Alabama Governor
George C. Wallace for president in 1968." The problem for the Austin campaign was that even though, as author B. J. Widick points out, Gribbs was
"not a 'Wallace man'; he didn't need to be. As a sheriff he automatically symbolized 'law and order.'"[49] The fear was that Beck's supporters easily would
swing into his camp after the primary. As Austin's supporters well knew, the
city's most conservative whites would never support their man now that
Beck was out of the race. As one such conservative white voter had written
to Austin before the election, "Your *BLACKNESS* is the only reason all
those *BLACK APES* voted in the primaries! . . . All you *BLACKS* know how

to do is have illegitimate children, drink, tear up schools, rob, rape, and constantly expect to get handouts from tax-paying whites! If by any fluke you become mayor of Detroit, you will be mayor of a dung heap because any *WHITE* who is able to do so will move out."[50]

But Detroit was saved, temporarily, from this threatened exodus because, on November 4, 1969, in what scholars have deemed the "closest political contest in the city's history,"[51] Gribbs became mayor of Detroit with 257,312 votes to Austin's 250,000.[52] And yet if conservative white Detroiters had hoped that the ousting of a liberal mayor with civil rights sympathies would restore the racial status quo or discourage black activism, the events that unfolded between 1969 and 1971 left them sorely disappointed. Gribbs's victory did not spell the end of social welfare and civil rights–sympathetic liberalism in Detroit, particularly because black and white progressives had managed to retain all six liberal incumbents and add three new liberals (including a third African American) to the City Council.[53] Gribbs's victory also did not quell the radical critics in the African American community. In fact, the combination of Gribbs' pro–law enforcement platform and Austin's defeat not only led poor and working-class blacks to become even more politically active, but it made them far more radical than Austin had ever been. While Cavanagh himself was pleased that the "almost demagogic" Beck had not won, even he was unprepared for the political fall out of Austin's defeat.[54]

After the Gribbs election, a full-fledged grassroots black revolutionary challenge to the existing racial inequities in the city came of age. After 1969, a key African American minority in both the city and the auto plants set about creating numerous militant organizations that advocated far more radical avenues for effecting change than Great Society–style liberals were willing to embrace and conservatives were willing to tolerate. As *Detroit Scope Magazine* reported in May 1968, "if anything, the conflict is in a more advanced state than it was in late July 1967," because "New Detroit's greatest grass-roots failure has been its inability to win support from the black militants."[55]

After November 1969, black militants became determined to lead the Motor City forward on their terms. The polarization that Detroit experienced after 1967, by 1969 had generated several new leadership possibilities. Although the first leaders to emerge were revolutionary black nationalists, they were soon joined by radical whites. And, in opposition to the solidification of this biracial Left front, conservative activists began mobilizing to take power in the Motor City as well.

A key reason that the election of Gribbs, even more than the uprising of 1967, had spawned such political factionalism was that in January 1971 the police department, with Mayor Gribbs's blessing, formed a special undercover unit called "Stop the Robberies, Enjoy Safe Streets," or STRESS. STRESS was just what Gribbs had promised his overwhelmingly white constituency—a tougher DPD division targeting crime in the city's poor neighborhoods. According to the CCR's Police-Community Relations Committee, the STRESS program "involve[d] one officer acting as a decoy, often disguised as a woman, a drunk or some other likely robbery victim, while two or three officers conceal themselves nearby to protect the decoy officer and to help with the apprehension of criminals."[56] Notably the approximately one hundred officers in STRESS, including between thirty to forty decoy officers, who volunteered for the program, were "often officers known to use excessive force."[57] After the birth of STRESS, the already severely strained relationship between the police and the black community deteriorated further. Between January and September 1971, STRESS made 1,400 arrests, and its officers had killed ten suspects, nine of whom were black. By September 1973, STRESS had a total of twenty-two suspect fatalities to its credit.[58] Of those fatalities, 95 percent came from the decoy operations (even though decoy operations comprised only 20 percent of STRESS activities), and six STRESS officers were responsible for the majority of the deaths.[59]

Almost overnight city blacks came to view STRESS as little more than an all-white, DPD-sanctioned vigilante organization. As more and more African Americans met an ugly fate at the hands of STRESS, such as Clarence Manning Jr., Dallas Collins, James Henderson, Ken Hicks, Howard Moore, Horrace Fennicks, Harold Singleton, Herbert Childress, Donald Saunders and teenagers Ricardo Buck and Craig Mitchell (none of whose deaths at the hands of STRESS were investigated in a manner satisfactory to the victims' families) the tensions between city blacks and the DPD reached an all-time high. With STRESS, black citizens' faith in the strategies of the established civil rights leadership, or liberal organizations like the CCR, was irreparably breached.

Sensing black Detroiters' outrage and discouragement, African American radicals met many times after the 1967 rebellion to decide how best to provide coherent alternatives to the policies of white and black liberals. These young radicals, several of whom had been migrants from the South—among them John Williams from Louisiana, Luke Tripp from Tennessee, and Mike Hamlin from Mississippi[60]—had been civil rights activists in the South and Detroit, had participated in Detroit study groups run by old leftists, and had taken courses at Wayne State University (WSU). Scholar James Geshwender notes that these activists "read Marx and Lenin; but they also read Mao-Tse-Tung, Frantz Fanon, Malcolm X, and Che Guevara among many others. They [also] became acquainted with various black and white radicals in and around Detroit . . . [and] in every case they read and/or listened with a critical orientation."[61] As Detroiter Ron Lockett remembers, "Wayne [state] was so incredibly fertile. There were the cultural nationalists, the nationalists who embraced socialism, the Marxist-Leninists, the Communists. It was just an incredible time."[62]

Inspired by their political education, young black radicals in Detroit decided to take their knowledge and new political perspective to the growing number of community blacks who were no longer sure that liberals could respond satisfactorily to their grievances.[63] One way to do this most effectively, they decided, was to start their own city newspaper to report on and analyze the current racial and political situation in the city as well as to map out a program of urban revolution for the "masses." In October 1967, the *Inner City Voice* hit the streets. Its masthead, "Detroit's Black Community Newspaper" and "The Voice of the Revolution," made it clear that this was not just any city paper. Its stated purpose was "to be a positive response to The Great Rebellion, elaborating, clarifying, and articulating what was already in the streets,"[64] as well as to be "a vehicle for political organization, education, and change."[65] Around the paper's editors a revolutionary and black nationalist Left began to gravitate and grow. Black radicals associated with the *Inner City Voice* soon became involved in virtually every move for social and political change in the city.

By 1968, the *Inner City Voice* was truly a community-oriented paper, albeit a most radical one. It reported on events such as the outrageous acquittals of police officers who were charged with murdering black teenagers at the Algiers Motel during the 1967 uprising, and it also followed the activities of black middle-class liberals in city politics while exposing any weakness or perceived hypocrisy among them.[66] The paper routinely reprinted statements from Detroit's other left-leaning community organizations that were also critical of liberal plans for the city. In addition, the paper chronicled the continuing incidents of white violence in high schools and repeatedly offered examples of how other revolutionary freedom fighters around the world had handled their similarly oppressive conditions.[67]

When Austin lost his bid for mayor in 1969, the disenchantment that initially prompted black radicals to publish the *Inner City Voice* escalated dramatically. The editors of the paper quickly stepped up distribution efforts and suggested to their readers that Austin's defeat was actually not a bad thing. In the November 1969 issue, the paper's editors argued that "Austin represented the most backward, right-wing, conservative wing of 'Negro' leadership in the city."[68]

After 1969, the black nationalists affiliated with the *Inner City Voice* started Black Star Press, so that all persons and organizations considered too left by mainstream printing houses could be published. They also started a production company called Black Star Productions, which, in 1970, came out with a full-length documentary on the black revolutionary struggle in Detroit, *Finally Got the News*.[69] Also in 1969, the black radicals affiliated with the *Inner City Voice* staged a takeover of the WSU student newspaper, the *South End*. According to one of these black radicals, Marian Kramer, the refusal of local presses to print the *Inner City Voice* planted the idea of commandeering the *South End* so that they could "continue to get the word out concerning the situation in the plants, the communities, and the students in the inner city of Detroit."[70]

In 1968, WSU had 68.9 percent of all the black students attending the three biggest universities in the state.[71] If educating greater numbers of black Detroiters was the goal, then reaching WSU's large working and commuter student body made sense. When *Inner City Voice* staffer John Watson ran for the position of editor at the *South End* and won, his editorial team announced that the *South End* would be overhauled completely with the "intention of promoting the interests of the impoverished, oppressed, exploited, and powerless victims of white monopoly capitalism and imperialism."[72] They went on to note that this paper also would "present that portion of the news which rarely receives coverage."[73] Like their counterparts at the *Inner City Voice,* the *South End*'s writers often went beyond news reporting to offer an education in black revolution. Also like the *Inner City Voice,* the *South End* routinely editorialized on the dangers of black middle-class "Toms," "honkie students," "frat freaks," "racist fat asses," and "pigs" alike.[74] The language of the black radicals was not pretty, but this, too, was deliberate. These revolutionary activists in Detroit were determined to "tell it like it is," unlike the liberals whom they felt too often glossed over the Motor City's ugliest elements.

While some black radicals were attempting to tap into and redirect black disaffection in Detroit through the press and visual media, others chose the pulpit. That there now were blacks willing to question traditional doctrinal conventions, reject mainstream theological explanations for their condition, and consider a new revolutionary black theology first became apparent after the 1967 rebellion. Just hours after that uprising began, a stone statue of Christ that stood in front of the city's Sacred Heart Seminary was mysteriously painted over in black. According to the *Detroit Free Press,* "three men tried to whitewash the statue several weeks after the rebellion but they were shooed away by a black woman who lived in the area. Someone came back later to finish the job and the statue went through several paintings in the weeks following the riot."[75] By 1967, even the religious icons of the city had been both racialized and imbued with political significance.

Like many other African Americans across the U.S. when the National Committee of Negro Churchmen called for the development of a theology relevant to the "Black revolution," black Detroiters responded to this call.[76] In fact, Detroit became the site of some of the country's most dramatic struggles over black theology. While it is well known that Detroit was the birthplace of the Nation of Islam in the 1930s and a hotbed of Muslim activism in the late 1960s, with Malcolm X as a regular visitor and speaker, few recognize that the city also was home to the country's most serious black Christian challenge to religious as well as political accommodation and moderation.[77] In 1967, Detroit's Reverend Albert Cleage gained national attention when he founded the Shrine of the Black Madonna, a place of worship that "attracted more persons committed to Black Power than any single institution still connected to the Christian churches."[78] Cleage also pioneered a new religious doctrine for the black community that influenced African Americans across the country. In a series of dramatic sermons published in *The Black Messiah* (1969),[79] Cleage argued that Jesus was a black revolutionary, that the Promised Land could be reached only through grassroots struggle, and that the Scribes and the Pharisees were just like "the established Uncle Toms who were profiting from the system of oppression."[80] After 1969, Cleage wielded increasing of power in Detroit. Even the city's more traditional black ministers had to concede that he "produced a political theory that has shaped Detroit in the 1970s."[81]

Cleage did not just reinterpret the Bible. He spoke to his parishioners routinely about various controversial events in the city and called on them to take a revolutionary approach to registering their concerns. Cleage knew that "the Black Church must recapture the loyalty of the black youth if it is to be significant in the Black Revolution," and he intended to do just that. One of his sermons, "An Epistle to Stokley,"[82] maintained that "like today's young black prophets," Jesus was "a dangerous revolutionary,"[83] and that even Jesus recognized that "conflict and violence are inevitable."[84] Referring specifically to the key struggles for equality still being waged in Detroit, Cleage argued that "conflict is inevitable unless the white man agrees to transfer power."[85]

That the rebellion of 1967, and the mayoral election of 1969, spawned a revolutionary black press, media, and theology was clearly an important turning point in the political history of the Motor City. But these black revolutionaries might have been confined to preaching to the converted had they not also begun to mobilize within the community around issues relevant to both poor and working-class blacks. After 1969, Detroit's black Left self-consciously involved itself in virtually every community action designed to reform education, economics, or the police. As a result, it soon was a very potent political force for every Detroiter to reckon with.[86]

Of course, disaffected Detroiters had already been mobilizing in radical ways even before the black revolutionaries took up their cause. For example, both black and white teachers in the Detroit public school system had long complained of the poor educational resources in the black schools and routinely protested these shortages. Some teachers, such as Lynn Konstat, were not shy to call attention to the paucity of materials available to students such as those at Cooley High School. As she noted, the twelfth-grade English book there had been printed in 1939 and it had only one black author in it.[87] And by 1968 teachers had also begun to demand action, not just attention, from the School Board. One group of black educators in Detroit issued a "Declaration of Black Teachers," which insisted on concrete changes to "the present system of education [that] is not organized for the benefit of black youth." It recommitted black teachers to the process of lifting black students "from the hell of ignorance, confusion and despair in which racist society has placed them."[88] Black students around Detroit had been taking matters into their own hands even more boldly than were their teachers. On October 18, 1968, black students at McKenzie High School staged a walkout during which they demanded more black teachers and a more Afro-centric curriculum, among other things. Then, on October 25, 1969, black students from Cooley High marched to the School Center Building, where they demanded a meeting with Superintendent Norman Drachler as well as immediate satisfaction for their demands, which mirrored those of the students at McKenzie. Meanwhile, student leaders from ten other high schools and one junior high had been holding regular meetings to determine what their more radical strategy would include for overhauling the educational system.[89]

In response to such escaling black discontent on July 1, 1969, Abe Zwerdling, the liberal president of Detroit's School Board, suggested that "the state Legislature redraw all the school boundaries in the Detroit area to create five or six new school systems, completely integrated."[90] Contrary to the hopes of Zwerdling, the Cavanagh administration, and the black middle class, this new strategy did not bring peace to Detroit schools but touched off a firestorm of protest. Indeed the combination of preexisting teacher-student militancy in the black community, as well as the deep citywide dissatisfaction with the liberal proposal to decentralize and desegregate the city's schools, offered black revolutionaries the perfect opportunity to step in and provide leadership, advice, and support.

As the liberal School Board saw it, black "extremist groups" were soon exploiting the "school situations to recruit membership, sell their ideas and eventually replace the present system and institutions with their own."[91] This view was not far off the mark. As soon as Detroit's School Board suggested its decentralization plan, twenty-five black community groups came together to form an umbrella organization called Parents and Students for Community Control (PASCC). And, from PASCC's inception, black radicals from the *Inner City Voice,* the *South End,* and the black clergy played a key leadership role. Indeed, it was their hard work that brought these groups together in the first place.

Guided by black radicals, PASCC not only rejected the School Board's plan, but it also proposed one of its own, the Black Plan, which "would divide the school system into eight districts, six of which would be in a black controlled and nonracist school board."[92] The parents in PASCC made it clear that they wanted their children to be educated by teachers and overseen by administrators, with whom they could identify and trust. The June 1970 issue of the *Inner City Voice* reprinted an open letter from PASCC, which had been drafted with the help of *Inner City Voice* editors. According to this letter, "control of education in the black community by reactionary middle class whites had no right to exist. . . . To leave the education of Black children in the hands of those who have so miserably failed, despite their control over resources, would be suicide. Community Control is education for survival."[93]

According to PASCC literature, after 1969, the organization "increasingly began to campaign, to educate the black community. . . . [M]eetings and rallies were called; literature was distributed, [and] PASCC spokesmen appeared at over 100 community meetings."[94] PASCC's goal was to develop proposals for the School Board's new decentralization guidelines, which would give the black community more power and would make sure that enough of the city's school budget went to the mostly black schools. The Black Plan incorporated these objectives. Because the existing Board of Education, one that PASCC members reviled for being "controlled by white liberals,"[95] wanted total integration, it found the Black Plan unacceptable. PASCC members felt it particularly ironic that the board had taken sixteen years after the legal mandate for desegregation to make this decentralization move intended to facilitate integration. They decided that it was the whites' "method for maintaining control in the city."[96]

In fact, white liberals had always supported the principle of integrated education, but only now had they been forced to think of new ways that they might accomplish it. The fear of losing the votes of conservative whites, which had prevented city liberals from being aggressive on the school integration issue before, now was being overshadowed by their fear of losing control of the schools to black radicals. Ironically, only a few years earlier, most PASCC parents would have fully supported the liberals' integration plan. The fact that they came to reject it so vehemently is evidence of just how disillusioned they had become with liberal coalition politics.

On April 7, 1970, when the Detroit School Board formally adopted its original plan to integrate city schools, many community blacks were furious. For them, according to PASCC, "the Board's plan was one of the worst in terms of black control." As far as PASCC was concerned, the board's plan actually fueled white racial violence.[97] PASCC members were outraged to report that after the board's plan went into effect, "mobs of white students and their parents brutally attacked the small groups of blacks who had punitively been sent to the white schools."[98]

After the failure of their Black Plan, and again with the guidance of black revolutionaries such as *Inner City Voice* staffer Mike Hamlin, PASCC became even more radical. Not only did it continue to run candidates against members of the Detroit Board of Education (receiving upwards of 70,000 votes),[99] but it also began agitating in the schools directly through a separate but closely linked group called the Black Student United Front (BSUF). The BSUF was the brainchild of Hamlin and other black leftists who recently had come together to create a formidable black revolutionary umbrella organization called the League of Revolutionary Black Workers, or "the League." Soon the BSUF had branches in twenty-two high schools, each of which demanded the removal of police from the schools and the end of all-white curricula and predominately

white faculties. At Osborn High School, where, according to the BSUF, "rov-
ing packs of white adults and white Osborn students charged a group of about
100 black students . . . [throwing] bottles, pieces of metal, and various deadly
objects at the black students,"[100] BSUF leaders submitted twelve demands to
the school administration, including that it add twenty more black instructors
and a Black Studies curriculum.[101] The BSUF at Northeastern Senior High demanded that "supplements to the current textbooks must be added that include today's social problems and current politics like *Black Rage, The Rich
and the Super Rich,* and *Soul on Ice.*[102] And at Northern High, members of
the BSUF demanded that "all pictures and artifacts in Northern be directly in
line with the percentage of black students . . . that the Black nationalist flag of
unity be displayed . . . that the library of Northern High be filled with an abundance of books dealing with the Black Experience . . . that a room in Northern be set aside and named the Malcolm X Reading Room . . . [and] that
Northern be renamed Rap Brown High."[103]

As black students, led by black revolutionaries, were voicing their increasingly radical demands throughout the school system, city liberals pan-
icked. The educational committee of New Detroit, as well as the CCR and
the Detroit Public Schools Commission on Community Relations (DP-
SCCR), each began working overtime to conduct interviews and take surveys to figure out what was going on. When students at Northern High
School launched a protest that made headlines as the "Northern High Revolt of 1969," the liberals' fear that they were losing control of the situation
only intensified. The increasing unease of white liberals was mirrored in the
black civil rights leadership. In earlier years, the NAACP had been willing to
support the social activism of students in city schools, and the local NAACP
had even issued a press statement on April 22, 1966, that "it support[ed] the
Northern High School students" in their efforts to end discrimination.[104] After the Northern High Revolt of 1969, however, and after black students at
Central High School wrote a vitriolic attack on the relationship between
middle-class blacks and white officials in City Hall, civil rights leaders dis-
tanced themselves from all student activism.[105]

If the revolutionary black nationalist activism in the educational arena
threatened the politics of liberalism, so did its mobilization around questions
of economic justice. The black nationalist theologians, with the support of
black radicals from the *Inner City Voice* and the League, once again turned
revolutionary rhetoric into action when they hosted a national meeting of
civil rights activists called the Black Economic Development Conference
(BEDC) on April 26, 1969. The BEDC brought together black radicals from
around the country, including the director of international affairs for the Student Nonviolent Coordinating Committee, James Foreman. The BEDC made
national news when Foreman proposed the adoption of a highly controversial "Black Manifesto," a scathing attack on the "hypocrisy" of "the white
man's religion" and of all churches, black and white, that followed the doc-

James Foreman speaking at Black Economic Development Conference, December 3, 1969. *Walter P. Reuther Library, Wayne State University.*

trine. This document, written in dramatic language, not only outlined the elements of Christianity that "excused oppression," but it also called for $500 million in reparations from white churches and synagogues to be used for economic development in the black community.[106] Significantly, this manifesto was ratified by a vote of 187 to 63 at the BEDC, and thereafter black churches were split wide open over the question of how politics and religion should, or should not, intersect. The Black Manifesto's call for concrete and immediate action to eliminate inequality—combined with the growth of the Nation of Islam, the new militant theology of Reverend

Cleage, and the radical theology espoused by prominent black intellectuals nationally[107]—meant that many blacks were now determined to take economic justice rather than ask for it.

In addition to the black radical theologians as well as *Inner City Voice* staffers and League leaders, soon a Detroit branch of the Black Panther party was engaging in militant economic activism. According to the DPD, in 1970 "there [were] only about 25 hard core Panther members in Detroit with another 50 sympathizers serving as community workers."[108] But the police also conceded that their estimate might not be accurate. And even if there were few actual Panther members in the city, Joe Dulin, the principal at St. Martin de Porres black Catholic High School in Detroit, warned that "if things don't change soon every eleven and twelve year old will end up a Black Panther. Potentially every black is a Panther."[109] The Detroit Panthers were particularly active in the arena that made the greatest difference to black residents: economic justice in their neighborhoods. According to Nadine Brown at the mainstream black newspaper the *Michigan Chronicle,* "The Panthers get food donations from all merchants in the community . . . [and] if they refuse, they tell them that they are not going to be allowed to stay in the community if they don't put something back into it."[110] Even though they sometimes accomplished their goals through threat and intimidation, the Panthers won a degree of respect in Detroit's black community because they operated programs to feed poor children and educate citizens of their rights under the law.[111]

By 1969, radical activism to eliminate economic and racial inequality in the Motor City was not engaged in solely by male revolutionaries. Black female revolutionaries were also extremely active in Detroit. Some mobilized poor women in the community to demand better treatment and services from the welfare system, or they urged working-class women to demand more humane treatment on the job in the city's health care industry. Black women also worked in groups, such as the West Central Organization, to save neighborhoods threatened by urban-renewal initiatives. As African American radical Marian Kramer remembers, "we were not the typical women in the NOW movement. . . . We were always in the streets, fighting urban renewal, forming tenants' unions, protecting people against police brutality, and so forth."[112]

While the post-1969 escalation of such revolutionary black activism in Detroit deeply disturbed liberals and conservatives alike, what most alarmed them was the fact that, increasingly, black radicals were not working alone. As community opposition to STRESS in particular mounted, black men and women from the *Inner City Voice,* the *South End,* the Panthers, and the religious community found themselves closely allied with a growing number of white revolutionaries. Indeed, it was the broad-based nature of anti-STRESS activism in the Motor City after 1971 that most transformed the city's black radical challenge to liberalism and conservatism into a biracial revolutionary challenge.

Detroit activist Marian Kramer. *Walter P. Reuther Library, Wayne State University.*

From the moment that the DPD formed STRESS, it was obvious that city blacks were most upset that this tiny unit was responsible for 39 percent of the DPD's citizen deaths during its first year of operation. But STRESS officer behavior soon generated much white criticism as well. Indeed the high numbers of questionable deaths made the DPD "the department with the highest number of civilian deaths per capita in the country,"[113] and this was hard for any Detroiter to ignore. In 1971 Chief Inspector James Bannon of the DPD actually admitted to the Michigan Civil Rights Commission that

The crowd at the March 26, 1972, anti-STRESS rally. *Walter P. Reuther Library, Wayne State University.*

thirteen STRESS officers already had been cited by the Citizen Injury Board at least two times: "Five officers had between five and eight contacts [with the board], and Officer Peterson was reported with 22 contacts, 21 one of which occurred prior to his STRESS assignment."[114]

Ultimately the police brutality witnessed during the New Bethel incident, the Cobo Hall incident, and that which was perpetrated by STRESS led local whites to the left, just as it had led blacks. Some of these whites formed radical organizations such as the Ad Hoc Coalition and People against Racism (PAR) specifically to address racial discrimination in the Motor City. The Ad Hoc Coalition was formed by white Detroiters such as Sheila Murphy, whose family long had been active in the city's Catholic Workers Movement.[115] Likewise, the white Detroiters who organized PAR in 1968 had long been involved in civic civil rights initiatives in the city.

It is significant, however, that local white radicals were soon joined by other whites from around the country who were convinced that the racial and political polarization in the Motor City suggested significant revolutionary possibility. Believing that Detroit was ripe for revolution, groups broadly identified as "New Leftists," "Trotskeyists," "Socialists," "Communists," and "Maoists" began leafleting and selling papers in the city after the 1967 rebellion. Organizations such as the International Socialists, the Revolutionary Communist party, and the Socialist Workers party, to name but a few, formed Detroit branches after 1967 and soon began mobilizing in both the community and the auto plants. As scholar Robert Mast writes, "In the 1960s and early 1970s a number of progressive-minded whites came to Detroit to join with native-born white Detroiters; they wanted to mold a political moment, in cooperation with Black progressives. . . . Detroit would be one of the opening shots in a protracted war with the holders of power—maybe the Fort Sumter of the late twentieth-century People's Movement."[116] This is exactly what white radical Jim Jacobs thought when he moved to Detroit in 1968. As he saw it, "this is a city where the black liberation struggle was an objective reality."[117] Likewise white radical Rick Feldman moved to the Motor City in 1970 because "we were going to make the revolution in Detroit. We were welcomed and challenged and criticized by everybody who was here before us."[118] White radical Dave Riddle also was a part of that generation who saw Detroit as a very significant place: "We looked at it as a labor center and a center of the movement for black liberation."[119]

White radicals first had the opportunity to work with black radicals in several community organizations, such as the aforementioned West Central Organization (WCO), "an amalgamation of white liberals and activists and poor of all colors . . . with radical Saul Alinsky as tutor."[120] The WCO, an umbrella group "representing 55 churches, block clubs and other organizations,"[121] had been around before the 1967 rebellion and convened to make civic urban-renewal efforts more sensitive to the needs of those who would be removed.[122] By 1969, however, as the WCO became more embroiled in other civic battles, such as that over school desegregation, it also became far more radical. Indeed, when the WCO decided to place black revolutionary John Watson in charge of its community action efforts, the group attracted numerous city radicals, both white and black.

But while radical whites in Detroit clearly had contact with black radicals before 1971, it was the excesses of STRESS after that year that gave these whites the opportunity to be a genuine part of the black liberation movement. In fact, after STRESS killed teenagers Ricardo Buck and Craig Mitchell, black and white revolutionaries together organized a State of Emergency Committee (SEC), which soon became the coordinator of all anti-STRESS activism in the city. The day after the murders of Buck and Mitchell, for example, the SEC met at the Northland Family Center, where both boys had been employed, and demanded that the mayor disband STRESS immediately. The gathering was attended by virtually every black and white radical in Detroit, as well as middle class black Detroiters such as the editors of the *Michigan Chronicle* and representatives from the Michigan State Board of Education, the Detroit Branch NAACP, and the Southern Christian Leadership Conference.[123]

Such new cooperation between city radicals and black liberals had not escaped the attention of Detroit's white liberal leaders. Radicals clearly now led the most determined grassroots activism against police brutality, and

The September 23, 1971, anti-STRESS rally. *Walter P. Reuther Library, Wayne State University.*

black liberals supported them at least in this cause. As the CCR noted after the debacle at the New Bethel Church, "the generalized civil rights community (which under ordinary circumstances have little or nothing to do with the people involved in the Republic of New Africa group) [is] rising to the general defense of the right of any group to exist that speaks to the issue of racial and social change in this country and community."[124] It did not surprise the CCR that when the SEC organized an anti-STRESS rally in Kennedy Square, more than 5,000 Detroiters—leftists and black liberals—came there to protest.

Because black and white radicals were running the SEC, other community groups and individuals wishing to work with the SEC also became more radical in their activism against STRESS. For example black police officers who had fought against racism within the DPD for years became more outspoken and more radical with a push from the black and white revolutionaries in the SEC. The Black Guardians of Michigan, an all-black organization of police officers, went on record in 1972 demanding that the founder of STRESS, Police Commissioner John Nichols, immediately disband that "'murder' squad," and that if he did not, they would "comply with our obligation to the community by identifying those members of this Gestapo Murder Squad to the public." These officers also noted publicly that "we, as black officers, feel no more secure in our person than the Jews did under Adolph Hitler."[125]

Not surprisingly, the fact that black and white revolutionaries were capturing the loyalties and interest of growing numbers of poor as well as working-class black Detroiters, and that they were advocating a future city based on socialist or communist premises, deeply angered white Detroiters who always had been racially conservative and had only grown more so since the upheaval of 1967. Just as that rebellion had spawned both black and white revolutionary groups seeking to lead Detroit in an entirely new direction, the 1967 uprising had also made the city's white conservatives increasingly determined to shape Detroit's destiny.

That a new white conservative movement had been gaining momentum since 1967 became particularly apparent in the city's educational arena. Just as the liberal School Board's plan to decentralize and desegregate Detroit's public schools ignited radical black militancy, it also fueled conservative white activism. In the fall of 1969, when the Detroit School Board held public meetings so that parents could come and register their opinions about the proposed decentralization plan, not only did members of PASCC show up in large numbers, but so did scores of white parents who were also deeply opposed to school integration. Then, on April 7, 1970, when the board announced that its decentralization plan would be implemented, "750 white parents, some carrying picket signs, quickly filled the 250 seats and crowded in hallways." It amazed the School Board that by the time that the meeting got under way, "hundreds of citizens packed the meeting facilities and the lobbies and halls of the School Center Building. Closed circuit television was set up for those who could not get into the crowded meeting room."[126] And when it became clear that the integration plan would become formal policy in that meeting, despite the fact that several conservative members of the board who were not liberals and had voted against it, white parents were incensed and decided to mobilize against integration on their own.

Over the issue of school decentralization, and specifically mandated busing, numbers of previously moderate whites in Detroit also found themselves gravitating toward the conservative camp. Consequently, longtime racial conservatives found themselves vindicated and energized. Indeed their post-1967 activism indicated clearly that conservative whites were as politically committed and as determined to effect the course of history in the Motor City, as any black or white radical. In 1970, several parents on the East Side, the home of Osborn High School, where PASCC had noted extraordinary white violence against black students, came together to stop the desegregation plan—or at least the busing of children within it. The mothers among them created an organization called North East Mothers Alert (NEMA), and in time this group became one of the most vocal anti-busing groups in the city.[127] Before long, parents on the West Side were also mobilizing against busing, and NEMA consolidated with these West Side forces to form Mothers Alert Detroit (MAD).[128] MAD was certainly an organization to be reckoned with. It attended School Board meetings, circulated petitions, went to

Detroit woman with "Wallace" and "No Busing" buttons at the Flemming School.
Walter P. Reuther Library , Wayne State University.

the media with its views, and even picketed the Detroit grocery store chain, Farmer Jack, because the store contributed community service money to the NAACP.[129]

Conservative white Detroiters made their political presence and strength known in the city's educational arena in other ways as well. On April 7, 1970, when the proposal to decentralize Detroit's public schools became policy, a controversy erupted after conservatives accused School Board liberals of hatching their plan during a secret and closed meeting on March 31, 1969, and then presenting it as fait accompli at the April 7 gathering. The covert nature of this vital meeting outraged parents of both races, and around the city, 2,200 students boycotted four Detroit schools in protest. White parents such as Aubrey Short went much further than this, however. On May 4, 1970, Short kicked off a petition drive to recall all four of the liberal members of the School Board who had voted for the desegregation plan. By June 1970, Short presented the City Election Commission with more than 130,000 signatures demanding that the issue of recall be put on the ballot. On July 27, 1970, Wayne County Circuit Judge Thomas Roumell ordered the recall off of the ballot because all signatures had not been verified, but the Court of Appeals put it back on the ballot in August. On August 4, 1970, the conservative white community, ironically with the assistance of more than a few black nationalist voters, succeeded in removing all four liberal members from the Detroit School Board.[130]

While some of Detroit's conservative whites expressed their views by voting in the School Board referendum, others opted for more extreme actions. Even though these whites should have felt more secure when Gribbs became mayor in 1969, it had not escaped their notice that it had been since Gribbs took office that black and white revolutionary sentiment had flourished, becoming both more popular and powerful. In response, many of these whites began embracing a politics far to the right of Gribbs as the only way to combat the perceived threat. After 1969, the United Klans of America in the Michigan cities of Detroit, Flint, Southgate, Ponitac, Lapeer, Dearborn, Bancroft, and Owosso stepped up their public presence, and KKK Youth Corps leaflets began showing up in inner-city schools. These leaflets called on whites "to organize a fighting corps of white students from your friends and classmates," and often they set off just the sort of violence that had so brutalized black students at Cooley High in September 1969.[131] In addition to supporting the Klan, some of Detroit's conservative whites gravitated after 1969 toward Donald Lobsinger's John Birch–like organization, Breakthrough, "which held rallies all over white Detroit. . . . [T]he slogan of Breakthrough was 'SASO' standing for 'Study, Arm, Store Provisions and Organize.'"[132] In one such rally at Cobo Hall, in this case to show whites' support for George Wallace, utter chaos ensued once again when black and white counterprotesters experienced the DPD's wrath. Writers from the *South End* described this incident, known as "COBO II": "As the people fled the clubs and mace, they were pushed and thrown over the ten foot drop to the ground where even more pigs waited to club them. Dozens of people were injured with split heads, broken bones, lacerations, cuts and abrasions."[133]

As conservative whites began mobilizing politically, an all-out war for the future of the city was on, and little had inflamed the passions of conservative whites more than the activism of Detroit's black nationalists. As one white Detroiter responded to the Black Manifesto at the BEDC, "I owe the black man nothing," while another, a thirty-two-year-old city white, claimed that "the Negro wants to enslave the white man like he was enslaved 100 years ago. They want to take everything away from us."[134] A twenty-four-year-old white woman concurred wholeheartedly. She deeply feared a "Black Takeover—Take Over is the word because that is what they want to do and they will."[135] And finally, yet another white Detroiter argued that "its Brown, Carmichael, and that crowd" who should be blamed for "communism" reaching "the uneducated Colored."[136] Ultimately the most committed conservative whites were willing to go to great lengths to stop the black nationalists. For example, in response to John Watson's ascendancy to the editorship of the *South End,* Donald Lobsinger's organization, Breakthrough, expended a great deal of effort in obtaining more than 2,000 white students' signatures on a petition demanding that the president of Wayne State University "fire student newspaper editor John Watson."[137]

It is important, however, to note that white revolutionaries angered these white conservatives as much as did the black radicals.[138] They were slightly heartened by the fact that the Detroit and Michigan State Police contained a "Red Squad," which had been in existence since the 1930s, but had become particularly active since 1967. Operating out of the fifth floor of Police Headquarters on Beaubien Street, Red Squad informers zealously infiltrated Detroit's radical community groups, both black and white. According to the media, the "Detroit police and other law enforcement agencies kept tabs on groups such as the Republic of New Afrika [*sic*], the Black Panthers, the Socialist Workers Party, the Communist Party and [even] the Girl Scouts of America," because they had "heard the organization was championing a unified world government."[139]

White racial and political conservatives were not only glad to see this crackdown; they were also encouraged that law enforcement was busily rooting out threats to community security with STRESS. While such Detroiters felt that Mayor Gribbs had made many mistakes since taking office, they appreciated the fact that he actively supported this undercover decoy unit. Whereas the formation of STRESS had outraged and politicized city blacks in radical ways and had captured the attention of revolutionary whites as well, conservative whites felt that STRESS was the only group working to control chaos and disruption in the Motor City. And, as the black and white revolutionaries in the SEC mobilized to disband this undercover police unit, conservative whites mobilized with equal fervor to make sure that STRESS was there to stay.

In response to the large anti-STRESS rally organized by the SEC in Kennedy Square, conservative whites, led by autoworker Richard Grant, held a pro-STRESS rally to let the mayor know how much they appreciated what he had been doing in the city.[140] Several other pro-law enforcement white Detroiters expressed their views in local newspapers. As Christine Kojowski wrote to the *Detroit Free Press* on September 20, 1971, "STRESS has done a tremendous job in trying to make our streets safer. They deserve praise and citizen support." Writing to the same paper, a Mr. Smith said, "It is interesting to note, in passing, that so-called leaders of the black community (only the black community) are trying to sabotage STRESS, which leads to the inevitable conclusion that it is only young blacks that are doing the mugging. I hear no outcries from the white community."

To the dismay of conservative whites, however, an event took place in 1972 that seriously jeopardized STRESS's longevity. On the morning of March 9, "STRESS officers unknowingly targeted and killed, not a private citizen, but a Wayne County Sheriff Deputy, and wounded two additional Deputies" as well.[141] Not surprisingly, this shocking episode caused Mayor Gribbs great embarrassment and led even him to question the wisdom of a decoy task force like STRESS.

On March 9, Wayne County Sheriff Aaron Vincent was hosting a poker party in his apartment at 3210 Rochester Street in Detroit. Vincent's neighbor Albert Sain was there, as were his law enforcement coworkers Harry Duval, David Davis, Henry Henderson, and James Jenkins. And unbeknownst to this group, outside of Vincent's apartment building a STRESS crew was patrolling. When STRESS officers saw a man enter 3210 Rochester Street with a handgun, two of them, Ronald Martin and James Harris, followed the man into the building after calling the DPD for backup. For reasons that never became clear, Martin and Harris, along with DPD officers Shiemke and Marshall, burst into Sheriff Vincent's apartment with guns blazing. According to later deputy testimony, these officers from STRESS and the DPD then forced Deputy Henderson to stand up against the kitchen wall, where allegedly Officer Dennis Shiemke proceeded to kill him. Before Henderson was shot, he had been waving his Wayne County Sheriff's ID above his head, trying to identify himself to Shiemke, and reportedly he had cried, "'Man, you are all wrong, why are you doing this?'" before a fatal bullet ripped through his body.[142] What finally brought an end to the shooting spree (but not before one man had been killed and two others critically injured) was Deputy Sheriff David Davis's ability to persuade DPD officer Marshal that he, too, was a member of law enforcement. "This is D.E.," Davis shouted to Marshall from behind a door, "you know me from the Argyle Bar!"[143]

When the shooting spree finally ended, other police officers arrived to report on the carnage there. One of these reporting officers later testified that when he arrived on the scene, he "observed the STRESS officers hold a private conference with DPD officers Shiemke and Marshall . . . allegedly to synchronize their accounts of the raid."[144] All of the synchronizing in the world, however, could not mitigate the fact that STRESS had murdered fellow members of law enforcement and that this was a public relations disaster for the mayor. Under pressure from the SEC, which immediately held a 2,000-person anti-STRESS rally at the University of Detroit, prosecutors pressed charges against STRESS officers for the first time, and virtually every city agency called on Police Commissioner Nichols to explain why they should not force STRESS to disband.

Detroit Police Commissioner John F. Nichols and Mayor Roman Gribbs, October 15, 1970.
Walter P. Reuther Library, Wayne State University.

Conservative whites did not sit by passively as this political pressure against STRESS mounted. These citizens again went to the newspapers to register their strong feeling that STRESS must stay, despite the unfortunate mistake that black and white radicals were calling the "Rochester Street Massacre." As a Mrs. Wsp wrote, "I beg Detroiters not to be carried away by sympathy for criminals! We need STRESS! The choice is between STRESS and crime!" And, in response to the notion that STRESS only had brought chaos, not crime reduction, to the Motor City, a Mrs. Orb wrote, "STRESS has, rather, created an atmosphere of hope and confidence among the honest and law abiding citizens of Detroit."[145] It was a good sign to these whites that Mayor Gribbs publicly refused to disband STRESS when asked to do so on March 17, 1972.[146] They were not certain, however, that Gribbs would have the last word. Despite the growth of a viable white conservative politics in Detroit, radicals clearly were quiet powerful as well. And, of course, black and white liberals hostile to STRESS still held a number of influential positions in the Motor City. Thus, white conservatives reasoned, they must keep fighting for their law enforcement vision.

Indeed, despite the solidification of both a radical and a conservative political challenge in the Motor City from 1969 to 1972, black and white liberals did not give up their claim to lead Detroit. From the minute they extinguished the fires of the 1967 uprising, liberal leaders never wavered from their commitment to integrate all city schools, never stopped questioning the

DPD's tactics, and never stopped believing that moderate political solutions to social, economic, and racial distress were the most practical in the long run. As Detroit had become a war zone after 1969, however, both their benevolent attitude toward black radicalism and their dismissal of white conservatism as a fringe element did change. Between 1969 and 1972, the New Detroit–style liberal position that black militants must be given a voice and that white conservatives, while disruptive and counterproductive, could be ignored, crumbled.

White and black liberal leaders alike were late to recognize the very real political threat posed by the city's conservative whites. Even though Roman Gribbs had defeated their candidate in the 1969 election, and even though Gribbs clearly was a conservative, city liberals tended to focus on the fact that the extreme conservative candidate Mary Beck had lost, and that they continued to hold an enormous degree of power in the city. Indeed liberals still controlled the City Council and still headed virtually every official committee in the TAP, MDT, New Detroit, and the School Board. But when conservative whites successfully mobilized to remove every liberal representative on the Detroit School Board, liberal leaders finally acknowledged the power of their adversaries. In response, civic liberals decided to take conservatives on directly. For example, after the recall of the four liberal School Board members, leaders of the NAACP filed a lawsuit that, at least initially, resulted in an even more comprehensive desegregation plan than the one white conservatives had so vehemently opposed. Not surprisingly, such liberal counterattacks upped the ante in the ongoing war for control of the Motor City.[147]

Likewise, conflict escalated as black and white liberal leaders in Detroit began to change their tune about the city's black militants. It soon began to dawn on these liberals that New Detroit's plans to listen to, and even to fund, black radicals had seriously gone awry. In 1967, black militants still were relatively marginal figures who liberals believed only posed a long-term threat if they ignored civil rights matters in the city. By 1968, however, such "marginal" black radicals had managed to take over the media of key liberal institutions such as WSU, and were encouraging black students to take over the very schools that liberal School Board members were trying to integrate. And, worse yet, black radicals had joined with whites in the call for an all-out urban revolution. Liberal leaders soon were just as determined to prevent black or white revolutionaries from taking over as they were to stop white conservatism in its tracks. A case in point is the battle touched off between radicals and liberals after John Watson of the *Inner City Voice* became editor of the WSU student paper, the *South End*.

When Watson took over the *South End*, he made no secret of the fact that he was going to turn that paper into a vehicle for revolution and that its pages would be filled with news and editorials to that end. But because he was elected, and because this was a newspaper protected by constitutional mandates, Watson felt that he was on pretty safe ground with the liberal administration at WSU: Surely, it would not tread on the democratic process and the sacred American principle of freedom of the press. On February 13, 1969, though, the university's Board of Governors stated publicly that "we, individually as alumni and collectively as directors of the Wayne State Fund, are deeply concerned about the posture of the University-sponsored newspaper, 'the South End.'" The board specifically noted the paper's "vulgar expressions" and "its hate-mongering verbiage"[148] Member Arthur Greenstone went further to suggest that, "the newspaper has been inflammatory and racist" and also "anti-Semitic. There is no other word for it. Goebbels would be proud."[149] The WSU board officially went on record "that a small politically motivated group has captured control of the *South End* under the guise of freedom of speech."[150] And when a self-described "hippie," Cheryl McCall, became the editor of the *South End* for a brief moment in 1969, the president of WSU officially suspended the paper on July 10, 1969, "until the Student Newspapers Publications Board can review and investigate the entire problem of vulgarity and obscenity and lack of reference to the student community in this paper."[151]

Some liberal leaders were very uneasy about the civil liberties implications of shutting down the paper and of the WSU board's open hostility to Watson's editorship of the *South End*. For instance, board member and UAW leader Leonard Woodcock noted uncomfortably in 1969 that "there was not this gathering of opinion at the end of a full year of control of the *South End* by a white group."[152] To many other liberals, however, the war for the control of the Motor City now had become so ugly that going to extreme lengths in order to defeat radicals was, in fact, reasonable.

Between 1967 and 1972, as radicals, conservatives, and liberals each came to fight for their distinctive vision of Motown's future, Detroit had become a war zone. The racial and political polarization that was in evidence as the Motor City burned in 1967 only deepened thereafter. After that year, serious political alternatives to postwar liberalism emerged, and the fate of the Motor City was most uncertain. Even by 1972, no one yet could have predicted who was ultimately going to win the seemingly intractable battle for civic control. The city's fate was made even more unpredictable because the new political power bases that had emerged in the urban center between 1967 and 1972 had also emerged in the auto plants. These two worlds still were inexorably linked.

5: Workers, Officials, and the Escalating War for Detroit's Labor Future

> It seems kinda strange that a relatively small group of black workers can put such huge outfits as these in a dither, especially since both the companies and the UAW are thoroughly experienced infighters, but these DRUM, FRUM, ELRUM, JEFFRUM and all the rest of the RUMs have these people all shook up.[1]

As Detroit became increasingly conflict-ridden after its urban uprising in 1967, James Johnson Jr. was finally realizing his dream of attaining a job in an auto plant. On May 8, 1968, Johnson began working at Chrysler's Eldon Avenue gear and axle plant, and although he had applied for the position of janitor,[2] Chrysler hired him to be a conveyor loader, making $3.10 an hour.[3] Chrysler was running three shifts around the clock, and it needed as many unskilled line workers as it could get.

Johnson's main task at Eldon Avenue was to feed six brake shoes a minute into a 380-degree oven while standing no farther than six to eight feet away from the inferno.[4] This was one of the most despised jobs at the plant, and once again all of the workers performing it were black.[5] According to Johnson's employee medical records, the intense heat of this work site took a toll on his health. As company doctors reported on August 20, 1968, Johnson "allege[d] nausea and chest pains from heat," and on August 21, 1968, he again "allege[d] nausea from heat . . . [and] state[d] he thinks [the] chest pain is strain from work."[6]

Much to his relief, in January 1969, Chrysler moved Johnson from the oven line to the cement room, where he began making over $3.40 an hour. Johnson knew that this was a real promotion, not only because of his increase in pay, but also because his six co-workers now were white. According to Chrysler auditor Don Thomas, "the cement room was very nice and cool in the summer. . . . The cement job is the best."[7] Everything seemed to *be looking up for Johnson. He was finally in a job that he could tolerate, he was able to start saving for the house that he had always wanted to buy, and he was even training in his spare time for the respected position of job setter, thanks to a skilled worker named Robert Baynes.*

But despite being promoted to the cement room, things were far from ideal for Johnson. As he later alleged, his foreman, Bernard Owiesny, routinely "used abusive, insulting and degrading racial slurs toward [him] such as calling him 'nigger' and 'boy' and saying such things as 'You niggers can't catch on to nothing' and 'Do this right now boy and I mean right now boy.'"[8] As a result of such treatment, Johnson was very much on edge at his workplace. Regardless of what good things happened to him, such as getting a promotion, he always had to endure racial slurs and poor treatment from management. Like other black workers on Chrysler's shop floors, he was getting more and more frustrated and eventually would rebel.

During the summer of 1967, the shop floors of Detroit's auto plants strongly resembled the city's riot zones. Indeed, because of the amount of violence erupting in city plants, and because the violence there was equally rooted in disappointments with the strategies of liberal leaders, Detroit's labor arena soon experienced the same political polarization as the city. Just as city leaders felt vulnerable to grassroots frustration after 1967, so did labor leaders. Also, as had happened in the city, liberals' legitimacy in the labor movement had eroded among both whites and blacks, which meant that the political challenge brewing in the plants had a particularly threatening character. But despite the rising crescendo of dissident voices on the shop floor, like their civic counterparts the labor liberals stuck steadfastly to their pre-1967 plans for improving plant life—which only served to fuel greater rank-and-file opposition to their rule.

But this is where the similarities between the civic and labor liberals ended. Whereas city liberals at least initially attempted to assuage the black militants gaining ground after 1967, and only became outwardly hostile to them when the power pendulum began to swing leftward, labor leaders consistently made discrediting and eliminating shop-floor revolutionaries their central and unwavering goal. And yet, just as police brutality continued to fuel revolution and counterrevolution in the city, so did foreman abuses and the ever-deteriorating working conditions undermine any attempt on the part of these union officials to quell shop-floor dissent. Like the city proper, Detroit's auto plants became a war zone between 1967 and 1972 as new political power bases began vying for control. In this case also no obvious victor was yet in sight.

* * * *

Ironically, the 1967 Detroit rebellion had handed union leaders a new opportunity to improve life for the city's African American workers. After extinguishing rebellion fires, the Cavanagh administration subsequently called on urban employers to create new, better, and more numerous jobs for the discontented. Because both city and federal officials had also decided that chronic black unemployment was one of the key factors precipitating the upheaval, they, too, turned to companies like Chrysler and demanded a renewed commitment to hiring minorities. On July 21, 1970, the Detroit Chamber of Commerce reported that it "ha[d] obtained a commitment for 250 jobs in the near future with the automotive industry."[9] Chrysler not only agreed to hire more blacks, but it also participated in "the operation of a Chrysler and UAW federally supported job-training program"[10] and received additional incentives from the federal government to hire minorities. Union leaders were pleased to see that such governmental pressure to hire minorities in Detroit soon resulted in many new union jobs for black Detroiters. Indeed, by 1971, 60 percent of Chrysler's workforce at Dodge Main plant was black.[11] And, by the mid-1970s, blacks represented almost 70 percent of the workers on the urban assembly lines of other auto companies as well.[12]

Although more union jobs was a step in a positive direction, liberal leaders in both the UAW and the TULC knew that they would have to be ever vigilant to ensure that such jobs were both safe and well-paid for black workers. Of course, this would be difficult to accomplish because, even in the city's largely black plants, almost every person with the power to see to this remained white. Indeed, so little progress had been made in desegregating the most desirable positions within Detroit's auto industry that, in December 1969, UAW leader Douglas Fraser noted, "after all this effort, we only had a miserable percentage of 4.4 percent blacks in [the] skilled trades."[13]

By 1969, TULC officials were even more cognizant of the racial inequities still plaguing Chrysler's plants than were UAW leaders. While the TULC was proud that there was finally a black presence on the union's International Executive Board (IEB), and while it was gratified to see that a number of UAW locals now had blacks in leadership positions, it also had to concede that the number of African American union leaders lagged well behind the overall percentage of black workers in the UAW. But both the TULC and the UAW still believed that the way to achieve greater equality in the union and on the shop floors was to work through the existing procedures for dispute resolution—namely, the grievance procedure. Therefore, leaders dealt with racial discrimination by telling black workers to continue to file complaints when they faced offending managers, as well as to run for positions of influence within the union. TULC leaders also assured these workers that, meanwhile, they would continue to levy pressure on the International UAW to bring more African Americans into its fold.

The problem for the TULC and the UAW alike was that, by 1967, many black line workers had become too angry to follow such prescriptions for change. Not only did shop-floor violence escalate after that year, but it also increasingly stemmed from incidents of racial harassment. For example, in February 1969, African American autoworker Rushie Forge committed a particularly violent act at Chrysler's Jefferson Avenue assembly plant that shocked even seasoned union leaders. When Forge arrived at work, he found his time card had been taken, and that his foreman, William Young, had suspended him for five days. When he asked Young why he had been suspended and received no response, "Rush managed to slap William Young back thirty feet into a stock skid where he cut his hand."[14] He went on to stab Young twice with a chisel. Then, on September 7, 1969, when plant guards attempted to examine the lunchbox of black worker Willie Brooks, yet another violent altercation ensued. After plant security guards jumped on Brooks, and Brooks chose to fight them, management called in the police. When the "police entered they were greeted by a hail of washers, bolts and cat calls thrown at them by the workers on the line."[15]

In response to such racialized shop-floor violence, TULC leaders attempted once again to impress upon the UAW's leadership the seriousness of the situation and the necessity of acting decisively. Specifically, TULC leader Robert Battle III organized the Ad Hoc Committee of Concerned Negro Autoworkers, which warned UAW President Walter Reuther that without "full equity," the growing number of frustrated black workers would create even more chaos.[16] As this committee put it bluntly to Reuther, "it is precisely because of our faith in your integrity and commitment that we seek to resolve these matters with you at the conference table, rather than, as many powerful voices have suggested, take the issue to the streets and the public press."[17]

By and large, however, UAW leaders felt that the union was already taking the plight of Detroit's blacks seriously, and that it had a commendable track record of supporting civil rights. If only Chrysler would rein in its discriminatory managers and stop running its plants without regard for workers' safety, these leaders reasoned, the union's civil rights efforts would be apparent to black line workers. But Chrysler did neither of these things. Not only did it continue to run its plants with little attention to safety,[18] but because so many of its assembly and foundry workers were black, blacks tended to pay the highest price for abominable working conditions. One such black worker, Mamie Williams, was having such serious health problems on the job that her doctor insisted that she stay home from work. Soon after her leave began, however, Williams received a telegram from Chrysler ordering her to return to work lest her employment be terminated. She did return to work the next day and, one week later, paramedics took her from Chrysler's Eldon plant in an ambulance. She died that night. Soon after Williams's death, according to the UAW, another black woman, Rose Logan, "was struck in the right leg by a jitney whose vision was obstructed by an improperly loaded shoe box. . . . Eventually she developed a thrombophlebitis in her right leg. . . . [A] blood clot loosed from her leg and traveled to her heart with fatal results."[19] Like Williams, Logan had suffered physical injury while working for Chrysler, and when she died, many workers assumed that this was because the company had forced her back to work prematurely.

While workers were still reeling from the deaths of Williams and Logan, on May 26, 1970, twenty-two-year-old black worker Gary Thompson met a similar fate. Thompson was working the midnight shift at Eldon when he received a new job assignment from his foreman. The foreman wanted Gary to drive a forklift jitney to another part of the plant, rather than work his regular job as a crane operator for maintenance. According to the union, managers gave Thompson this assignment because they needed him to empty a hopper of scrap steel weighing three to five tons into a railroad car.[20] It was well known by the workers in this department that the jitney Thompson was ordered to drive was faulty. But, with a baby on the way at home, when Gary was asked to drive the jitney, he knew he needed his job too much to refuse. One-half hour before Gary was supposed to end his shift, he drove the faulty forklift, and the next morning his body was discovered buried under five tons of steel that the jitney had tipped over onto him.[21]

As far as Thompson's parents were concerned, "Chrysler treated [Gary] no better than a machine," and even though the UAW filed a grievance after her son's death, his mother Helen nevertheless believed that "the union did not give him fair representation."[22] Of course in the union's mind, filing grievances was exactly what the union thought it was supposed to do to represent workers like Thompson. Yet filing a formal complaint brought neither the UAW nor the Thompson family any satisfaction. Chrysler denied this grievance, writing in its rebuttal that "the fact is that conditions in the plant had nothing to do with this tragic accident. . . . [Thompson] backed away from the gondola car *without the mast and loaded hopper* (this is contrary to rules governing the operation of jitneys),"[23] and told workers to "rest assured that our continuing efforts to make our plant a safe place in which to work will be intensified."[24]

By the time that Thompson died, however, many workers at Chrysler had already reached the breaking point. For years, they had followed the rules by filing grievances and by registering complaints with the Michigan Civil Rights Commission (MCRC). Other workers had protested the situation in the plants by staying home or by taking matters into their own hands with their fists and other weapons. Believing that all of these approaches were futile, numbers of workers, both black and white, had begun to form rank-and-file organizations designed to combat the safety hazards and the racism on the shop floor without the union.

The city's grassroots organizations that became active after 1967 came from across the political spectrum and color line. Some were multiracial and relatively moderate, like the Black Polish Conference, while others were held together by a black revolutionary ideology, like the Black Student United Front and the staff of the *Inner City Voice*. The dissident groups that arose in the plants in the late 1960s were equally diverse. Between 1967 and 1972, groups of black and white revolutionaries, as well as a biracial group of politically moderate but UAW-critical trade unionists, all began mobilizing on shop floors, thus creating new possibilities for the plants' future.

Just as the city rebellion encouraged many residents to expend more effort on finding better biracial solutions to the ever present urban problems, many autoworkers also believed that the violence erupting on plant floors by 1967 called for biracial solutions more aggressive than those put forth by labor leaders. In 1967, such workers gravitated toward a new in-plant organization called the United National Caucus (UNC). The UNC was originally organized by skilled tradesmen and, specifically, by Irish-born worker Pete Kelly from UAW Local 160. According to Kelly, "when I first heard Walter Reuther speak I thought that the sun shone out of his ass. He was a very impressive orator. He was probably the most progressive labor leader in the country at the time."[25] But when Kelly came to feel that the UAW was passively standing by while management tried to chip away at hard-won union gains such as its Cost of Living Allowance (COLA) benefits, and when the UAW seemed incapable of getting the auto companies to put their abusive foremen in check or make the plants safer, he got fed up. In short, Kelly formed the UNC in order to push the UAW in a more militant direction.[26]

According to UNC founders, their group was a "caucus" within the UAW and, as such, was not interested in overthrowing the union. Indeed, as UNC members put it, "we are not trying to split our union, but, to bring back the dignity and loyalty our great Union was built on."[27] The UNC's commitment to reforming the UAW and making it more responsive and democratic soon attracted both black and white, skilled and unskilled workers. What appealed to many black workers, despite the UNC's predominantly white and skilled-worker origins, was that its co-chair was an African American who made sure that the UNC took racial equality in the UAW very seriously. Owing to its growing popularity, the UNC soon had offshoot groups in many plants, including the United Justice Caucus (UJC) in the Jefferson Avenue assembly plant, the Mack Safety Watchdog in the Mack Avenue plant, Strike Back in the Hamtramck assembly plant, Shifting Gears in the Chevy gear and axle plant, and the Democratic Caucus within Local 155.[28]

As the UNC quietly gained a following in the plants between 1967 and 1972, the UAW leaders grew more leery of it. According to Kelly, when UNC members went to the 1970 UAW International Convention and set up a UNC headquarters "right beside the convention," "it irritated the hell out of the union leadership."[29] Even though the UNC initially confined itself to publishing in-plant newsletters that answered worker questions about plant safety and informed them of their rights under the contract, it also challenged the UAW's political control.[30] For example, at the UAW's Twenty-third Constitutional Convention in Atlantic City, Pete Kelly nominated black co-chair Jordan Sims for the presidency of the union, and Sims reciprocated by nominating Kelly as international secretary-treasurer of the International UAW, saying, "In going to the Caucus I found in the people there the general sentiments of the rank and file, the dreams of the rank and file. I found there a need for some meaningful form of democratic recognition within this great UAW. [Pete Kelly is] my man to help reestablish what our union is supposed to really mean and represent."[31]

But the top leadership of the UAW was as yet undaunted by the UNC's bid for power. In fact, incumbent UAW President Leonard Woodcock soundly defeated Sims, while Emil Mazey, incumbent secretary-treasurer, trounced Kelly as well.[32] The fact was that between 1967 and 1972, UAW officials believed that they had a far greater threat on their hands than the UNC. Indeed, numbers of workers had been gravitating not to the politically moderate and biracial UNC but toward in-plant black nationalist organizations as well as toward those of white revolutionaries. These groups set out to challenge the UAW leadership far more aggressively than the UNC ever intended to.

The first of these groups was called the Dodge Revolutionary Union Movement (DRUM), and it was the brainchild of several staff members of the *Inner City Voice* who had connections with some workers at Chrysler's Dodge Main plant, including a particularly outspoken worker named General Baker. Baker was born to a family of sharecroppers who had migrated to Detroit from rural Georgia in 1941. As a young man in the Motor City, Baker was introduced to politics when he took classes on political theory at Wayne State University (WSU). Baker started an organization on WSU's campus called UHURU, which means "freedom" in Swahili, and then met other black radicals at the *Inner City Voice* when he joined a rally to protest Detroit hosting the Olympics Games when it still had no effective open housing legislation. After the anti-Olympics protest, Baker then went to Cuba with eighty-four other Americans, eleven of whom were black. Because of his exhilarating and inspiring experience meeting freedom fighters in Cuba, including Castro himself, Baker was determined to bring black liberation politics to Detroit. He felt he could do this when he began working at Chrysler's Dodge Main plant upon his return.[33]

Not only Baker but also the entire staff of the *Inner City Voice* wanted to organize workers within the auto plants. Their opportunity came on May 2, 1968, during a wildcat strike at Dodge Main plant that had actually been started by a group of white women frustrated with management's intense line speedup as well as its treatment of female employees.[34] On that morning in May, women in the plant's bumper room decided to walk off the job after their lunch break. They were immediately joined by other workers in their department, including several black men. But Chrysler ultimately chose to fire only two of the white women for instigating the wildcat, while it fired five black men for doing the same. The company targeted one of these black men, Baker, in particular because it believed him to be the real provocateur. But Chrysler had misjudged this autoworker. After being fired Baker, along with autoworker Chuck Wooten and nine others, including activist Marian Kramer, decided to form DRUM. After founding DRUM, on May 29, 1968, the twenty-four-year-old Baker wrote the following warning to Chrysler: "Let it be further understood that by taking the course of disciplining the strikers you have opened that struggle to a new and higher level and for this I sincerely THANK YOU. You have made the decision to do battle with me and therefore to do battle with the entire black community. . . . You have lit the unquenchable spark."[35]

Once Baker started DRUM, the staff of the *Inner City Voice* lent its full support to the new organization. DRUM also received support in the form of $8,000 from the city's Black Economic Development Conference (BEDC).[36] But it was the *Inner City Voice* staff who most consistently stood by DRUM. Indeed, many articles in the paper explicitly encouraged all Detroiters to support this in-plant organization. After 1968, the staff of the paper placed the words "The emancipation of labor is the emancipation of man and the emancipation of man is the freeing of that basic majority of workers who are yellow, brown, and black" directly on the masthead of the *Inner City Voice*.[37] Its support of DRUM stemmed from a larger commitment to, and long-standing practice of, supporting almost any black radical group struggling for social change. *Inner City Voice* staffer Mike Hamlin put his energies into the community and student activist groups the Black Student United Front; Ron March was the liaison between the *Inner City Voice* and DRUM; and Luke Tripp and John Watson were the links between the *Inner City Voice* and WSU's student paper, the *South End*.

But while DRUM had key ties to the *Inner City Voice,* the organization soon took on a life of its own. Most of DRUM's members saw themselves as revolutionary black nationalists whose program was rooted firmly in shop-floor politics. DRUM advocated the complete overhaul of the UAW because it felt the union had become the company's lackey. It made unheard-of demands, such as calling for the union to directly allocate autoworkers' dues to the black community in order to aid in black self-determination.[38] DRUM also attacked the perceived union timidity toward the reviled line foremen.[39] Likewise, DRUM criticized Chrysler for hiring whites "straight out of the Deep South" for its plant security force and then equipping them with "tear gas, night sticks, riot helmets, and the new untested chemical MACE which might blind you on plant property."[40]

Like its counterparts in the *Inner City Voice*, the shop-floor revolutionaries in DRUM prided themselves on "telling it like it is." At several other workplaces in Detroit, DRUM-like groups sprang up almost overnight: JARUM, FORUM, ELRUM, CADRUM, CHRYRUM, FRUM, and UPRUM. The RUM message was also resonating outside Detroit as well.[41] During these years, RUMs also could be found in New Jersey auto plants, in Georgia auto plants, in the New York and Chicago transit systems, in San Francisco's Muni-Railway, in the U.S. Steelworkers union, in the Building Service Employees International union, and in the American Federation of Teachers.[42]

The members of the Detroit-based RUMs not only shared the original DRUM's belief that city and plant activism must be combined (indeed, members of CHRYRUM noted their mission to tackle "not only problems that exist in the plants but problems that exist within the black community"),[43] but they also felt that the attack on racism in the plants must go far beyond the TULC's program.[44] Because they were revolutionaries, the RUMs and their supporters would inject a new militancy into the familiar discussion of race and racism by insisting on a "necessary" link between capitalism and racism. Because the RUMs saw the UAW as a key structure upholding the capitalist system, they concluded that union bureaucrats were one of their most significant adversaries.[45] Indeed, as DRUM's official constitution put it, "we must gear ourselves in the days ahead toward getting rid of the racist, tyrannical, and unrepresentative U.A.W. as representation for the black workers, so that with this enemy out of the way we can deal with our main adversary, the white racist management of Chrysler Corporation."[46]

The RUMs' hostility to the UAW additionally was fueled by their belief that the collective-bargaining apparatus itself prevented autoworkers from having any real power in dealing with management, particularly in dealing with racism. As one RUM group put it, "everyone knows that our grievance procedure is a fraud. . . . And most grievances are settled the company's way because we do not use our strike power to settle them our way."[47] And, according to the RUMs, the UAW leadership actually was perpetuating and feeding off of such shop-floor racism. Every issue of a RUM newspaper included some reference to the union leadership's alleged complicity in in-plant racism or substandard working conditions. When both the UAW and the TULC reminded them that there were a number of African Americans in positions of union power, RUM members were not impressed. Even though eleven presidents of UAW locals were black by 1970, along with a noticeable number of local union officers and shop committeemen, black radicals on the shop floors believed that blacks still had no real power in the union.[48] The RUMs felt that the few blacks who were in positions of company or union authority did very little to improve working conditions for ordinary black workers, and thus racial discrimination in Detroit's auto plants still flourished.

Black revolutionaries on the shop floor made it clear that they were as deeply set against black union officials as white. They reviled the black leaders within the union for not using their new positions to stand up for the black rank and file strenuously enough, and they accused these black leaders of selling out to the needs of the UAW "machine." As the RUMs saw it,

"Wake up brother. Yes! A black man can be squeezing you to death too."[49] And, as members of DRUM stated more bluntly, "It seems as though every time the white power structure is shaken another grinning and shufflin Uncle Tom will come running to their rescue."[50] Over time, the RUMs were not content just to criticize black union officials for supporting the white union administration. They were determined as well to identify these "sellouts" by name and department and then to oust them from their positions.[51] According to DRUM, black middle-class apologists for the union leadership were "the proven enemies of Black workers at Hamtramck assembly, and they shall be dealt with."[52]

Given such RUM rhetoric, TULC and UAW leaders were equally appalled that these groups kept spreading. By the close of 1969, each of the RUMs had become more vocal and better organized and, at the end of that year, they all united with *Inner City Voice* staffers to form the League of Revolutionary Black Workers (or "the League," as it was known). Black radicals legally incorporated the League in 1969 as a self-described "black Marxist-Leninist organization."[53] According to League members, their organization "emerged specifically out of the failure of the white labor movement to address itself to the racist work conditions and to the general inhumane conditions of black people."[54] The League's seven-man executive board included *Inner City Voice* staffers Mike Hamlin, Luke Tripp, John Watson, General Baker, and Chuck Wooten, as well as John Williams and Kenneth Cockrel, a young black attorney. According to the League, the group was "not a cultural nationalist organization, although some people apparently think so. What the League does is to use black identity and anti-colonialism—which are legitimate concerns in the first place—as part of a more general struggle."[55]

Nevertheless, just as most of Detroit's black radicals were deeply suspicious of working with whites after having watched black liberal efforts to do so, so were many of the in-plant black revolutionaries. In its founding constitution, the League noted that its "sole objective is to break the bonds of white racist control over the lives and destiny of black workers," and that "we must gear ourselves up in the days ahead toward getting rid of the racist, tyrannical, and unrepresentative unions as representatives of black workers." Therefore, according to the constitution, "membership is denied to all honkies due to the fact that said honky has been the historical enemy, betrayer, and exploiter of black people. Any relationship that we enter into with honkies will be only on the basis of coalition over issues."[56] At least initially, all members of the in-plant RUMs supported this view.[57]

From the League's perspective, black workers had endured white privilege in the plants for so long that it could not imagine whites ever being willing to work aggressively for black empowerment on the shop floor. Likewise, members and supporters of the RUMs believed that "a disease called racism has poisoned their stupid little pea brains beyond help," and that as long as whites kept getting preferential treatment, they would be an enemy.[58]

In 1969, ELRUM at the Eldon Avenue gear and axle plant where James Johnson was employed was one of the most vocal and active RUM groups in Detroit. According to students writing about ELRUM in 1969, black revolutionaries founded this group in November 1968 after "the ELRUM people . . . came to DRUM for advice and assistance in setting up an organization in their plant."[59] ELRUM held its first meeting on November 10, 1968, and it was not the only dissident group at Eldon.[60] The extremely outspoken UNC co-chair, Jordan Sims, had also formed a UNC group in the plant called the Black Shop Stewards Committee. But it was ELRUM, originally started by workers Fred Holsey and James Edwards, that most captured the spotlight between 1968 and 1972.

Like all of the League units, ELRUM espoused a revolutionary critique of Chrysler and deteriorating working conditions on the shop floor. When Mamie Williams died after coming back to work at Chrysler's insistence, ELRUM contended that "she was murdered by the racist corporation and its lackeys."[61] After Rose Logan's death, ELRUM reported that "a few weeks ago a sister in Department 25, Rose Logan, was run over by a honkie driving a forklift."[62] And when Gary Thompson was killed on the job, ELRUM noted that "Gary Thompson a 22 year old veteran of Vietnam, who had a pregnant wife and a son, was murdered May 26, 1970 at approximately six o'clock a.m. by Chrysler Corporation. . . . Once again ELRUM says to Chrysler Corporation, 'YOU HAVE MURDERED ANOTHER ONE OF OUR BROTHERS.'"[63] Members of ELRUM visited Thompson's parents after his death, and, according to Helen Thompson, "there was a gang of them at the funeral."[64] Even though Eldon's plant manager did come to Thompson's funeral, he never got up to say anything because, as Thompson's mother said, "I think that he was scared to death of these ELRUMs; he was scared to death to say anything."[65]

Members of management and union alike were fearful of the RUMs, primarily because they did not just write about shop-floor problems; they had also been holding numerous demonstrations and rallies and repeatedly shut down auto plants in their attempt to force both the union and the company into action. One of the most dramatic work stoppages took place at Chrysler's Dodge Main plant on July 8, 1968. The day before that wildcat DRUM members had marched to Local 3 headquarters where a UAW Executive Board meeting was taking place. They demanded to meet with officials in the boardroom, which they did, but these officials refused to agree to a list of ten demands that DRUM provided them. It was then that DRUM decided to call an illegal strike for the next morning. On July 8 at 5 a.m., DRUM members positioned themselves around the gates of the Dodge Main plant, and 4,000 workers walked out. Even DRUM leaders were shocked by the high turnout. In response to this wildcat, both the UAW and Chrysler got injunctions forbidding any DRUM picketing, but such legal actions only fueled RUM militancy.[66]

On January 27, 1969, ELRUM also initiated a plant shutdown that "centered around 19 demands. Most dealt with racism."[67] But because this protest resulted in Chrysler firing twenty-five workers and then disciplining eighty-six others on charges of misconduct, on February 10, ELRUM decided to storm UAW headquarters, Solidarity House, to protest Chrysler's actions. Then, in 1970, after Chrysler fired black autoworker John Scott for his violent confrontation with white foreman Erwin Ashlock, who had routinely used racially discriminatory language with Scott, ELRUM once again shut the plant down. In this wildcat, several local union representatives from Eldon stood by the workers' decision to shut down the plant, but they paid dearly for their actions. During the two-day wildcat, 700 to 800 workers walked out of departments 78, 80, and 83 alone, and as a result, Chrysler did agree to rehire Scott. But immediately thereafter the company fired the thirteen union stewards who had supported the wildcat. In response, ELRUM initiated yet another wildcat.[68]

On May 23, 1970, ELRUM shut down the Eldon plant once again, this time to protest the "murder" of Thompson. In fact, the energy behind this particular wildcat is what led RUM members to form the League. As Mike Hamlin remembers, "that strike taught us a lot. We knew at that point that what we had to do was to begin to organize workers in more plants and begin to organize the black community to relate to the struggles in the plants, in the city, in the state, and eventually around the country."[69] Not only did dramatic RUM wildcats inspire radicals to create the League, but it also made them even bolder toward the UAW. Between the Scott and Thompson wildcats, for example, all RUMs in the League held a highly public rally outside of Cobo Hall, where the UAW was holding a special convention. With their bullhorns, RUM members shouted, "Walter Reuther and his henchmen are a bunch of phoney bigots; Reuther shed alligator tears when Martin Luther King was assassinated." At that point, RUM members called on Reuther to prove himself by acceding to several RUM demands, including the elimination of all health and safety hazards, speedups, and dues checkoff. The RUMs also called for a four-day work week of five hours per day, as well as an end to the Vietnam War.[70]

From the union leaders' perspective, however, agreeing to any one of these demands was out of the question. As UAW leaders saw it, giving in to the RUMs not only would validate those dissident organizations, but it also might fuel the growing anti-union activism of revolutionary whites. It had not escaped the UAW that after 1967, several of the white revolutionary groups that had been agitating in the streets and on campuses began taking their agenda and ideology into the plants as well.[71] As DRUM leader General Baker noted, "since the action seems to be in the auto plants, the white organizations want to be there where the ground has been made fertile."[72]

Some groups within the white Left had always believed that revolution must start "at the point of production." For others, particularly those that had focused most of their energies on organizing college campuses, this was a new strategy. A number of white leftist organizations had bitter factional fights when some of their members suggested that every effort should now be devoted to plant organizing.[73] Many white radicals were not easily persuaded that, as Detroiter Rick Feldman put it, "if there was going to be a revolution it had to be among 'real' people, not among students anymore."[74]

But a number of white leftist groups did decide to follow "the principles of Class Struggle Unionism," and they had their members "industrialize" in order to bring their revolutionary politics into the auto plants.[75] To "industrialize" meant applying for a working-class job in a place where there were known to be tensions and preexisting worker militancy. Once hired, the idea was to recruit members into one's own group and lend active support to the struggles indigenous to the plant. As one white radical described the post-1967 workplace activism of the International Socialists (IS), "part of the IS's political perspective was that they would send these working-class radicalized students to get jobs in the Teamsters, auto and mine workers, heavy industry."[76] In this vein, several members of the IS, for example, applied for jobs at Chrysler's Mack Avenue stamping plant because they had heard that it was particularly militant.

Because each of the white leftist groups now in the plants had their own newspaper or newsletter, they added considerably to what was already a growing body of dissident literature. The IS distributed its paper, *Workers Power,* which reported on both world and local plant events; the Socialist Workers party similarly distributed *The Militant;* the Progressive Labor party distributed *Challenge;* and the Revolutionary Communist party distributed *Revolution.* While each of these organizations was very different politically, the bottom line was that, between 1967 and 1972, Detroit's auto industry, like the city proper, was a magnet for white revolutionaries from around the country. As Detroiter Gene Cunningham noted, "we saw things being possible to do in Detroit that couldn't be done anywhere in the country . . . with Detroit's rich history of labor struggle and Detroit's concentration of heavy industry."[77]

Also as had happened in the city itself, black and white radicals in the auto plants increasingly began to work together between 1967 and 1972. Officially, of course, both RUMs and the League took the position that "we don't believe in Black and White together," and each was particularly vehement about not working with white line workers. But because every RUM and League member saw themselves as "Marxist-Leninists," they did participate in class-based struggles, provided that those struggling had a true revolutionary agenda. In addition, over time, it had dawned on the RUMs that there were in fact very practical reasons to work with the white Left. In-plant black radicals were often forced to rely on both white and black student radicals to distribute their literature at plant gates, because management either suspended or dismissed them if they did it themselves.[78] As RUM coordinator Mike Hamlin put it, as their battles with management and union leaders escalated, black revolutionaries "needed to mobilize some white allies."[79] While only one white worker, John Taylor, officially became a RUM member, the white revolutionary Left, and even white moderates in the UNC, both supported and contributed to many RUM and League efforts by attending rallies, walking picket lines, and reporting on black radical victories in their various publications.

Not surprisingly such an alliance between black and white revolutionaries in Detroit's auto plants soon antagonized white conservatives on the shop floors, just as it was alienating them in their neighborhoods. In that respect, white conservatives, like black and white radicals, saw their city struggles and plant battles as inexorably linked. Some white workers became even more conservative after 1967, precisely because they equated the city's growing radical activism with that erupting in their workplaces and vice versa. Whereas the revolutionaries at Chrysler's Jefferson plant, for example, believed that Rushie Forge had merely "lashed out in a torrent of hatred that had been stored up in all his years in Birmingham, New York, and Detroit" when he attacked a line foreman, conservative white workers believed that black workers like Forge were simply violent and crazy.[80] And as many of these workers' fear of blacks on the assembly line increased, they refused to concede the possible legitimacy of both African American shop-floor complaints and black grievances in the city. Indeed, to Detroit's racially conservative white workers, black "rebellion" in either the plants or on city streets was merely an excuse for engaging in racially motivated violence.

Likewise, when conservative white workers saw the proliferation of in-plant black revolutionary groups, which routinely attacked white privilege in the most vitriolic language, they were easily persuaded that black radicals were themselves racist and anti-democratic. Thus, when they simultaneously heard the pronouncements of right-wing politicians like George Wallace in their communities, they had yet another direct and personal connection to his anti–civil rights, anti-radical, and anti-black message. White support of Wallace was so noticeable on Detroit's shop floors that this was one of the reasons why black radicals were so leery of working with shop-floor whites. As members of DRUM noted, "the white workers are not getting any better; they are getting worse. Check out the support white workers gave the peckerwood George Wallace."[81] With entire UAW locals supporting Wallace, in addition to individual white workers, auto plants were witnessing the same discriminatory rhetoric that was common across the city during this same period. As members of FRUM noted, "The UAW is beginning to expose itself from top to bottom. As you know, in Flint today they have already endorsed Mad Dog Wallace for president without opposition."[82]

Just as white conservatives in the city wrote their own newsletters and printed their own leaflets in opposition to black radicals, they were equally prolific in the plants. One leaflet passed out by white workers at a plant in Local 809 exhorted other whites on the line to come to a "White Rights Rally. . . . If you are tired of sex-crazed Blacks pawing young white girls, if you are tired of terror in our schools and in our streets."[83] Other white UAW workers printed and distributed around the Dodge assembly plant a scathing parody of DRUM's newsletter called "D.U.M.B." as well as a similar "M.A.P.U.M.B" leaflet around the Mack Avenue plant. Not only did these leaflets ridicule the RUM demands, but they also made it very clear that conservative factory whites were persuaded that "Wayne State University types" had instigated the growing conflict in their plants.[84]

But despite their hostility to the presence of the in-plant black and white revolutionaries, the fact that these radicals did fight the universally hated company most aggressively did pose a dilemma for even the most conservative white workers. Indeed, because Chrysler had been driving production so relentlessly throughout the 1960s, white workers were not necessarily unsympathetic to the idea of plant shutdowns. Between 1964 and 1967, many of them had also believed that such bold actions might be necessary. But because the black radicals in Detroit's plants were so obviously hostile to working with shop-floor whites, any alliance between mainstream or conservative white workers and militant blacks was, at least in this period, virtually impossible. As RUM member John Taylor recalls, ELRUM "would always refuse to give [its] leaflets to white workers,"[85] and as UNC activist Jordan Sims noted, ELRUM's view of whites was "'motherfucker, we don't want you in here'—they would alienate them, and this was ridiculous."[86]

Between 1967 and 1972, as support for the RUMs, the UNC, and segregationist George Wallace was surfacing across the auto industry, liberal leaders of the UAW and TULC watched Detroit's shop floors descend into a political crisis. But despite the very real challenges to their control initiated by both the UNC and the Wallace supporters in the plants, the UAW and TULC were most concerned about the black revolutionary threat to industry stability and their own authority. As one journalist put it, "DRUM was a panic button and both the union and the company reacted."[87]

During this period, the UAW battled the RUM groups almost exclusively even while other plant dissidents, namely members of the UNC, routinely challenged the union as well. Indeed, the UNC was a real threat to union authority. As one UNC booklet (with the UAW insignia on its cover) commented, "since 1967 the United National Caucus has been busy exposing the mistakes, weaknesses, and betrayal of trust by the UAW. The UAW record is a sad and sordid one."[88] As another UNC document stated, "We intend to fight the bureaucrats who run this union and put control back into the hands of the rank and file worker."[89] And with regard to the conservative whites also mobilizing on its shop floors, the UAW was well aware that they also could pose a serious threat to union stability. On January 16, 1969, leaders at UAW Local 600 warned Walter Reuther himself that "in the recent Presidential Election activity, Wallace supporters did their bit to stir up racist's feelings." They assured Reuther, however, that "the Wallacites [in contrast to the RUMs] . . . used a more subtle method of whisper and hand-to-hand distribution of material."[90] Obviously, the UAW leadership did not believe white conservatives to be as threatening as the in-plant radicals. Even though "Local 600's General Council, on Sunday, January 12, 1969, in open and frank discussion, condemned the activities of [both] white and black racists," the UAW worked far harder to rid the plant of the latter than the former.[91]

In certain respects, it was easy for union leaders to justify their focus on the black revolutionaries, because these dissidents were the most open about their hostility to the UAW. Members of the Mack Avenue plant RUM, MARUM, maintained, for example, that "there are more PREJUDICES in the UAW than there are in Chrysler Corporation," and DRUM leader Ron March unabashedly stated that "there seems to be no place you can turn for any type of restitution as far as your grievances are concerned because of this coalition between union and management."[92] But, of course, UNC affiliates also attacked the UAW leadership quite openly. As authors of the *United Justice Train* wrote, "we are now aware of some of our rights as UAW members. We feel that the evil features of this wicked leadership must be exposed and faced up to by the members in order to give everyone—regardless of race, creed or color—their UAW constitutional rights."[93] And yet, the UAW never expended a fraction of its efforts to dismantle the RUMS on eliminating the UNC in this period.

In addition to believing that the RUMs most seriously challenged their leadership role, union officials particularly despised the fact that the RUMs made them look so impotent in front of management. For example, between 1960 and 1974, there were 122 wildcat strikes at Chrysler, which the UAW had been powerless to prevent.[94] Some of these strikes were large, like the Dodge Main plant walkout of May 1968. Others were small, like numerous "heat" walkouts that would idle a shift or two when workers refused to labor in inhumanely hot conditions. Whatever their size, wildcats had a dramatic impact on company productivity. Chrysler repeatedly made it clear to the UAW that it must prevent such work stoppages and, when the union could not do so, its leaders feared that their bargaining authority with the company was eroding.

In addition to not being able to control its membership, the UAW was humiliated when Chrysler intimated that certain UAW members—namely, black radical members—were nothing but dangerous thugs. According to Chrysler, "by the end of August, 1968, the Plant Protection Department had recorded no less than ten cases of assault when the attackers were black men," and when the management personnel at Hamtramck assembly

(DRUM's stronghold) told the union that it had also received numerous threats, UAW leaders were thoroughly embarrassed.[95] Although it was never established that such intimidation was perpetrated by members of a RUM, given the many threats that peppered RUM literature, both Chrysler and the UAW assumed that it was. About black officials in the UAW, DRUM members had written that "we must try to bring them over to our side or do them like we are going to do the white pig honky."[96] Regarding its in-plant strategy, at least one *DRUM* author had suggested that "it should be obvious that the correct tactic to use is the ambush thing."[97] Finally, as the RUM-affiliated *Inner City Voice* wrote, in addition to printing a recipe for making a bomb, "it is necessary, therefore, that every black man in the community possess at least one rifle of a high-powered caliber."[98] And when DRUM held a raffle on November 17, 1968, the first prize offered was a new M-1 rifle, the second prize was a new shotgun, while the third prize was a bag of groceries and a turkey.[99]

Even though League leader Mike Hamlin had publicly declared that black radicals had "no intention of destroying [the plants],"[100] the UAW shared Chrysler's conviction that the RUMs were violent. Wanting to save face with the company as well as assert its own authority, the union was soon conducting surveillance on these groups. Irving Bluestone, the director of the UAW's General Motors Corporation department, received a letter from Don Rand on November 13, 1969, that had as an attachment RUM leaflets as well as "a listing of the license numbers of those who were driving cars and who parked n UAW property." "You will note," Rand wrote, "that attorney Ken Cockrel [of the League] was identified as one of the participants."[101] And correspondence from worker Jacob Przybylo sent to the offices of UAW leader Arthur Hughes indicates just how much of a tab the union was in fact keeping on the RUMs. As Przybylo wrote, "Dear Sir, I was sick with the flu and these are a week late. That man Edwards is the ELRUM Membership Chairman also of late Wayne State University West End Leftist that was ousted and came into our plant. . . . If you want any other information you can call me at home before 2:00 p.m."[102] Again, however, even though the UNC wrote articles on subjects, such as "Can a Plant Guard Put His Hands on Me, and What Can I do if One Does?," and although this group was also behind a number of heat walkouts in the plants, the UAW never implicated the UNC in any incidents of in-plant intimidation, and it did not put this group under surveillance during these years.[103]

The energy that the UAW eventually came to expend on keeping the RUMs under surveillance suggests that they touched an even deeper nerve than one of embarrassment and intimidation. The simple fact was that the RUMs were the UAW's greatest *political* threat on the shop floor. Indeed, far more than the UNC or the Wallace supporters, the RUMs most reminded union leaders of the Communist party–associated dissent that they had defeated in the 1940s and were determined not to let surface again.

Importantly, before it was apparent to UAW leaders that the RUMs were so politically threatening, several of them did try to find out what RUM leaders wanted, and they hoped to respond to the frustration that brought these groups into existence. For example, Walter Dorosh, president of Local 600, wrote to Walter Reuther, "Local officers, together with unit representatives, for a number of months sought out the representatives from FRUM; the purpose was a meeting of the minds on the alleged charges."[104] And when members of DRUM asked to meet with TULC leader Shelton Tappes to explain their purpose, some in the UAW leadership were glad to see them talk. Tappes did meet with DRUM leaders in early 1969, at a rally that they were holding at the United Methodist Church. For one and a half hours, Tappes listened while DRUM members spoke of "bad working conditions, the attitudes of supervisors toward Negroes in the plants, discrimination on shop upgrading and the lack of consideration of Negro employees in the skilled trades classification."[105] Even though UAW leaders insisted that Tappes attend the meeting with DRUM, he then got flack from UAW leaders for having appeared too sympathetic to the black radicals there.[106] Nevertheless, Tappes dutifully submitted a report to UAW official Bill Beckham on that event. According to Beckham, "Shelton advised us that there were approximately 300 to 350 people in attendance at this meeting."[107]

Despite the small numbers, Beckham encouraged Reuther to engage in a meaningful dialogue with DRUM, although he went on to concede that his view "is not shared by many, since the attitude generally expressed in the building is to crush them."[108] And Beckham wasn't the only union leader suggesting early on that it would be prudent to keep communication lines open with the RUMs. Union official Frank Menendez also noted that "a question naturally comes to mind as to the cause of the deep-rooted discontent that is prevalent in the Hamtramck assembly plant. It is my considered opinion that supervisors must be instructed in human relations. There is an utter disregard for the feelings of the hourly workers. It makes no difference what color a person is; they are all treated badly and there is definite room for improvement."[109]

By and large, however, this inquisitive and potentially sympathetic perspective on the RUMs quickly became a minority view among UAW leaders. These officials, including such figures as Irving Bluestone and George Merrelli, considered black radicals in both the city and in the plants extremely dangerous to the union and therefore did not think accommodation was the answer. In 1968, Bluestone shared this view with UAW President Walter Reuther after calling his attention to a recent television show featuring black radicals in Detroit and their "specific references to the UAW . . . including the call for a revolutionary party to destroy our current social system."[110] And, as Merrelli told student interviewers in 1969, DRUM was "carrying out the mandates of Communist China. . . . It became quite apparent, knowing and being familiar with Communist operations. . . . [T]his happens when they worm themselves into positions of leadership and then out comes the program. . . . [This is an] Old Commie trick. We had to fight the same thing in the early days of our organization."[111] To UAW leaders, radicals were once again threatening control of Reuther's brand of trade unionism.

Indicating just how threatened top UAW officials were by the RUMs, an intense internal discussion about the inner workings of these groups had in fact been well under way well before Shelton Tappes attempted to determine what DRUM wanted. On October 4, 1968, Douglas Fraser encouraged black UAW leaders Nelson Jack Edwards and Marcellius Ivory to come to a meeting in which "unquestionably we will be talking about D.R.U.M.'s activities."[112] And, on July 15, 1968, top UAW leaders again called a special meeting to discuss DRUM's most recent activities. According to meeting minutes, President Reuther told those assembled that "this is a group of black nationalists and they are tied in the with the Chinese Commies at Wayne State University. We are going to see more of this [activism,] which is organized by the black nationalists."[113] While he did not disagree with Reuther's assessment of the RUMs at this meeting, Fraser cautioned that "we have to handle this delicately [because] in the last issue of DRUM there are indications that they have the support of other plants." And then, as somewhat of a voice in the wilderness, black IEB member Jack Edwards suggested to fellow officials at this gathering that "we can't isolate ourselves from their ideas."[114]

But as RUM activism escalated, union leaders became increasingly unsympathetic to such notions. By 1969, the UAW was keeping even closer tabs on the RUMs. For example, Ken Morris, director of UAW Region 1B, amassed an extensive collection of RUM newsletters, while the director of UAW Region 1, George Merrelli, also had begun a large file on the RUM materials being circulated in the plants.[115] Indeed, when top UAW officials came across RUM literature, they often forwarded it to President Reuther himself, as well as to other high-ranking leaders. For example, Bluestone sent copies of DRUM literature to Reuther on July 2, 1968, because "this group represents a growing and serious problem."[116] That same year, Merrelli sent Fraser copies of both the *South End* and the DRUM Constitution, while Fraser sent Emil Mazey, Ken Morris, Pat Caruso, and E. Bruce "a copy of the first issue of *MARUM*" as well.[117]

Just as it was important for union officials to keep abreast of what its black dissidents were writing, it soon became equally necessary that they figure out exactly who was behind the RUM insurgency. Clearly, these leaders did not believe that RUM dissent was indigenous to the auto plants. As Reuther's statement to the IEB on July 15, 1968, indicates, UAW leaders suspected that it was campus radicals who actually were instigating the RUM activism in the plants. Merrelli seemed to agree with Reuther, as he wrote to Ed Liska, president of Local 3, expressly so that he could share with him "a copy of the 'South End,' an official Wayne State University Student publication," believing that Liska would "find the story quite interesting."[118] And the suspicion of top union leaders that the RUMs were run by outsiders was certainly fueled by leaders at the local level. In 1969, William Gerbe of Local 3 wrote Merrelli about a stormy meeting that had taken place at his union hall because Gerbe wanted Merrelli to know that, in his opinion, "there were four hundred in the hall and about seventy-five percent were not our members."[119]

But suspecting that the in-plant RUMs were following the "China Commie philosophy" of outside groups because the "Inner City Voice publication [is the] same source as D.R.U.M."[120] was not the same as proving such a connection. Efforts to identify plant dissidents as outside agitators or DRUM/WSU conspirators, so that they could successfully be exposed and thus eliminated, met with varied success. When two employees at Hamtramck assembly were involved in an altercation with officials there, Frank Menendez of that plant was able to let Merrelli know that "both employees in question were very high in the leadership structure of DRUM."[121] Yet in another case, official Bill Beckham had to report, "I am not sure this will answer the question that you are asking, in that this active group in the UAW cannot be laid, based upon the evidence, at the door of the individual you are asking about. He may be involved, but we are not aware of such involvement."[122] Regardless of what they could prove, as students interviewing union officials in 1969 noted, "there appears to be widespread consensus attributing the Wayne State *South End* newspaper as being a main instigator" in stirring up shop-floor dissent.[123] These officials tended to agree further that they were not going to let such student activists in any way affect their labor relations system.[124]

The UAW's determination to expose the RUMs as the tool of white student radicals and as a dangerous threat in their own right is revealed in several mass mailings that it sent to members after 1968. In its open letter to "All Local 961 Members," UAW leaders of that local not only accused EL-RUM of being the tool of WSU student radicals and of anti-establishment types like Tom Hayden, but it also reminded workers that "the UAW is the greatest Democratic Union in the world. You can hold office regardless of your race, color, or creed."[125] Not just local union leaders but leaders from the UAW International as well decided to approach members directly about the RUM threat. In an open letter from the International UAW to "All Members of the UAW Local 3," UAW officials argued that the in-plant black radicals were the "voice of a worldwide propaganda network. . . . [They call] for bloody and violent revolution over and over. . . . This group—whatever it is and whatever it stands for—has no legal or moral right to bargain with the Chrysler Corporation. . . . Negro members are too intelligent to permit themselves to be used as pawns by an outside group of extremists who want to divide us and create chaos and revolution."[126]

By March 1969, the IEB of the UAW had decided that it was necessary to write not simply to members of UAW locals where the RUMs were active, but also to every UAW member in the country. Officials at Solidarity House had begun to receive RUM leaflets from leaders of UAW locals in cities other than Detroit, and this was alarming. One such city was Atlanta, where RUM activists at a General Motors plant had put out a leaflet exhorting "all brothers and sisters of the PLANT-TATIONS" there "to listen and speak to Brothers from the Revolutionary Movements of the AUTO PLANT-TATIONS of Detroit, Michigan."[127] As ominously to union leaders, members of GM-RUM in Atlanta had also noted that "after nine months of giving out the 'Voice' we've found that not only do white workers have an interest in the paper and the things that its saying but they even feel left out."[128]

Just as the Reuther caucus of the UAW had believed itself to be the only logical choice to lead the union in the 1940s, so it did in the late 1960s. And just as it had put enormous effort into undermining its Communist-supported Martin-Addes-Leonard caucus opponents by accusing them of being anti-democratic and dangerous during those years, the heirs to Reuther's labor relations vision once again came to put enormous effort on eliminating the new threat from the Left. Indeed, as UAW official Emil Mazey put it in an interview with the *Detroit News*, the "black militants in Detroit's auto factories pose a greater peril to the UAW than the communist infiltration did in the 1930s."[129]

The UAW leaders of the 1960s and 1970s were proud of the liberal-Democratic union that they either had worked so hard to build or had inherited. These leaders took pride in the fact that they had delivered high wages and good benefits to their membership, and also that they had "been in the vanguard of the legislative fight for civil rights [and had] marched in Detroit, Washington, D.C., Selma, Jackson, Mississippi, Memphis, Tennessee for justice and equality."[130] They were proud as well that they had "been in the leadership of the crusade against poverty."[131] More so than any other dissident impulse on the shop floors of Detroit between 1969 and 1972, the in-plant black and white revolutionaries had undermined the *political* premises on which the postwar labor-management accord had been constructed. Even more determinedly than their counterparts in city government, Detroit's liberal labor leaders were unwillingly to accede power to these challengers.

Between 1968 and 1972, the liberal leadership of the UAW dramatically escalated its attempt to undermine the black and white revolutionary insurgency. Over time, however, it became clear that neither collecting information on the dissidents nor writing exposés of them for the benefit of the general membership, had rid the plants of the RUMs. In fact, it may have even fueled their activism. When the UAW wrote to its general membership about the RUM threat, one leadership-oriented worker accused officials of paying too much attention to the militants and thus encouraging them. As this "confused UAW member" wrote in disgust to the leadership of UAW Region

1, "you seem to have given a bit of legal status to the DRUM movement by recognizing and 'negotiating' with them."[132]

Whether they were being spurred on by attention from the UAW leadership or by their own sheer determination, the fact was that Detroit's RUMs were growing in power and influence between 1968 and 1972. Clearly, the radical view that "at the height of the civil rights struggle, Reuther was always found at the head of the line, while never really raising any struggle against the racism that existed in his own union or the plants, where blacks constituted a majority," was shared widely on the shop floors.[133] Much to the UAW's dismay, through their in-plant organizations, black and white radicals were presenting line workers with a vision for how postwar labor-management relations might be conducted that was more militant than the one long defended by labor liberals. As the mainstream black newspaper the *Michigan Chronicle* noted, "no matter what the actual number of DRUM members, many other black auto workers knew this mess for what it is and while they may not be DRUM members, they sure as hell support some of the DRUM goals."[134]

One black autoworker knew firsthand the plant problems that made the RUMs so attractive. This worker, one who would become a cause célèbre to black and white revolutionaries, and whose popularity on the shop floor would convince the UAW leadership that it must reassert control of the workplace at any cost, was James Johnson Jr. While the city and workplaces of Detroit were becoming war zones of racial conflict as well as sites of new political possibility after 1967, Johnson continued to go to work every day, simply trying to make a living. But even though his plant had become a hotbed of RUM activism, Johnson was completely uninvolved in the controversies and conflicts at Eldon. He was not a member of ELRUM, and he had never walked out in a wildcat. He was, however, deeply frustrated by the treatment he had endured since Chrysler hired him.

On May 9, 1970, for example, Johnson had a serious car accident in which he sustained injuries to the back of his head and neck. After taking time off from work at his doctor's insistence, he "received a telegram from [Chrysler] to return to work or be terminated." Against the advice of his physician, Johnson did come back to work, but when he returned he discovered that Chrysler had denied him benefits to pay his medical expenses. Then, on May 29, 1970, he took a few days off from work after getting the approval by a foreman in his department. But when Johnson came back to work, he could not find his time card because it had been removed from its usual place. When he finally tracked the card down, someone had stamped it "Clear AWOL."[135] When Johnson questioned this, Chrysler's personnel department maintained that he had never told the foreman of his intention to take a vacation and therefore he had been absent without permission.

In time, Johnson was able to have both the insurance and the vacation decisions rescinded. As foreman Bernard Owiesny said later, "I didin't know about him having permission to take a vacation at the period."[136] Nevertheless, these incidents had a profound impact on him. Johnson was certain that he had endured these bureaucratic complications, as well as the constant verbal abuse from his foreman, because he was a black man in an all-white department. Not surprisingly, experiences such as these all too often "conjured up childhood experiences in Mississippi" and aggravated Johnson's already precarious mental state.[137]

In June 1970, yet another incident occurred in Johnson's work life that only confirmed his suspicion that he was being victimized on the job. During that month, job setter Robert Baynes took a two-week vacation and recommended that Johnson fill in for him, given that he knew how to do the job already. Because the job setter was like an assistant to the foreman, this was quite an honor. Johnson was also excited by the opportunity to make $5 an hour while he filled in for Baynes. To Johnson's disappointment, "Mr. Owiesny, however, placed a Ronnie Jasper, a white man and a close personal friend of his on [the] job setter's job."[138]

As a result of the times during which he had been forced back to work after his car accident, denied his medical benefits, cleared from the company's rolls after his vacation, and blatantly passed over for a white man in a temporary job promotion, Johnson was under increasing emotional stress throughout May and June of 1970. In July, he finally snapped.

On July 15, Johnson came to work as usual at 2:30 p.m. and went directly to his job in the cement room. He performed his regular job for forty-five minutes. A foreman named Hugh Jones, who was filling in for Johnson's foreman, Owiesny, came over to Johnson and assigned him to work the number 2 oven, his old and despised job. As Johnson well knew, the oven line was one of the worst jobs in the plant, and "he believed that he had, by hard and meritorious service, worked his way out of such a job."[139] Johnson was doubly upset because Jones was one of the few black foremen in the plant, and it bothered him a great deal that Jones would betray another black man in that way.

Despite his anger at being told to do so, Johnson went to the oven line. Yet once he got there, he did not begin the job. According to later testimony, Johnson "didn't refuse to do the job . . . [but he] didn't have the proper gloves. The gloves [were] not laying for the employee to take."[140] Johnson then asked foreman Jones to call his union steward, Clarence Horton. When Horton arrived, managers were summoning Johnson to the personnel office. Horton attempted to get a heat pass for Johnson, as it was 90 degrees in the plant and more than 120 degrees near the ovens, but instead Johnson received a suspension for "insubordination." According to the supervisor's report completed by foreman Jones, Johnson "was told to do a job that he refuse to do so, and went and sit down and number 2 oven was off until I could find another man to start up. All this happen[ed at] 3:15 p.m. This employee is now being suspension as of know 3:30, 7/15/70, and sapose to report to Labor Relations 3:00 o'clock 7/16/70."[141] Steward Horton later testified that there was nothing he could do; management had already made its decision.[142] According to one state official who later commented on these events, "when suspended (which he [Johnson] considered fired) he was convinced his persecutors had won."[143]

As an indication of how utterly disillusioned autoworkers had become with the labor relations system, Johnson did not even bother to file a grievance before he left the plant that day.[144] After he was suspended, he "appeared very nervous and upset," but he left the plant peacefully.[145] But at 4:55 p.m. that same day, with a fury that shocked the nation, he came back to the Eldon plant with a gun, went to his department, and opened fire. According to the general foreman at Eldon, Wallace Moore, "Someone then stuck their head in [my] door and yelled 'Hey you guys better get out of here, he's shooting at anything with a white shirt on.'"[146] After shooting foreman Gary Hinz twice, Johnson then asked, "Where's Jones?"[147] He found Hugh Jones and fired at him twice before the man fell. Even after Jones fell, Johnson "fired at point blank range then four times."[148] Johnson next pointed his gun at a worker named Melvin Cooper but walked away because "Melvin Cooper was not in a white shirt."[149] On his way to the Jordan street exit, Johnson ran into a job-setter named Joseph Kowalski. According to a stock chaser named Ed Lacey, "Kowalski came out and tried to talk to him but he couldn't. Kowalski turned around and was shot in the back and fell down."[150] After shooting Kowalski, Johnson allowed himself to be handcuffed by plant security. He said little as security guards escorted him from the plant, and he found himself charged with first-degree murder.

But the in-plant radicals had much to say about Johnson's deed. In fact, Johnson had become a shop-floor celebrity because, as the *Inner City Voice* editorialized, "like the heroic black workers in the past who decided to put an end to the racist harassment which is unavoidable, Brother James accepted the challenge to his manhood; and as a result, this courageous Brother was forced to wage an armed struggle at the point of production. . . . It was then that Brother decided that justice would be served."[151] The July 1970 issue of *ELRUM* was equally celebratory. Its front-page headline read, "Hail James Johnson."[152]

Reaction to the murder in the city's black community was equally intense and equally, if more subtly, sympathetic. As even the mainstream black newspaper the *Michigan Chronicle* noted, "anyone familiar with Detroit's auto 'plantations' would not be entirely surprised [at] what James Johnson did," primarily because of the "hoax" of Equal Employment Opportunity and the fact that someone like Johnson was just another "'mule,' a man machine."[153] The *Michigan Chronicle* was also quick to point out that "Johnson's union, or to put it more accurately, union failure, enters into this grisly story."[154] One radical Detroit paper, *The Metro,* actually suggested that "Johnson got the wrong men. . . . [T]he real criminals sit in their offices in Highland Park [Chrysler], Dearborn [Ford], and the General Motors Building, and Solidarity House [UAW]. . . . [T]hey don't have to worry about being shot down by an angry worker. Yet. But they should."[155]

Of course, Detroit's conservative whites and its liberal politicians and labor leaders did not see the Johnson murders at all in the same way that the radicals did.[156] In fact, these murders and the ensuing trial only served to transform Detroit's bitter war for civic and labor-movement control that conservatives, liberals, and radicals had been fighting for years into an even more bitter affair. As city residents began to focus their attention on the potential outcome of Johnson's and several other controversial trials, Detroit's war at home quietly moved from its streets and shop floors to its courtrooms with quite surprising consequences for the city's political future.

6: From Battles on City Streets to Clashes in the Courtroom

> The principle of Reparation is recognized in international law. . . . [W]e must
> consider recognizing reparations now as a domestic principle.[1]

*While Detroit's residents and its auto plant workers were buzzing about the
murders committed by James Johnson Jr., the accused sat in the Wayne
County jail awaiting his trial for first-degree murder. Although Johnson was
but one of many autoworkers who recently had exploded violently on Detroit's shop floors, his shooting spree attracted national media attention because it so dramatically symbolized the chaos that still enveloped America's
urban centers and plants, even after civic leaders had extinguished the fires
of urban rebellion and labor leaders had redoubled their efforts to improve
the quality of work life for their most unskilled laborers. Johnson's deed also
clearly illuminated the fact that powerful forces to both the left and to the
right of liberalism had emerged in Detroit since 1967 and did not appear to
be going away. Although Johnson was completely apolitical, his murder trial
would become one of the most politically charged events in Detroit's history,
as radicals, liberals, and conservatives sought to have their views of "justice"
prevail.*

Johnson's murder trial followed closely on the heels of several other equally
controversial trials and was followed by still others. In fact, between 1969
and 1973, both the civil and criminal courts of Detroit became a new bat-
tleground on which radicals, conservatives, and liberals waged their war for
control of the city.

In every one of these highly charged court battles, Detroit's black and
white revolutionaries hoped to use the legal system not only to acquit black
defendants, but also to prove conclusively just how discriminatory and unjust the city of Detroit still was. Simultaneously, the city's white conserva-

tives, who had long suspected that liberals had become too soft on crime and violence, still hoped that the court system might harshly penalize defendants such as Johnson. And for Detroit's liberals, who had come to feel that their ability to govern the city depended on defeating the challenges emanating from both the Left and the Right, these trials were a pivotal opportunity to show, once and for all, that they were the city's most fair-minded arbiters of justice.

To prove this, Detroit's liberals—be they judges, hearing referees, politicians, or administrators—chose not to stand in the way of the black radical lawyers like League leader Kenneth Cockrel, who repeatedly tried to push the city's legal system to its most progressive limits. Indeed, they decided to celebrate, and take credit for, the victories that such attorneys managed to secure for their clients. And this decision proved pivotal for Detroit politics, as, much to the Left's dismay, it netted these liberals new legitimacy among the city's previously disenchanted poor and working-class blacks.

* * * *

The first controversial and pivotal trial to hit Detroit's criminal courts stemmed from the night of March 27, 1969, when two police officers were killed during their raid on the New Bethel Church. While initially the Detroit Police Department (DPD) had rounded up 142 African Americans and brought them to the city jail, ultimately prosecutors decided to charge four black men—Alfred Hibbitt, Kirkwood Hall, Raphael Viera, and Clarence Fuller—with either assault with intent to kill and murder or murder in the first degree.[2] These men would not all be tried together. One trial date was set for Hibbitt and Kirkwood, and their case came to be known as New Bethel One. Another date was reserved for the trial of Vera and Fuller, known as New Bethel Two.

As soon as the police arrested this foursome and bound them over for their respective trials, a young black attorney from the League offered these defendants his services. This man, Kenneth Cockrel, was "at 34, the most talked about lawyer in Detroit."[3] As a member of the League's executive board and an unapologetic Marxist, Cockrel certainly stood out. But he also was well known and respected as an attorney who consistently defended poor Detroiters, regardless of their notoriety. Still, it was Cockrel's political ideology, as well as his radical litigation style, that virtually guaranteed that New Bethel One and Two would become highly public and controversial events.

Cockrel made headlines even before New Bethel One began. Once the police charged his clients, Cockrel's first order of business was to get a lower bail for them so that they might be released pending their trials. On April 19, 1969, Cockrel came before Recorder's Court Judge Joseph E. Maher to argue for thirty-eight-year-old factory worker Al Hibbitt's release. During these proceedings, the prosecution maintained that Hibbitt's bail should be extremely high because he had attacked a member of law enforcement. But Cockrel argued that his client was not the man that police were looking for, and that bail therefore should be reasonable. After hearing both sides, Judge Maher sided with the prosecution and set bail at $50,000. Cockrel was outraged. He stormed out of the courtroom, where reporters then overheard him criticize Maher for doubling Hibbitt's original bail, which Cockrel already thought was "confiscatory." Ears perked up as Cockrel went on to call Maher "a racist monkey, a honkie dog, a racist pirate and a bandit" under his breath.[4] As soon as Cockrel left the courthouse, the reporters who had heard his inflammatory comments went to the judge to ask his opinion of the outburst. Infuriated, Maher promptly charged Cockrel with contempt of court and ordered the attorney to present himself to Judge Joseph A. Sullivan for a hearing.[5]

But upon learning of the contempt charge against him, Cockrel immediately went on the offensive. With the city's many black and white revolutionaries offering their support, and with liberal organizations such as the Wolverine Bar Association and black liberal congressmen such as John Conyers Jr. standing by his right to free speech, Cockrel decided that he actually welcomed the chance to defend his charges against Maher in open court. It particularly gratified Cockrel that city residents and autoworkers alike were flocking to his aid. As DRUM members announced, "at 2:00 p.m. Monday every black worker who is on the afternoon shift should make it their duty to be at Recorders Court in support of Brother Ken Cockrel. Time and time again it has been Ken alone in our behalf."[6]

Setting out "to prove beyond a reasonable doubt that Judge Joseph Maher is a criminal, a racist, a bandit and a thief," Cockrel's office immediately began calling on linguists, etymologists, and civil liberties experts to help draft a case.[7] Even the well-known lawyer F. Lee Bailey was "one of the many who have volunteered and will testify."[8] Apparently, Bailey agreed with Cockrel's view that the contempt "charges are designed to deter, intimidate and prevent prospective clients of defendant [Cockrel], or are reasonably calculated to have the effect of doing so, from engaging in litigation . . . all in violation of the First, Sixth and Fourteenth Amendments to the Constitution of the United States."[9] The amount of rigorous research that went into the Cockrel contempt defense was staggering. Hundreds of pages of information on racism, civil rights, civil liberties, and the use of the English language flooded the law office where Cockrel's law partner, Harry Philo, was drawing from such materials to draft a "Memorandum of Authorities in Support of Motion to Dismiss" the contempt charges.

When the contempt proceedings began, the courtroom was packed and nearby Kennedy Square was filled to capacity with pro-Cockrel demonstrators. After two days of hearings, prosecutor Michael O'Hara bowed to public and media pressure and quietly suggested a voluntary dismissal of all charges to Cockrel's defense team.[10] In turn Judge Sullivan dutifully dismissed the contempt case and the New Bethel Trials proceeded. Significantly, however, the Motor City Left had already capitalized on the educational potential of that contempt charge. Harry Philo's planned defense of Cockrel was printed and distributed around the city, thus giving Detroit's radicals much publicity and making it clear that they were committed to exposing the injustice of "the system." Almost overnight, Detroiters learned that "Ken Cockrel is one of the most sought-after speakers and commentators on our society in the State of Michigan at colleges, law schools, churches, high schools, political organizations, youth groups—a featured speaker for the Michigan ACLU—a frequently cited candidate for Mayor of Detroit—a leader of many organizations on the side of the people."[11] Thus, as a result of Maher's attempt to censure Cockrel, and the defense that Cockrel

Kenneth V. Cockrel, March 1970. *Walter P. Reuther Library, Wayne State University.*

mounted, Detroiters came to know more about this young attorney and his ideas than they otherwise might have.

As New Bethel One and Two played out, Cockrel and the inner-city Left received only greater attention. When, for example, the initial group of prospective jurors in New Bethel One came from a predominately white pool, Detroiters watched in amazement as Cockrel pushed his allowable challenges during jury selection to the limit in order to get a sympathetic panel. By probing so deeply into the racial perspectives of the prospective jurors, Cockrel successfully seated a jury far closer to being the "peers" of his defendants than was usually the case. Indeed, jury composition mattered a great deal to Cockrel. He had decided early on that the best way to defend each of those accused in the New Bethel murders was to remind members of the jury that these were black men being charged with attacking white police officers—officers, he maintained, who had a well-known reputation as being violent, untrustworthy, and racist every time they stepped foot into the black community.

As the Cockrel defense team saw it, "the full scope of police-community relations in Detroit has been and is fraught with racial polarity and tension and New Bethel fits into this entire framework."[12] Cockrel insisted that every New Bethel defendant be judged within this particular social context—a context in which black men always were assumed to be guilty when in fact, he argued, it was white officers who kept breaking the law. Perhaps because they related well to the picture that Cockrel painted, or perhaps because they simply were not persuaded by the prosecution's case (indeed, one black officer on the stand admitted that he couldn't "swear to the fact that this was the individual I seen in front of the church doing the shooting"),[13] the jury of six blacks and six whites in New Bethel One ultimately voted for acquittal. In doing so, they sent shock waves through the radical and conservative communities of the Motor City alike.

But before anyone could digest the implications of the verdict in New Bethel One, other dramas were unfolding in the New Bethel Two trial that also had begun in 1969. From the beginning, New Bethel Two was more newsworthy than New Bethel One because both defendants were self-proclaimed black nationalist separatists who had gone public with their radical views in publications such as the *Inner City Voice* and *Black Consciousness*. Indeed, the Republic of New Africa that had been meeting at the New Bethel Church on the fateful night often proclaimed its desire to turn five Southern states into a country for blacks and defendant Clarence Fuller was an admitted RNA member known as "Brother Chakka." Defendant Raphael Viera not only admitted to being an RNA delegate from New York, but he also proudly proclaimed his membership in the Young Lords party of Puerto Rican revolutionaries.[14] Given their clients' political views and that they had not managed to obtain a jury as representative of their clients as they had in New Bethel One, Cockrel and fellow defense attorneys Milton Henry and Sheldon Halpern were concerned about the case.

Clarence Fuller, April 15, 1969. *Walter P. Reuther Library, Wayne State University.*

From the moment that the New Bethel Two trial got under way, the defense team was disturbed to note that prosecutors Robert Harrison and Owen Galligan produced a nineteen-year-old witness, David Brown Jr., who testified that Viera and Fuller indeed had shot at the New Bethel victims, officers Michael Czapski and Richard Worobec. Although the defense pointed out that Brown's father had received a healthy fee for persuading his son to testify on behalf of the prosecution, this testimony was nevertheless damaging to the accused. Undeterred however, Cockrel was determined to use Brown's testimony to his clients' advantage, and he did so by directing the jury's attention to what he argued was the police-induced chaos and violence of the New Bethel incident. On cross-examination, Cockrel asked Brown to tell the jury what his experiences had been on the night of March 27, 1969, which, the jury found out, included being repeatedly kicked in the head by the officers in the church.[15] By getting Brown to detail his injuries and his subsequent repeated trips to the doctor, the Cockrel-led defense team successfully focused the jury's attention on the grievous actions of the police.

Despite employing a "police brutality" defense strategy similar to that used in New Bethel One, Cockrel was not altogether sure that the New Bethel Two jury was going to be very sympathetic, as he had not succeeded in getting a large black presence on it. Midway through the trial, Cockrel decided to get to the bottom of why, with almost 50 percent of Detroit's population being black, there were so few blacks on Recorder's Court jury panels such as this one. Cockrel, along with his radical white partner, Justin Ravitz, went to the jury commissioner's office and demanded to see the questionnaires that were used to compose the panels of prospective jurors. What they found chilled them and would change the course of legal history in the Motor City.

As soon as Cockrel and Ravitz began looking carefully at the jury pool questionnaires, they discovered that often the forms were headed with handwritten buzz phrases such as "on ADC," "long hair," or "community activist."[16] Cockrel and Ravitz further discovered that nonurban white residents made it into the pool of prospective jurors far more often than did inner-city residents, and that recent migrants from the South, usually black, were dismissed from potential service disproportionately.[17] Because the Jury Commission was still using the 1967, not the 1968 or 1969, voter rolls, Cockrel and Ravitz were also enlightened as to why so few young people— their clients' peers—had made it on to the New Bethel Two jury.

Armed with their findings, the Cockrel defense team filed a "Joint Motion to Quash Jury Panel and for Other Relief and Affidavit Thereon" before Judge Horace Gilmore, the New Bethel Two trial judge.[18] They alleged in their motion that "the Jury Commissioners' determination of jurors' qualifications did not meet constitutional standards of fairness, objectivity or freedom from discrimination racial and otherwise."[19] Judge Gilmore suspended New Bethel Two until a full investigation into potential Jury Commission improprieties could take place.

The New Bethel Two trial was on hold for a month as Judge Gilmore heard testimony from the Jury Commission itself. After Cockrel's team subpoenaed Jury Commissioner Karl McKeehan to testify, and Ravitz grilled him for over four hours, according to the *Detroit Free Press*, it was "confirmed that many persons were excluded from service for such reasons as having a beard, wearing miniskirts, being on welfare, or chewing gum."[20] Specifically Cockrel and Ravitz proved "824 total cases of exclusion which were 'consistent with our contention' that the process is 'illegal, unconstitutional and racist.'"[21]As a result of the testimony in this Jury Commission hearing, Judge Gilmore called for a thorough investigation by the Wayne County Prosecutor, a special investigator, or by the Wayne County Circuit Court.[22] Then, rather than seek a mistrial in New Bethel Two, Cockrel and Ravitz requested that Gilmore recall and seat wrongly excused jurors in that case. After the judge agreed to this, Cockrel and Ravitz were able to merge a new group of previously excused jurors with members of the original jury and "for the first time ever in Detroit . . . a majority Black jury" sat in the box at Recorders Court.[23]

Not surprisingly, while the Cockrel defense team's victory in the jury-selection process heartened city blacks, it angered white conservatives around the city. As Cockrel and Ravitz had hoped, when the New Bethel Two trial resumed, after deliberating twenty-eight hours the new jury of twelve black and two white Detroiters acquitted both Viera and Fuller. And, of course, this was exactly the outcome that conservative whites most feared.[24] As they well knew, the implications of this challenge to the jury selection process, and this verdict, went far beyond the New Bethel trial itself.

Indeed shortly after the New Bethel Two defense team filed its motion before Judge Gilmore, the Presiding Judge of the Recorder's Court, Robert E. DeMascio, felt compelled to issue an order overhauling the way that *all* Recorder's Court juries were chosen from then on. The order significantly curtailed the discretion of the Jury Commission to arbitrarily exclude people from jury service on discriminiatory or capricious grounds. Henceforth, the Jury Commissioners could excuse individulas from prospective jury service only for the specified reasons and grounds enumerated in the law. Any interview that might lead to excusal from jury service for discretionary reasons had to be held in open court before a court reporter, and the names of all individuals who had theretofore been excused on discretionary grounds had to be accumulated and relisted as persons to be called for jury service.[25]

Because of the dramatic outcomes in the New Bethel One and Two, and particularly because now every poor black defendant awaiting trial would have much better odds of being judged by a jury of his or her peers, when the James Johnson Jr. murder trial finally hit the court docket, Detroiters from across the political, class, and color spectrum watch with bated breath.

With Cockrel and Ravitz agreeing to defend Johnson, every citizen knew that this would be a particularly important proceeding. Feeling a new sense of optimism after their victories in the New Bethel trials, radicals hoped that in the Johnson trial Cockrel could once again achieve a real triumph for the city's African Americans. Simultaneously, conservative whites hoped that the New Bethel trials had been a fluke and that the Johnson judge would harshly penalize this criminal. City liberals of both races hoped that the Johnson trial would vindicate the rationality and fairness of the legislative system, just as they believed that the New Bethel trials had.

Voicing the sentiment of much of Detroit's liberal leadership after the New Bethel trials, Director of the Commission on Community Relations (CCR),

Richard Marks had argued that "black citizens genuinely mourn the death of a police officer . . . and genuinely support the apprehension of the killer . . . [but] they are simply unwilling to abandon for any reason, the traditional struggle by which any citizen would advance to protect and assert his common humanity."[26] "Negro citizens," Marks continued, "are as desperately concerned that there will be proper policing in their communities as any other citizen in our city."[27] To liberal leaders, the fact that black and white Detroiters were resolving their differences in courtrooms instead of on city streets was testimony to the strength and very successes of liberalism. They intended to drive this point home. If blacks accused of serious crimes in Detroit could now receive a fair trial before a jury of their peers, then their liberal agenda had indeed made in-roads into entrenched racial discrimination. The New Bethel trials were not about criminals winning out over cops; rather, they were glowing examples of how any violation of black civil rights—even by members of law enforcement—would effectively be censured in the judicial process.

But when Cockrel and Ravitz took on the Johnson defense, they had no intention of having this trial bolster the credibility of Detroit's liberals. They approached Johnson's defense by insisting that his actions be viewed and judged within the broader, and quite ugly, social context of the city and country in which he lived. While they agreed that Johnson, the individual, was on trial, they also insisted that he did not live or act in a vacuum, and that therefore his surrounding environment would be as relevant as his personal history in deciding this case. Not only did Cockrel and Ravitz decide to use a strategy similar to that in the New Bethel trials, but they also capitalized on their legal victory regarding jury selection. Johnson's fourteen jurors were similar to him in terms of class and race. Several were migrants from the South; nine were black (five women and four men), and five were white (four women and one man).[28] All of the men were hourly workers, and five of the women were wives of auto employees.[29]

Johnson's trial began on April 30, 1971, in the courtroom of Judge Robert Colombo, with Prosecutor William Galligan laying out the facts as starkly as possible:[30] Because Johnson had killed three people, he now should be convicted of first-degree murder.[31] Cockrel, on the other hand, opened for the defense with a treatise on how Johnson, an ordinary black Detroiter, was driven to an emotional state in which murder was the tragic yet inevitable outcome. He went on to argue that the entire case, and thus the question of guilt or innocence, was far more complicated than the prosecution had suggested. While Cockrel readily conceded that Johnson had indeed pulled the trigger of the gun that killed Hinz, Jones, and Kowalski, and he agreed wholeheartedly that the act was vile and irrational, he also argued that there was an explanation for these brutal murders—one that would require the jury to look carefully at the life of the accused.[32]

Cockrel went on to summarize the most dramatic examples of the depri- vation and resulting mental instability that characterized Johnson's life. He touched on Johnson's formative years in Starkville, where he and his siblings were raised under conditions "not so terribly different from the conditions of life of their forefathers and foremothers who were slaves."[33] He then made several bold and controversial statements, such as that even medical science could not adequately "assess the organic brain damage caused by a wholly inadequate diet."[34] He went on to briefly chronicle Johnson's experi- ences in the army, his move to Detroit, and finally the events at Chrysler that precipitated his breakdown. In closing, Cockrel pointed out that, even if ac- quitted, Johnson would not go free—he would be committed to the Ionia State Hospital for the criminally insane.[35]

In arguing for a verdict of not guilty by reason of insanity, Cockrel had a huge task ahead of him.[36] Even for the best defense attorney, it would have been difficult to divert the jury's attention from the chilling fact that three auto employees were dead as a result of Johnson's actions. Cockrel had to persuade the jurors of three key things. First, he had to convince them that particular aspects of growing up on a sharecropping farm could scar a de- veloping individual. Second, he needed to show that the debilitating mental effects of discrimination in the rural South also existed in the urban North, where Johnson moved as a young adult. Of course, to persuade the jury of either of these things, Cockrel also had to convince them that mental illness was almost entirely a social construct, that there was a direct relationship be- tween racism and mental illness in African Americans like Johnson. Finally, Cockrel had to convince the jury that a series of key events that Johnson ex- perienced while working at Chrysler stemmed directly from issues of race, thus exacerbating Johnson's existing mental instability and driving him to the breaking point.

Cockrel and Ravitz called Johnson's mother, Edna Hudson, as their first wit- ness.[37] It was her testimony that laid the foundation for a key component of the defense strategy: Johnson's life story. Hudson was a petite woman who came into court wearing "an orange dress, white coat and grey patent leather pumps."[38] As the *Michigan Chronicle* put it bluntly, "her appearance and de- meanor gave no advance notice of her testimony about the bleak, almost hope- less life of a Mississippi sharecropper."[39] The defense team was counting on just such testimony, as it wanted to take the jurors back to the moment John- son was born and have them see exactly what his life had been like. Eventually, the jurors would hear every pertinent and recoverable detail of Johnson's life. But it was Hudson's testimony about her son's earliest years in Starkville that most riveted the courtroom. As a journalist from the *Michigan Chronicle* later reported, "none of the studies of sociologists, psychologists, and congressional committees have illustrated the grinding poverty and hunger of the 'other America' as vividly as Mrs. Hudson did in that courtroom."[40]

Cockrel then asked Hudson to explain how these conditions specifically affected James as a child. She replied that his health was "poor" as a child. She said that he was a very nervous child who had terrible "spells." He would wake up at night crying and screaming. He would say that he was afraid of dying and that he kept seeing gruesome and distorted faces. She said that she would hold him close to her for about thirty minutes until these spells passed. She told the jury that she always worried terribly about her son. Intuitively, she knew it had been very bad that he had never been allowed to play as a child because there were never any toys, and the children always had to work like adults.

When Cockrel had finished questioning Hudson, the prosecution began an in-depth cross-examination attempting to show that Johnson's problems as a child did not stem from deprivation but rather from the violent relationship between his mother and father, from the impact of his father subsequently leaving the family unit, and from the fact that Hudson left James alone so much when she went to work in Starkville. The prosecution also attempted to show that Johnson always had an abnormally violent temper even as a child. Hudson responded to this cross-examination by saying that she knew "of no attacks that he [James] made upon other persons with weapons or does not know of his ever having thrown things at persons." In her opinion, her son "was like any ordinary child when he lost his temper." She also pointed out that when she had to go off to work in town, she was only trying to provide her children with "something of their own."

Next to Hudson, the second most powerful witness whom Cockrel and Ravitz called was Johnson himself. After he told the jury about growing up in Starkville, he was asked to describe the terrible hallucinations that he had suffered as a child. He said that these hallucinations would come at night and occasionally during the day. He heard voices beckoning him, and he would see distorted faces with eyes missing or eyes and mouths in the wrong place. He told the jury of his terror of people dying and of dying himself. He explained that whenever someone in the community died, it was his or her face that he would see in his nightmares. He testified that the more depressed he was, the worse his spells became.

Under cross-examination, the prosecutor attempted to show that Johnson was inventing the mental illness of his childhood and adulthood in order to get an acquittal. In prosecuting attorney Weisswasser's opinion, for example, Johnson had "put on an act for the Army psychiatrist."[41] It soon became clear, however, that Johnson did not understand psychiatry and seemed to be completely unaware of the extent of his mental dysfunction. By the time he left the stand, it seemed unlikely that he had fabricated his tales of mental distress merely as a defense ploy. Indeed, even after the rigorous cross-examination of him and his mother, it was clear that Johnson had indeed been an emotionally disturbed child. The roots of his distress, however, were still not evident.

The prosecution continued to suggest that Johnson's problems, if as severe as the defense suggested, were the product of an abusive home life. Thus, there could be no links between his breakdown at Chrysler years later and his life in the South as a child. But then the defense called Johnson's first cousin, Maggie Taylor, to the stand. Taylor was born in Crawford, Mississippi, near Starkville. As a child, she had been very close to Johnson and had seen him every day. Her testimony corroborated that Johnson was an extremely troubled child, that death was one of his primary fears, and that this fear had remained with him to the present day. Taylor's testimony was most important, however, because it introduced poignant evidence that Johnson's mental instability had direct roots in the racial discrimination that he had endured and witnessed all of his life.

In fact Taylor's testimony offered the jury the first concrete explanation of what had most precipitated Johnson's awful fear of death, his terror of white people, and his chronic hallucinations. After conceding that Johnson had been fearful and had nightmares since the age of four or five, Taylor explained the terrible impact on Johnson of having seen the gruesome lynching of her brother Henry. In her words, "he was forever changed by it."[42] She told the jury that Henry had been accused of being in love with a white girl, and that a mob of whites chased him down and beat him until he was dead. According to Taylor, the nine-year-old Johnson had witnessed the entire event. She explained that he was so terrified by this violent act that he went into a "nervous rage." Right after the murder, everyone in the family went to Johnson's grandfather's house across the street. Everyone was very distraught, she recalled, but Johnson was in a terrified stupor. While the other family members stayed at the grandfather's house for five days and eventually came to terms with Henry's death, Johnson could not eat or sleep and had awful visions. Taylor told the jury that from the moment of her brother's lynching, Johnson's fear of death, dying, and white people became more acute, as did his hallucinations, nervousness, and inability to function normally.

Cockrel and Ravitz hoped that the testimonies of Hudson, Johnson, and Taylor would convince the jury that there was a connection between childhood deprivation, the brutal effect of American racism, and Johnson's mental illness. But they did not leave this to chance. The second key pillar of their defense strategy was the testimony of black psychologist Clemens H. Fitzgerald. They called Fitzgerald to the stand first and foremost to persuade the jury that Johnson was indeed mentally ill. Fitzgerald confirmed that Johnson exhibited "schizophrenic reaction, chronic undifferentiated, with marked paranoid features,"[43] and that he was "an individual who has been chronically depressed and who probably as an adolescent, prior to service, was functioning as a schizoid personality."[44]

But Cockrel also hoped that Fitzgerald's testimony could persuade the jury that Johnson's illness was directly rooted in poverty and discrimination.

And Fitzgerald did chronicle the scarring effects of economic deprivation on the developing child, explaining that the effects of racism (such as witnessing a lynching or being called "boy" and "nigger" one's whole life) seriously compromised the mental health of African Americans like Johnson. As Fitzgerald told the jury, "oppression and institutional racism had produced [in Johnson] the type of stress that is unknown to most."[45] He stated further that Johnson's "schizoid personality"[46] stemmed not just from "pathological family experiences" but also from the "results of racism with the feelings of being oppressed in an unwelcome society."[47] After Fitzgerald's testimony, prosecutor Weisswasser remarked that he thought Fitzgerald "was making too large an issue 'over a couple of hundred years of slavery.'"[48]

Cockrel and Ravitz also placed into evidence other psychological reports of Johnson, including the evaluations of psychologists, L. L. Mackenzie, Barbara Stewart and William Bowen. These official reports gave further evidence that Johnson was mentally ill because of the society in which he lived. Armed with these evaluations, Cockrel intended to prove that it was white people and white authority figures in particular whose behaviors exacerbated Johnson's condition. As Stewart had reported, Johnson felt that it was not he alone who was unduly discriminated against by white people; so were many other blacks in America.[49]

Midway through the trial, the burden was still on Cockrel and Ravitz to show that Johnson's specific background was directly connected to the murders. Perhaps it would have been enough to convince the jury that Johnson was insane in order to have him acquitted. The defense team, however, wanted to bring a certain logic to Johnson's acts of 1970, and not just paint him as a schizophrenic ticking time bomb that could have exploded anywhere at any time. They wanted to show the jury that certain events in Johnson's work life drove him to commit murder precisely because these events stemmed from the same social and racial discrimination that had made him mentally unstable in the first place.

This part of the defense strategy thoroughly outraged prosecutors, who could not believe that Cockrel and Ravitz were asking the jury to focus their attention on what it was like to be an autoworker, particularly a black autoworker, in Chrysler's Eldon Avenue gear and axle plant. When prosecutors complained, however, Judge Colombo ruled that "all those factors are relevant under the law."[50] Cockrel and Ravitz then proceeded to call witness after witness who worked in the Eldon plant and who readily testified to the horrendous working conditions, shop-floor violence, and racial abuse that black workers endured there daily.[51] Cockrel and Ravitz brought the stories of Gary Thompson and Maimie Williams to the jury's attention in dramatic detail and elicited testimony about the numerous Eldon wildcats that had been sparked by shop-floor discrimination. The jury also heard testimony from Chief Union Steward Johnny Moffet that workers like Johnson feared for their lives in the plant because "the union was not adequately responsive to safety issues." They heard from Johnson's union steward, Clarence Horton, that there were "38 safety problems in department 78 alone."[52]

Cockrel and Ravitz used all of this testimony to show that, although Johnson had attempted to escape southern racism and deprivation by moving to Detroit to "find a better job in the auto industry,"[53] once at Chrysler he found as much discrimination and a similarly degrading work situation. When Johnson was on the stand, he had described how unsafe it was to work at Chrysler and how blacks always had to do the least safe and lowest-paid jobs. As he said, "the more dollars and cents you could demand the more there were racial overtones," and, although he denied that "all white people tend to be racist" at Chrysler, he stated firmly that "all persons that he has seen subjected to harassment have been black."[54]

Before long, prosecutors could no longer contain their anger at the direction the trial had taken. Weisswasser told the *Detroit News* that "the defense is cloaking its real intentions. . . . [I]t is our theory that this trial is being used to abet the purpose of a certain radical, and, by their chosen word, revolutionary labor groups. . . . Johnson is being used as a cat's paw in a mockery of legal defense."[55] Not surprisingly, when it came time for prosecutors to begin their cross-examination, they repeatedly asked Johnson whether he himself had been a member of ELRUM or the League when he worked in the plant and whether he had read the radical newspaper *Inner City Voice*.

The trial took a new turn, however, when the prosecutors began questioning Johnson's politics. Prosecutors were attempting to discredit Johnson, and all of the people who testified on his behalf from the plants, by suggesting that they were black militants bent on revolution. In the end, this new tactic was a grave mistake, as it allowed the defense the opportunity to show that political, as well as racial, discrimination existed at Chrysler, and that this political discrimination also had a deleterious effect on Johnson's mental health. To support this point, Cockrel introduced a report from a certified psychologist who had examined Johnson before the trial began. Johnson had related to this examiner that he felt "that supervisors at the Chrysler Corporation thought, perhaps, that he was a member of a subversive group and that this was the likely reason that he was getting what he felt was a 'raw deal.'"[56] The defense also submitted a letter from Fitzgerald, who had written, again before the trial, that Johnson believed "management wanted him out because they felt he was a 'revolutionist.'"[57] Cockrel and Ravitz reminded the jury of Johnson's testimony that he "was not a member of the League or ELRUM," and that he did not even know who put out the *Inner City Voice*. The prosecution persisted, however, and asked whether Johnson was influenced by any of these radical organizations when he worked at Chrysler. Johnson replied that they only "affected his attitude on the job . . . in so far as that which he read [by them] was true," and he knew "some of that which [their papers] contained is factual because he has seen it himself inside of the plant."[58]

Of course, many black autoworkers had endured a childhood of poverty and racism and had grown up to face much overt racial, and even political, discrimination in the workplace. Thus it was necessary for Cockrel and Ravitz to explain why, in Johnson's case, this lifetime of oppression resulted in murder. To do this, they attempted to link the testimony about Johnson's mental illness to that about the workplace protest of the other Eldon workers. They pointed out that life at Eldon was clearly so difficult that it drove many Eldon workers to wage group protests like wildcatting and individual protests like staying home from work. They then argued that the same events that only frustrated and angered other workers drove Johnson, with his particular psychological profile, to commit an insane act of violence.

Because of Johnson's background, he already had "a suspicion, fear, distrust, and dislike of white people, such as plantation owners and other white people."[59] Thus, when he arrived at Chrysler, he was especially sensitive to and bothered by the fact that "all of the men on the oven line are Negroes," and that his foreman routinely verbally abused him with racial slurs. According to Cockrel and Ravitz, the longer that Johnson worked at Chrysler, the more he became convinced that he was being persecuted. When Johnson took his vacation and then received a telegram from Chrysler saying that he had been absent without properly notifying the plant and that his employment was terminated, he was devastated. Likewise, when he was denied medical benefits after his car accident, he felt singled out and vulnerable. When he was not allowed to fill in for his friend Robert Baynes as a job setter because his foreman "went over and got one of his friends and gave him two weeks on company time to learn the job,"[60] he became even more emotionally distressed. When supervisors finally ordered Johnson to go back to his old despised job on the oven line on July 15, 1970, he had finally reached his breaking point.

Clarence Horton testified that "no one once asked James Johnson why he didn't want to go that oven,"[61] and even though he tried to get Johnson a heat pass, there was nothing he could do. Chrysler managers had "already made their mind up"[62] to suspend Johnson for insubordination. General Foreman Ellsworth J. Rhodes testified that "Hugh Jones was determined and the decision was really made by him quickly."[63] Johnson thought he had been fired and that his persecutors had won. Losing his long-sought-after job was an indescribable blow to his pride. According to the defense, Johnson's already precarious hold on sanity finally slipped away.

To illustrate Johnson's terrible psychotic state on the day of the murders, Cockrel reminded the jurors of Johnson's testimony that he didn't even know Joe Kowalski and that he and Gary Hinz actually had "a friendly relationship." Two summers before the murders, Hinz had come to Johnson's house to sell him a lawn mower for thirty dollars, even though Hinz had paid a hundred and forty dollars for it himself.[64] The fact that Hugh Jones was only Johnson's temporary foreman and that he, too, was black was further evidence, according to the defense, that Johnson had truly snapped.

The trump card in the Johnson defense strategy was the decision to take the jury to the scene of the murders. Early on in the trial, Cockrel had told the jury that "we have asked that you have an opportunity to view department 78, the cement room [and] the oven. And we will ask you to judge those conditions as the testimony develops them, as James Johnson felt them and as you view them, remember[ing] always that the standard is *not* any person's capability to withstand stress, but James Johnson's given his history, his background, his weaknesses and his state of mind."[65] The judge granted this unusual request. Perhaps more than any other evidence presented in the trial, the trip to the Eldon plant had the greatest impact on the jury.

On a Thursday morning, Judge Colombo, the entire jury, and Johnson boarded a bus and went to the Eldon plant. Covering the jury's sojourn to the plant, the *Michigan Chronicle* reported sarcastically that "going and coming from Eldon Ave. Thursday morning, Johnson sat on the back of the bus."[66] It noted further that on the day of the jury's tour, Chrysler had made sure "the plant was spic and span," and although "they didn't roll out a red carpet for the jurors . . . the walls were freshly painted in bright colors and the aisles were open and . . . Eldon Ave. looked as if Mr Clean, Snow White and the Seven Dwarfs, and the White Tornado had gone through it." Once inside the plant, Johnson looked around him and quietly stated, "it wasn't like this when I was here."[67]

Despite the fact that Eldon was spruced up considerably, and was much cooler both in and outside of the facility than it had been on the day of the murders,[68] the jury was noticeably appalled by the plant's atmosphere and work conditions. The jurors who were, or who had been, auto employees looked around with grim recognition, and the jurors who were wives of auto employees looked around the plant with a sober appreciation for their husbands' work life. Chrysler had shut down the assembly line for the jury tour, but the assembly line workers were still there, staring on in silence. As the jury began to watch the ovens being loaded, and as they paused to examine the asbestos-lined gloves needed to perform the oven-line job, the workers standing by raised their fists in solidarity with Johnson. As the *Michigan Chronicle* reported, "a young black man yelled . . . 'hey Brother Johnson,'" and according to *Time Magazine*, the gazes of the workers there "reflected little anger and much sympathy; there were muffled cries of 'Hey, Brother Johnson . . . Right on, Brother Johnson.'"[69]

The trip to Eldon was the most important moment in the trial. Better than all of Cockrel's and Ravitz's eloquent words, the experience of being inside the plant impressed upon the jury the alienating and dangerous nature of the oven job. They could better understand why Johnson had been devastated when he thought that he had been demoted to that job on the morning of July 15. Better than all of the passionate testimony provided by other workers on Johnson's behalf, the sight of the workers with fists raised at Eldon impressed upon the jury that even if Johnson was insane, other workers in Detroit obviously understood why he had snapped. Undoubtedly jurors already were becoming more sympathetic to the defense, particularly after "the prosecutor [had been] talking of 'black boys' and asking one of Johnson's cousins whether she ever slept with him," but the trip to Eldon seemed to cement the defense's case in their eyes.[70]

On the last day of the trial, after Weisswasser referred to Johnson as "just a big baby" in his closing remarks,[71] Cockrel once again approached the jury. He summarized the abundance of testimony they had heard on Johnson's deprived childhood, on the racial harassment that he had always endured, on his related mental instability, and on the particular events that led to a complete breakdown on July 15. Cockrel then reminded the jury of all the possible verdicts, highlighting what proof was necessary for an insanity acquittal. He left the jurors to their deliberations with the closing remark, "the defense maintains that the prosecution has not proven, as is their clear and undisputed burden, James Johnson, legally sane beyond a reasonable doubt." Therefore, he went on, Johnson deserved the verdict not guilty by reason of insanity, even though this verdict was not "just," as real "justice escaped James Johnson in a very real way three and a half decades ago back on an American plantation."[72]

The jury deliberated for only three hours and forty-six minutes. The jurors argued and yelled so loudly while coming to their decision that they were often overheard.[73] According to *Time,* one juror was heard to exclaim, "Did you see that cement room in the plant? Working there would drive anyone crazy!"[74] Another more skeptical juror was heard saying, "I've worked in a factory all my life and I didn't kill anybody," to which a another juror replied, "you weren't born in Mississippi and I was; you don't know what you're talking about!"[75] Before deliberations ended, a fourth juror was heard saying loudly, "the man needs help. You know he won't get it in prison. It's up to us to help him."[76] As the jury returned to the courtroom, Johnson sat quietly wondering what lie ahead of him while the Detroiters who packed the courtroom also sat on the edge of their seats. As the media looked on, the jury delivered its verdict: not guilty by reason of insanity. According to the *Michigan Chronicle,* this jury verdict "electrified the courtroom" while "James Johnson slumped over, hands clasped behind his neck ... wept. The sobs shook his body."[77] After reading their verdict, members of the jury crowded around Cockrel. According to one of the jurors, those on the panel felt warmly toward Cockrel and wanted to talk with him.[78] As writers for the *Michigan Chronicle* noted when the trial ended, "no television production could match this case for sheer drama."[79]

As a result of his successes in the courtroom during New Bethel One and Two, and then the Johnson murder trial, Cockrel became one of he most famous and infamous attorneys in the Motor City. That Cockrel was a self-avowed Marxist and a leader of the League did not escape his critics or supporters. In every civic and labor battle since 1967, from those over shop-floor relations and working conditions to those in city schools or involving police-community relations, the Left in Detroit had been a powerful force to reckon with. This fact was underscored when, in December 1971, mere months after the Johnson acquittal, Cockrel successfully defended another young black man, Nathaniel Johnson, accused of assault with intent to rob officers of the STRESS unit. During this trial before Judge Roy N. Gruenburg, an all-black jury of nine men and three women deliberated only forty minutes before acquitting Cockrel's client.[80]

Without a doubt, the New Bethel and Johnson verdicts made Detroit's revolutionaries feel that they were making genuine headway in the city. Spurred on by their courtroom victories, Cockrel, other leftist groups, and the family of STRESS victim Clarence Manning Jr. decided to file a civil lawsuit against Mayor Gribbs, Police Commissioner John Nichols, and Wayne County Prosecutor William Cahalan, so that the trio would be forced to disband all STRESS operations.[81]

In the anti-STRESS suit of 1972, plaintiffs detailed the circumstances leading to five civilian deaths at the hands of STRESS officers in one "dreary, soot-dirty block of transient hotels, bars and unrazed century-old homes . . . an area populated with a large number of alcoholics, panhandlers and derelicts—mostly harmless people who are guilty only of [the] institutionally created crimes of poverty, unemployment and disease."[82] The official complaint of this suit laid out the events leading to the murder of Manning in the most detail, because on May 28, 1971, at 10:30 p.m., STRESS officers had fired eighteen shots at the unarmed Manning and one of the seven that actually hit him was fatal. In addition, this suit compiled dramatic statistics on the number of deaths that particular STRESS officers had caused. And because so many fatal STRESS actions had gone unpunished, plaintiffs took the opportunity in this suit to officially accuse Prosecutor Cahalan of knowing that "the Detroit Police officers connected with the unit known as STRESS have engaged in illegal, wrongful, criminal and unconstitutional beatings, shootings and killings," and that he "has failed, refused and prevented any criminal prosecutions against such officers."[83]

For white conservatives such as Mayor Gribbs and Commissioner Nichols, as well as those who either were themselves or actively defended members of the DPD, the anti-STRESS suit of 1972 was a serious threat. Not only were civic radicals challenging them, but so were a number of well-established liberal organizations such as the NAACP and the ACLU. And while these groups were signing on as plaintiffs, workplace organizations such as the UNC also began speaking out in support of the suit.[84] This biracial challenge to law enforcement became even more unsettling to white conservatives when the anti-STRESS suit showed up on the court docket of a black judge.[85] Although this judge, Edward Bell, was hardly a left-leaning liberal himself, he was African American, and every city conservative knew well what a poor reputation STRESS had among Detroit blacks, regardless

Kenneth V. Cockrel speaking at the March 26, 1972, anti-STRESS rally. *Walter P. Reuther Library, Wayne State University.*

of their class position or political persuasion. But just as it began to appear that radicals and civil rights–oriented liberals would score another victory on the legal battlefield of the war-torn Motor City, Judge Bell stepped down to pursue his own political ambitions, and thereafter the controversial anti-STRESS suit was reassigned to Judge John O'Hair, former counsel for the Detroit Police Officers Association.

The implications of this turn of events were vast. Radicals such as Ken Cockrel experienced a real set-back when, after four days of graphic testimony, Judge O'Hair decided he need not render an emergency decision, and thus the case was destined for the regular docket, where it could languish for years. And liberals also felt defeated by O'Hair's ruling because it thwarted their attempt to prove that the legal system would indeed resolve thorny social problems in expeditious fashion. But while the de facto victors in the anti-STRESS suit—white conservatives and the Gribbs administration—should have been elated, they were still uneasy. To them, as long as blacks or liberals—or, worse yet, black liberals—were on the bench in the Motor City, their interests were not secure. Only fueling this fear, a biracial group called the Labor Defense Coalition, the first-listed plaintiff in the anti-STRESS suit Cockrel, vowed that the citizens of Detroit "will not wait two years for 'justice.'"[86] Indeed, city radicals did not have to wait hardly any time at all to reseek "justice" in their campaign against STRESS. Despite the number of reforms that Mayor Gribbs had insisted on after the debacle on Rochester Street,[87] an event transpired on December 4, 1972, between four STRESS officers and three young black men that once again brought this police unit into the media spotlight and once again allowed Cockrel a chance to challenge STRESS in court.

Because Mayor Gribbs's new reforms were intended to make STRESS more efficient and organized and did not eliminate its undercover features, black fear of the police only escalated after 1971.[88] Well aware of this fear, a local newspaper *The Community Reporter* took the time in 1972 to inform black Detroiters about "what to do in the case of STRESS."[89] But the problem with such advice was that in every STRESS maneuver that ended in a citizen death, the victim did not *know* that he or she was being accosted or questioned by a member of law enforcement, as STRESS officers were always dressed as hippies or street people. And because STRESS patrolled areas already full of hippies and street people, ordinary citizens had no reason to believe that a strange individual approaching them was anything other than he or she appeared to be.

One such neighborhood, which not only was filled with the eclectic and the down and out but also with an active drug trade, was home to three young black men: Hayward Brown, Marcus Clyde Bethune, and John Percy Boyd. Brown was an eighteen-year-old who had joined the Sons of Malcolm X in the twelfth grade. Brown's first cousin, Boyd, was a student at Wayne State University who worked with underprivileged kids at the Detroit Department of Parks and Recreation. Bethune was also a college student at WSU. [90]

By his senior year of high school, Brown had become deeply influenced by Malcolm X's position that young black men had to be free of drugs in order to fight most effectively for black liberation. According to Brown, in 1972, he, Bethune, and Boyd "decided that someone needed to move on the dope men" in their neighborhood. As he put it, "we saw the situation getting worse. More and more dope was coming into the community and making more junkies, and the designated authorities weren't doing their jobs."[91] Within a few months Brown, Bethune, and Boyd were known in their community as foes of the drug trade.[92]

On December 4, 1972, Brown, Bethune, and Boyd decided to escalate their anti-drug activism and go to a known heroin house in their neighborhood, run by a man named Jack Crawford. They had intended to oust this big-time dealer and thus arrived with guns "for the purposes of self-defense because it is a known fact that dope men are armed."[93] Unbeknownst to the trio, however, four STRESS officers—Richard Grapp, Eugene Fuller, Robert Rosenow, and Billy Price—had also decided to take their unmarked four-door Plymouth sedan to stake out Crawford's house that night.[94]

As soon as Brown, Bethune, and Boyd arrived at Crawford's house in their Volkswagen Beetle, Crawford saw them and sped off in his car. The trio chased him, and in turn, STRESS officers followed the VW in their white sedan.[95] According to Brown, as he and his friends were following Crawford, a white car started to force them to the side of the road, and they believed that the vehicle contained Crawford's henchmen. Eventually, the STRESS car collided with the VW. Whereas the STRESS officers claimed later that they then showed Brown, Bethune, and Boyd their badges (which they forgot to note in the police report they eventually had to file), the young black occupants of the VW claimed that these scruffy-looking men pulled guns on them. Within minutes, bullets were flying, and someone in the VW managed to wound several occupants of the white Plymouth.

After the shooting melee, Brown, Bethune, and Boyd drove the VW to Dexter Avenue, where they abandoned the car and decided to take a cab to the house of one of their mothers. Deeply fearful of retaliation from Crawford's drug runners, the three men "started staying in motels for the first few days" and then moved from one friend's house to another "for their own security."[96] Meanwhile, the DPD had put out an all-points bulletin on these three men and were combing the streets of Detroit for them. On December 7, STRESS officers burst into the apartment of Patricia Ragland and forced her to undress while they searched her home for Brown, Bethune, and Boyd. As her fiancé, Carl Ingram, exclaimed incredulously while the search was taking place, "there ain't three men hiding in her clothes!"[97] On December 8, DPD officers stormed the home of Durwood Forshee while looking for the fugitives and, in the process, managed fatally to shoot Forshee as he slept in his bed. After the Forshee murder, on December 15, 1972, the family members of Brown, Bethune, and Boyd went to the Wayne Country Circuit Court to get an injunction against the DPD for its raids on black homes. Judge Thomas Foley readily granted the injunction forbidding the DPD from entering any home without a warrant except in an emergency,[98] but on January 4, 1973, "police burst into Reverend Leroy Cannon's house without a warrant on a false tip that the fugitives were hiding there, yelling 'Nigger if you breathe too loud, I'll blow your brains out!'"[99]

One of the reasons that the police did not heed Judge Foley's injunction was that on December 27, 1972, four STRESS officers had experienced yet another deadly run-in with Brown, Bethune, and Boyd. On this day, four plainclothes STRESS officers—Robert Dooley, Robert Bradford, Charles Sauvage, and Donald Lewis—in another unmarked car surrounded the apartment where Brown, Bethune, and Boyd were hiding. When the unsuspecting trio came out of the building, Officer Dooley grabbed Brown to use him as a shield while he shot at Bethune, who then ran up to Dooley and shot him in the face. Meanwhile, someone fired a shot that killed Officer Bradford. According to the later testimony of twenty-eight-year-old Dooley, who ultimately lost one eye and was paralyzed from the waist down as a result of his injuries, "Bethune was kicking me and I could see, he like walked like stomping on my leg and my back and he was saying 'we're going to kill all you white Mo-F pigs, all you white pigs are going to die in this town, we're going to kill you all!'"[100]

In the midst of this chaos, Brown, Bethune, and Boyd somehow managed to escape once again, which set in motion "the most massive manhunt in Detroit's history."[101] The DPD not only continued to comb Detroit's black neighborhoods looking for the three fugitives, but it also extended its search around the country. The DPD sent descriptions of the three men to authorities in cities such as Charlotte, North Carolina; Chicago; and Cincinnati.[102] It also maintained surveillance on every member of the trio's family when it heard a rumor that someone at the University of Greensboro was going to help Boyd leave Detroit.[103]

Despite this extensive dragnet, however, Bethune and Boyd allegedly disguised, respectively, as a priest and a nun, managed to flee to Atlanta, where they were subsequently killed under highly suspicious circumstances in a blazing shootout with police between February 23 and 27, 1973.[104] Before Bethune and Boyd met this fate, however, the DPD still believed them to be in the Motor City, and they escalated their search operations there accordingly. They soon arrested a man named Ivan O. Williams for harboring the fugitives, but they still were unable to apprehend the "Mad Dog Killers" as Police Commissioner Nichols had referred to them. Overnight, citizens began flooding the Police-Community Relations Commission of the CCR with complaints about out-of-control police brutality. In response, the Detroit City Council decided to call a public hearing to allow citizens to voice their

Police manhunt of Hayward Brown at a house on Trumbull Avenue, January 12, 1973. *Walter P. Reuther Library, Wayne State University.*

grievances and, in turn, to give Police Commissioner Nichols the opportunity to explain his officers' actions. Initially, the council planned to hold this meeting in the auditorium of the City County Building, but the overflow of 900 to 1,000 people forced it to move the hearing to Ford Auditorium.

At this mass event on January 11, 1973, black Detroiters crowded the microphones provided to read their complaints. The principle complainants were there on behalf of John Boyd including Melba Boyd and John Clore; his mother, Dorothy Clore; a family friend, Sandra Overstreet; and relatives of Ivan Williams. But many who were neither friends nor relations of the fugitives also spoke at this meeting, while Cockrel attempted to present the City Council members with a box containing 30,000 citizen signatures calling for the abolition of STRESS. Eventually, it was time for Commissioner Nichols to respond to the numerous grievances voiced, but when he tried to speak, "the crowd became quite angry and noisy," and after several attempts to read a prepared statement, he was forced to leave the stage because of the audience's jeers and shouts.[105]

As fate would have it, the next day, two of WSU's Public Safety officers, Robert Oliphant and Leonard Corsetti, located Hayward Brown. As Corsetti attempted to arrest Brown, he fired a shot that prompted Brown to return fire. But because DPD backup was almost immediately on the scene, this time the police apprehended Brown, who subsequently was charged with seven counts of assault with intent to commit murder and one count of first-degree murder. Because Chief Prosecutor William Cahalan refused to consolidate the charges, Brown prepared to stand trial three separate times.

Although attorney Richard Soble represented Brown at his arraignment, Cockrel soon took on the defense. And, when Brown's trial began, it immediately became a media circus. Assisting Cockrel was his partner, Ted Spearman Jr., as well as a court-appointed associate, Geoffrey Taft. Thomas Behan was the assistant prosecutor on this case, and the judge randomly assigned to the first trial was none other than George Crockett. A jury of seven black women, three black men, and two white women sat in this first trial in which Brown stood accused of four counts of assault with intent to commit murder from the December 4 shootout with STRESS officers Price, Grapp, Rosenow, and Fuller.

As transcripts reveal, however, from the moment that Brown's trial began, it was STRESS in the hot seat, not the eighteen-year-old defendant. It was not that Brown was irrelevant to the trial; indeed, many witnesses, including a priest from St. Francis De Sales, came to refute Commissioner Nichols's characterization of him as a "Mad Dog Killer." Most of the testimony, however, involved establishing exactly what STRESS was doing on the night of December 4, why it had such a high suspect fatality rate to its credit, and how the undercover nature of its operations could lead so easily to tragedies such as the Rochester Street murders and the shootings of December 4.

Police manhunt of Hayward Brown near Wayne State University, January 12, 1973.
Walter P. Reuther Library, Wayne State University.

When Cockrel questioned Officer Rosenow, for example, jurors heard the following exchange:

Q: Did you have any legal reason to stop that car? Had they violated any law in your judgement and experience as a police officer?

A: No Sir. They had not violated any law.

When questioning Officer Grapp, Cockrel asked:

Q: You just decided to stop it, isn't that right?

A: I decided I would stop them because of their activity in the neighborhood.

Q: Their activity is that they were operating, I assume lawfully, a motor vehicle in the neighborhood, isn't that correct?

A: Yes.[106]

In yet another telling exchange, Cockrel additionally asked Rosenow to explain why he carried a .44 magnum on the night in question instead of the standard-issue .38 special. Rosenow replied, "I feel that the .38 Special lacks penetrating power."[107] The jury also heard testimony that all STRESS officers present that night were dressed nothing like members of law enforcement and that there was no corroborating evidence that these officers ever identified themselves as such to Brown, Bethune, and Boyd.[108] But the most exculpatory evidence on Brown's behalf was that none of the STRESS officers who testified had actually seen him shooting at them.[109] Trial transcripts reveal that the prosecution was not very well prepared or effective in making its arguments during the trial, whereas the defense's portrayal of STRESS's vigilante-like and dangerous secrecy came through loud and clear. On May 10, 1973, the jury acquitted Brown on all charges after ten hours of deliberation.

But Brown's tribulations were far from over. He once again had to stand trial for the December 27, 1972, altercation between himself, Bethune, Boyd, and STRESS officers Dooley, Sauvage, Lewis, and Bradford. In this case, prosecutors charged him with first-degree murder and assault with intent to commit murder. For days, the jury of eight blacks and four whites heard testimony from Prosecutor Leonard Gilman's police officer witnesses, and then it was transported, as the Johnson jury had been, out of the courtroom to hear the testimony of Officer Robert Dooley, who lay paralyzed and blinded in his hospital bed. During this portion of the trial, Cockrel strenuously objected that, unlike Johnson, Brown had been taken to the hospital in chains and thus that the judge, Clarence Laster Jr., was not so subtly lending credence to the "Mad Dog Killer" image of Brown that the prosecution was trying to promote.[110] But apparently, Cockrel was not too rattled by the prosecution's presentation of witnesses because, in a shocking move, he ultimately decided not to call *any* witnesses for the defense. He maintained that the prosecution had not even come close to proving the murder charge, and that there already was sufficient evidence to indicate that the assault charge was bogus as well. While Judge Laster agreed to dismiss the murder charge, he still insisted that the jury rule on the assault charge. After only two hours of deliberation, the jury acquitted Brown of assault as well.[111]

After this acquittal, Brown then stood trial on the final charges stemming from the shootings of the two safety patrol officers at WSU, who finally had apprehended him that January. For this trial, William Cahalan, head Wayne County prosecutor, personally got involved. Cahalan did not like the fact that the presiding judge, Samuel Gardner, had previously been a partner in the law firm that had represented Brown before Cockrel took his case.[112] Cahalan was not alone in showing particular interest in Brown's last trial. As conservative talk-show host Lou Gordon told his Detroit listeners, "I'm going to have a great deal to say about Hayward Brown when his trials are over. . . . It seems to me that having been present [in the other trials] he should not have been let off completely free."[113] But despite Cahalan's active assistance of the prosecutor in charge of this third case, James E. Lacey, a jury of nine men and three

Hayward Brown, May 11, 1973. *Walter P. Reuther Library, Wayne State University.*

women nevertheless acquitted Brown of any wrongdoing after a two-hour deliberation, including a dinner break, on July 7, 1973.[114] According to the *Detroit Free Press,* "about 40 spectators in the courtroom of Judge Samuel Gardner cheered when the verdict was read."[115]

The verdict and courtroom reaction infuriated Prosecutor Cahalan and many other supporters of law enforcement in Detroit.[116] Cahalan argued publicly that the verdict was both "wrong and a miscarriage of justice"[117] As one journalist opined, "Cahalan is angry because the people who prosecutors traditionally counted on to bring in guilty verdicts—white, middle class men—aren't showing up on Detroit juries as much as they used to."[118] After the third Brown acquittal, Cahalan and others began to suggest the appointment, rather than the election, of criminal court judges. As Cahalan stated in a press conference after the acquittal, "his [Judge Gardner's] instructions to the jury sounded like those of a defense attorney. Gardner should not have been the judge in this case." Cahalan then went on to suggest that the state legislature revisit the rules regarding jury selection.[119]

The white conservatives' fear that the judicial system was fast slipping into the hands of Detroit's white and black radicals was fueled not only by the New Bethel, Johnson, and Brown verdicts, but also by the fact that, the previous November, Detroiters had elected radical Justin Ravitz, Cockrel's law partner, to a ten-year term as a judge for the Detroit Recorder's Court. A co-counsel with Cockrel on the New Bethel and Johnson cases and a lawyer for the anti-STRESS suit of 1972, Ravitz now would preside over the trials of hundreds of blacks accused of criminal offenses. Detroit's conser-

vative whites believed firmly that the popular support behind jurists like
Ravitz was an ominous sign for the city's political future. They were appalled that Ravitz's enormous support among poor and working-class black
Detroiters had allowed him to come in second, with 130,514 votes out of
the fourteen candidates running.[120] They were equally troubled by fact that
Ravitz had won by reminding these voters of his "successful defense of the
two New Bethel cases, including the exposé of the wholesale and criminal
exclusion of thousands of qualified jurors," and of his "successful defense
of James Johnson . . . who was proven to be no more than a victim of racism
and corporate greed."[121]

That Ravitz had not been supported solely by Detroit's African Americans
nor only by radicals clearly added to conservative whites' disgust. The Ravitz
campaign had also been endorsed by top liberal politicians at the local and
state level, including State Senator Coleman Young, State Representative
Jackie Vaughan III, City Councilman Carl Levin, and the First, Thirteenth,
Fourteenth, and Seventeenth Congressional District Democratic party organizations. Reflecting conservatives' deepening antagonism toward Detroit's
liberals after Ravitz's election, a spokesman from the Detroit Bar Association proclaimed that such an election "indicates the necessity for further removing the selection of judges from the people."[122]

The city's conservative whites found the cumulative legal losses between
1969 and 1973 staggering. They were humbled during the New Bethel trials,
but they still held out hope that these cases were an anomaly. By 1973, however, they felt deflated by how many times the police had been censured in
the judicial process, and they were thoroughly persuaded that liberals were
conspiring with radicals to turn Detroit into a crime zone. As one A. J.
Kalber put it in a letter to the *Detroit News* after one such censuring of the
police in the legal arena, "was it by luck or arrangement of counsel that the
black groups . . . had their case assigned, through the so-called blind-draw
assignment system, to the only black judge in the Wayne Country Circuit
Court? Now how about abolishing the present court assignment system
which obviously permits litigants to select their own judges."[123] And it
hardly alleviated the concerns of men like Kalber that black jurists like
Crockett had gone on record saying, "I happen to know from my own experiences that a policeman will tell a lie in court. I happen to know that
they'll crack somebody's head—especially if it is a black head—and then
bring that person into court expecting the judge to convict him so that the
policeman can't be sued for damages."[124]

It was Hayward Brown's three acquittals, however, far more than the
words of a black judge, that most alarmed conservative white Detroiters. As
the more conservative of the two major Motor City newspapers, the *Detroit
News,* editorialized on June 10, 1973, because of "Kenneth Cockrel's play
upon racial emotion and presentation of Brown as a victim of oppressive society . . . Brown emerges from all of this as a sort of ghetto folk hero . . . [and

this] has served to damage public confidence in the legal processes."[125] The various authors of letters to the *Detroit News* on July 16, 1973, couldn't have agreed more. As Richard Haefner of the white suburb of St. Clair Shores wrote, "Kenneth Cockrel has proven conclusively that the jury system is no longer responsive to the people and needs immediate revision if justice is to prevail." S. K. Pullen of suburban Belleville wrote, "The next time anyone is tried for murder in Detroit why don't they pick a jury from among the convicted murderers serving terms in Jackson State Prison? Detroit is a city run by emotion and minorities. The law is just a name in Detroit." And as another writer G. F. Parsons maintained, "Hayward Brown's victory in a courtroom verdict by a black judge and jury may turn out to be one of the most disastrous events in the history of Detroit's race relations."[126]

By 1973, conservative whites firmly believed that radicals were taking over Detroit and that liberals were no longer simply fueling dependency through their myriad community programs—now they actually were catering to black criminals in their own courtrooms. For example, Conservative whites found it outrageous that in the 1971 trial of black Detroiter Nathaniel Johnson, which daily drew "standing-room-only crowds," the presiding judge "refused to allow the prosecution to bring into evidence fragments of a broken glass bottle, alleged to be one of the weapons used by Johnson and Manning against one of the STRESS officers. The Judge ruled that the bottle fragments could not be brought into evidence because police had remained on the street for several hours and could have tampered with it."[127]

The legal battles from 1969 to 1973 convinced conservative white Detroiters that something had fundamentally changed within the liberal agenda. With liberals now in cahoots with radicals to promote black interests over white, conservatives considered it even more imperative that both be ousted from any sphere of influence. As a writer in the Detroit Police Officer Association paper, *Tuebor*, put it, "DETROIT is Number One in Rapes/Number One in Murder/Number One in Chicken-hearted Judges," and another cautioned that before long Detroiters would see "Kenneth Cockrel as mayor . . . George Crockett as head of the Supreme Court, or the Black Panthers in charge of Community Relations."[128]

But just as white conservatives were shocked by the acquittals of black defendants and the legal setbacks of the DPD over the period 1969–1973, so were city blacks. For years, black Detroiters had deeply distrusted the judicial process, as white police officers routinely went free after victimizing African Americans. As Detroiter Rosetta Sadler wrote after white jurors acquitted the white police officers charged with murdering the young African Americans at the Algiers Motel in 1967, "the American courts have done it again. It was done like it has always been done since black people came to this country. . . . Not a court in this state would have accepted an all-black jury to sit on the jury for a black man."[129] After the New Bethel trials, however, just such an "impossibility" became possible. As the *Inner City Voice* put it, "The change in the jury selection process, which was by far the greatest victory to come out of the New Bethel Incident and trials . . . many people, especially blacks will continue to benefit. Already, scores of lawyers have filed appeals on behalf of clients to grant them new and fairer trials."[130]

And the Johnson verdict in 1971 only fueled the dawning hope among many still-suspicious city blacks that maybe the New Bethel trial verdicts had not been a fluke. While not every black Detroiter agreed with the *Inner City Voice* that Johnson had rung "the bell of justice" when he committed murder (indeed, many condemned his violent act), they were pleasantly surprised nevertheless that "the system" actually was able to see men like Johnson not simply as "black criminals" but as victims of the social ills of racism and oppressive employment.[131]

Just as city blacks supported the Johnson verdict even while many of them disliked the actions that Johnson himself had taken, so were they pleased by the outcome of the Brown trials without necessarily believing him to be a saint. Indeed, the severe injuries suffered by Officer Dooley in altercations with Brown and his cohorts gave many a Detroiter pause. But given the historic and outrageous offenses committed by STRESS officers against city blacks, the question of Brown's "innocence" became secondary to that of whether the police would finally be censured in court. City blacks supported the Brown acquittals first and foremost because they represented a victory for the black community over the police—no matter what the particular circumstances that had led to that triumph. And because these legal triumphs had been facilitated and celebrated by city liberals, city blacks previously disgusted with liberalism began to look at it more favorably. They, too, assumed that Detroit's liberals must have really changed.

But while black radicals conceded that black judge George Crockett was "just about the most together Brother on the bench," they themselves were not seduced into the liberal fold.[132] As Cockrel had put it about Crockett's New Bethel judicial activism, "everyone is going around saluting Judge Crockett for having followed the law which was not a revolutionary act, but had revolutionary consequences in a state who is not accustomed to the law being followed."[133] But Detroit's radicals feared that, unlike them, Detroit's poor and working-class black residents were perhaps exaggerating the long-term benefits of such legal victories, which is what was really luring them back to liberalism. To combat this trend, the Detroit Left sought to make it abundantly clear that they, not liberal judges or officials, were the reason why the down and out were finally being heard in the Motor City. As some radicals had put it after the New Bethel victories, "Those who are now saying that 'the fact that the New Bethel trials wound up as they did is an illustration of the extent to which genuine democracy operates within the system' are liars. The fact of the matter is that the defense in all of the cases, and the persons involved in the defense in all of the cases, had to force the system . . . to produce the results over which the 'liberals' are now clucking and which have the conservatives, especially those who are alive, turning over in their graves."[134]

Overall, however, city radicals made little progress when they tried to keep average black Detroiters from feeling more charitable toward liberals, particularly black liberals like Crockett. Not only did the city's black community come to see "the system" more favorably after the New Bethel, Johnson, and Brown verdicts, but it was equally heartened by the election of Justin Ravitz to Detroit's Recorder's Court. After this election, the Ravitz camp had noted that "Detroiters proved then that an independent people's political movement with real roots in the community can engage in the electoral process and win," and that "it is possible to struggle and win power to concretely improve the lives of people while utilizing their system."[135] And, of course, the victories over the police in the Brown trials only cemented community optimism in what could be achieved by working through established channels. Detroiters were thrilled that "no longer would police testimony necessarily be accepted above that of the citizen. No longer would the court's rulings necessarily support the judgement of police. No longer could law enforcement be above the law."[136]

While the Detroit Left worried deeply about this renewed African American faith in liberalism, the civic liberals who had felt under siege by both radicals and conservatives since 1967 welcomed it. Indeed, even though a conservative mayor still ran the city, with another mayoral election on the horizon, liberals felt newly hopeful about their chances to lead Detroit into the future. To city liberals, it had been a key victory that the bulk of radical political and social activism had been channeled from the unwieldy, dangerous, and unpredictable arena of the city's streets into a much more civilized and familiar arena—its courtrooms. Liberals were delighted that they had finally proved the legal system capable of responding fairly to the concerns of Detroiters who long had been discriminated against.

Even though so many Detroiters now believed that, for better or worse, liberal leaders had changed their stripes by 1973, liberals themselves maintained that they were responding to urban problems just as they always had. To a significant degree, they were right. As their myriad TAP programs illustrated, Detroit's liberal leaders had repeatedly tried to channel dissent from the streets and into established institutions. And, as the civil rights legislation of the mid-1960s makes clear, they also had been known to encourage flexible interpretations of the law in order to fight discrimination. Even the controversial stands that these leaders had taken during the New Bethel and Johnson trials were not as radical as they might at first appear. From their perspective, these trials were simply a practical application of the long-held liberal principle that white atonement for past racial sins was a component of making progress toward racial equality.[137] As Mayor Cavanagh had stated to the Kerner Commission several years earlier: "We must frankly face up to the need to consider and accept a new principle . . . the principle of reparation for long standing injustice dating back to the generations preceding ours . . . The price that they [blacks] have paid has been incalculable. Now the nation must, I believe, begin to make reparation—for the deeds of past generations, and of our own."

Whatever the ideological continuity in the liberal agenda, civic liberals clearly had pursued racial equality through the court system more aggressively between 1969 and 1973. City liberals had become more activist both because they were forced to and because the trials gave some of them the opportunity to act on convictions that they had always held. Nevertheless, the fact was that white as well as black Detroiters from across the political spectrum were surprised when these liberals responded to urban crisis by allowing their agenda to be pushed to its most progressive limits. These citizens believed that liberals had recently experienced a dramatic change of heart. These perceptions about shifting liberal loyalties had enormous implications for the direction that Detroit politics would soon take.

Many city radicals had hoped that their successes in the judicial arena—like the election of Ravitz—would further radicalize Detroiters and make them more "committed to ongoing non-electoral efforts."[138] They hoped that they could "utilize their [the liberals'] system and at the same time maintain and strengthen non-electoral political work."[139] But, in fact, these successes were reconvincing black Detroiters that the way to social change was through the ballot box. Sensing the direction in which black politics were headed in 1973, Cockrel wondered publicly whether all of the effort expended on trials like Hayward Brown's meant "that much in terms of furthering the movement, educating the people, or building an organization. . . . [W]hat if that same time and energy had been devoted toward building an organization? Would the effect have been broader and more important?"[140]

Cockrel's question was particularly timely because, within a few months, a critical mayoral election would take place in Detroit, and the Left needed to decide what, if any, role it was going to play in it. Not surprisingly, the fate of the radical dissidents in city plants was relevant to these calculations. Given liberal desires to steal its thunder, the city Left would need the labor Left if it still hoped to influence Detroit's political future.

7: From Fights for Union Office to Wildcats in the Workplace

> Detroit is a high-octane town. If the mixture is right, it doesn't take much to spark a wildcat walkout at its auto or supply plants.[1]

After James Johnson's dramatic murder trial, Judge Robert Colombo placed him in the custody of the Michigan Department of Mental Health. As he was bounced between various institutions thereafter, Johnson had no idea that his criminal trial had played such a key part in altering the course of Detroit's political history. A mere two years later, Johnson was unwittingly thrust into the political limelight once again, when a liberal hearing referee for the Workman's Compensation Bureau decided on a claim that he had filed against Chrysler Corporation during his incarceration at Ionia State Hospital for the Criminally Insane. Indeed, Johnson's fate at the hands of the Workman's Compensation Bureau informed the battles still raging for control of Detroit's auto plants and labor movement just as his acquittal in the criminal court had shaped the battles for control of the city itself.

In both the city and its plants, long-disenchanted blacks had gained enormous hope from Johnson's experiences in the legal system during the summer of 1971. But whereas the city's liberal leaders sought to capitalize on this new hope, liberal labor leaders did not. Ultimately, Johnson's explosion in the Eldon plant and his subsequent experiences with the criminal and civil courts only reinforced the union leadership's belief that it must reassert its control in the labor movement at any cost. And, between 1969 and 1973, this is exactly what it attempted to do. During this period, UAW leaders placed tremendous effort and expense into discrediting the black revolutionaries who had been mobilizing on Detroit's shop floors.

In several key local union elections the UAW leadership succeeded in eliminating worker dissent by 1971—or so union officials thought. In fact, although Detroit's RUMs and the League largely did fall apart by that year, shop-floor dissent was not completely extinguished. Fueled by the continuing egregious conditions in Detroit's plants, the biracial and politically broad-based activism of the United National Caucus (UNC) blossomed in the wake of the RUMs' demise. Notably, however, the UAW leadership's bitter fight against the in-plant black revolutionaries prior to 1971 blinded it to the legitimacy of, and widespread mandate for, the more broad-based reforms advocated by the UNC. Thus, unlike their liberal counterparts in the city, labor leaders did not choose to harness this militancy and make it their own.

* * * *

Because of their aggressive tactics, their venomous criticism of the union hierarchy, and particularly because of their revolutionary political agenda, Detroit's RUMs had greatly unnerved the UAW by 1968. Despite their relatively small numbers, the RUMs had managed to halt production in several auto plants and win a noticeable degree of sympathy and support from autoworkers. Between 1968 and 1971, union leaders in Detroit came to feel that they were at war with the RUMs. In September 1968, April 1969, March 1970, and May 1971, the UAW had the opportunity to battle black dissidents in several union elections that dramatically intensified the war for control of the labor movement.

In September 1968, a trustee of Local 3, the epicenter of DRUM activism, died while in office, and the UAW scheduled an election for September 26, 1968, to determine who would succeed him. In a surprising move, one that was born of intense internal debate and of consultation with leaders of the League, DRUM decided to run a candidate for this office "to test the strength of the organization . . . to get publicity for the organization and to better identify it in the eyes of other black workers . . . [and] to be able to use the election as an organizational tool."[2]

To the shock of UAW officials, the DRUM candidate, Ron March, won 563 votes to the 521 for his opponent, Joe Elliot.[3] Because March did not win by enough of a margin to meet the UAW Constitution's requirements governing elections, the union scheduled a runoff election for October 3, 1968. This gave Local 3's leadership time to mobilize. Implicitly warning UAW President Walter P. Reuther of the danger of a DRUM victory, in early October 1968, Irving Bluestone "attached the kind of material being distributed by DRUM at Local 3"[4] in a memo that he sent to Reuther. And, specifically to prevent DRUM from winning, Local 3's leadership approached its large pool of Polish retirees and encouraged them to vote in the runoff election. Given the Local's ethnic composition prior to becoming more African American, the supply of white Polish retiree voters in Local 3 was extensive. Yet since retirees normally did not exercise their voting rights in such minor union elections, the union solicitation of their support was highly irregular. But union leaders well knew, based on their close surveillance of DRUM literature that relations between black revolutionaries and white Poles at Chrysler were troubled, and that a high retiree turnout could influence the election.[5] However, the leadership of the UAW did not count solely on the retirees' anti-black biases to bring them to the polls; officials also sent a letter urging them to vote because a DRUM victory might lead directly to the termination of all retiree benefits.[6]

Despite such leadership maneuvering to discredit him, March nevertheless received 1,386 votes in the October runoff election. Joe Elliott, the underdog in the first election, managed to receive 2,091 votes, which made him the new trustee of Local 3.[7] Not surprisingly, union leaders breathed a sigh of relief at this outcome, while DRUM leaders were furious. Immediately after the election, DRUM distributed a flier blaming the "underhanded" tactics of both the UAW and the police of Hamtramck (the city completely within Detroit where Local 3 was located) for preventing a fair election. According to DRUM, moments after March had won the initial trustee election, "the Polish pigs of the Hamtramck police department jumped into their cars and rode to the back of the bars on Jos Campau and Clay to wantonly beat over black brothers with double-edged axe handles and spray them with deadly mace."[8] According to DRUM leader General Baker, several DRUM supporters were arrested in this melee, and DRUM leaders then went to the police station and union hall to find out what was going on. As Baker reported in a 1969 interview:

> Once we got into the union hall, in comes the mayor and the police commissioner of the city of Hamtramck ... [then] ... one of the white union officials runs outside and calls [more] police and about the whole 50 man police force ran in with mace and ax handles and started spraying and beating everybody in the hall under the guise that we were attacking the mayor and police commissioner.... All the doors were locked, so it obviously had been set up some kind of way, except the doors they came in. Everybody in there just got wasted.[9]

During the runoff election, DRUM maintained that the police repeatedly stopped or ticketed cars carrying black DRUM voters so as to keep them from the polls.[10] According to DRUM, in addition to the police upsetting their chances in the runoff, the UAW "racists" had literally stolen the election.[11] As Baker put it, "we figured there was cheating in the voting machines. That's the only way. Even with the retirees voting ... we had the majority down there to vote."[12]

But despite its disappointments in 1968, DRUM had another opportunity to challenge UAW leaders in the electoral arena. In March 1969, the vice president of Local 3, Charlie Brooks, vacated his position to take a job with the UAW International. When the UAW scheduled a special election for April 9 to determine Brooks's successor, DRUM immediately entered Don

Jackson as a candidate. This time, DRUM maintained, the UAW would have to come to terms with the fact that "more and more black workers are finding it necessary to take the D.R.U.M. road."[13] Such bravado clearly unsettled the UAW leadership. On March 10, the International Executive Board (IEB) sent a letter to every UAW member to point out that it had made great strides at Dodge Main plant, where 66 percent of full-time union officials were black and 56 percent of the elected stewards were black noting also that 65 percent of the elected stewards and committeeman at Local 3 were black as well.[14] In addition to sending this letter, the UAW leadership decided to throw its support behind a black candidate in the upcoming Local 3 vice presidential election.[15]

But not every black member of the UAW was appeased by this endorsement, nor did all of them agree that it was the union who should be taking credit for the recent rise in the number of black authority figures on the shop floor. Some observers outside of the labor movement thought that "more blacks are now on the staffs of both institutions [union and company] than before DRUM made its appearance" precisely because of DRUM's activism.[16] As DRUM members themselves saw it, Chrysler simply had "switched black 'management' all around the plant to make it seem as though a number of brothers have been upgraded."[17] They went on to accuse the UAW's choice for vice president, Andy Hardy, of being "Uncle Remus himself."[18] March directly approached Local 3 voters with DRUM's message that "the time has come for Black workers to wake up and refuse to be fooled by the tactics of professional negro sell-out artists. The time has come for us to support men for their political positions, not for their family or social relationships."[19] These views clearly resonated with some non-DRUM black workers. As one such autoworker put it when explaining his support of Jackson, "I do not agree with all of the tactics and strategies of D.R.U.M., but it is here for all who want to see it. . . . [Black promotions] and also the attitude of the white foremen has changed his approach toward the black workers, since the 'DRUM guys' started beating the DRUM against racism last May!"[20]

Despite such worker support, however, the April 9 election between Jackson and Hardy was a virtual repeat of the earlier election for trustee. Once again, a victor was not determined right away because the votes cast required a runoff election. And in this second election, during which Jackson received 1,254 votes to Hardy's 2,800, once again the UAW was relieved while the leaders of DRUM were outraged.[21] Both groups knew, from the large numbers of votes both March and Jackson had recently received, that DRUM was a legitimate contender for power in Local 3. Indeed, DRUM was firmly convinced that it was the UAW's fear of this power that had led it to take extraordinary measures to ensure a black radical defeat.

According to DRUM, both the DPD and police from Hamtramck, allegedly with the tacit approval of the UAW, had worked together to prevent a Jackson victory. DRUM claimed that the DPD came to Jackson's house on the morning of the election and "confiscated his license plates from his car under the pretense that they were stolen even though he produced his registration. They held his plates for a couple of hours and [then] returned them stating it was a mistake."[22] DRUM also maintained that a car with DRUM members Ray Johnson and Ron March was followed by both the DPD and the Hamtramck police. According to DRUM, "they were stopped at Lawton and Pasadena, taken out of the car at shot-gun point and arrested for allegedly assaulting an officer and resisting arrest."[23] On April 30, 1969, Jackson and March wrote a letter to the president of Local 3, Ed Liska, asking him to investigate the improprieties that they thought had taken place during the runoff election, but they received no satisfaction from this quarter.[24] DRUM, which initially had been ambivalent if not downright hostile to the idea of entering the electoral arena, was amazed at the hostile reaction that its campaigning had touched off among the union traditionalists. DRUM hoped, however, that any irregular maneuvering on the part of the union leadership would merely serve to net DRUM more supporters from the still-disenchanted auto workforce. As DRUM noted optimistically, "the election demonstrated clearly to workers that the UAW bureaucracy was willing to risk outright scandal rather than to allow blacks to control their own union."[25]

The UAW leadership, however, had no intention of allowing DRUM to capitalize on what was unequivocally a UAW victory. In 1970, the UAW faced DRUM once more in an electoral battle, and this time it hoped to neutralize completely the black radicals at Local 3. In March 1970, virtually every top leadership position in Local 3 was up for grabs as the elections for its Executive Board loomed and, once again, black revolutionaries geared up to battle union traditionalists. In the race for the presidency of Local 3, DRUM member March challenged incumbent Liska. In the race for vice president, Jackson faced off against incumbent Hardy. DRUM also ran Raymond Johnson for financial secretary, Gracie Wooten for recording secretary, and Carlos Williams for treasurer. DRUM members Betty Griffith, Charles Roberts, and Grover Douglas also ran for open trustee positions.[26]

Clearly, DRUM had not been cowed by its defeats in the elections of 1968 and 1969. Its bold electoral push in 1970 and its optimism that it would triumph can only be understood in the broader context of the tremendous inroads that other League components were simultaneously making across the Motor City. From city schools and universities to city streets and courtrooms, black and white radicals were on the move and were enjoying noticeable victories. As League leader Mike Hamlin put it, "the League had dizzying success. . . . [W]e felt that nothing could stop us. . . . [O]ur historic moment had arrived."[27] As one of the League's most important organs, DRUM believed that it, too, would succeed in wrestling power from its arch nemesis in the auto plants just as the League's urban components successfully were taking on city liberals and conservatives alike. As *DRUM* put it, "our movement has begun and it will not be stopped. VICTORY IS INEVITABLE."[28]

But when DRUM geared up for the Local 3 elections on March 18, so did the UAW. In this final ugly battle between black revolutionaries and UAW traditionalists, the union leadership once again emerged victorious. Liska won the presidency with 2,732 votes to March's 973. Jackson lost to Hardy, who received 2,470 votes. Wooten lost with 896 votes to Jerry Shelton's 1,585. And Raymond Johnson received 666 votes to A. Newkirk's 743. Only DRUM members Griffith, with 880 votes, and Williams, with 847 votes, had enough ballots in their favor to allow them a second chance at victory in a later runoff election.[29]

Even though the UAW traditionalist's slate had defeated DRUM's top candidates through the electoral process, never before had such controversy surrounded a UAW victory. Immediately after the victors were announced, workers at Dodge Main plant reported widespread improprieties in the election and registered their complaints with the UAW's Credentials Committee. Such workers claimed that many retirees had been allowed to vote without proper identification and that only two or three balloting machines were working so that many active UAW members never had the chance to vote. They maintained as well that the machines that were working regularly were tampered with by union election officials and repairmen without the required challengers present, and that there was improper campaigning by Local 3 leadership candidates who were present illegally on the election floor. Some suggested that DRUM challengers were ignored, that the DRUM levers were often not working, and that there was a piece of metal over March's lever in at least one polling booth. Finally, the complainants charged that ballots had been counted the next day even though the proper number of challengers was not present.[30] DRUM members detailed these charges in the newsletter article "Liska Won at the Point of a Gun."[31] And at least thirty workers from Dodge Main plant eventually signed affidavits detailing the election fraud that they also claimed to have witnessed.[32] In the end, however, "the Credentials Committee of the 22nd Constitutional Convention of the UAW [which] investigated protests of members of Local 3 ... found insufficient evidence to order a new election."[33]

That the Credentials Committee took this position is not altogether surprising, as DRUM members were not alone in chronicling what had taken place during the Local 3 elections.[34] The leadership of Local 3 also kept its own detailed notes on what had transpired on March 18 and 19, and it made sure to forward its accounts to President Reuther and Region 1 Director George Merrelli on March 24. According to one of these reports:

> Problems developed as soon as the polls opened Wednesday morning at
> 4:45am. . . . DRUM candidates were in and out of the hall[,] constantly badg-

ering voters. . . . [Q]uite a bit of drinking was taking place, and certain challengers were seen using pills of an unknown nature. . . . [O]n both days in the afternoon DRUM candidates plus about a hundred or so SDS [Students for a Democratic Society] people campaigned in front of the hall using bullhorns, stopping traffic, and using threats and scare tactics against the voters. . . . DRUM challenger Lewis Zachary, in a fit of anger, tipped over the retirees' voting table and tore the voting log book. He also dragged a voter out of the booth while he was voting, under the pretext of challenging his vote. . . . In my opinion, the conduct of the DRUM people was disgraceful, and their sole purpose was to usurp the prestige of a peaceful honest local union election.[35]

The various "Election Notes" that arrived in Reuther's office not only offered an account of the events of March 18 and 19 but also offered personal profiles and risk assessments of several DRUM members present on those days:

All news about this individual [Ron March] reveal that he is a complete failure and is using the black issue as the cause of his own failure. . . . [He is] a fiery type of man. . . . [General Baker] is a huge strong built guy with a very ugly face. . . . [H]e is not a speaker but a planner. . . . [Charles Wooten] is a tiger with emotions. . . . Wooten is a fiery speaker and a dangerous man. . . . [W]herever the leaders of DRUM go, he is right in the middle of the group. . . . [Raymond Johnson] is not intelligent in any way but is a hater all the way. . . . [Donald Jackson] is a quite nice guy and appears to be a nice guy. . . . [H]e doesn't fit with the DRUM group but is with them all the time.[36]

Even though the UAW had successfully defeated the DRUM slate at Local 3, it did not relax thereafter. There was, after all, a runoff election coming up, and two DRUM members were candidates. Even though the UAW maintained that "the most dangerous DRUM people are the few young men who are hellbent on destruction,"[37] the potential electoral victory of black DRUM women like Betty Griffith was obviously threatening as well. Right before the runoff election, Local 3 President Liska sent a telegram to Reuther in which he "urgently request[ed]" a meeting "with yourself and Brother Merrelli to discuss protection for this Local union in the forthcoming run off election. DRUM forces in the first election deliberately tried to sabotage election proceedings as well as results by direct force against membership."[38] But Liska need not have worried. During the Executive Board runoff, both DRUM candidates lost, and DRUM had clearly suffered a huge setback in every election that it entered. DRUM continued to maintain that these defeats were highly suspicious. As DRUM member John Watson put it, "DRUM suspected that the union would cheat," but it was the effort that the union allegedly had expended on defeating DRUM that Watson found most shocking.[39] According to Watson, the most appalling moment was when "George Merrelli, the regional UAW leader, stormed into the hall with his entire 50-man staff. They were armed and had the additional support of a contingent of police."[40] Whatever had actually happened during these elections, the fact remained that after March 1970, DRUM was certainly in decline. Because DRUM failed in its attempt to take power in the local, and because the company subsequently fired several key DRUM leaders, including March, black radicals in the other plants were deeply unsettled.

To increase their unease, after the defeat of DRUM at Local 3, the UAW leadership noticeably geared up for elections at Local 961 in May 1971. Local 961 included the Eldon Avenue plant, the home of ELRUM. The tensions between the UAW and ELRUM were perhaps even greater than those between the UAW and DRUM. ELRUM had escalated its attack on the union ever since Gary Thompson's death, and also ELRUM already had run candidates, and did quite well, in an earlier Executive Board election.[41] In addition, the union was even more defensive at Eldon than at Dodge Main because ELRUM was not the only vocal dissident group there. A UNC affiliate, the Eldon Safety Committee, had repeatedly joined ELRUM in its criticism of the UAW and of the union leadership at Eldon in particular. The union, however, did not make many distinctions among these dissident groups.

Members of ELRUM and members of the Eldon Safety Committee (led by UNC Co-Chair Jordan Sims) had only a loose connection, and the latter group often made it clear that it disapproved of the RUMs' exclusionary policies. But to the union leadership at Eldon, there was little difference between these groups, and both had to be stopped. One leaflet put out by a pro-administration group in the plant indicates the degree to which Sims's opponents saw him and ELRUM as one and the same. According to this leaflet, which authors claimed was penned by Sims himself in order to discredit him, "I organized E-L-R-U-M in December 1968. In January 1969 I led them in a wildcat, that got 22 of them fired."[42]

Undeterred by such propaganda, black dissidents passed out questionnaires to Eldon employees asking them to note "wrongs that might have been committed by union or management" so that they could better "act in serving the needs of the workers."[43] Simultaneously, the leadership of Local 961 appealed directly to its membership to denounce the plant dissidents and to stand behind union loyalists in the upcoming election: "We would like to talk to you about DRUM and ELDRUM and the hate literature that they have put out in the plant." They went on to say that Eldon's workers should be wary of the RUMs because these radicals intended to take over the entire United States, not just the local.[44] Because the union leadership was astute enough to realize that the appeal of the RUMs lie in their commitment to fighting racism, they further told the Eldon workers that "we like to point out to you that this LOCAL union has sent people to Lansing and Washington many times to help lobby for anti-discrimination legislation. . . . [I]t's also interesting to note that we have worked closely with the NAACP in helping push through these liberal programs."[45]

Even with all of these appeals to the rank and file at Eldon, however, in May 1971, ELRUM and the Eldon Safety Committee both enjoyed much support on the shop floor. This made it even more important for union traditionalists to prevail electorally as they had at Local 3, and campaigning became quite passionate as election day drew near. A group calling itself the Concerned Eldon Avenue Employees (known by ELRUM as "The Invisible Honkeys Slate") put out a leaflet calling Sims, the Eldon Safety Committee's choice for president, "an atheist who wants an all black union." The group went on to say that Sims "is mentally ill. He is a cruel, selfish, uncouth nappy chinned BLACK MAN," and it questioned that if he and his supporters "hate the UAW so badly and want an all black shop—why don't they find employment elsewhere?" At the end of its newsletter, the Concerned Eldon Avenue Employees encouraged fellow workers to "support your local union and its hard working officials."[46]

Unfazed by such negative campaign literature, Sims approached the voters of Local 961 with the following campaign agenda and response to his critics: "Line speed, health and safety violations from dirty floors to defective safety switches and poor ventilation are unbearable and unresolved. Nothing has been done about the excessive noise. If elected I'm going to use established procedures and I'll see to it that federal and state laws are enforced. . . . I am not anti-International. The International exists to serve the membership and not the other way around as some people think."[47] In response to criticism that he was a front man for ELRUM and was seeking a UAW takeover, Sims wrote his own leaflet, in which he noted, "I am only one MAN seeking ONE OFFICE and I am willing to HONESTLY put my case before this MEMBERSHIP!"[48]

Sims campaigned against both the Local's black incumbent, Elroy Richardson, and a white union steward named Frank McKinnon. Local 961's election took place on May 12, 1971, and like the earlier election at the Dodge Main plant, at the union leadership's request, there were armed guards on the premises to "prevent extremists and outsiders from disrupting the election process."[49] Also, as at Dodge Main plant, the votes in the Local 961 election were split, requiring a runoff election two weeks later between Sims and McKinnon, who had finished first and second, respectively. After the first election, the incumbent union president Richardson complained publicly that there had been many "'outsiders' in front of the hall," and there were "black militant workers . . . among election challengers."[50] Sims responded to Richardson's allegations by filing his own complaint with the Michigan Civil Rights Commission, charging that the election process at Local 961 was being jeopardized by red- and race-baiting. Such unsavory tactics proved successful, as, on May 28, 1971, McKinnon won the runoff election, albeit by an extremely narrow margin.[51]

With the election of McKinnon, it appeared to UAW leaders that the black militants at Eldon finally were in retreat. Despite the *Michigan Chronicle*'s

1969 warning that if union reformers were "kept out of power, the UAW may well be adding to the list of dissidents who seek to rectify grievances with the company and union through channels such as DRUM and other militant groups have chosen," by May 1971, UAW officials were thoroughly relieved that they had succeeded in stemming the tide of shop-floor dissent.[52] With many RUM members fired or blacklisted from the industry, with the defeat of March and Sims, with Chrysler hiring more blacks into management, and with more moderate blacks winning union office around the city, the union leadership was newly confident that it had regained the upper hand on the shop floor and that labor relations soon would stabilize.[53]

Although the UAW may have been naive to think that its electoral successes had quelled shop-floor dissent, especially because management would continue to push autoworkers to the breaking point after 1971, it was right to believe that the RUMs had little remaining power. But while the union felt that it had played the decisive role in ridding the plant of RUM dissidents (and while leftist critics of the union often voiced the same opinion), the RUMs' demise stemmed as well from limitations in their own agenda as from outside forces. Between 1967 and 1971, black autoworkers had admired the RUMs for their bravery when dealing with the company and the union. They also recognized that the RUMs were usually the first to speak up on their behalf when something egregious occurred in the workplace. But it is significant that so few of these workers actually became RUM members during these years. Ultimately the RUMs' rhetoric, style, and racially exclusive and ill-planned tactics, as well as the fact that its male-dominated leadership too often saw the RUM struggle as a means to fulfil the destiny of "black manhood," had severely weakened these organizations over time.

In their efforts to "tell it like it is," the RUMs often offended autoworkers, particularly the older ones. As the only white RUM member, John Taylor, put it, "the older people had a lot of trouble with the whole tone."[54] RUM leaders' reaction to any discomfort with their tone was simply to say, "if anyone becomes easily offended when they hear or read cursing or cussing words, profanity, etc. Don't read this article!"[55] Yet, even while older black workers generally agreed with the RUMs that the racism in the plants was intolerable and that those who allowed the discrimination to flourish were absolutely in the wrong, many were turned off when the RUMs accused black union officials of being "Sambos" and "Uncle Toms" and called them "Mother Fuckers."

The off-putting rhetoric of RUM leaders directly undercut the worker cooperation that they sorely needed if they wanted to lead the labor movement. In the April 3, 1968, *ELRUM*, for example, ELRUM leaders chose to criticize the union for the very real problem of white women getting preferential hiring treatment over black women by calling the white women "White Bitches" who worked for "Elroy's [Richardson] prostitute service." They went on to say that these "Honkey Whores" "turned tricks" for the "Uncle

Toms and dumb Honkeys" in Local 961, and especially for the "Fat old Honkey Butch pollack Backavatich."[56] To black workers who had long fought against the cavalier use of racial epithets and to female workers (both black and white) who had always condemned sexist rhetoric, such language was inexcusable. According to Taylor, this particular *ELRUM* article "really turned people off."[57] In response to this piece, one black Eldon worker wrote to RUM leaders about the "obscene pamphlet you gave me yesterday morning": "Your pamphlet displayed disrespect for your fellow workman and was a disgrace to every black woman who works here. . . . [Y]our expressions make you a discredit to the black man and the black cause. . . . [W]e black men of the Eldon Ave. Axle don't need nasty talk and cuss words to express ourselves. . . . [T]hen you come along with those terms 'House Niggers' . . . but I am no nigger now and I never will be one."[58]

Not only did RUM leaders routinely use racially inflammatory and sexist language, but they also made poor choices with regard to organizational style. For example, when RUM leaders chose to wear black berets and carry weapons, many of the older women in the Eldon plant felt "physically afraid of the ELRUM people."[59] During the Local 961 election, "most of the people counting the ballots were female and older . . . and they thought the EL-RUM people had guns and were going to go berserk."[60] These women were not necessarily paranoid since RUM leaders had made no apologies when they publicly stated that "those who oppose us will be dealt with through any means necessary."[61] This did not bode well for the RUMs' longevity. As Taylor said, after seeing this fear in the Eldon women, "I knew right then that there had been a tremendous failure of ELRUM."[62]

RUM leaders came to alienate workers not only in the realm of rhetoric and style but also with some of their tactical decisions regarding which workers to court within the plants and when to engage in direct action. From the RUMs' inception, for example, their leaders insisted that members refuse to work with whites in the plants, and yet whites made up at least 40 percent of every plant that RUMs were in. ELRUM, for example, rarely gave its leaflets to white workers.[63] Such insularity not only persuaded the UAW that the RUMs were anti-democratic, but it also alienated numerous white workers who might otherwise have been sympathetic to the RUMs' call for reining in management. As UNC leader Sims noted, "when ELRUM first started, all the workers could understand was the hostile belligerent or condescending attitude of management to workers . . . [and] the whites wanted to help push the program, even though it was black."[64] But when RUM leaders refused such help, many plant whites became openly hostile to them. The RUMs' racial exclusiveness also alienated black workers. As the African American who wrote to ELRUM about its controversial "prostitute" newsletter put it, "until we unite and work as one, and I don't mean black and all black; I mean black and white together; we will always be building and others will be tearing down."[65]

Also, when the RUMs engaged in direct-action initiatives on the shop floor, such as wildcat strikes, they often opted for macho flare over detailed planning. After Gary Thompson was killed at the Eldon plant, for example, ELRUM leaders quickly moved from calling Chrysler a "murderer" to initiating a wildcat without first thinking through how they would generate sufficient worker support. As Taylor remembered, "we hadn't organized our base correctly. We weren't ready for the strike hit. We should have agitated more around the issue of Gary Thompson and safety in general."[66] Not only did ELRUM fail to secure the necessary support for its wildcat on an ideological level, but it also ignored the economic considerations that were in many Eldon workers' minds at the time. According to Taylor, Thompson's death "just verified [what] we had been saying and we were kind of self-righteous. In our ignorance, we failed to note that Memorial Day was on Friday that day. . . . [S]o they [the workers] were getting triple time and we had picked that day for a strike."[67]

RUM leaders' strategies for union elections turned out to be as flawed as their strategies for work stoppages. On the one hand, RUM leaders' tactical decision to enter the union's electoral process was based merely on a desire to upset the status quo in the plants. As DRUM's Baker put it, "we never really ran to win."[68] Thus, when RUM leaders made a bid for union office, they did not attempt to work with progressive black or white union committeemen or stewards; nor did they work very hard to win support from mainstream black and white workers. On the other hand, by running candidates in union elections, the RUMs had entered the UAW's turf and thus had exposed themselves to public attack. Ironically, not only did the RUMs suffer in these local elections, but so did the non-RUM dissidents who also ran for office and were trying to improve shop-floor life along biracial lines.

The fact that the RUMs and the League were completely male-dominated, and that leaders often rationalized the broader workers' struggle in terms of securing the privileges of black manhood, also severely compromised these organizations' viability. It was not unimportant, for example, that ELRUM's caustic denunciation of Chrysler's role in Thompson's death specifically noted that this worker had a pregnant wife at home. Indeed, much of the RUM leadership's hostility toward auto companies and the UAW alike directly stemmed from its belief that both groups actively denied black men their sanctified role as men, husbands, and fathers. RUM literature often couched the shop floor's struggles taking place across Detroit in terms of the black man's need to assert his manhood so that every white man—and black woman—would be prevented from seeing him as inferior. As DRUM leaders put it, they had listened to Stokely Carmichael and H. Rap Brown and "were inspired by the sentiment and ideas of manhood expressed by their words."[69] After repeatedly outlining what the role of "black men" should be, RUM leaders instructed members and supporters alike to "keep your head up, look whitey in the eyes and say, 'I'm just as good as you.'"[70] In addition, RUM leaders specifically noted that such manhood must be asserted so that white workers no longer would disrespect "their" black women.[71] As one RUM official put it, "all white men think our women are whores and can be had. . . . [B]lack men must protect their women and children."[72]

Not surprisingly, the numerous and highly dedicated black women in the RUMs and the League did not appreciate such patronizing rhetoric, and when the men in these organizations refused to tackle their own sexism, internal group tensions mounted. Just as there was a women's revolt within the Black Panther Party between 1969 and 1970,[73] women in the RUMs and the League also rebeled against the practices of the men in these groups. As one female member put it, the League and the RUMs let women do "much of the work in the movement—typing, cleaning, making leaflets . . . but when it came to 'shine time' we were not anywhere."[74] Over time the RUMs' and the League's stated quest to empower black men, as well as to have white men and black women alike give black men their due respect, came to alienate many of the women in these organizations. According to activist Miriam Kramer,

> A lot of us got pulled into the League of Revolutionary Black Workers and we were its backbone. But male supremacy was rampant and we never got proper credit. . . . [W]omen like Cassandra Smith, Edna Watson, Dorothy Duberry, Diane Bernard, and Gracie Wooten played tremendous roles. . . . [W]e were forceful but we were played down. . . . [W]e endured a lot of name calling and had to fight male supremacy. Some would call us the IWW: Ignorant Women of the World.[75]

League member Edna Ewell Watson had a similar assessment of women's position in that organization:

> The role of women in the League was traditionalist in terms of black patriarchal ideology and political priorities. Women were positioned and constructed to be supportive of the male leadership. . . . Many of the male leaders acted as if women were sexual commodities, mindless, emotionally unstable, or invisible. . . . There was no lack of role for women in the League as long as they accepted subordination and invisibility.[76]

Kramer and Watson were not exaggerating the subservient position to which black men had relegated women in the League and the RUMs. The League, for example, routinely assigned women to internal committees such as the "Youth Committee," the "Clean-up Committee," and the "Cooking Committee" in disproportionate numbers. Leaders placed "Cassandra, Sandra, Julia and Jerome" on the Cooking Committee and "Julia, Cassandra, Waistline, Evette, and Cadesia" on the Clean-up Committee. The Youth Committee likewise was comprised of "Diana, Gracie, Julia, Trisha, Ilena, Cassandra, and John."[77]

Given the central role that securing the privileges of "black manhood" played in their desire to tackle shop floor discrimination, not surprisingly, the male leaders of the League and its RUM affiliates were largely unapologetic about their position of dominance. It angered leaders John Williams, Rufus Burke, and Clint Marbury, for example, when anyone in the organization tried "to elevate the problems of women on par with capitalism by calling it sexism."[78] Whereas some men in the RUMs felt benevolent toward the women over whom they felt dominance (noting that black men should be "respectful in relationships with women and children"),[79] other equally domineering RUM men were less charitable. They maintained that "our Sisters on the other hand must first respect themselves before they can ask for 'respect.'" They went on to suggest that black women needed to be more circumspect about their "dress, language and disposition."[80] Years later, Watson speculated that "perhaps the different handling of gender issues might have made the League more viable, but history was against us."[81]

While the RUMs' gender politics weakened the organizations, larger political divisions within their parent group, the League, dealt the death blow. On June 12, 1971, the League split in an ugly factional fight. As League scholar James Geschwender has argued, "the contradictions in the League version of the capitalist-colonial exploitation model suggested incompatible tactical lines, which were a constant source of strain in the organization." When they split from the League, Executive Board members Kenneth Cockrel, Mike Hamlin, and John Watson argued that the organization always had been based on three distinct forces: the "proletarian revolutionaries" like the three of them, who advocated simultaneous and equal organizational efforts in the plant and the community; the "backward reactionary-nationalist lumpen-proletarians," such as General Baker and Chuck Wooten, whose efforts at plant organizing included anti-white sentiment and had too many "cultural nationalist tendencies"; and the "petty-bourgeois opportunists," such as Luke Tripp, who sought "refuge in the ivy-covered halls of white capitalist universities."[82]

As it turned out, the Baker / Wooten group most often clashed ideologically and strategically with Cockrel, Hamlin, and Watson.[83] To Baker and the other "lumpen-proletarians," the Cockrel group's legal work and many of its community-based efforts were too reformist and spread the League too thinly. Baker, in particular, felt that with Black Star Productions, Black Star Printing, two Black Star Bookstores, and a Black Consciousness Library, the League drained too many of its resources away from the all-important shop floor.[84] Of course, the Cockrel group could not have disagreed more. Referring to the extensive work that Cockrel had done in the Motor City's courtrooms, one supporter said, "Our work did not consist of a mere defense of cases in court, but mass education and agitation through rallies [and] the structuring of the Labor Defense Coalition to show the class nature of the system. . . . The court was used to educate the community to contradictions between labor and capital [such as] in the James Johnson case."[85]

Indeed, the Cockrel group felt that the League had earned substantial support within the black community precisely *because* of its legal activism, whereas the organization's other factions "used their position in the League as a basis for an arrogant, condescending parade inside the black community."[86] According to Cockrel, Watson, and Hamlin, the League's long-term potential was destroyed by those who were too steeped in "exclusionary" black nationalism. As they said, "the Leagues' failure to promote the extension of proletarian consciousness among the masses of whites in the United States will be fatal to our struggle."[87] In their opinion, "the politics of black nationalism had been injected into the workers' organization through gossip and behind the back conversation rather than through the vehicle of open political discussion."[88] They argued that certain exclusionary members' "conduct as regards to other human beings, especially women, was on a level wholly inconsistent with continuance in the ranks of a revolutionary organization."[89]

Even though the League's final split was couched in purely political and strategic terms, the experiences of the RUMs in the plants clearly indicate that the roots of its demise were social and cultural as well. One need only look at the League's "code of conduct"—in which members were reminded not to "hit or swear at people," not to engage in "excessive drinking or getting high in public," and to be "respectful in relationships with women"[90]— to see a key reason why there was little RUM presence in the plants after 1971. It was not that all League members engaged in such inappropriate behavior; it was simply that enough of them were guilty of it to cause a serious public relations problem for the organization. As the League's Executive Board noted on March 29, 1971, "such conduct damages our organization's reputation and drains legal and other resources needlessly," after it again reminded members that there would be "no loafing around the offices . . . no unnecessary fights or abrasive contact with the public or member in our ranks."[91]

Whatever "officially" killed the RUMs, when the UAW looked around Detroit's auto plants in 1971 and concluded that shop-floor dissent was on the wane because of the RUMs' defeat, it underestimated the average worker's desire for a more humane and less racist workplace. Historian Steve Jefferys has written that, in the plants at this time, there were "two tendencies among the black workers . . . those influenced by black nationalist and socialist politics of the black power movement, and those blacks who had entered the local UAW machine."[92] Mistakenly, the UAW leadership saw the in-plant political situation in this same dichotomous manner. Because UAW leaders could only see shop-floor politics in terms of those who were "commies" or those who were union loyalists, they were blind to the legitimacy of another shop-floor dissident movement of distressed autoworkers that flourished in the wake of the intense management speed up which was neither black nationalist nor communist, nor safely within the leadership fold.

The UAW did not adequately take into account the implications of the fact that working conditions in city plants kept deteriorating between 1971 and 1973. Chrysler's plants in particular had become nothing short of hazardous, as that company ran production around the clock and put most of its workers on inhumane overtime schedules to meet an unprecedented demand for its cars. Chrysler's sales and earnings between April and June 1973, for example, were nearly double that of the previous year. Yet its prosperity came not through an expansion of its operations or by updating and modernizing its existing facilities, but rather from an intense speedup.[93] Although the UAW leadership no longer had to contend with the vocal attacks of the RUMs during these years, it still was bombarded with grievances about safety and production standards.[94] And while the RUMs weren't there to draw attention to it, the fact remained that workers were still suffering serious injuries on the shop floor.[95]

By 1973, safety conditions were deplorable in virtually every Detroit auto plant. On August 15, 1973, the *Detroit Free Press* detailed the substandard conditions found by the UAW at twenty of them.[96] By that year, health and safety had become such a prominent issue that the UAW's national publication, *The Washington Report*, also addressed the issue of safety, workplace chemicals, and on-the-job accidents on a regular basis.[97] But as had been the case between 1960 and 1967, the issue of health and safety had become most pressing in Chrysler plants after 1971. Notably the Michigan Civil Rights Commission (MCRC) had deemed safety conditions "abominable"[98] at Chrysler's Eldon Avenue plant, which "covered over a million square feet and housed 2600 machine tools of over 170 types"[99] This was not an altogether surprising assessment, considering that there was only one safety representative responsible for as many as 2,500 automotive machines and between 75 and 80 pieces of mobile equipment, such as jitneys and trucks.[100] And, according to one scholar, "it seems to be the practice of foremen, when equipment is needed, to pull the tags off of the equipment in the repair area that badly need corrective maintenance and put them back into service on the floor."[101]

During the early 1970s, as more and more workers were injured on the job at Eldon, the plant was subjected to an increasing number of workplace inspections. Following the particularly grisly on-the-job death of Gary Thompson in 1970, UAW Safety Director Lloyd Utter inspected the Eldon facility, noting a "complete neglect of stated maintenance procedures in this plant. The equipment is being operated in an inexcusably dangerous condition."[102] As a result of such reports, Chrysler acknowledged in August 1970 that it must correct "a number of safety and housekeeping items." But a few months later, Utter once again reported that "there seems to be no concern about housekeeping in this plant and the safety program reflects this lack of concern."[103]

Between 1971 and 1973, nearly every Detroit autoworker was dealing with oil slicks on shop floor, faulty cranes, presses without guards, fumes, and hundreds of other safety violations. Journalist Rachel Scott was so astounded by working conditions during this period that in 1974 she wrote a powerful exposé of the auto industry.[104] Scott discovered that in Chrysler plants "on an average day . . . ten to twelve workers were injured seriously enough to be sent to Workmen's Compensation lawyers at Chrysler for evaluation."[105] According to Joseph Baltimore, a former Workmen's Compensation Board adjuster for the company, Chrysler so desperately wanted to protect its "lost-time" record that there were "a number of cases where people had operations, fingers cut off, and they [brought] them back to work the same day."[106]

Once again UAW leaders did not ignore such terrible shop-floor conditions. In June 1972, for example, President William Gilbert of Local 7 spoke to members about numerous in-plant problems that existed and then "put management on notice that this will no longer be tolerated. . . . [S]erious problems exist in health and safety."[107] Likewise, in August 1973, UAW Region 1 leaders decided to go over management's head when they sent the Occupational Health and Safety Administration a telegram demanding an inspection of Chrysler's Forge plant, where "three times within a two week period, a defective overhead crane dumped tons of steel in pedestrian areas."[108] But the union leadership still did not want to hear what workers themselves thought should be done to correct these problems. When the United Justice Caucus (UJC) on August 31, 1972, submitted "a petition signed by over 800 members of local 7 to President Bill Gilbert calling for a special meeting to deal with problems," Gilbert refused to accept it.[109] Not surprisingly, then, as safety conditions did not improve, and as worker injuries mounted, UAW members came increasingly to believe that their leaders' efforts were completely inadequate. As one worker with a pregnant wife and five children, Nathaniel Williams, wrote to UAW President Leonard Woodcock in 1973:

> I was under the impression that the union (UAW) was establish to protest the inalienable rights of its individual members from certain injustices related to his employment. . . . But from what I have seen and for what I have had to endure from the inadequacies of the union—have cause me to believe the relationship the higher union officials has with the lower union members, is that of being the other end of the company's VISE by which workers are . . . SQUEEZED INTO THE MIDDLE WITHOUT RETRIBUTION.[110]

Worker Beulah Wallace voiced a similar sentiment in another letter to Woodcock: "I cannot get representation from the local union . . . when I ask my foreman to call my committeeman, he just laughs at me and tells me to catch the committeeman at the coffee machine. . . . What is happening to the U.A.W., which at one time under President Walter Reuther was one of the greatest unions in the free world?"[111]

As a result of such hazardous conditions on Detroit's shop floors, as well as workers' growing perception that the UAW was still not tackling plant problems aggressively enough, shop-floor dissent did not die with the RUMs. Yet because the union had so heavily attributed shop-floor dissent to the League and the RUMs, it was slow to realize that such dissatisfaction had a life independent of revolutionary black or white agitation. Indeed to the company and the union, the shop-floor labor-relations system, unlike between 1967 and 1971, now seemed to be operating quite smoothly. While each well knew that problems still existed in the auto plants, at least everyone appeared to be following the established rules for addressing them. It was not until March 1973, when a Workman's Compensation Bureau hearing referee ruled on Johnson's claim against Chrysler, that the UAW finally realized how fed up its workers really were with these "rules." The union responded to this realization, however, by gearing up for battle.

Back in 1971, when James Johnson, Jr. retained the services of white radical attorney Ronald Glotta to represent him in his workman's compensation case against Chrysler Corporation, no one could have predicted that his actions would once again shake up Detroit. Chrysler had rejected Johnson's claim outright and, thus, it would be two years before anyone would hear of him again. After years of legal wrangling, however, Glotta and lawyers for Chrysler had the opportunity to present their arguments before a hearing referee of the Workman's Compensation Bureau in a very eerie reprise of the Johnson murder trial. Although Glotta presented much of the same evidence in this hearing as Cockrel had done in the murder trial, including calling many of the same witnesses, Glotta's legal strategy had a slightly different slant.

Whereas attorneys in the murder trial focused on the life history of Johnson, in the compensation case, Glotta honed in far more on the actions of Chrysler. Glotta essentially put the corporation on trial. Using as his legal precedent a case argued in 1960 by attorney Donald Loria, *Carter v. General Motors*, Glotta argued that working at Chrysler, and specifically working under the inhumane conditions and overt racial discrimination that Chrysler condoned, had exacerbated Johnson's precarious mental state and caused him to have a breakdown.[112] In short, Glotta forcefully maintained that Johnson's breakdown was a work-related injury. It was not until the *Carter v. General Motors* case that mental disability qualified for compensation benefits under Michigan law, and Glotta hoped to show that the working and racial conditions at Chrysler indeed had mentally disabled his client.

The details of Johnson's compensation hearing closely mirror those of the murder trial, except that in these proceedings, Johnson's "insanity" came under far more scrutiny than it had in the criminal trial. For starters, Chrysler's lawyers did not allow the psychological evaluations from the defense team in the criminal trial to go unchallenged. These attorneys had Johnson reevaluated by a Dr. Gorden Forrer, who categorically rejected Dr. Clemens Fitzgerald's original diagnosis that Johnson was schizophrenic. Forrer claimed that Johnson had a mere "characterological disorder with paranoid trends," and that his only real problem was that "his psyche causes him to view reality as a racist plot."[113] In Forrer's opinion, Johnson's goal was to "destroy white representatives of society" not because of racist behavior toward him, but because "he views [them] as an extension of the repressive, depriving, threatening authority of his childhood father."[114] Once again, the question was raised whether Johnson was indeed scarred by American racism—in this case imparted by Chrysler—or whether he was simply plagued by an "ever-present race consciousness."[115]

On February 28, 1973, Hearing Referee John J. Conley handed down his ruling. In his twenty-eight-page landmark decision, Conley, whom Glotta described as a "liberal with a good heart," ruled in favor of Johnson, ordering Chrysler to pay compensation benefits to him. Additionally, Conley ordered that "said defendant shall furnish, or cause to be furnished to said employee, medical (including psychiatric treatment and counseling and group therapy as recommended by Dr. Fitzgerald in his testimony.)"[116] To justify his decision, Conley outlined the various events at Eldon relating to Johnson's breakdown, including the fact that on the day of the murders Johnson had been told to go to work in "the dirtiest, the hottest, hardest, and most menial in the department . . . and he believed that he had by hard and meritorious service worked his way out of such a job."[117] When he was suspended for not going to that job, Conley concluded, Johnson believed that he had been fired. As Conley put it, Johnson "was convinced his persecutors had won and when he shot the three men he was acutely and overtly psychotic. . . . [H]is actions were not the actions of a sane criminal."[118] In his concluding remarks, Conley stated that although the case had received "considerable publicity and created considerable interest in it, such tragic results, of an employment caused or aggravated mental illness, does not in any way change the legal issues, or influence, or affect plaintiff's entitlement to workman's compensation."[119] Conley then awarded Johnson workman's compensation benefits of $75 per week, dating back to the day of his "injury"—the day of the murders—July 15, 1970.

From the moment that he heard about Conley's decision, Johnson tried to distance himself from the media hype surrounding it. "I am no hero," he said. "I never wanted to be a hero. I just wanted to be left alone to do my job and make an honest living. . . . [I]t was either that job or I went on welfare."[120] Johnson's attorney, however, deliberately highlighted the controversial implications of his client's case. As Glotta told the *Detroit Free Press,* "this landmark decision is a direct indictment of the racism and inhuman working conditions at Chrysler. Chrysler pulled the trigger which resulted in Johnson's insanity and the death of three men."[121] In another press release, Glotta pointed out that "the workman's compensation decision shifts the burden of economic responsibility from the tax payers of Michigan, who have been paying for Johnson's incarceration and treatment, to the real culprit, Chrysler Corporation."[122]

In light of speeches such as Glotta's, and anticipating the outrage of many conservative Detroiters with the workman's compensation ruling, Ernie

Fackler, Director of the Michigan Bureau of Workman's Compensation, stated that although "it appears the state is giving cash to criminals . . . we are not condoning his crimes, which are serious indeed. But we are saying that this man was mentally disabled, in part, due to his job."[123] He went on to say that "this was an especially agonizing decision because of the less than aggressive defense put up by the Chrysler Corporation. In fact they said nothing to refute the facts in this case."[124] But statements like Fackler's, and even articles in national publications like the *Wall Street Journal,* which suggested that this ruling had "carefully separated the killings from the workman's compensation issue,"[125] had virtually no impact on the storm of criticism that followed the Conley ruling.

Some critics of the Johnson ruling placed as much blame on Chrysler as on the liberal official who had handed it down. As an editorial in the *Detroit News* put it, while Conley's decision took Detroit back to the "dark ages," "Chrysler's non-defense in this case is almost as shocking as the final judgement." The *Detroit News* editorialized that "Chrysler Corporation, for whatever internal corporate reasons, has done a disservice to business in Michigan and the employment of many disadvantaged workers."[126] Most critics of the Conley decision were not as restrained, however. To them, his decision was "a ruling against reason," and they suggested further that "for the sake of common sense, this ruling needs reversing."[127] Indeed, to conservative white Detroiters, Conley's decision was not just a blow to Chrysler; it was the most offensive example to date of liberals catering to blacks in the city's legal system. In their minds, the Johnson compensation ruling, following as it did a string of equally "outrageous" legal maneuvers since 1969, was final confirmation that black interests had superseded white in Detroit.[128]

Whites in Detroit's surrounding suburbs were equally incensed and surprised by the Johnson ruling. As a letter to a newspaper in the virtually all-white Macomb County noted, "Ever since we read last week about the horrendous decision imposed on Chrysler Corporation . . . we have wondered if sanity and justice prevail anymore anywhere. . . . [I]t wouldn't be out of order either to have the Bureau examine the credentials of its hearing referee."[129] More than all of the other controversial legal decisions between 1969 and 1973, the Johnson compensation ruling had given substance to the lofty liberal principle of "reparations." It had not been particularly threatening when liberal leaders had espoused the *principle* of reparation, but when "reparations" meant dollars in compensation payments, white conservatives were incensed.

According to one auto industry scholar, the Johnson verdict had particularly "ugly overtones among white workers."[130] But in fact, there were white workers who could see that something positive might be made of Johnson's unprecedented compensation award. Maybe, they thought, the UAW would use this case as ammunition in its battle to clean up the auto plants. Indeed, not a few workers at Chrysler held this hope. But the UAW was not at all inclined to do this. From its perspective, anything connected to Johnson seemed only to be a lightening rod for shop-floor destabilization and an erosion of its authority.

Back in July 1970, when James Johnson actually had committed the murders, the union had been noticeably silent on the matter.[131] Embroiled as it was in the election battles with DRUM and ELRUM, the union did not want to call further attention to Johnson, as he was so popular with the plant dissidents. It irritated local union leaders immensely that shop-floor militants were "playing brother Johnson up as a hero." Leaders of Local 961 pointed out that "this local union believes that brother Johnson was sick" and that the attention on him was creating "a false image of your local union [and of the] working conditions in the Chrysler Eldon Avenue Axle Plant."[132] It also troubled union officials that, after the murders, line foremen reported that workers were saying things like "this evens things up" and seemed to be proud that foremen were now afraid of them.[133] Such fallout was precisely what local union leaders wanted no part of. They thought that the hype around the Johnson case would simply fade away, especially after the RUMs were ousted from the plants. But when Johnson's compensation ruling made headlines in March 1973, many workers, both black and white, believed that their complaints about the conditions in the plants had finally been validated. By 1973, numerous autoworkers could agree with a legal spokesman who said that "it is hoped that the Johnson case will become the spearhead for a new effort to improve working conditions not only at the Eldon Plant but in all the plants in the United States," and that "this victory can become even more meaningful if it is seen as the result of a united effort by many people and [it is] used to launch an even greater effort to fight the very conditions which drove James Johnson to the insane act of shooting and killing three other employees."[134]

Disgruntled workers who had been relatively silent for the previous two years were energized by Johnson's victory in 1973. When a radical group called the Motor City Labor League put out a leaflet exclaiming that "the James Johnson case is a victory for all of us. WE SHOULD TAKE ADVANTAGE OF IT,"[135] its message found receptive ears. Six days after the verdict, three autoworkers fired from the Eldon plant for wildcatting in 1969—Jordan Sims, John Taylor, and Fred Holsey—wrote to UAW president Leonard Woodcock saying they wanted to meet with him to reevaluate their own discharges. They told Woodcock, "we were fired because we fought the conditions which Chrysler has chosen to maintain at the Eldon Plant which led to the psychotic breakdown of Mr. Johnson and the death of three fellow employees. . . . [T]he recent Johnson decision is a vindication of the position we took prior to our discharges."[136] On March 15, these workers also wrote to the *Detroit Free Press:* "We are dismayed at your recent editorial regarding the James Johnson workman's compensation decision. . . . [W]ith humane, nondiscriminating employment practices, Chrysler would still have four good tax paying workers at the Eldon Plant."[137]

Although the UAW leadership considered itself to be a pillar of the liberal coalition in the city that clearly welcomed the implications of the Johnson award, labor liberals did not see the Conley ruling in a similarly positive light. Indeed Sims, Taylor, and Holsey met with so little success in their meeting with Woodcock that the next day they decided to try talking to another UAW leader, Douglas Fraser. In their meeting with Fraser the trio discussed not only their specific discharges but also problems with the UAW contract. Sims wanted the UAW to push for inclusion of Section 502 of the National Labor Relations Act in the upcoming contract. As Section 502 stated, "nor shall the quitting of labor by an employee or employees in good faith because of abnormally dangerous conditions for work at the place of employment of such employee or employees be deemed a strike," and Sims felt that workers desperately needed such powerful language in their agreement with Chrysler.[138] But having recently spent so much energy to bring about Sims's defeat in the 1971 election at Local 961, the UAW was reluctant to see the Johnson ruling as an opportunity to push for his reinstatement, and union leaders certainly were not going to take seriously his suggestions regarding contract language or bargaining strategy.

But Sims was not the only Detroit autoworker who saw the Johnson decision as an opportunity for the union to push the company or the labor relations system in more worker-oriented directions. Only days before Conley announced his decision in the Johnson case, a group of workers at Chrysler's Jefferson Avenue assembly plant had become fed up with the conditions there and decided to walk out in protest. These workers were still out on a wildcat days later when Conley announced his ruling and they felt a surge of optimism that their union would authorize their illegal strike since it was over many of the same issues that had broken James Johnson. They knew it would not be unheard of for the UAW to call such a strike during the term of the contract, as it had done just that in the highly public Lordstown strike of 1972.[139] But the leadership of Jefferson Local 7 did not support its workers. Instead, on March 8, 1973, local union officials issued the leaflet "Walk outs: unauthorized strike must stop!!!"[140] and looked on as Chrysler subsequently fired several of the Jefferson workers who had wildcatted.

Because of its bitter and recent battles with the RUMs between 1968 and 1971, the UAW was immediately hostile to the dissent and militancy it saw resurfacing in 1973. Union leaders saw a revolutionary black nationalist agenda behind every shop-floor push to humanize the plant or to liberalize the labor relations system, and they were determined not to facilitate that agenda at all costs. Even though top union leaders knew that it was generally in their interest to address the issues that created shop-floor dissent, in 1973, they ignored this wisdom.[141] Blinded by political paranoia, the union opted to block dissent at every turn. In fact, the militancy among autoworkers in 1973 was not born of black nationalist agitation. By that year, autoworker dissent had become broad-based, multiracial, and politically diverse. Ironically, like its liberal counterparts in the city, the union leadership could have embraced its members' energy and determination without compromising its beliefs.

As union leaders might have remembered, there had in fact been a biracial and broad-based group of dissidents in the auto plants who were not affiliated with the RUMs for a long time. While workers attracted to the politics of black nationalism and revolution joined the RUMs between 1968 and 1971, others had been joining the United National Caucus (UNC) and its various offshoots in plants around Detroit. As the RUMs' presence declined in the plants, the UNC only grew. The UNC and its affiliated groups were attractive to workers primarily because they agitated very effectively and consistently around the issue of workplace safety. They published informative newsletters such as the *Mack Safety Watchdog* and the *United Justice Train,* which kept workers apprised of the many hazards on the shop floor and instructed them of their rights under their contract. The July 1972 issue of the *United Justice Train,* for example, reported that "worn out sockets slip off the bolts, peeling skin off the knuckles. . . . Overhead motors are fastened to the cables with homemade wore gadgets. When these slip off it means a broken head for whoever is underneath."[142]

The UNC had always welcomed both black and white trade union activists, and while it was extremely critical of the racism in the plant and agitated against it, it never espoused black nationalist rhetoric so politically moderate black workers could participate comfortably. It was not that the UNC had been hostile to the black nationalists and revolutionaries in the RUMs when they launched workplace protests. Indeed, the UNC often courted RUM support as it clearly did during the election at Local 961 in 1971. But the relationship between the RUMs and the UNC had nevertheless been fraught with tension. While the RUMs often saw the UNC as bourgeois opportunists, the UNC felt that the RUMs were making a huge tactical mistake by not including whites and not attempting to reform, rather than overthrow, the UAW. Although the UNC did not like UAW policies any better than the RUMs did, it did support the institution of the UAW and wanted to bring it back to its earlier, more militant days.

But the UAW did not take the UNC at its word, nor did it understand that the UNC's appeal was growing among Detroit's autoworkers. Indeed, while UNC co-chair Sims had lost to McKinnon in the May 1971 runoff election at Local 961, Sims had received 1,142 votes to McKinnon's 1,178, indicating the considerable support he enjoyed even in that early year. But because the UAW leadership did not recognize the key differences between the UNC and the RUMs, when the RUMs fell apart after 1971, the union leadership mistakenly assumed that the support for activists like Sims also would fizzle.

Workers' support for the UNC, and for UNC representatives like Jordan Sims, only spread after 1971. Between 1971 and 1973, the UNC managed not only to win over many more shop-floor workers, but it also began to work with many of the remaining black and white revolutionary activists whenever a major dispute with the company or the union erupted. Black radicals, for example, had come to respect the UNC for its active support of black workers in their confrontations with foremen. When black worker Tilden Engle shot his foreman, Regis Lantz, in Chrysler's Jefferson plant, the remaining black nationalists stood by him, but so did the UNC. As the January 1973 *United Justice Train* put it, "maybe the important question is: why does a worker become so desperate that he can think of no solution except shooting a foreman? The answer to that question is that the worker has no confidence in the willingness or ability, of Local 7 in particular, to deal with his problems."[143] White leftists also grew more willing to work with the UNC because, as members of the International Socialists put it, "the UNC has regularly propagandized against racism and unemployment" and "is still the only cross-local oppositional group that exists inside the UAW."[144]

This new cooperation between various dissident strains within the plant was born not only of necessity but also of a significant ideological shift within the minds of the remaining RUM activists. With the League in tatters, many black labor militants in 1973 began to reconsider their previous position of refusing to work with whites. As the remaining members of the Jefferson assembly plant RUM eventually decided, "we must refuse to fight our own class allies,"[145] and they began to call "for the unity of the working class against the capitalist class."[146] The RUM members remaining at Chrysler's Dodge Truck plant also had changed their view on working with whites: "The old RUM movements had a very positive aspect in that they organized workers into a force to get something done. But why didn't the RUM movement last? . . . [Y]ou just can't organize black workers alone because white, arab, Mexican, Puerto Rican, etc. all workers' face the same conditions as black workers . . . the new RUM movements understand that it's not just a black-white struggle . . . but a struggle between the classes."[147] Over time, many original RUM members even began to support the UNC's position on the need for claiming, rather than rejecting, the UAW as an institution. Some remaining RUMs, such as JARUM, actually decided to place the UAW insignia on the masthead of their dissident paper. As members of JARUM told fellow workers, "it is your union and it is my union. We see that we can run it together and we must run it together."[148]

Equally significantly, by 1973, white leftists in the plant also became more vocal about their long-held position that the struggle in the plants should be understood as a worker, not purely a black liberation, enterprise. While it was far easier for dissidents to work together across racial and political lines in 1973 than it had been in 1967, this did not mean that there were still no serious political differences between the UNC, the remaining RUM activists, and the white leftist dissidents. Indeed, as some members of the virtually all-white International Socialists saw it, "without any question, the UNC might tomorrow become an obstacle."[149] It did mean, however, that shop-floor dissent over the poor working conditions and racism in the plants was now grounded in coalition efforts. As the UJC wrote, "we workers often are divided along race, age, and sexual lines [but] . . . those divisions serve only to weaken us."[150]

And indeed the shop-floor dissent that began to grow after 1971 was remarkably broad-based. On February 6, 1972, for example, the UNC held a "conference on racism" at a local union hall that attracted approximately 200 representatives from various organizations, including the remnants of the League, to educate people about racism in the economy, on the shop floor, in the community, and in the labor movement. These conference attendees also sought to pass resolutions on what should be done about inequality and discrimination. When some who still called themselves League members asked conferees also to endorse a resolution that workers must "overthrow the bourgeois state and fight for socialism and communism," members voted it down, and the "resolution that was adopted was similar to the one proposed originally by the UNC leadership, speaking to workers' control of their working conditions."[151] In January 1973, another "rank and file caucus" of both black and white workers from numerous political camps came to discuss "the unwillingness and inability [of the UAW] to provide a winning strategy for the battles we face."[152] At this event, as at others, the UNC wanted "to make one thing clear. We're not trying to 'wreck the UAW' [UAW president] Woodcock and company are doing a good job of that. We're trying to make the UAW stop serving the company and start serving the workers."[153]

Still, UAW leaders continued to believe that the post-1971 dissent was orchestrated by outside revolutionary activists, particularly because plants like Jefferson assembly had been idled by at least four work stoppages since January 1973.[154] Even though it was the UNC at Jefferson that routinely engaged in shop-floor protests in which "workers black and white, young and old, male and female, demonstrated the kind of militancy and solidarity necessary to defend us from corporate abuse," the union simply could not believe that it was witnessing legitimate worker protests against the speedup and unsafe conditions that existed in every plant by that year.[155] And although UNC members continually told UAW leaders that it was "not a political group" or "a substitute for a political party," the UAW decided that the UNC was indeed composed of socialist and communist agitators and soon began keeping tabs on the UNC almost as vigorously as it had on the RUMs [156] UAW leader Emil Mazey sent Ken Morris a letter in which he enclosed "a Caucus letter from Local 7, which you should find of interest."[157] Later that year, George Merrelli sent Douglas Fraser a letter with a paper "attached which is probably an advanced copy of a letter which is to appear in the United National Caucus Newspaper. Thought it might be of interest to you."[158] Perhaps Merrelli sent this letter to Fraser because union official Walter Wallers already had written to him saying, "George, I have talked to you before about this situation. I feel that Jordan Sims is making Local 961's Hall a haven for United Caucus headquarters."[159]

While UAW officials found it hard to believe that shop-floor dissent was now politically broad-based, they found it equally hard to believe that the dissent could be biracial. But the shared enemy of inhumane speedup, overtime, and horrible working conditions had managed to unite Detroit's blacks and whites in common cause. After 1971, Detroit's autoworkers could see their shared class interests on the shop floor in ways that they still could not in their neighborhoods. As Detroiter Roger Robinson put it, "I think the brutality of the auto industry caused people in this geography to recreate community. Even with the racism and the craziness, you go into most plants and the black workers and the white workers generally look out for one another. . . . [T]here's a political subculture in the industrial unions where coalitions are made based on real power. And they don't even necessarily *like* each other."[160]

Indeed, between March 1973, when the Johnson compensation ruling sparked workers' hopes that the UAW would push the company to clean up its plants and tackle shop floor racism there, and May 1973, a formidable biracial dissident force emerged. UNC leaders had managed to package their plan for leading the labor movement in a way that blended every worker's desire for more shop-floor power with the desires of black workers in particular for more racial equality in the plants. In 1973, the UNC articulated the inexorable connection between these goals, and its commitment to them, by demanding that "iron clad provisions must be written into the next contract that prohibit all discriminatory hiring, promotion, and upgrading policies" and "that our union fight for workers control over production standards."[161] Such UNC rhetoric won it a great deal of respect from line workers. As one worker, Willie F. Pride, wrote, "what the *Justice Train* stands for is good. . . ."[162] And as a result of worker support, Jordan Sims, the UNC co-chair and longtime nemesis of UAW officials, won the presidency of Local 961 in May 1973.[163] As scholar Dan Georgakas explains, "Jordan Sims, even after being fired in 1970 for his shop floor agitation, went to union meetings regularly and organized his forces as he might have had he still been working in the plant."[164]

Sims's ascendancy to the presidency of Local 961 reflected not only the newfound power of shop-floor dissidents but also the changed nature of that dissent. Sims was neither a revolutionary nor an outside agitator: He was a trade union reformer who believed that the union still could and should stand behind its workers and fight aggressively for their rights. Again, however, UAW leaders did not take Sims's victory as their cue to become more militant; rather they saw his win as evidence that union control was once again slipping into the hands of a radical sect. After Sims's win relations between the UAW and its rank and file only deteriorated further.

By the summer of 1973, as heat and speedup took their toll, workers dramatically escalated their attack on union leaders for the way they dealt with the company. Of course, the UAW had tried to rein in management when conditions got particularly bad, but it was still not willing to halt production. And this is what workers now believed was the only way to force the company's hand. When the UAW's promises of change were no longer enough, its own rank and file at Chrysler once again exploded. Between July 24 and August 13, 1973, autoworkers rocked Chrysler and the UAW with two of their most dramatic wildcat strikes to date. These walkouts, at Chrysler's Jefferson Avenue Assembly and at Detroit Forge, respectively, were sparked by the same issues of workplace racism and intolerable working conditions that had been causing wildcats since 1968 and had fueled the broad-based dissident movement that put Sims in power in 1973. Wildcatting was not the chosen strategy of all workers in 1973, but by that year, if a handful of dissidents initiated a work stoppage, other workers readily went out with them.[165] As Georgakas noted about the 1973 wildcats, "The most significant aspect of these strike[s] was that black radicals had maintained a working alliance with white, mainly Polish workers, something that had not occurred at Dodge Main in 1968, at Eldon in 1969–70 or at the Chrysler Sterling Stamping Plant where white workers had rebelled in a week long wildcat over working condition grievances similar to those voiced by DRUM and ELRUM."[166]

The Jefferson wildcat began on July 24 at 6 a.m., when Isaac Shorter, a twenty-six-year-old black migrant from Mississippi, and Larry Carter, a black twenty-three-year-old from Florida, locked themselves in a six-foot power cage in the metal body shop where they worked. They cut off the power to the feeder lines that ran through their department and demanded the immediate discharge of their white foreman, Tom Woolsey, for his allegedly blatant racist practices on the shop floor. Woolsey was despised by many black workers within his department because he had a reputation for belittling black workers by calling them names and by threatening them with bodily harm. He had received five grievances at Jefferson and had already been transferred within the Chrysler system several times.[167]

Trying first to work through the system, Shorter and Carter got 70 percent of their department—214 people—to sign a petition calling for Woolsey's discharge. Carter gave this petition to his union representative so that the he would file a grievance on the workers' behalf. But when nothing happened to Woolsey, Shorter and Carter decided to take matters into their own hands. According to Carter, "I turned my petition in Monday to my Chief Steward, Tom Matthew, and I didn't hear anymore about it, so we had to move to a higher level to demand it."[168] According to Shorter, neither he nor Carter were "members of any party" and neither ever had been a member of a RUM, although they did consider themselves communists.[169] But even though Shorter and Carter were black and were admitted leftists, more than 150 workers surrounded the structure where the duo had barricaded themselves and actually placed their hands on its cable to prevent a Chrysler maintenance crew from removing them from the power cage. As Shorter re-

Supporters of Isaac Shorter and Larry Carter at the Jefferson Avenue assembly plant, July 24, 1973. *Walter P. Reuther Library, Wayne State University.*

ported, "it wasn't just me and Larry—it was the individual thing until we pushed that button, and when we pushed that button in the cage, it became a worker's thing. A people's thing."[170]

It should not have surprised the UAW that these men enjoyed such broad-based support in this plant. As the Jefferson UNC group had noted after another recent work stoppage in the plant, "We workers at Jefferson Assembly often find ourselves divided along race, age and sexual lines. These divisions serve only to weaken us . . . last Friday these divisions broke down. 85% of the workers in Department's 9173 and 9160, and with the support of the rest of the plant, fed up with being treated like children, put down their tools and walked off their jobs. . . . These workers, black and white, young and old, male and female, demonstrated the kind of militancy and solidarity necessary to defend us from corporate abuse. . . . [W]here is our leadership when we need them?"[171] But the union refused to recognize the significance of the biracial cooperation in that wildcat or in Shorter and Carter's July shutdown. Indeed, as Shorter and Carter staged their protest,

Isaac Shorter (left) and Larry Carter at the Jefferson Avenue assembly plant, July 24, 1973. *Walter P. Reuther Library, Wayne State University.*

UAW leaders were making every effort to end the wildcat and "to get Shorter and Carter to leave the cage."[172] But the workers crowding around the cage booed them and told them to leave the area. By midday, Shorter and Carter had expanded their list of demands to include a written guarantee of amnesty for all wildcatters. And, by 7:15 that evening, Shorter and Carter managed to get Woolsey fired and also obtained a written guarantee from Chrysler's plant manager and the production manager that they would not be fired after the wildcat.

The UAW was stunned and appalled by the day's events. It could not believe that the company had capitulated to what it saw as a small group of troublemakers. As Shorter explained in a later interview, "Douglas Fraser said that we were hijackers. We don't consider that we were hijackers for the simple reason that hijacking is an individual thing."[173] Shorter could not fathom why the UAW refused to concede the broad-based worker support that he and Carter's action had received: "The workers supported us, I'd say ninety-five percent. . . . [W]orkers even went to sleep around the cage and ten minutes after we were in the cage workers were bringing us chains, locks, and even wanted to escort us to the bathroom. Workers stayed there with twenty-five years seniority, some of them probably retiring in the next couple of months. They were in there until we got out."[174]

Significantly, after Shorter and Carter's wildcat, the UNC, not a RUM, hosted the victory celebration.[175] Shorter spoke to the politically and racially diverse audience gathered there about the need to stand together to bring better conditions to the plants.[176] Several editorials in the *Detroit Free Press* also reflected the broad-base support that Shorter and Carter enjoyed.[177] Not surprisingly, the UAW was deeply concerned that the actions of Shorter and Carter would only encourage further illegal protests. And in the article "A Precedent in Chrysler Shutdown," the *Detroit News* voiced the same concern. As it turned out, both the UAW and the media were correct. On August 7, 1973, the midnight shift of Chrysler's Detroit Forge plant initiated its own illegal work stoppage.

Of all Chrysler's plants, Detroit Forge had been the site of some of the most intense speedup and forced overtime. For six months, 60 percent of Chrysler's shop-floor employees had been forced to work a seven-day week.[178] Because the plant was running at full productive capacity, there was little time left for cleanup and maintenance, and workers' injuries rose noticeably. In July 1973, worker Harvey Brooks had his arm crushed in a conveyor belt. In August 1973, thirty-five-year-old Tony McJennet had a finger amputated in a faulty crane. Another worker was severely injured when an axle flew off a conveyor belt into his chest, and the next day, management insisted that another worker resume the job on the faulty belt despite the fact that the belt had not been fixed and there was still blood on the equipment.[179] Even though there had been a RUM at Forge called FORUM, by 1973, the horrific safety conditions and work schedules had created a dissident movement much bigger than this RUM ever was. Indeed, in August, Forge workers united across the color line and the political spectrum.

As had been the case at other Chrysler plants across the Motor City, union officials had already tried valiantly to deal with the preponderance of safety hazards at Forge. On July 29, 1973, for example, UAW leader Hank Ghant (undoubtedly spurred on by the July 24 shutdown at Jefferson) personally had toured the Forge facility and was so dismayed by what he found that he attempted to force "management to change and improve conditions."[180] By August 3, however, even he had to concede that management was moving too slowly, so he went straight to members of the UAW national bargaining committee, which was in the process of preparing for the expiration of the National Agreement, and told them that something had to be done. Clearly, however, the workers at Forge were not interested in any more meetings or negotiations. They wanted action.

As soon as the midnight shift walked out, other Forge workers refused to go inside the plant, and by the next day, there were approximately 1,397 workers out on an unauthorized strike. Chrysler's response to the walkout was to file an injunction against the picketers *and* the leaders of UAW Local 47.[181] Embarrassed by such legal censuring, Leon Klea, president of Forge Local 47, instructed these workers to return to work immediately, but he was "jeered and booed and told they weren't going back to work."[182] Klea was convinced that this work protest, like the others before it, had been engineered by outsiders who had, as Douglas Fraser put it, "been reading Marx and Engels."[183] Fraser admonished the wildcatting workers to "repudiate these people who are creating a serious problem at Forge."[184] Angry Forge workers told reporters that Fraser's opinion about the origins of the strike was absurd, and they invited anyone to see the conditions for themselves.[185] Fifteen of the Forge workers who had shut the plant down said in a leaflet that they distributed, "you all know that as members of Local 47 you refused to work in an unsafe plant, and not any militant *or* any other group was behind it."[186]

Despite, and perhaps because of, the union's attempt to discredit the strike through its red-baiting tactics, Forge workers refused to end their wildcat.[187] Instead, they asked the union to call a strike vote to authorize their protest. On August 9, 1973, "an interracial group of about 250 workers consisting mostly of older workers" met with officials from Local 47 to make just such a suggestion.[188] For a time, their request fell on deaf ears, but on August 11, 1973, with the strike continuing unabated, Fraser finally decided to take his own personal tour of the Forge plant. After the tour, Fraser agreed that the conditions there were horrendous. He then told workers that if the company did not clean up its plant, he would authorize a strike vote for the following Friday.[189] For a moment, striking workers at Forge were optimistic that their protests would be legitimized.[190] But when striking workers met with UAW leaders to discuss the vote on August 12, Fraser told them that no strike vote would be authorized until everyone first went back to work. As a special leaflet signed by Fraser, Merrelli, and Klea informed Forge workers, "the UAW is a union that listens and responds to the interests of its membership," and it assured the workers that "progress is being made by the UAW at Detroit Forge."[191]

Indeed, the UAW was addressing working conditions at Forge more aggressively in light of the wildcat. Leaders not only compiled a detailed handwritten account of the health and safety conditions, but they repeatedly brought it to management's attention.[192] Additionally, these leaders sent an urgent telegram to OSHA inspectors requesting a "safety inspection of Chrysler Detroit Forge Plant, which has forced 1500 hundred workers out of the plant with the immediate threat that deadly working conditions may set off a chain reaction that could involve 40,000 other Chrysler workers."[193] The UAW maintained that "management's refusal to correct outrageous conditions is responsible for the plant closings."[194] But when it spoke to Forge's workforce, the union blamed the wildcat on "outsiders [who] have no input or influence upon your grievances nor upon your union."[195]

Understandably, Fraser was very concerned that this unauthorized strike would jeopardize the UAW's bargaining position, as the contract was expiring the next month.[196] Because Chrysler had already fired eighteen workers for participating in the wildcat, however, most strikers were outraged at Fraser's suggestion that they go back to work.[197] But the UAW stood firm and eventually convinced the wildcatters to return.[198] While the workers did go back, they did so with a great deal of resentment. As a *Detroit Free Press* headline put it: "Wildcatters Go Back, but Not Kittenish."[199] After the wildcat was over, the union never authorized the much-awaited strike vote. The Forge wildcat lasted six days and forced Chrysler to cut the production in three of its engine plants by 50 percent. But the UAW did not capitalize on the company's weakened position to demand satisfaction for its constituency. Instead, it stood by the company's ultimatum that anyone who continued to wildcat would be immediately discharged. Reflecting the sentiment of more workers than it probably realized, the *Detroit Free Press* commented that "the UAW was lately known for donning the velvet glove instead of the iron fist."[200]

Despite such media chiding, however, the UAW's leaders were greatly heartened by their success in ending the 1973 wildcats and once gain began to feel optimistic about the future. The UAW had successfully eliminated some of the most dangerous challengers to its authority in the Jefferson and Forge plants and this was no small feat. Labor officials had been in a bitter and protracted war with black and white revolutionaries ever since 1967, and, for a significant period of time, it appeared that they might be losing, particularly as numbers of their politically moderate constituents became increasingly enamored with the determination and direct action activism of those radicals. Rather than attempt to co-opt their enemy or to claim credit for their enemy's inroads against managerial abuses as civic leaders had done with police abuses, labor leaders decided to crush radical dissent by whatever means necessary. After the 1968–71 union elections, it appeared that they had been successful.[201] But as was the case in the city, as long as abuses continued future dissent was almost assured. After 1971, when shop-floor dissent resurfaced as both a biracial and a politically diverse entity, the UAW was most hostile to it. Ultimately the UAW's deep-seated, and historically rooted, opposition to a revolutionary politics blinded it to the legitimacy and potential usefulness of the militancy increasingly exhibited by its own constituency.

Because the UAW successfully quelled shop-floor dissent at Jefferson and Forge, the influence and power of its critics was on the wane by mid-August 1973. The UAW leadership's actions in July and August made it clear to Chrysler's workers that their union would spare no effort to keep them on the job despite their workplace grievances. Although it would take one more major showdown between the UAW leadership and shop-floor workers to decide conclusively who had won the battle for control over the future direction of the labor movement, the events that had transpired at Jefferson and Forge led both black and white radicals, as well as moderates, to suspect that it was highly unlikely that their more militant, anti-management vision would triumph.

8: Urban Realignment and Labor Retrenchment

An End to Detroit's War at Home

Detroit was the future in terms of Black politics.[1]

Whites walked away from this city, literally abandoning all that they had built, rather than make reasonable accommodation.[2]

Instead of harnessing the groundswell of radicalism to strengthen unionism, International officers made common cause with management to suppress it.[3]

While James Johnson's vindication within the workman's compensation system meant a great deal to auto workers, to Johnson, inside the Ionia State Hospital for the Criminally Insane, it meant very little. After May 26, 1971, Johnson was bounced between three mental institutions: the Center for Forensic Psychiatry (CFP), Ionia, and the Ypsilanti State Hospital for the Criminally Insane. Although he connected with the outside world for a moment when his compensation award was announced, by and large, he remained removed from society.[4] But while little changed in Johnson's life after his fifteen minutes of fame in 1973, the city that he had migrated to back in 1953, and the auto industry where he began working in 1968, each underwent a dramatic, and ultimately quite costly, transformation that same year.

By mid-August 1973, Detroit city and labor liberals felt more optimistic about the future than they had in almost a decade. These leaders sensed that they were well on their way to eliminating the most serious barrier to their ability to take Detroit and its labor movement forward. When civic liberals allowed Motor City radicals to push the legal system to its most progressive limits between 1969 and 1973, and when in turn these liberals took credit for every radical courtroom victory, the black community's faith in both liberalism and change "through the system" was renewed. Accordingly, the power of the Detroit's Left began to wither. And, when labor liberals successfully defeated shop-floor black radicals in the electoral arena and then beat back biracial and politically diverse worker dissent in the summer wildcats of 1973, the most serious challenge to their authority and leadership agenda was also similarly on the wane.

In time, however, it became clear that these liberal victories were less conclusive than they first may have appeared. Even without a Left presence in the 1973 mayoral election, civic liberals still faced a serious challenge from conservatives mobilizing on a massive scale to take political control. To defeat this bold challenge, white civic liberals had to accede control of Detroit's liberal coalition to African Americans. And although a black liberal mayor emerged victorious in the 1973 election, the continuous attacks that he endured from racially and politically conservative whites, now residing primarily in the suburbs, made his triumph bittersweet. African Americans finally had real power in Detroit, and liberalism had survived a conservative attack. But because the national conservative war against liberal, and particularly African American, power never ended, Detroit was doomed to experience severe economic distress and social isolation.

Despite the quite different way that they handled their challengers from the Left, labor and civic liberals faced a long-term fate that was similar in key respects. Although labor leaders successfully mounted yet another assault on shop-floor dissent to secure their leadership position in August 1973, their victory soon rang hollow as well. Labor liberals hoped to use their newly secured power to win greater gains from auto companies, but this did not happen. In fact, after 1973, auto companies mounted their own increasingly aggressive attack on the bargaining prerogatives of the UAW, and, having already killed off much of its militant base, the union leadership was in no position to resist this assault. As a result of leadership decisions in the tumultuous period between 1967 and 1973, between 1973 and 1985, Detroit's labor movement suffered a tremendous setback at the hands of management for which workers paid dearly.

* * * *

Without question, Motor City radicals found themselves in a very difficult position by 1973. Because civic liberals, both black and white, were trying to capitalize on their post-1967 victories, the Detroit Left had to decide what position it would take in the upcoming mayoral election. Some leftists argued for entering the electoral process in order to remain a force in shaping the city's future. And because Kenneth Cockrel's courtroom successes had made him a public figure, as well as had amassed him quite a following in the black community, there were serious discussions about a possible Cockrel candidacy for mayor in 1973.[5] The hope among black Detroiters that Cockrel would replace Gribbs as mayor manifested itself in a "Draft Cockrel for Mayor Committee" effort among those who believed that "no other candidate announced or unannounced . . . has displayed the kind of courage, honesty, and dedication to the people of Detroit than Ken Cockrel symbolizes."[6] Accompanying this organized call for Cockrel to enter the race was a stream of letters from ordinary black citizens.[7]

The decision of whether or not to run for mayor was a very difficult one for Cockrel. On the one hand, he genuinely felt that a strong mayor could effect substantive change for the black community and felt as well that it would be much better for Detroit if the future mayor was a leftist, not a liberal. On the other hand, as a revolutionary, Cockrel questioned whether entering the electoral arena might force him to compromise his beliefs and thus preclude his agitation for even more substantial long-term and overarching change. That there was much community support for his candidacy did not alleviate Cockrel's concerns about running for mayor, because the very idea of him running also appalled many black radicals whose views Cockrel respected.[8] An even more important factor to Cockrel was that one of his closest friends, Justin Ravitz, expressed concerns about him entering the race. As Ravitz wrote to Cockrel, "I think this is real—you would run well—and that obviously we would learn a lot thru the entire process too. We've never really measured our support. In a sense the last few years have taught us that in terms of supportive personnel we are sorta thin qualitatively; at the same time I suspect that quantitatively we are some bad motherfuckers. . . . [Nevertheless,] until we have more substantive cadre and programs dispersed thruout the strategic sectors of this city . . . someone would have a helluva burden in persuading me that we have the capacity to do it in a way that makes objective, political sense."[9] In the end, Cockrel agreed with Ravitz's analysis and decided not to run. But while Motor City radicals intensely debated the problems and possibilities of entering a candidate in the upcoming mayoral election, black middle-class liberals wasted no time in trying to capitalize on the renewed community faith in the ballot box.

Determined by 1973 that Detroit would be governed not only by a liberal mayor but specifically by an African American, the black middle class in the city chose its candidate carefully. Sensing the desire in the larger black community for a political figure more daring than Austin had been, black leaders decided that Coleman Alexander Young would fit the bill perfectly. Indeed Young had been in the public eye throughout the 1950s and 1960s but he, unlike Austin, had been a highly controversial figure for most of these years. For example in 1937, when the UAW was engaged in its most bitter battles for union recognition, Young was an organizer for this militant labor organization. And, though he then served in the Air Corps during WWII, his outspoken criticism of racial discrimination in the military, as well as his vocal support of Henry Wallace by 1948, netted him the reputation of troublemaker.

Throughout the decade of the 1950s Young's choice of friends and his organizational affiliations caused many to view him not only as a rabble rouser but, more seriously, as a subversive. And Young certainly did have close relationships with several politically controversial figures such as W. E. B. Du Bois and Paul Robeson. During these years he also lent his hearty support to groups such as the National Negro Labor Council which, by 1951, had been deemed a subversive organization by none other than U.S. Attorney Herbert Bromwell.[10] Although Young stated publicly on numerous occasions, that "I am not now and never have been a member of any organization that was subversive or whose design was to overthrow the United States in any way," many nevertheless considered him to be far on the left of the political spectrum. In 1954, for example, the head of the Detroit office of the FBI wrote to J. Edgar Hoover, noting that "this man is a dangerous individual and should be one of the first to be picked up in an emergency and one of the first to be considered for future prosecution."[11]

But as the 1950s drew to a close Young's political reputation began to change. In 1959 he decided to run for a seat on Detroit's City Council and, though he lost, during his candidacy he became a popular figure among many working-class black Detroiters on the East side of the city. In Young they saw a man with whom they could relate. Never a member of the black bourgeoisie in Detroit, Young was familiar as one who worked numerous menial jobs and thus could understand the needs of ordinary city residents. Grass roots admiration of Young eventually translated into votes, and in 1961 Detroiters elected him as a Democratic candidate for the state constitutional convention. Three years later he won a seat in the Michigan State Senate representing the East Side district of Detroit, and in 1968 he became one of the first black members of the Democratic National Committee. Throughout the 1960s Young also played a prominent role in the NAACP and the American Civil Liberties Union and he worked aggressively to secure a state open housing law as well as to create the Michigan Civil Rights Commission.

Because Young and Jerome Cavanagh shared a deep commitment to civil rights, Young stood firmly behind this white liberal when Detroiters elected him mayor in 1961. But, by 1968, Young's support of the Cavanagh administration had become qualified. As Young put it, "I've been for Jerry [Cavanagh] until recently. . . . But the one thing I've got against him is he has been capitulating to the police."[12] Needless to say, as white liberals geared up for the election of 1969, such pointed remarks made Young less attractive than Austin as a potential candidate.

But Young was not to be deterred from speaking out critically. Indeed as the Cavanagh administration gave way to the Gribbs administration, and as police brutality escalated, state senator Young became even more vocal about the need to rein in the police department. By the early 1970s Young was not only speaking out against police power but he also was arguing publicly that blacks needed a stronger voice within the local liberal coalition. As he saw it, the Democratic Party of Detroit was dependent upon the votes of white and black city residents alike, yet blacks were still second-class citizens within the party. Specifically Young shared the frustration of Detroit's black community that racial discrimination continued to flourish under the aegis of liberal coalition politics in the Democratic Party. When black civil rights leaders in Detroit began looking for a candidate whom they trusted to keep the struggle for racial equality at the fore, who was firmly within the liberal Democratic fold, who was committed to reforming the police department, and whose passion would inspire black voters, Coleman Young was an obvious choice. Young had assured them that he was "a Negro first and a Democrat second."[13]

But as middle-class black liberals mobilized the poor and working-class African American community to support Young, Detroit's white racial conservatives were initiating their own dramatic effort to keep a law enforcement advocate in the mayor's office. Soon they approached none other than Detroit's own police commissioner, John F. Nichols, to run for office. White racial conservatives appreciated Nichols's aggressive stance against crime as well as his staunch defense of the police department's independence. Notably, after the 1967 riot while state senator Young spoke in favor of establishing a civilian review board for the police department, then-superintendent Nichols argued vehemently that the department must have the right to oversee its own affairs.[14] Indeed it was Nichols's vocal protection of the police department in the face of mounting community criticism that made him a natural to become the city police commissioner in 1969. And in turn, Nichols's no-nonsense approach to the maintenance of law and order led him, personally, to create the highly controversial STRESS unit in January 1971. Even though Nichols had never run for political office, and despite the widespread unpopularity of his STRESS unit with the black community of the city, the *Detroit News* opined on October 8, 1973 that "if white voters follow their usual pattern of higher turnout than black voters . . . Nichols will be the next tenant in the Manoogian Mansion."[15] In fact, the Detroit media overestimated how easy a Nichols victory would be, as the well-liked white liberal president of Detroit's City Council, Mel Ravitz, was a top mayoral contender as well.[16]

In August 1973, the *Detroit News* reported that Nichols and Ravitz, not Young, were leading in the mayoral field.[17] Ravitz was very popular, particularly with white liberals from the Cavanagh days, because his election strategy was to "put together a coalition of white and black votes" rather than appeal to one or the other.[18] According to Ravitz, "if this election brings us a mayor who is supportive of only a segment of the community—any segment—then heaven help Detroit . . . because the next four years will be spent in further polarization."[19] This message resonated loudly within powerful liberal institutions, such as the Detroit AFL-CIO, the Detroit Association of Fire Fighters, and AFSCME Council 77, each of which chose to endorse Ravitz in the primary.

Surprising many, however, Ravitz came in third, behind Nichols and Young in the September primary, despite the labor endorsements.[20] As the *Detroit News* put it, "Ravitz's popularity is straining under the weight of the uncertainty and the desire by voters to elect a black candidate."[21] In rejecting Ravitz, black voters made it clear that they still were highly suspicious of white liberals, as they had so recently lost faith in whites' ability to represent them in the Democratic party. In voting for Young, however, black Detroiters had sent the equally strong message that they had not rejected liberalism per se but would now insist that a *black* liberal mayor be at the helm. In this primary, the conservative white voters had made it just as clear that they still opposed a liberal mayor of any color running their city.

Indicating the complex intersections of race and politics in the Motor City by 1973, according to a *Detroit News* poll, Young received 77 percent of the black vote and 15 percent of the white, while Nichols received 13 percent of the black vote and 75 percent of the white. In yet another *Detroit News* poll, Young received 80 percent of the black vote and 21 percent of the white, while Nichols received 9 percent of the black vote and 69 percent of the white.[22] In the primary itself, Nichols received 96,655 votes to Young's 68,075. In citing such figures, however, Detroit's media had overlooked the fact that Ravitz also had done quite well in the primary, receiving 52,527 votes.[23] By turning out in large numbers for Ravitz, white liberals made it clear that they were still committed to running the city in the Cavanagh tradition. Indeed, after their candidate was defeated in the primary, Ravitz voters swung into the Young camp, as their only alternative at that point was Nichols, whom they considered out of the question.

As the Young and Nichols campaigns unfolded after the September primary, it was Young who most defined the election issues. Although Young campaigned for housing reform, educational reform, and other issues that long had been central to blacks and progressive whites alike, his primary pledge to Detroiters was that he would create a "people's police department."[24] According to the Detroit Commission on Community Relations (CCR), so little progress had been made in reforming the DPD because of "evasions in the communication of information by police," and Young was determined to rid the city of such recalcitrant law enforcement personnel.[25]

As a result of Young going public with his police-reform message, before long, police-community relations in Detroit had become the central issue for both candidates. By making law enforcement a campaign focus, Young ran the risk that Nichols would use the bogeyman of escalating "black crime" and would exploit the pervasive argument that such crime must be combated by a stronger police force. In a surprising move, however, it was Young who went on the offensive with regard to crime, leaving Nichols in the curious position of having to argue that Detroit really was not that dangerous. Young challenged Nichols to explain why the level of crime in Detroit was so high, which forced Nichols to defend his own track record as police commissioner. In response, Nichols maintained that "Detroit had been controlling crime and that it had dropped over the last years,"[26] which, ironically, meant that the law enforcement candidate was the one arguing against the popular conservative preoccupation with urban crime. As Nichols told voters, "most of the murders recorded in Detroit are of the type—justifiable homicide and violence among families and friends inside their homes—that could not have been prevented by police, regardless of what they did."[27] When Young pointed to Detroit's high crime figures to argue that the existing law enforcement system was ineffective, he stole Nichols's thunder.[28] Again ironically, Young had capitalized on crime statistics that had been artificially inflated by the police department itself during a vigorous bid, years earlier, for more federal funding.[29] Nevertheless, armed with these figures, Young persuaded many voters on the fence that, while STRESS had contributed immeasurably to the city's racial tensions, it had not solved its crime problem.[30]

Still as election day approached, the outcome remained quite difficult to predict. Both Young's and Nichols' chances depended on how many blacks turned out to vote, on how many liberal whites would in fact vote for Young, and on how many black votes Nichols could win from Young. Significantly, in the September primary, Young had won fewer white votes than had black candidate Austin in the 1969 race which did not bode very well for his chances. On the other hand, Nichols could not rely solely on there being more registered white voters in the city than black to secure his bid for power as his predecessor Gribbs had done. In fact, by election day, the city had 79,624 more registered voters than in 1969 when voters put Gribbs into office and the bulk of these new registrants were African American.[31]

On November 7, 1973, tensions ran high as voters went to the polls. Detroiters waited anxiously for the votes to be tabulated because they knew that this election would change the city forever. When the final ballots were tallied, Young became Detroit's first black mayor, with 233,674 votes to Nichols's 216,933.[32] Significantly, however, because Young had won by a very slim margin, he would face many critics from the moment he took office.

Although Young was victorious because he had put "together a coalition of blacks, unions, and white liberals," the fact remained that the city's racially conservative whites had backed Nichols and were vehemently against a liberal, let alone a black liberal, mayor.[33] Even many pro-Young voters soon found his victory bittersweet. According to radical Detroiters like Gene Cunningham, while Young had needed their support to win office, thereafter "the more radical elements were told 'thanks for your help in getting us here, but we don't need you now.' A lot of us were jettisoned."[34] And even some of the white liberals who had thrown their support behind Young came to feel slighted when he took office. Overnight, white liberals lost the bulk of civic power to the black leaders within the liberal coalition.

But of all Young's critics, white conservatives would prove to be the most troublesome for his administration. As Young prepared to take office on January 6, 1973, he issued "a warning to all dope pushers, rip-off artists and muggers [that] it's time to leave Detroit. Hit the road! . . . I don't give a damn if they're black or white, if they wear super fly suits or blue suits with silver badges."[35] The city's criminal element, of course, did not take Young's victory as its cue to abandon the city, but the city's white racial conservatives did—at least those with the economic means to flee. And for those financially unable to participate in the post-1973 exodus, "There remain[ed] a virulent racial bias that many believe[d] [to be Young's] biggest challenge."[36] As one of Nichols's campaign workers told reporters after Nichols read his concession speech, "The city will go to hell now."[37]

Any blame or credit for Young's victory could not be laid at the doorstep of the UAW. Indeed, the UAW had failed to endorse both Young and Ravitz in the primary as it was expected to do in the summer of 1973. On August 9, at a UAW-CAP (Community Action Program) meeting "marked with controversy" and at which fifty delegates stormed out, the UAW chose to endorse only Ravitz. As Young's campaign manager, Rob Millender, remarked bitterly, "Changing the Union's rules had permitted non-Detroit residents to help endorse Detroit's candidates . . . [and] I think this action tonight was a severe blow to the labor-black coalition we've worked for years to build. . . . [T]he UAW seems to think that endorsing five blacks for the [City] council races (out of nine candidates) is some kind of trade for not endorsing Coleman Young."[38]

But the reality was that in August 1973, the UAW was far more concerned with events taking place on the shop floors than in defending its decision to endorse Ravitz. No sooner had the dust settled at Chrysler's Forge plant than the UAW leadership was faced with yet another unauthorized strike at Chrysler's Mack Avenue stamping plant. But whereas the UAW had been caught offguard in the Jefferson wildcat and had been firm but calm during the Forge wildcat, the Mack strike of August 14 touched a raw nerve in the union leadership, prompting its decision to end work stoppages like this once and for all. By the time the Mack wildcat erupted, union officials had lost any desire they might still have had at Forge to understand the cause of this rash of illegal strikes. And in the Mack wildcat, the union was blinded more than ever by its notion that the dissent in the plant was part of a left-wing conspiracy.

And yet, of the three plants that had recently been plagued by severe labor trouble—Jefferson, Forge, and Mack—Mack was the oldest, dirtiest, and most dangerous plant with the highest number of work-related injuries, and it also had the largest UNC presence. Trouble had been brewing at Mack since at least September 1972, when a die-setter was killed after a bolster plate blew off of a faulty machine, cutting off the top of his head. Then, in early 1973, a woman on the cab-back line had her fingers severed because the machine she was operating had a broken protective guard. On August 4, 1973, a worker in the pressroom lost four fingers because "the automation device that was supposed to remove stock from the press had never been repaired."[39] As had happened in the other auto plants, Mack workers first took their grievances to the union, hoping that it would pressure the company into making their jobs safer. When the grievance procedure did not force management to correct the safety hazards in the plant, however, many on the line turned to UNC publications like the *Mack Safety Watchdog*, which attacked both the company and the union on the issue of safety and educated workers about the plant's unsafe conditions.

But workers did not just read the *Mack Safety Watchdog* and file grievances; they also were willing to initiate work stoppages in areas of the plant that were particularly hazardous or where the speedup was inhumane. In June 1973, just such a walkout occurred after union steward Malcolm Woods had been fired for standing by his worker constituents in a speedup dispute. But even after this wildcat in June, and even with all of the pressure from the UNC, the Mack plant still was known around Detroit as a "hell hole." On August 10, a group of workers from Mack actually picketed leaders at their Local 212 union hall to let them know that, as union members, they wanted a strike vote to be authorized over safety. Because this also netted them little result, on August 14, workers once again decided to take matters into their own hands.

On that day, shortly after the first shift began at 5 a.m., white autoworker Bill Gilbreth and black autoworker Clinton Smith went into the stubs frame-welding department, sat down on the conveyor belt, and deliberately halted production. These two men were members of a tiny leftist organization called the Workers' Action Movement (WAM). Gilbreth had been fired in an earlier seventeen-person walkout over poor ventilation, and, in shutting down the plant on August 14, he and Smith hoped to demand his reinstatement as well as to call attention to the poor working conditions and intolerable speedup at Mack.[40] Even though the political organization that Gilbreth and Smith belonged to had virtually no following in the plant, when they began their sit-down, workers flocked to support them and to protect them from Chrysler's security guards. Shortly after the sit-down began, two plant guards managed to break through the crowd, and a bloody fight began. Security guards Paul DeVito and Gene Prince ended up in the hospital with their injuries. Captain Prince needed 16 stitches to close a head wound and Captain DeVito sustained bruises to the head, neck and shoulder.[41] Meanwhile, the sit-in continued.

By 7 a.m., Chrysler sent home the 2,650 workers from its second shift and called the DPD to come and arrest Gilbreth and Smith. By the time the police arrived, however, so many workers had crowded around the duo that the police were forced to withdraw. One hour later, Gilbreth, Smith, and forty-two other workers, almost all of whom were either members or supporters of the UNC, went to the plant cafeteria to discuss their wildcat strategy. Because many of these striking workers felt that WAM was nothing but an opportunistic group that did not represent them politically, they granted this organization very little role in the strike when the wildcat moved to the cafeteria.[42]

As the wildcatters gathered in the cafeteria, other Mack workers crowded outside the plant gates. And before long, representatives from the International UAW also arrived on the scene. Doug Fraser told the growing crowd of workers outside the plant that the strikers were simply "agitators" who "represent only a very tiny fraction of the total Chrysler workers in the Detroit area and I advocate a policy of no surrender."[43] He then told reporters that the union had "agreed that these people were not going to take our union and the plants where we represent workers."[44] Because two members of WAM had initiated the wildcat, it was easy for the UAW to discount the protest. Fraser truly believed that "an overwhelming majority of the rank and file just won't put up with this nonsense."[45]

But as some workers remained on strike in the cafeteria, workers outside the plant circulated a leaflet informing the UAW that "it was not WAM or any other organization that caused the struggle, but rather the anger of Mack workers at our unsafe and inhumane working conditions."[46] These workers recognized the danger of the UAW insisting that the strike was the work of a few radicals: "we know why our enemies try to say the whole thing was caused by a few troublemakers. They do this to discredit us. They are trying to hide the fact that it was a genuine worker's protest against the unbearable conditions in the plant."[47] They reminded those at both Chrysler and UAW headquarters that:

> Time and again workers have come to union officials and asked for help with our problems. All we ever hear in return is that we should go back to work and let the officials take care of things. People have been getting fired; conditions have been getting worse—and nobody feels they have anywhere to turn for help. This is what caused the situation at Mack and not a few outside "trouble-makers."[48]

But these words fell on deaf ears. The union leadership had been watching WAM for a while, and it was not inclined to shift its focus now. On June 12, 1973, for example, UAW leader E. J. Morgan had given Irving Bluestone, Ken Bannon, and Doug Fraser a report on WAM, along with copies of their literature.[49] During the Mack wildcat, the union refused to concede that, had it not been for conditions in the plant, WAM could not have initiated anything. Indeed, the union did not recognize the significance of the fact that, even more than at Jefferson and Forge, Mack was a UNC stronghold, and thus dissent there was both indigenous and broad-based. But even if it had recognized that the UNC, not WAM or a RUM, held sway at Mack, it would have mattered very little, for UAW officials consistently refused to believe the UNC's vehement claim that "we are not a political group, nor are we a substitute for a political party."[50] To the horror of Mack workers, the union did not object when the company decided to call in sixty Detroit police officers in full riot gear to forcibly evict the wildcatters from the plant. By the time the police stormed the plant, in a battalion led by Commissioner Nichols himself, there were only fourteen strikers still in the cafeteria. Twenty-eight others had already gone outside to generate support.[51] When the DPD set upon the strikers remaining inside the cafeteria, sheer chaos ensued.[52] Within minutes, the police had succeeded in evicting the wildcatters, but only a few hours later, they were shocked to see that even though the cafeteria sit-in was over, the Mack wildcat was not.

As Detroit police officers began to leave the scene of the wildcat, the many Mack workers who had been outside the plant descended on their union hall. Once there, a stormy meeting unfolded between union officers and the Mack rank and file. The president of the local, Hank Ghant, pleaded with workers to go back to their jobs and let the union deal with the company on the question of safety. But according to the *Detroit News*, "during the meeting dissidents and their sympathizers shouted down local and International officers who urged them to return to work, and [they] voted to continue their unauthorized walkout."[53] The meeting ended with the workers vowing to picket the plant the next morning despite the refusal of their union leaders to support them. To UAW officials, the Mack workers were out of control. Because they suspected the political motives of these workers, and because they saw worker actions as part of a conspiracy to disrupt plants all over the city and unseat the UAW, union leaders believed it was now time to end this kind of dissent once and for all.

After the August 15 meeting between the union leaders and the rank and file of Local 212, the UAW International decided to contact union officials from locals all over Detroit to assist in its efforts to end the strike at Mack. The next morning, at 4:30 a.m., one thousand union officials met at the Local 212 union hall and began to map out their strategy for ending the wildcat. With baseball bats, pipes, and an assortment of other weapons in hand, union leaders listened to many an inflammatory speech by their International leaders. For example, Emil Mazey, UAW secretary-treasurer, reportedly told the crowd, "they [the strikers] are a bunch of punks, [and] we are not going to let them destroy everything we've built."[54] Then, as dawn broke, the assembled union officials marched in groups of 250 to each of the four Mack gates and began to attack the picketing workers there. Within minutes, the Mack plant became the scene of a bloody fight between UAW leaders and UAW members.[55] These union leaders "reportedly chased

Gilbreth from the Canfield gate to the parking lot [where they] tackled him and punched him repeatedly until some of his supporters arrived."[56]

By early morning on August 16, the UAW had successfully broken the Mack wildcat. The irony that the union itself had physically ended the strike was lost on no one. Editors of the radical paper the *Black Voice* noted that a UAW "goonsquad" had broken the strike at Mack.[57] And Bill Bonds, a newscaster from WXYZ Channel 7, commented publicly that this had been "the first time in the history of the UAW [that] the union mobilized to keep a plant open."[58] After the melee at Mack, the commander of the DPD's Fifth Precinct was heard telling UAW officials, "I'm glad we're on the same side."[59] UAW leaders proudly told reporters that they were on call twenty-four hours a day to go to any other auto plant that workers might decide to disrupt.[60]

Although the events at Mack had greatly shaken the UAW leadership, union leaders were certain that they had acted appropriately. At a September 5 meeting of the UAW's International Executive Board, Ken Morris spoke directly about the wisdom of the UAW's decision to keep the Mack plant open.[61] A UAW leaflet circulated after the wildcat also made it clear that officials stood firmly behind their actions, and that they were thoroughly persuaded firmly that members of WAM had been behind the entire debacle. As UAW leaders Doug Fraser, Ken Morris, Hank Ghant, Joe Zappa, Bill Marshall, and Steve Despot wrote, "only the strong showing of support by over 1,000 UAW members put a stop to WAMs picketing so [that] any workers who wanted to go to work could do [so]—and they did."[62]

Just as the UAW leadership was unapologetic about its victory in 1973, so was the Young administration. Indeed, the tremendous hostility of white racial conservatives that he often endured did not cause Young to waver from the political agenda that he had outlined in his campaign. Young continued to embrace the programmatic agenda of the Great Society while infusing it with even more deliberate measures to promote racial equality. Young knew that voters had elected him precisely because he had long supported many key liberal initiatives. With regard to public aid, for example, Young had gone on record saying that "all welfare assistance should be extended and received AS A MATTER OF SOCIAL RIGHT. I am opposed to any and all efforts to degrade the recipients of public assistance and to their use as forced labor."[63] Indeed while he was a state senator Young was an outspoken supporter of a controversial bill designed to raise benefits to families on ADC.[64] Likewise he had made his support of broad-scale integration initiatives equally clear early on in his career. When he supported a Fair Housing Ordinance in Detroit Young argued forcefully that "segregation in the schools can never be eliminated while segregated housing is allowed to exist."[65] Young also played a vital role in enacting Michigan's abortion law while in the state senate. And, to his critics' dismay, Young did not waiver from these sixties-style liberal views even when the national political context in which he was trying to promote them grew increasingly inhospitable. Indeed he actively argued that the programmatic agenda of the Great Society, infused with far more deliberate measures to promote racial equality, was still a viable means to improve Detroit.

True to this perspective, once in office, Young decided to tackle the issue most burning among his constituents—deteriorating police-community relations—first by dismantling STRESS and restructuring the force in a more citizen-friendly direction and then by wielding the weapon of integration even when affirmative action was coming under severe attack elsewhere in the country. Young was as angered as his constituents that the DPD's STRESS unit had initiated four hundred warrantless raids within its previous thirty-three months of operation and had killed twenty-two citizens.[66] The fact that STRESS's most recent violence was aimed at fourteen-year-old Glenn Smith, fifteen-year-old Anthony Moorer, and a woman named Jewel Denice Gant only made Young more determined to put an end to the DPD's undercover decoy operations.[67] Young, whose office now wielded more power as a result of a recent revision of the City Charter, not only eliminated STRESS, but he also called for the establishment of fifty police mini-stations intended to be "open seven days a week, and will have one police officer, one police reservist, an officer trainee, and a citizen on duty [and] . . . each station will have a marked, equipped police car for emergency neighborhood response."[68]

By including citizens in his new initiatives to improve police efforts to serve the community, Young was deliberately embracing a liberal strategy for structuring law enforcement that heralded back to the days of Cavanagh's reformer police commissioner, George Edwards. By 1974, however, Young was well aware that such citizen-oriented law enforcement reforms would only work if the DPD itself was comprised equally of both black and white Detroiters. Thus, immediately after taking office, Young began the process of fully integrating the police force with his Executive Order number 2.[69] The mayor justified his integration efforts by noting that, as late as 1972, the 5,558-member force still was only 15 percent nonwhite, and he believed that "when the police department is fully integrated, all segments of the community will have a chance to feel more directly involved in the department because their sons and friends will be a part of the force."[70] Although Young retained white police chief Phillip Tannian, he quickly appointed a new body of police commissioners, three out of four of whom were African American, and eventually Detroit boasted a black police chief as well. Gradually, Young achieved a far more race- and gender-integrated police department than had any mayor before him. By 1981, 1,126 out of 5,013 police officers were African American, and 10 of the 20 police commanders were black as well. Whereas women comprised only 2 percent of the department in 1967, by 1987 they made up a full 20 percent of the force and, in addition, there were three female commanders and a female deputy chief.[71]

But Young did not rest with integrating the DPD alone. He also paved the way for countless African Americans to become heads of key city agencies and to staff these units in unprecedented numbers. He eventually would also "set a national record for awarding contracts to minority firms."[72] The fact that Young largely succeeded in his attempts to integrate Detroit, and also to bolster several Great Society initiatives for the city's poor, only affirmed his supporters' belief that liberalism was a sound political philosophy. Even though the federal government was busily dismantling Great Society programs like Model Cities throughout the 1970s and 1980s, Detroiters' voting behavior indicates that they still were optimistic about the possibilities embedded within LBJ's Great Society vision.[73]

Such optimism was only fueled as Young also embarked on several new projects designed to revitalize the city's economy and improve its image during his first and second terms. Not only did he build many new parks and recreation centers, and erected both low-income housing units and even a downtown Civic Center, in 1976 he also proudly unveiled a huge hotel, office, and shopping complex on the city's riverfront. This massive project, architecturally similar to the Peachtree Center in Atlanta, was appropriately named the Renaissance Center. Young intended it to draw both tourists and new businesses into Detroit. He also hoped to make Detroit thrive when, in 1977, he built the Joe Louis Arena and managed to keep Detroit's hockey team from moving to the suburbs. That same year, Young also purchased Tiger Stadium so that Detroit's major league baseball team would remain in the inner city.

Unfortunately for the Young administration, and thus for Detroit, the mayor's ambitious urban renewal projects did not offset the hostility of racially conservative whites. As Wilbur Rich has noted, many such whites "believed that Young would treat them like second-class citizens. This misconception among whites came from the belief that a black mayor cannot be even-handed in his approach to racial issues."[74] Clearly, Young did not remove all whites from positions of power. Not only did whites continue to comprise the majority of the DPD, but in Detroit's fire department, whites still made up to 90 percent of the highest-ranking uniformed officers and 51 percent of the 1,697 firefighters by the close of the 1980s.[75]

But as Young's mayoralty unfolded, conservative white hostility to him and to Detroit only grew. Perhaps not surprisingly, the city's white police officers were most vocal about their disgust with Young. In May 1975, "close to 1,000 white officers picketed the federal building" when Young's affirmative action plans for the city were being announced.[76] In addition to engaging in such protests, Young's police officers routinely lampooned and criticized him in the Detroit Police Officers Association publication *Tuebor*. Even though 90 out of 170 police promotions in 1976 had gone to white officers, the police still despised Young.[77] As officers Ron Jones and Ron Sexton had put it even before Young took office, "four years of Coleman Young and the animals would eat the buildings down to their foundations."[78] And when Young did become mayor and then insisted that all Detroit police officers actually live in the city that they policed, Officer Carl Parsell wrote, "I guess what the ol' boy means is that if you work in a sewer, you have to 'reside' in a sewer."[79]

But these white police officers were not the only ones hostile to living in Detroit after it came under black leadership. As Young began a second term as mayor, whites' hostility to his rule had escalated to such a degree that their ongoing exodus from the city that had begun slowly in the 1950s became a virtual stampede in the 1970s and early 1980s.[80] According to data collected by the city, whereas Detroit had 891,000 whites in 1969, by 1976, when Young was proudly unveiling his Renaissance Center, only 543,000 remained.[81] Reflecting the sentiments behind such flight, Theodore J. Popwitz argued in a letter to the *Detroit Free Press* that "Mayor Young has polarized the city to a greater degree of racism than was displayed in the two race riots the city has experienced."[82] As a result of the massive out-migration of urban whites, between 1970 and 1990, the percentage of blacks in Detroit rose from 44.5 percent to 78.4 percent, giving the Motor City one of the largest African American populations in the urban North.[83]

In time, the conservative whites who remained in Detroit, and the many more who had left, came to blame Young for every city problem and to accuse him of everything from reverse discrimination to corruption to downright poor manners and slovenly behavior. He soon tired of such criticism, which to him was clearly born of racist stereotyping. One popular charge was that Young was uncivilized and could not even keep the mayor's mansion presentable. This rumor particularly rankled Young, and he decided to defend himself publicly. In an interview with the *Detroit Free Press,* Young referred directly to the Manoogian Mansion comment and said, "I do resent though the implications that I didn't keep that place up. We spent over one million on it in that last couple of years."[84] When the local media later implied that Young was a corrupt mayor, he pointed out that the FBI had continuously kept close tabs on him, and, if he was doing anything illegal, they would more than happily have exposed that fact. The most prevalent criticism that Young faced, however, was that he was a reverse racist. To this, he always responded that his attempts to improve opportunities for urban blacks clearly had not altered the fact that whites still held the bulk of economic power in Detroit. Thus, he maintained, the charge of reverse racism was nothing short of absurd: "I view racism not as a two-way street. I think racism is a system of oppression. I don't [think] Black folks are oppressive to anybody, so I don't consider that Blacks are capable of racism."[85] Young's retorts, however, peppered as they often were with four-letter words and direct jabs at the suburbs, did not help his cause.

In fact, nothing Young ever said could stem the tide of white flight, and the effect of this exodus was to bring severe economic distress to Detroit.

When Detroit lost much of its white population, it also lost a significant portion of its economic base. Ironically, the city's poorest whites, those who had voted in record numbers for Nichols, were not always able to flee. As a researcher of Detroit's 1973 election, Michael Soules, found, "indeed, the only areas that seem to be resistant to white flight were the most pro-Nichols neighborhoods, like the old Italian Precincts of District 4, district 6 on the Northeast side, and, interestingly, the poorer pro-Nichols areas of Southwest Detroit (Districts 25 and 26)."[86] Just as ironically, many middle-class whites who had originally supported Young chose to leave the city within his first or second term in office. While some of these whites decided to leave because they grew uncomfortable with living in an increasingly black city, others left when it became clear how badly Detroit was suffering economically as compared with its suburban neighbors.

But whatever motivated middle-class whites to flee, their exodus only contributed to Detroit's economic malaise. As urban planning scholar June Manning Thomas has argued, "a white family did not have to be 'racist' to participate in a racist process."[87] According to social geographers Bryan Thompson and Robert Sinclair, when white Detroiters left the inner city, for whatever reason, they took with them "the majority of the important service, professional, and leadership activities of the Detroit Metropolitan system."[88] Soon it was no longer inner-city Detroit, but the surrounding suburbs, that housed the core of the region's auto industry. And, in time, industry foremen, supervisors, inspectors, and white workers no longer called Detroit their home. Increasingly, they moved to metro-area suburbs with few, if any, black residents.[89]

Whereas Detroit became more impoverished after 1973, neighboring Oakland County had become "the county with the nation's highest average household-effective buying income."[90] And by 1980, the median income in Detroit was $17,033, whereas in the bordering Wayne County suburb of Grosse Pointe Woods it was $35,673.[91] That same year, 27 percent of blacks and 6.8 percent of whites in the city were receiving some type of public assistance, and 25 percent of blacks and 7 percent of whites lived below the poverty level.[92] By 1983, "the $11,685 gap in average household income between the overall region of Metropolitan Detroit ($33,241) and Detroit City ($21,556) . . . was the widest of the 33 largest metropolitan areas in the United States."[93]

To be sure, the urban renaissance of which Mayor Young and his supporters had dreamed was not thwarted simply by white flight. The fact that the nation as a whole was heading into a major economic recession when Young took office also took its toll on Detroit's long-term economic health. As a result of this national downturn, in 1975 Detroit experienced "its worst fiscal crisis since the Great Depression."[94] That year, the city had to lay off more than 4,000 employees, and, in time, Chrysler's Jefferson Avenue plant (one of the city's largest factories) closed its doors. By 1977, the city had lost

56,400 jobs, and Detroiters clearly were suffering.[95] As Young put it, "no city in America has been harder hit by the national economic recession. Detroit's unemployment rate is three times the national average."[96] Indeed, black unemployment had reached a full 25 percent as Young began his third term.[97] Young wondered time and again, as labor scholar Martin Glaberman has also questioned, "how could a mayor prevent all the Chrysler plants in the city from going down, the economy from going down, the auto industry from going down?"[98]

But, of course, how Young chose to address the city's economic downturn was vitally important. Whereas city radicals had succeeded in pushing liberals toward adopting more aggressive and uncompromising approaches to achieving greater racial equality during the previous decade, they had not persuaded these liberals that the structural roots of economic inequality also indicated the need for more radical corrective measures. With the ascendancy of black liberals in Detroit, any voice suggesting serious limitations of a War on Poverty approach to eliminating economic inequality was drowned out by a renewed commitment to this liberal strategy for addressing economic problems. Detroit's problem, however, was that with dwindling federal dollars, even an intense commitment to a liberal War on Poverty was difficult to act on. As Mel Ravitz argued years later, "we never really had a War on Poverty; it was more of a skirmish."[99]

Ultimately, when faced with the exodus of capital from his city, Mayor Young did not actively question the power that capital wielded over the well-being of Detroit's citizenry. Rather, he tried to woo industry leaders back to the Motor City with many corporate welfare enticements that cost Detroiters dearly. In 1980–81, for example, he offered $200 million in tax abatements and other relocation incentives to General Motors so that it would build a new plant in Detroit's Poletown neighborhood. He offered Chrysler a similar incentive package so that it would build a new Jefferson Avenue plant.

The problem for Detroiters, however, was that these new facilities provided but a fraction of the jobs the companies had promised. Of the 6,000 jobs GM promised at its new Poletown plant, only 3,700 materialized. Ironically, even if the Poletown plant would have hired the 6,000 workers expected, given the debt that the city had gone into to attract these jobs, each position effectively would have cost the city between $40,000 and $50,000.[100] And to add insult to injury, after GM opened the Poletown facility, it then went on to close two other local plants, thus throwing "thousands of other workers" out of a job.[101] As Mel Ravitz commented in 1988, "the large corporations have directly benefited from these economic subsidies and political strokings and have eliminated over 50,000 jobs."[102]

But while Young's traditionally liberal approach to economic crisis may not have been the medicine needed to cure Detroit's ills, neither his Keynesian strategy of jump-starting capitalism nor the continuing national economic downturn can fully explain the devastation that befell the Motor City.[103] In no American city did urban politicians question the fundamental tenets of capitalism, and, of course, every major industrial city experienced the recession of the 1970s. But few urban centers became as economically distressed as Detroit. Clearly, it was when Detroit lost its white population, tax base, and political support, that its future was doomed.[104] As Manning Thomas has noted, it was "racial estrangement [that] kept the region fragmented and alienated. This context of alienation counteracted whatever improvement programs the city initiated."[105] Not coincidentally, while Detroit had lost 56,400 jobs by 1977, the suburbs had gained 36,500 jobs.[106] As the city grew poorer, its social deterioration escalated, setting in motion a vicious cycle of greater white antipathy toward the inner city and, in turn, greater social malaise. As the longtime NAACP leader and former deputy superintendent of the Detroit public schools system, Arthur Johnson, complained bitterly in 1990, "whites don't know a god damned thing about what's gone wrong here. . . . It's Apartheid. They rape the city and then they come and say, 'look what these niggers did to the city' as if they were guiltless."[107]

Not all whites, of course, fit this profile. Just as white Detroit had been divided politically before Young took office, so it was after his election. As *Detroit Free Press* reporter Bill McGraw has noted, "white Detroiters are impossible to pigeon hole. . . . [S]ome are rich, some are poor. Some white Detroiters hate the city, seethe at the perceived insults of the black majority and would leave if they could. But many other whites are among the city's biggest supporters and could not imagine living anywhere else."[108] Even Arthur Johnson had to concede in 1994 that "as much as people want to communicate the image of Detroit as a Black city, there are more whites living in Detroit than any other city in Michigan . . . and most of them are here because they *want* to be here, just like the middle-class Black people."[109] And indeed, this was the case. While numbers of whites still lived in the city because they felt economically imprisoned there, other whites who stayed did so either because they remained loyal to Young or because they at least remained committed to the dream of biracial coexistence. As white Detroiter Morris Gleicher put it, "I had greater hopes, as did all my friends, for what [Young] would do in this city. . . . He would generate activity. . . . [H]e would raise the level of understanding, not only of the Black community, but of the whole city."[110] Whereas to white Detroiter Moira Kennedy, living in the Motor City "was almost a political statement. I did not want to live and raise my kids in white suburbia."[111] And to white city resident Mary Sue Shottenfels, "it was such a warm, wonderful experience . . . to live in an integrated neighborhood, trying to make it work here, trying to be a part of the city, trying *not* to walk away." As she felt compelled to note, "this is *not* an all-black city."[112]

Detroit was, however, a *mostly* black city by 1985, and despite the social and economic deterioration it suffered between 1974 and 1985, the black

Coleman A. Young giving his second inaugural speech, January 1, 1978. *Walter P. Reuther Library, Wayne State University.*

community there remained fiercely loyal to Young. Although the Motor City was clearly losing ground in its War on Poverty every year that Young held office, Detroit's blacks and progressive whites could point to genuine gains in racial equality. In the end, Detroiters gauged the success of their black-led liberal leadership primarily in racial, rather than economic, terms. The mayor's real appeal was best summed up by the Detroit chapter of the National Negro Labor Council (NNLC) when it placed him firmly in the context of a broader struggle for African American equality. According to the NNLC, Young "'damned the odds,' he took up the cudgels, the causes, and the confrontations of those martyred souls of the past. . . . The torch that they carried to guide us through the dark tunnels of slavery and injustice has been taken from their fallen hands by Coleman A. Young to guide us to freedom and equality."[113]

Detroit's liberals and even some of its radicals, such as Ken Cockrel, benefited from the mayor's determination to place blacks in positions of civic authority. In 1977, Cockrel won a seat on the City Council, running as a Marxist. By that year, Cockrel was still critical of black liberals like Young, but he had concluded that they must be challenged in their own arenas of power. As he put it in 1980, "the municipal corporation, as a legal entity established to represent people, exercises decisive control over the allocation of a substantial amount of money and human resources . . . and that's objectively a piece of power that we perceive as being of great value to those concerned about transforming the relations of production in society."[114]

The leadership presence of advocates like Young and Cockrel in post-1973 Detroit made blacks and progressive whites hopeful about their future. Specifically it raised the expectation that even past civic injustices might now be rectified. And Detroiters were not disappointed on this score. In 1974, for example, city officials finally began to investigate the rumor that the DPD had for years been directly involved in the city's drug trade. Although such a possibility had been discounted in 1972, when the issue was raised by events such as the Rochester Street massacre and by men like Hayward Brown, two years later, Detroit's newly elected and appointed officials actually did begin to look into the allegation that STRESS officers were paid hush money by local drug dealers to the tune of $1,500 per month, which they then would give to officers higher up in the DPD.[115] Also, in 1975, the family of Clarence Manning Jr., the young man who had been killed by STRESS officers in 1971, won damages totaling $180,000 from the city. And, in the following year, the family of Durwood Foshee, who had been killed in his bed during the DPD manhunt of 1973, was awarded $1.4 million for pain and suffering.[116]

Sadly, for Detroit's autoworkers, finding such a silver lining in the cloud of economic devastation that soon also engulfed their industry was much more difficult. The fact was that Detroit's workers wielded very little power after their 1973 showdown with the UAW. It was telling, for example, that in the last bargaining session between the UAW and Chrysler before the national recession hit the auto industry full scale, workers were appalled by the contract that their union ultimately presented to them but felt powerless to reject it. According to the UNC, "Chrysler workers did not win a single improvement on working conditions. . . . [W]e won no protection on speed up . . . [and] the new contract has no new provisions which will end racial harassment and discrimination in upgrading and hiring."[117] But when UNC leaders advised workers to "vote NO on this contract" and tried to organize "mass picketing at Solidarity House to protest the sell-out 1973 agreement," few joined their protest.[118]

Although the UNC still agitated on the shop floors well into the next decade, by 1974, its power base had eroded noticeably. Workers in Detroit had been taught in the most graphic way that shop-floor dissent now would be met not only with serious opposition from the company, but also from their union—even when that dissent was broad-based and clearly fueled by plant problems not politics. And from 1974 to 1980, while labor relations in Detroit were indeed peaceful, workers watched helplessly as their labor movement weakened dramatically.

Detroit's liberal labor leaders were slow to comprehend their worsening situation. When the UAW leadership had gone to the bargaining table in 1973 with Chrysler, it was so relieved that workplace dissent was finally in check, that it once again had firm control over its inner-city members, and that labor-management relations finally had stabilized, it could see little else.[119] The union hoped, of course, that, with order restored on the shop floor, the 1970s could be a decade of greater membership gains, and thus that labor's power in the American economy would rise accordingly. But not only had the contract of 1973 turned out to be a disappointment; when the brewing national recession finally hit Detroit with a vengeance in 1974, the UAW found itself scrambling merely to maintain what it had already won for its constituency. The idea of expanding postwar benefits soon seemed absurd, because, in addition to the barrier created by the economic downturn, in many ways the union had become management's "partner." Certainly the UAW had moved dangerously close to the company years earlier when it broke the back of shop-floor dissent. But some workers actually accused labor leaders of also having made backroom deals with company officials in order to cement their new cooperative alliance. Specifically it was a lawsuit filed by workers against both the company and the union regarding their actions after the 1973 Forge wildcat that made this charge.

During the 1973 Forge wildcat, Chrysler had fired fifteen workers. At the bargaining table that fall, the company agreed to rehire twelve of the fifteen in exchange for the UAW's ratification of the local bargaining agreement. Before the agreement was ratified, however, the three Forge workers who remained jobless—Karl Williams, Jerome Scott, and Thomas Stepanski—had already filed grievances for reinstatement with their committeeman, Thornton Jackson. Jackson dutifully wrote grievances demanding that the trio "be reinstated and paid all lost time and to be made whole,"[120] but the company denied them. As part of its justification for keeping Williams out, Chrysler argued that, "On 8/9/73, at approximately 6:50am, Karl Williams was observed at the Huber West Gate with another employee diverting any traffic which attempted to enter. When he was approached by a process server of the World Investigations and Security, Inc., Karl Williams assaulted the server by striking him with his fist."[121] And regarding Thomas Stepanski, Chrysler maintained that, "On 8/8/73, T. Stepanski was observed at the main entrance to the Detroit Forge plant blocking traffic and telling other employees not to go into the plant because 'it is a pig pen and it was an unsafe plant to work in.' "[122]

After Chrysler denied the worker grievances, their fate was placed into the hands of labor arbitrator Gabriel Alexander.[123] In the arbitration hearing that followed, workers hoped that Alexander would see that "the grievants did not cause the plant to be shut down. . . . Rather the stoppage that did occur was a spontaneous reaction on the part of employees to the unhealthy and unsafe conditions in the plant."[124] Chrysler, on the other hand, forcefully alleged that the three fired workers, with Scott as the primary spokesman, had started the illegal wildcat when they told workers to "'Go Home, there is no work today, we are on a wildcat. We are closing the fucking place down.' "[125]

Ultimately, Alexander sided with Chrysler in this matter. He wrote in his decision that he was "constrained to deny the grievances [because] I am satisfied that grievants were active leaders of the stoppage, and were not mere participants."[126] After Alexander ruled against their reinstatement, Williams, Scott, and Stepanski formed a defense committee that pressured the union to take up their cause again. When it became clear that union leaders considered the matter closed, the fired workers went to civil court, where they filed a lawsuit against both Chrysler and the UAW leadership for allegedly engaging in a "conspiracy, agreement, understanding, plan, design, or scheme," which resulted in the permanent firing based on their race and political convictions.[127] Because all of them had been members of the Forge plant RUM, Williams, Scott, and Stepanski suspected that this was the real reason why each remained fired. Even though the UAW had taken their case all the way to the arbitration level, the trio nevertheless felt that union leaders had not argued their discharge case strenuously enough. Specifically, the fired workers felt that if the union was truly committed to their case, it would have tried to secure their reinstatement by invoking Section 502 of the National Labor Relations Act regarding a worker's right to refuse unsafe work.[128]

As the civic trial unfolded, deposition and trial testimony only fueled these workers' conviction that UAW officials had betrayed them. As they found out, Chrysler's original informal offer to the UAW leadership had actually been to reinstate the twelve fired Forge workers "plus plaintiff Karl Williams, if the union would drop its grievances of plaintiffs Scott and Stepanski."[129] And after Chrysler made this offer to the UAW, top union leaders met on October 9, 1973, to discuss the proposal in the conference room of the Detroit Forge plant. Present at this meeting was a mix of both International and local union leaders, including Anthony Canole, George Merrelli, Wally Wallers, Evans Ray, Dennis Baliki, Al Howe, Raymond Turner, and Thorton Jackson.[130] According to the testimony of Local 47's recording secretary, Dennis Baliki, Canole reported that he had agreed with Virgil Anderson of Chrysler's Corporate Labor Relations Division that ten of the fifteen workers fired should return after the ratification of the local agreement, three of the fifteen should return two weeks later, and that the union should withdraw the grievances of Scott and Stepanski.[131] At this point, Canole's statement was greeted with shouts of "no!"[132] According to Baliki, "Al Howe starts mentioning that: Not Carl Williams. We don't want that Communist back," and "Al Howe said he's not going to have his kids growing up under Communism."[133] Because it soon became clear that there was serious disagreement about whether the union should accept the company's proposal to let Williams come back to work, those present decided that a vote should be taken. As Baliki testified, "Raymond Turner, Thornton Jackson and Al Howe voted no, Carl Williams shouldn't return to work. Evens Ray, Sr., Robert Evans, myself Dennis Baliki voted he should be returned to work. That left it a split vote. Leon Klea [president of Local 47] says, well, it's my place to break the tie, And he voted no, Carl Williams shouldn't be returned to work."[134]

Although the plaintiffs did not win their case, the incidents reported during the course of it were nevertheless extraordinary. Of course, as with any of the trials that took place in postwar Detroit, one cannot ascertain the veracity of the testimony given. But if what deponent Baliki said under oath was truthful, then the UAW leadership consciously had chosen not to bring one of its own members back into the plant, even after the company had agreed to do so. In effect, the UAW leaders' desire to gain control of its constituency, to save the union from "outside" destructive elements like the black nationalist and communist Left, and to reinstate peace on the shop floor rendered them even more determined than the company to keep black militant workers out of the plant. As Baliki put it when questioned why the union leadership had acted as it did,

> A: I felt they thought he [Williams] would have been a political threat, if he was to come back to work and probably be held in high esteem . . . and possibly have been a political threat to one of the committeemen.
>
> Q: By running for office?
>
> A:Yes.[135]

In time, however, the UAW found that management was a far greater threat to its power than militant workers like Williams. Only two years after the three workers' lawsuit, and only six years after the ugly events at Mack, the UAW and Chrysler once again were hammering out an agreement. In November 1979, Chrysler forced the UAW to agree to $203 million in wage and benefits concessions and another $100 million in deferred pension plan payments. In these negotiations, the union also agreed to a six-month wage freeze and surrendered six paid holidays.[136] The following year, the UAW was forced to give up more paid holidays, and by 1981, the union accepted Chrysler chairman Lee Iacocca's demand of an additional spate of concessions totaling $673 million, including a wage cut of $1.15 per hour and a loss of three more paid days off.[137] By December 1982, the UAW had nearly 350,000 fewer production workers to represent than it had in December 1978, owing to a series of inner-city plant closings and company lay-offs.[138] The union did get something in return for its concessions to the company—a plethora of joint union-management committees and shop-floor programs—but in the end it paid dearly for this new, less combative moment in labor relations.[139]

Like the woes that befell the Young administration between 1973 and 1980, the problems faced by the UAW leadership obviously had much to do with the economic recession that was plaguing the entire country. The oil price increases of 1973 (which sparked an economic downturn in 1974), as well as a noticeable rise in foreign competition, had a devastating impact on auto companies. By 1980, the Big Three automakers (Chrysler, General Motors, and Ford) had posted staggering combined losses, and by 1989, their share of the world's car market had declined to 24 percent.[140] While Chrysler finally made money in 1976 and 1977, it still was recovering from its tremendous losses in 1974 and 1975, and then it suffered another economic plunge in 1978 and 1979. Chrysler's financial troubles were so severe in 1979 that, with the help of President Jimmy Carter, Congress, and the UAW, it received $1.5 billion in credits from the U.S. government and secured passage of the Chrysler Loan Guarantee Act. The Chrysler bailout of 1979–80 (and the fact that foreign producers were gaining ever larger share of the car market) in turn justified management's call for even more concessions from the UAW.

In many respects, the UAW had little choice but to agree to cuts in wages and benefits as the 1980s dawned. But it is vital to recognize that the union had begun to cooperate with Chrysler long before the company fell on hard times, and thus it had severely undermined its long-term bargaining strength. When the UAW leadership chose to side with Chrysler during the tumultuous days of 1973, it raised the company's expectation of even greater labor-management cooperation thereafter. In addition, because the UAW leadership had actively squelched the militancy of its own membership in 1973, by the time labor-management "cooperation" began to mean management's encroachment on union power, the UAW was in no position to resist the onslaught. As historian Steve Jefferys has argued, "by 1981 it was clear that the International Union would no longer place other than consultative restraints on company-wide managerial authority," and by that year, the UAW had abandoned "any pretense that it could harness whatever radical energy the late 1960s and early 1970s had possessed to a revival of unionism."[141]

In lieu of trying to resurrect such militancy, UAW leaders instead tried to reverse the hardship that labor was enduring in their own legislative way. Union leader Mark Stepp, for example, testified before the House Committee on Labor Standards to encourage passage of "comprehensive legislation that would stop 'the injustice of making workers and communities the victims' of economic dislocation that came from factory shut downs."[142] As the 1980s began, however, scores of union members already had lost their jobs, and all the legislation in the world could not change this. According to the UAW's public relations staff, by the spring of 1979, the total union membership of the Big Three automakers was 840,000, as compared with its high of 1,530,870 members in 1969.[143] By December 17, 1979, 115,000 Big Three employees were on indefinite layoff, and 70,000 were on temporary layoff, while by February 8, 1980, 174,000 were on indefinite lay off, with 37,325 on temporary layoff.[144] By April 4, 1980, a total of 211,000 Big Three workers were laid off, and by May 2, 1980, that number had climbed to 266,582.[145] By May 16, 1980, 304,144 workers at Chrysler, Ford, and General Motors were unemployed.[146] Amazingly, by 1982 the UAW had only 477,000 auto members—a shocking low for this vital American union.[147] And even for those workers still in the UAW, life was hardly rosy. By the mid-1980s, it wasn't just the economically troubled Chrysler that had taken advantage of the UAW's new cooperative posture and weakened bargaining position; Ford and General Motors had forced the union to grant sweeping concessions as well.

By 1985, Detroit's auto plants were calmer than they had been during any period in their history. Union leaders remained glad that the political crisis that had engulfed shop floors between 1967 and 1973 was over, but as workers well knew, the price leaders had paid for labor movement control was extremely high. Labor liberals were firmly in control of the UAW, but that union now was but a shadow of its former self. Likewise, by 1985, the Motor City itself was also calmer than it had been in decades. And civic liberals were pleased that the crisis that had engulfed city streets between 1967 and 1973 had been resolved in their favor. But, of course, the price that they had paid for political control was high as well. To be sure, liberals were now firmly in charge of the inner city and, since they were overwhelmingly African American, this was indeed an historic accomplishment. But sadly these black liberals had come to lead a city that was increasingly isolated and economically eviscerated.

Conclusion

Civic Transformation and Labor Movement

Decline in Postwar America

> What should disturb all Americans is that the analysis League founders offered regarding the future of the auto industry, the UAW, the city of Detroit, and African Americans now applies increasingly to the nation as a whole.[1]

Anyone looking out the window of a city bus headed downtown on Detroit's Grand River Avenue in 1985 might easily think that, mysteriously, he or she had been transported back to World War II and bombed-out Berlin. Every block passed held boarded-up storefronts, vacant lots where houses once stood, and homeless people searching in piles of rubble for wood and other salvageable items. Even such formerly vibrant sites as factories and union halls looked empty, as if evacuated in an emergency. But if one got off of that bus, perhaps to go into a school or to conduct business at a bank, Detroit's resemblance to war-ravaged Europe suddenly would evaporate. The most striking thing about walking into one of Detroit's educational or financial institutions in the mid-1980s was that a great many of the teachers, principals, managers, and tellers inside were African American. If, per chance, one needed to meet with the head of the Detroit public schools system or the branch president of a bank that day, these people were as likely to be black as white. This odd juxtaposition of historically unprecedented African American middle-class presence and civic power amid extreme urban decay and economic decline that was Detroit by 1985, also characterized many city centers across America by that year.

Observers of the present and scholars of the past, however, should take extreme care not to associate increased black presence and power with urban decline in some linear or causal way. Nor should they privilege the historical outcomes of either inner-city economic decay or widespread white urban abandonment over African American empowerment. As this book has argued, the legacy of the urban transformation that took place across the United States between 1945 and 1985 is much more complicated than it has been portrayed to be, primarily because the *roots* of urban transformation and labor decline also were more complex than most have appreciated. This study of Detroit has sought to retrieve and examine significant parts of the postwar urban and labor narrative that previously have been overlooked in order to better understand why urban America and its labor movement evolved as they did and to suggest that transformation and decline was neither synonymous nor inevitable.

While this book has reexamined the urban transformation and labor-movement decline that took place within the borders of one particular city, its narrative suggests key ways in which the fate of postwar urban America as a whole also might be reassessed. Although Detroit clearly is not an Every City, its long-term fate and the many details of its past are shared by urban centers across the United States, and thus a broader reconsideration of postwar urban development can be gleaned from this study. Like Detroit, for example, many northern industrial urban centers after World War II evolved from prosperous magnets for native- and foreign-born hopefuls to decayed centers where prosperity seemed unimaginable. Detroit's economic tailspin certainly was more dramatic than that which other inner cities experienced. As urban scholar June Manning Thomas has noted, by 1989, Detroit had the lowest labor force participation rate in the United States, at 46.6 percent; its median household income of $19,394 was the lowest of any city in the country; and its urban unemployment rate was America's highest, at 15.7 percent.[2] Such figures are perhaps not surprising, as Detroit is home to the auto industry. When General Motors shut down its Clark assembly plant and nearby Fleetwood plants in 1987, "6,600 autoworkers—mostly black" were permanently laid off.[3] Chrysler's workforce as well had dwindled from 28,000 urban employees in 1979 to 8,636 in 1990, after it also closed numerous plants.[4] But Detroit was not the only city dependent on, and eventually gutted by, big industry as the 1980s dawned. From Pittsburgh to Cleveland to the South Side of Los Angeles, inner-city residents struggled to survive economically where they once had imagined prospering.

Likewise, just as Detroit experienced a dramatic white out-migration during the 1970s, and thus housed an African American majority thereafter, so did many central cities in the United States. Again, Detroit's demographic metamorphosis was more extreme than in most other cities, but the white flight that it experienced was not unique. For example, while those analyzing census data for the University of Michigan's Detroit Area Study concluded in 1997 that metropolitan Detroit was the most segregated city of all 47 U.S. metro regions with at least one million residents, it did not escape them that many other American inner cities also revealed noticeable concentrations of African Americans within their borders and white majorities within nearby suburbs by the close of the twentieth century. Indeed, as several urban scholars have noted, although "Detroit's segregation index is higher than that of other metropolitan areas . . . many of them experience similar conditions."[5]

But to recognize that numerous urban centers in 1980s America, like Detroit, had become the sites of deep economic distress, had lost much of their white population, and also became inhabited by an African American majority, does not, in itself, really further our understanding of postwar urban history. Indeed, to date, urban scholarship's virtually exclusive focus on these "truths" about the fate of inner-city America is precisely what has obscured other equally important postwar urban experiences and outcomes and has led directly to the dismissal of inner cities as ultimately irrelevant to America's political future or toxic to its social relations.[6]

This book has argued that it would be a tragic mistake to see American urban centers by the mid-1980s as simply the doomed place that many whites left and where the economy took a nosedive. It suggests further that it would be an equal mistake to regard America's inner cities as the symbolic battlefields on which American liberalism died an ugly death. Indeed, this study has initiated an inquiry into postwar urban history that deliberately questions these very notions so that the political complexity and determination of American whites and blacks alike are not minimized, thus allowing the multifaceted implications of postwar urban transformation to be finally revealed.

It is only when one recognizes the complexity of postwar political and racial goals as well as alliances, for example, that one can see the extent to which the racially conservative whites who chose to abandon the inner cities in the 1970s and to vote for Ronald Reagan in 1980 did so as *losers,* not victors, of their battle to lead urban America into the future. Clearly, as important as it was for postwar evolution that many whites eschewed inner-city living and liberalism after the politically tumultuous and racially rancorous 1960s, it was equally important that urban centers across the United States in the 1970s witnessed the most dramatic ascendancy of black liberal political power ever seen in American history as a result of this same tumult and rancor. Indeed, by the 1970s and into the 1990s, not just Detroit but many American inner cities witnessed precisely this unprecedented rise of African American political power. According to Manning Thomas, between 1969 and 1974 alone, "the number of black elected officials in the United States increased 120 percent, to include 16 congressional representatives and 104 mayors." She points out further that, by 1974, Los Angeles; Atlanta; Newark, New Jersey; Raleigh, North Carolina; Gary, Indiana; and Detroit had black mayors, and together these cities contained 5.5 million people.[7]

The fact that black liberals were taking control of key urban centers after 1970 certainly did unnerve many Americans. To a significant number of others, however, black-led cities quickly came to represent the last bastion of an American commitment to more just and equitable social relations. It was significant to such Americans that, whereas Head Start programs and civic civil rights commissions were few and far between in suburbia after 1980, they still were a prominent feature of black-led inner cities and not because they merely were holdovers from an earlier, more optimistic, time. Not only did black-led liberal cities house the few remaining American institutions committed to economic and racial equity in the 1980s, but these enclaves also had become home to the largest, most economically secure, and most influential black middle class ever before in existence in the United States. Indeed, the fact that middle-class African Americans could be found in numerous positions of social, economic, and political power in America's urban centers by the 1980s—that more corporate executives, social welfare advocates, educational personnel, middle managers, and the professional staff of hospitals and city agencies were black than ever before—indicates that the inner city had also come to be one of the very few places in the country where "equal opportunity" finally had some meaning.

In addition to black urban liberals being among the few U.S. politicians to make African American advancement a reality, at least for those in the middle class, these leaders and their supporters also wielded power beyond the borders of their own cities. With their vision for a more socially and economically just future and their continuing commitment to many 1960s-style programs, urbanites would provide a vital electoral base to any Democrat hoping to take or keep power nationally. Urban voters continued to send liberal representatives and senators to Washington well into the 1990s, propelled numerous black and white liberal mayors to power across the country, and made it possible for the Democratic party to regain presidential power in 1992 and to hold onto it in 1996. Significantly, as well, this urban constituency, comprised primarily of African Americans but made up of scores of whites still deeply committed to a progressive politics both racial and economic as well, served as a check on the Democratic party itself—a constant reminder that it should not swing too far to the right if it planned on keeping its crucial urban electorate. Indeed, it is only by ignoring the complexity of how urban politics evolved after World War II, and by dismissing urban centers after 1980, that one could argue that postwar liberalism had fully collapsed and that conservative whites had become the only relevant political actors in America by the close of the twentieth century.

Without discounting the tremendous suffering urban America—and poor and working-class urbanites specifically—experienced as a result of the antiliberal backlash that swept the country after 1980, this book nevertheless has suggested forcefully that black liberal politicians, the black middle class, and white progressives had clearly won something out of their tumultuous battles with white conservatism before the 1980s. Indeed it maintains further that even America's urban Left had gained something out of its determined postwar struggles. Not only had the activism of inner-city radicals in the 1960s and 1970s fueled a promising political moment for postwar America, but the Left influenced the country's future in real and positive ways thereafter.[8]

One writer has noted that in Detroit, for example, "while many of the goals and objectives of the League of Revolutionary Black Workers may have been underdeveloped and much too audacious for the times, many of them now are vital components in groups and organizations far less radical than the League."[9] While it is undeniably the case that "the League's attempt to stimulate a mass reaction to race and class oppression was only minimally achieved," as Herb Boyd points out, nevertheless it had a "most practical invisible legacy [that] was realized through electoral politics."[10] According to Edna Ewell Watson, Detroit's radicals had deeply "influenced many of those who served as the backbone and lynchpin of Coleman Young's administration."[11] And the radicals who had long agitated in other black-led liberal cities (such as Los Angeles; Newark, New Jersey; and Washington, D.C.) influenced their civic administrations in subtle but important ways as well.

But if America's remaining urbanites had won several concrete as well as subtle things in their struggles since World War II, at first glance it appears that, as workers, they had achieved nothing. Indeed, the only group that appears to have emerged victorious in the ugly labor relations conflicts that developed after 1945 is the companies. Yet like the popular "truths" about the fate of the postwar city and liberal politics, this "truth" about the fate that befell the American labor movement also tends to obscure more than it illuminates. While American workers suffered mightily at the hands of capital as the 1980s dawned, such an eventuality was not inevitable. Indeed, to see it as such both denies postwar workers their determination to better their lot and ignores union leaders' complicity in helping to usher in the very pro-company environment that would prove so costly to their membership.

Nevertheless, it does appear that America's dissident laborers had won little that they had fought for. But in fact, in Detroit and elsewhere, while it is true that American trade unions weakened dramatically in the 1980s, it is not true that dissident workers had no impact on the long-term character of their labor movement. As journalist Thomas Brooks pointed out, for example, it was black activism that forced the UAW in Detroit to desegregate its upper leadership, and this phenomenon also played out in other American unions that had witnessed rank-and-file African American dissent.[12] As Brooks noted about Detroit, in the 1970s, "more blacks are now on the staffs of both institutions [company and union] than before DRUM made its appearance,"[13] and as early as 1971 eleven local presidents were African American. [14] Likewise, although black revolutionaries lost their bid for electoral power at Local 3 in the 1960s, soon thereafter, four out of six union officers and 56 percent of the union shop stewards at that local were African American.[15] And, as Detroit Councilwoman Sheila Murphy Cockrel noted in 1998, even though "to this day, the League's role in opening up the United Autoworkers leadership to people of color and focusing the UAW on racial issues remains unheralded," this radical organization nevertheless did cause such a union transformation.[16] Not only did the plant dissidents push the Detroit labor movement in a more racially progressive direction, but, as Judge George Crockett noted in 1994, "it was in the framework of the trade union movement that Detroit's black leadership got its start in politics."[17]

Although it is beyond the parameters of this study to examine the character of American labor relations in much detail after 1985, one final point bears mentioning. The desire for a more worker-friendly and racially just labor movement, which had surfaced with a vengeance in the late 1960s and was squelched in the early 1970s, may appear to have evaporated thereafter, but this is not so. Indeed, by the latter half of the 1980s, dissent not only surfaced once again in the ranks of the UAW (this time directed against the consessionary bargaining strategy of the International, and this time based in a biracially supported organization called New Directions), but labor dissent also began to reappear outside of the auto industry as well. For example, by the mid-1980s, in the dissident organization Teamsters for a Democratic Union (TDU), workers in the International Brotherhood of Teamsters were dramatically escalating their efforts to democratize their union and to make their leaders more aggressive with owners.[18] Also in that decade, another dissident organization, Labor Notes, came of age, which brought together workers from virtually every American workplace who were committed to putting company abuses firmly in check.[19]

Although the autoworkers in New Directions ultimately lost out in their battle with the UAW International in several bitterly contested regional elections, both TDU and Labor Notes grew markedly during the 1980s and into the 1990s. In addition, by the early 1990s, even the more traditionally conservative leaders of the American labor movement, specifically those in the AFL-CIO, also began to reassess the wisdom of unions continuing to take a cooperative posture with management. With the upsurge and activism of TDU and Labor Notes, and with the ascendancy of the more militant John Sweeney to the presidency of the AFL-CIO, management was put on notice once again that a new day of labor activism was dawning—one that, like its predecessor in the 1960s, would take the needs of white as well as nonwhite workers seriously and one that now would expand beyond the boundaries of traditional blue-collar and industrial workplaces. Despite the labor movement's undeniable decline in the mid-1980s, in later years, corporations were once again alerted to the fact that they would not be allowed to determine the future solely or indefinitely.

While this study of postwar Detroit suggests the necessity of reexamining the complex roots and the legacy of urban transformation and labor movement decline, it does not pretend to predict the future of either America's inner cities or its labor relations. Through a more penetrating look at America's urban and labor past, however, we can at least get a more nuanced and balanced perspective on who won, who lost, and who *might* shape the next millennium. By digging more deeply into the history of urban America and its workplaces, and by reexamining their respective fates, we can clearly see that U.S. inner cities did not become simply abandoned wastelands by the 1980s; that they had never been divided primarily by race because they always were politically complex; that the radicals, conservatives, and liberals who had been agitating within them each impacted upon the future to an equal degree; and, finally, that the American labor movement always had more power over its destiny that its leaders imagined.

Epilogue

The trial of James Johnson is over but the implications will reverberate throughout this Motor City and its factories for years to come.[1]

Just as Detroit's dramatic civic and labor movement transformation between 1973 and 1985 was rife with irony—primarily because those who won the wars for urban and shop-floor control had paid such a high price for their victory—so was James Johnson's life over this period.

Any hope that Johnson would finally get real help for his serious emotional problems by being institutionalized was never realized. From virtually the moment that he entered Michigan's mental health system, the two psychiatrists with whom he had the most regular contact were Dr. Lynn Blunt and Dr. Ames Robey. Both had impeccable credentials and impressive clinical experience, and each had taken the time to familiarize himself with the facts in Johnson's criminal trial.[2] Also, both disagreed with the diagnosis that had landed Johnson in their care. In one of his first psychiatric assessments of Johnson, Blunt found absolutely no evidence "whatsoever of schizophrenia or any other psychotic illness."[3] Likewise, after Robey evaluated Johnson, he decided that Johnson's "major problem was a long-standing character disorder of explosive, passive-aggressive, or schizoid type," not "real" schizophrenia.[4] These determinations were not just a matter of semantics. In Robey's opinion, during Johnson's trial, the defense's "psychiatrist exaggerated or he, the patient, exaggerated and lied about symptoms to expedite a release from his charges."[5] It appeared to irk Robey that Johnson was "projecting all of his problems, his past crimes, and the rest of any difficulties in his life into the more or less socially acceptable 'wastebasket' of racial discrimination," and that Johnson showed "no insight into any area of difficulty in his own psychopathology and continues to emphatically insist that the entire situation arose out of one based solely on racial prejudice."[6]

The extent to which Blunt shared Robey's conviction that Johnson was manipulative, and that he had exaggerated the impact of racial discrimination on his life, seemed obvious to Johnson himself on August 19, 1971, when he met with Blunt to discuss the possibility of a transfer from the Center for Forensic Psychiatry to the far more prisonlike Ionia. According to Johnson's recollection of this meeting, Dr. Blunt asked him point blank whether he felt he had been justified in pleading not guilty by reason of insanity and, Johnson alleged, Blunt then told him that he personally felt Johnson should have gone to the state penitentiary on a second-degree murder charge. In lieu of a jail sentence, Blunt recommended a transfer to Ionia because, in Johnson's opinion, Blunt felt that he would be "put under extreme pressure" because "sometimes the best way to cure a patient is to break him down all the way."[7] Johnson was so appalled by this discussion about his transfer that he later wrote down every sentence uttered in it and sent the dictation to his sister so that there would be a record. According to Johnson's notes, Blunt came right out and told him that he should have just gone on welfare instead of killing the people at his job. To this Johnson allegedly replied, "Dr., this is an insult; I have never been on any welfare and never want to be on it as long as I have health and strength to work for a living."[8]

When it became clear that Johnson was being sent to the dreaded Ionia, he asked Blunt a key question: "Tell me. What kind of medical treatment can you recommend, or therapy for a matter of fact, that will make a person more resigned to the type of harassment, exploitation and you name it, and finally complete loss of job that I had suffered for the past two years?" According to Johnson, Blunt allegedly responded by saying, "Well, if I lock you up for the next twenty years you are not likely to kill anybody now, are you?"[9] And lock him up they did.

During the next four years, Robey became Johnson's primary treating psychiatrist. In one of his many evaluations of Johnson, Robey argued that "there was no specific treatment for [Johnson's] type of personality disorder."[10] Blunt had concurred that it was quite difficult to treat someone with Johnson's "sociocultural" profile, particularly when it appeared that "his behavior had surpassed what would be expected of person's with his background."[11] When Johnson got into a scuffle on his floor one night, during which he tried to stab another patient for making homosexual advances toward him, Blunt apparently did not see such behavior as dysfunctional. He considered it natural behavior for persons who had grown up as did Johnson. As Blunt said about Johnson's stabbing attempt, "knives were not uncommonly used in fights between people of his particular sociocultural background, but in such fights, both parties usually have a knife."[12]

Over this period, Johnson continued to insist that he was racially victimized, and doctors eventually decided to deal with this by giving him medication. For example, after having made numerous comments to a staff psychiatrist such as "it's rough, living in this country if you are this color," Johnson was put on a regimen of 50 milligrams of concentrated Mellaril three times a day to calm his anxiety.[13] When he still couldn't control his racial fixation and began "impulsively acting out" in front of a staff social worker, he was injected with 75 milligrams of Thorazine.[14] Over the course of Johnson's stay in the three mental hospitals, doctors responded to his obsession with racial discrimination by putting him on Chlorpromazine, Stelazine, and Darvon. Try as they might, however, doctors could not cure Johnson of his illness—what company doctor Gordon Forrer described later as Johnson's habit of bending "his recall and his self-serving manner based on an ever present racial consciousness."[15]

Indeed Johnson's conviction that he was being racially victimized only became more entrenched the longer that he was institutionalized. Johnson became increasingly outspoken about the injustices that he felt he endured while hospitalized. For example, when he was severely beaten for refusing to put on a body shackle during the transfer from the CFP to Ionia, he contacted outside authorities to investigate. According to Johnson, he had been "kicked, punched by personnel and also choked with a towel around his neck."[16] The medical doctor who treated him on his arrival at Ionia confirmed that, indeed, Johnson presented with "extensive subconjunctive hemorrhage," that "both of his wrists are still slightly swollen," that "the left little finger now appears swollen and bluish in color," and that Johnson "still occasionally spits up red blood."[17]

By and large, however, Johnson's complaints about how he was being treated continued to fall on deaf ears, so he eventually sought an early release from the hospital. The opportunity for such a release came accidentally in 1974, as a result of a case known as People v. McQuillen. In this landmark case, the Michigan Supreme Court ruled that mental patients who had been institutionalized under not guilty by reason of insanity acquittals could not be held indefinitely in mental institutions unless they still were deemed mentally ill. As soon as the justices handed down the McQuillen ruling, Johnson's attorneys applied for his release.

Johnson was eventually freed under McQuillen in 1975, but his release was filled with much controversy and irony. The McQuillen rule put Johnson's treating doctors, Blunt and Robey, in a quite curious position. After all, they had consistently maintained that Johnson was not really insane, only racially obsessed. And yet, the idea that Johnson now would go free was intolerable. According to Johnson Blunt had made it clear that he should pay for his crimes even if it had to be in the mental health, rather than the penal, system. And, although Robey apparently did not believe Johnson was insane any more than Blunt did, he nevertheless wrote to the court that his recommendation for Johnson's release would not be given. Yet the fact that these psychiatrists long had maintained that Johnson was not "schizophrenic," as his committing diagnosis suggested, made his release a virtual certainty. But while Johnson finally won his release from the Department of Mental Health, his ordeal with both the mental health system and the legal system was far from over. As it turned out, Johnson's 1973 workmen's compensation victory came back to haunt him.

Johnson's compensation victory had angered many people, but few were more outraged than officials at Chrysler. Just before Johnson was released from Ionia under the McQuillen decision, Chrysler filed an appeal with the Workman's Compensation Appeal Board, arguing that "fraud was committed at the trial and during the workman's compensation hearing," that the "plaintiff [Johnson] makes inconsistent claims in different forums for different purposes," and that, in order to be released under McQuillen, Johnson had admitted that he was not schizophrenic, that he only suffered from a "personality disorder." Because this was the position that Chrysler's doctors had taken in the compensation trial in which Johnson had been awarded his benefits, the company demanded that Johnson's compensation award be rescinded.[18] In essence, Chrysler had rejoined not only the issue of compensation, but also the continuing battle over whether Johnson was or ever had been insane.

In support of its argument before the Appeal Board, Chrysler argued that Johnson's only problem was that "his psyche causes him to view reality as a racist plot," and to prove this, it urged the board to accept the original compensation trial testimony of Dr. Forrer over that of the plaintiff psychiatrist, Dr. Clemens Fitzgerald.[19] But when Fitzgerald went before the board to vehemently restate his opinion that Johnson's feelings about societal racism were in fact based in reality (as evidenced even at Johnson's mental institution, Ionia, where "the entire staff of Ionia State Hospital was Caucasian and, as a result, they frequently mishandled, misused, and actually physically abused and beat some black inmates"),[20] Chrysler decided to introduce new psychiatric testimony to persuade the Appeal Board to reverse Johnson's award. Remarkably the company enlisted the support of Robey, Johnson's longtime treating physician, to make its case.

In February 1975, attorneys for Chrysler submitted an affidavit from Robey stating that "James Johnson, Jr. following the criminal and compensation trials expressed the deep satisfaction at having been able to [subvert] the principles in the trial by his self-serving narrating."[21] Robey then went on record with his long-held belief that the diagnosis on which Johnson was awarded compensation was bogus. Most surprising of all, however, was Robey's statement in this affidavit that Johnson "revealed to me and other members of my staff that he was drunk at the time of the triple homicides committed by him."[22] This assertion was critically important because, if Johnson had indeed been drunk on July 15, 1970, when he killed three men, then his insanity plea might well have been disallowed.

While Johnson's attorneys worked feverishly to prevent Chrysler from introducing Robey's affidavit into the appeal proceedings, Johnson himself began writing letters to a number of authorities to protest Robey's actions. He wrote to members of the Compensation Appeal Board, assuring them that he was willing to take a polygraph test in order to prove that he had never told Dr. Robey that he was drunk on July 15, 1970.[23] Johnson also filed complaints with the ACLU and the NAACP in which he requested a full investigation of Robey and of the veracity of his affidavit while urging that the proper legal action be taken against Robey for what Johnson referred to as a "criminal act."[24] *But despite Johnson's letters—and despite the curious fact that, midway through the appeal process, Dr. Robey had managed to "misplace" the case notes on which his affidavit was based—the Workman's Compensation Appeal Board admitted Robey's affidavit into evidence. It was then up to Johnson's attorney—once again, Ron Glotta—to address Robey's allegations on the stand. For days, Glotta hammered away at Robey's testimony. Finally, after one day of particularly grueling examination and cross-examination, Robey admitted that Johnson never actually said he had been drunk. Robey then alleged that he had objected when Chrysler's attorney presented him with the affidavit—because "technically [it] wasn't really correct"—but he was urged to sign it anyway because Chrysler was under a deadline.*[25]

Once Robey admitted that he had signed a false affidavit and alleged that a Chrysler attorney knew it was untruthful,[26] *Johnson's troubles should have been over. To his dismay, however, the Workman's Compensation Appeal Board ruled substantially in Chrysler's favor and limited Johnson's benefits to sixteen months instead of life.*[27] *Johnson was very discouraged by this ruling. As he pointed out, "I had barely been in Ionia for a month when 16 months were up. . . . [I]f I was recovered, what was I doing there for the next four years?"*[28] *But the backlash against Johnson's 1973 victory did not stop there. In July 1979, after yet another Chrysler appeal to the Workman's Compensation Board, the board went even further and actually struck "out earlier references to racism at the plant as a factor contributing to Johnson's mental derangement."*[29] *That the board had removed any language from the 1973 decision indicating Chrysler's culpability in his breakdown truly saddened Johnson. As he well knew, the complete reversal of his original compensation verdict indicated that, as the 1970s gave way to the 1980s, the State of Michigan now saw him as just another black criminal in the city of Detroit who had got away with spending four years in a mental institution instead of a prison.*

But while state officials no longer regarded Johnson as a sympathetic character, to many Detroiters, his life story was still a metaphor for all of the disappointments, frustrations, and hopes that had characterized their own lives in the Jim Crow South, the Motor City, and the auto plants between 1945 and 1985. Johnson's experiences of brutal racial discrimination in Mississippi, in Detroit, and while working at Chrysler had been sadly familiar to many inner-city residents. His vindication in both the criminal and civil courts of Detroit, in turn, had reflected the degree to which their struggles to force the system in more radical directions had paid off. And, finally, when officials eventually stripped Johnson of his earlier victories, these same inner-city residents could relate, with grim recognition. As conservatism outside of Detroit's city limits rose by the close of the 1970s, they risked losing too much that they had won over the previous tumultuous years.

Notes from the Author

Every history book begins with a set of questions that an author feels is particularly worthy of greater attention and investigation. This book is no different, although perhaps the questions that fueled its creation are more closely linked to my own history than most. My desire to understand Detroit dates back to the late 1970s, when I was growing up in the city and was a student at Cass Technical High School in the heart of downtown. Because I loved living in the city, I often wondered why it was that most of the suburban white kids I knew were so vocal about their hatred of Detroit as well as so hostile to the African Americans who lived there. For that matter, I wondered why there were so few white kids in Detroit or in my school when, according to old yearbook and city photos, there used to be many. Finally, I tried—as I rode the Grand River bus home from school each day—to figure out why Detroit, the home of the American auto industry, looked increasingly abandoned and rundown.

When I went away to college, this adolescent puzzling soon turned into a scholarly inquiry. In my junior year, I came across the book *Detroit: I Do Mind Dying,* by Dan Georgakas and Marvin Surkin, which directly shaped how I thought about the Motor City. This book chronicled numerous dramatic events that had taken place in Detroit and its auto plants during the 1960s and 1970s, and it immediately seemed to me that these events held the key to understanding the city's present. Thanks to this treasure, I went to graduate school knowing exactly what I wanted to study and write about: Detroit and its labor movement after World War II.

In the course of writing this book, I have leaned on many people, and I am happy now to be able to give them the public acknowledgment that they each deserve. The first person I want to thank for encouraging my work is Terrence McDonald at the University of Michigan. This project began with him and has unfolded with his initial words of advice in mind. I also want to thank Carol Karlson at the University of Michigan for her early support of my work. Scholars Nell Irvin Painter, Gary Gerstle, Liz Lunbeck, and Sean

Wilentz of Princeton University were also most helpful and inspiring to me during my years in graduate school and I want to thank them most sincerely.

As I began to research and write my dissertation, I had the good fortune to meet Detroit attorney Ronald Glotta, as well as Walter P. Reuther Library archivists Carrolyn Davis, Mike Smith, Bill LeFevre, Louis Jones, Pat Bartkowski, Tom Featherstone, and Mary Wallace. Ron Glotta graciously shared his time and his voluminous collection of documents about James Johnson Jr., and because my many attempts to locate Johnson himself failed these sources proved invaluable. Likewise the Reuther librarians' wide knowledge of Detroit's archival collections was a godsend.

I am deeply indebted to a number of my fellow historians who have commented on, and encouraged, my work as it has evolved. I am particularly grateful to Robin D. G. Kelley, Nelson Lichtenstein, Darlene Clark Hine, David Colburn, Robert Self and David Farber. I am also thankful that there were other historians who had become as fascinated with the past and present of the Motor City as I had. Thanks to the dynamic works of Kevin Boyle, Tom Sugrue, Suzanne Smith, Karen Miller, David Riddle, and David Freund, I became even more convinced that Detroit is worth thinking about. This belief was furthered by the enthusiasm of several undergraduate students who participated in various "history of Detroit" research seminars that my colleague Charlie Bright, or I offered at the University of Michigan between 1994 and 1997. Thanks to these students' energetic digging in local Motor City archives, many of the stories told in my book are far more interesting and colorful than they otherwise would have been. I particularly want to acknowledge University of Michigan students Amy Carroll, Ellen Schweitzer, Sean Gilbert, Tim Sabota, Greg Parker, John Bauman, Amy Dinges, Charlie Walker, Devon Perez, Rachel Paster, Mike Soules, Katherine Brady, and Brian Dunn. Likewise I want to thank scholar Robert Mast. The interviews he conducted in *Detroit Lives* were invaluable to my work and to the history of the city itself.

The most recent chapter in my book-writing saga unfolded at the University of North Carolina at Charlotte, where I now teach. Moving from Detroit to Charlotte was difficult, but my colleagues have made life here wonderful. I especially want to thank Donna Gabaccia, Cindy Kierner, and David Goldfield, as well as John Smail and my previous UNCC colleagues Lisa Lindsay and Paul Betts, for their support and friendship. I also thank the UNCC administration for awarding me several research grants, which allowed me much-needed resources to finish the book. And speaking of finishing the book, sincere thanks to Cornell University Press and to Sheri Englund in particular for believing in this project and putting so much energy into it.

I would also like to thank several key people in my personal life for their amazing support as I wrote this book. My forever-friend Tamara Smith spent many hours helping me to get my text into type and helping me to meet deadlines ever since this project first began. My friend Eric Beste was a sounding board for this project since the early 1980s. And my friends Marcus Daniel and Patricia Schechter have always been there to listen as well.

To Agnes Spitzer Greig, and to her husband, Robert Greig, I must give special thanks. Robert, you are a saint to have put up with me sighing, swearing, pacing, and fretting at your breakfast nook table summer after summer as I tried to make my dissertation into a book. Agnes, you are my sanity, my deepest confidante, and, of course, my lifelong scrabble/yahtzee/cards/musing-about-life partner. Without the long, late talks, I would never have been able to stick to this. I am so grateful for your wisdom, loyalty, wit, and understanding.

The love and support of my in-laws and family has been equally invaluable to me while completing this book. Daniel and Betsey Wells, as well as my sister-in-law, Caroline Wells, have always encouraged me, stood by me, and believed in me. I thank them for this as well as for welcoming me and my children into their family so lovingly and willingly. They have taught me just how kind and generous the human spirit really can be. My own parents, Frank Wilson Thompson and Ann Curry Thompson, are equally deserving of my gratitude. Their curiosity about the world and anger at injustice have formed the core of who I am and have inspired this book. Thanks to their faith that wrongs can be righted, I have learned to see the past as well as the future in new ways. From my sister, Saskia LoRee Thompson, I have learned that a commitment to Detroit, and to any inner city for that matter, goes deeper than mere loyalty to a locale. Saskia's dedication to improving cities and the lives of inner-city residents is based on her larger faith that unpopular causes are worth fighting for. For that, and giving me a beautiful niece, Isabel LaBarrie Thompson, I am so thankful that she is my sister.

There are four more people that I want to acknowledge in these pages: my sons, Dillon Thompson Erb and Wilder Thompson Erb, my new daughter Ava Thompson Wells, and my husband, Jonathan Daniel Wells. Dillon, I began this project when you were only five months old, and I knew then that you would have to endure a years-long journey with me as I found my way as a parent and historian. In many respects, you and I have grown up together, and you, more than anyone, can appreciate that the saga of writing this book is finally over. I love you; I am so proud of the young adult you have become; and I promise to stand by you as *your* life journeys unfold. Wilder, you, too, have weathered many of my book-writing years with patience and love. I want you to know that having your sweet presence around me is what has made these difficult years most wonderful as well. I love you; I am so proud of you; and I can't wait to help you become the world's first major league baseball player archaeologist! Ava, having you arrive (unexpectedly!) right as I was completing this book was the most wonderful and magical gift I could ever have received. Jon, you also are a gift that I will never take for granted. Your love and support of me, Dillon, and Wilder is ever-present and unqualified. Your daily words, notes, help, companionship, and laughter have been vital to me and to them. I want to thank you for these things, as well as for bringing Ava into the world with me and for willingly taking on more than your fair share of the parental work and responsibility, so that I could finish this book. As a fellow historian and an incredible person, I admire you, lean on you, and love you. Thank you.

Notes

Introduction

1. Jordan Sims, "Going for Broke," in *Rank and File: Personal Histories by Working-Class Organizers,* ed. Staughton and Alice Lynd (Princeton, N.J., 1973), 261.
2. *New York Times,* 16 July 1970; *Washington Post,* 16 July 1970; *Chicago Tribune,* 16 July 1970; *Time Magazine,* 7 June 1971.
3. Several noted historians have illustrated the use of "microhistory"—viewing larger historical events through the lens of an individual, or reconstructing a historical moment around a personal narrative. On the uses of microhistory, see Carlo Ginzburg, "Microhistory: Two or Three Things I Know about It," *Critical Inquiry* (Autumn 1993). For an example of how historians have blended micro with macro history, see Natalie Zemon Davis, *The Return of Martin Guerre* (Cambridge, Mass., 1983), or Sean Wilentz and Paul Johnson, *The Kingdom of Matthias* (New York, 1994).
4. The writings of Thomas Byrne and Mary D. Edsall, Tamar Jacoby, Alan Matusow, Charles Murray, Jonathan Rieder, Fred Siegel, and Jim Sleeper best articulate the tale of white urbanite disenchantment with the Great Society and illuminate—albeit with a critical gaze—the significance of black militancy in the 1960s.
5. For some of the best examples of this literature, see: Arnold R. Hirsch, *Making the Second Ghetto: Race and Housing in Chicago, 1940–1960* (Cambridge, Mass., 1983); Thomas Sugrue, *The Origins of Urban Crisis: Race and Inequality in Postwar Detroit.* (Princeton, N.J., 1996); and Gary Gerstle, "Race and the Myth of Liberal Consensus," *Journal of American History,* 82 (September 1995).
6. By the mid-1970s, in urban centers all over America, political power had shifted into the hands of African Americans. By 1973, there were 48 black mayors in the United States, and by 1990 there were 316. According to the Joint Center for Political and Economic Studies, in 1991, African Americans headed 30 cities with populations of 50,000 or more, and 16 led cities with white majorities. See Frank McCoy, "Black Power in City Hall," *Black Enterprise,* August 1990, 148–151, and Alex Poinsett, "The Changing Color of U.S. Politics," *Ebony,* August 1991. See also David Cochran, *The Color of Freedom: Race and Contemporary American Liberalism* (Albany, N.Y., 1999).
7. The body of work that considers why the U.S. labor movement was in dire straits by the 1980s is vast. Some, such as the authors published in Staughton Lynd's edited volume, *"We Are All Leaders": The Alternative Unionism of the Early 1930s* (Urbana, Ill., 1996), debate with other scholars such as David Brody, "The CIO after 50 Years: A Historical Reckoning," *Dissent* (Fall 1985), 457–72 whether excessive centralization and bureaucratization early on in the movement may be to blame. Others scholars, including Martin Glaberman, Nelson Lichtenstein, Ronald W. Schatz, Joshua B. Freeman, Martin Halpern, Herbert Hill, and Michael Goldfield,

Ronald L. Filippelli and Mark McColloch, have instead called attention to the ill effects of red-baiting and racial discrimination on and within the labor movement. The works of Michael Piore, Charles Sabel, Steve Jefferys, Karl Klare, Katherine Van Wezel Stone, Judith Stein, and others have instead attributed the weakness or decline of the American labor movement to economic, legislative, or political events and forces largely external to organized labor.

8. A few other scholars have also rejected labor history's recent tendency to minimize the relationship between postwar union choices and labor decline in the 1980s. The works of Michael Goldfield, Mike Davis, Kim Moody, Samuel Bowles, David Gordon, and Tom Weisskopf stand out in this regard.

9. Many have already narrated important parts of Detroit's story. This book owes a tremendous debt to these scholars and draws generously on their work. Particularly valuable accounts of the city's recent history have been advanced by Steve Babson, Kevin Boyle, John Bukowczyk, Joseph Darden, Dan Georgakas, James Geschwender, John Hartigan, Steve Jefferys, Christopher Johnson, Nelson Lichtenstein, Robert Mast, Jeffery Miral, Suzanne Smith, Mary Stolberg, Marvin Surkin, Thomas Sugrue, June Manning Thomas, and B. J. Widick.

Chapter 1

1. Box 5, Ronald Glotta Collection, the Walter P. Reuther Library of Labor and Urban Affairs, Detroit.

2. The marriage license of James Johnson and Edna Hudson Johnson, 16 May 1933, Marriage Licenses and Affidavits, Marriage Record Colored, 4 January 1930–22 December 1933, Book 7, Oktibbeha County Courthouse.

3. Testimony of Edna Hudson (p. 55) and memo from Kenneth Cockrel to Dr. Clemens Fitzgerald (based on interviews with the Johnson family, 9 May 1971); trial transcripts and summary of Case No. 70–04631, *The People of the State of Michigan v. James Johnson, Jr.,* Box 5, Ronald Glotta Collection, the Walter P. Reuther Library of Labor and Urban Affairs, Detroit.

4. Marva was born on 16 October 1945.

5. Memo from Cockrel to Fitzgerald and testimony of Edna Hudson (p. 59), RGC.

6. Miscellaneous attorney notes (p. 4), RGC.

7. Even though members of the Johnson family were still discussing the horror of the lynching of Henry Foster as late as the 1970s, this event never made it into the local press. Perhaps it is not surprising that the local paper, the *Starkville Daily News,* did not report this event because very little black news ever made it into that paper. The same can be said of the neighboring *Columbia Commercial Dispatch.* But even the area's two black newspapers, the *Jackson Advocate* and the *Mississippi Enterprise,* were silent despite their avowed commitment to reporting statewide black news. It is worthy of note, however, that during the same week that Johnson's relative was lynched, the Detroit Race Riot of 1943 received front-page coverage in the *Mississippi Enterprise.* Clearly, racial violence in the "Promised Land" of the North was more shocking news than the all-too-common lynchings in the South.

8. On James Johnson's emotional state during this period, see memo from Cockrel to Fitzgerald (p. 4), RGC. Ironically, James Junior's own doctor was well connected to the same powerful white families in Starkville who consistently turned a blind eye to the very sort of racial violence that had so emotionally damaged James. Dr. Hunter Ledbetter Scales was married to Virginia Mills Saunders, first cousin to Johnson's landlady, Elizabeth Saunders Gunn. For more on Johnson's doctor, see the Hunter Scales Collection, Mitchell Memorial Library, Mississippi State University. See also M. Saunders, *Saunders Family History,* Mitchell Memorial Library, Mississippi State University.

9. Report from Fitzgerald to Cockrel, 15 February 1972, Box 5, RGC.

10. Testimony of James Johnson Jr., 11 May 1971, RGC.

11. Ibid.

12. Trial testimony in Michigan indicates that this woman's name was Obera Powers. Research in Starkville, however, indicates that no one by that name lived in Starkville during this time. It is more likely that Edna worked for this woman, Obera Powell, as this name does appear in the record.

13. Memo from Cockrel to Fitzgerald (p. 6), Box 5, RGC.

14. Ibid.

15. Miscellaneous attorney notes, Box 5, RGC.

16. Johnson had repeated problems with getting to work on time because he had to ride the bus. When he finally saved enough money to buy a 1955 Buick Century for $1,200, he couldn't afford the base parking sticker and had to walk two miles across the base to his job. See testimony of James Johnson Jr. (p. 62), Box 5, RGC.

17. Information gathered for these years of James Johnson's life (in Mississippi, while in the army, and in Detroit) comes from an assortment of documents, letters, and miscellaneous notes found in RGC.

18. *The Kerner Report: The 1968 Report of the National Advisory Commission on Civil Disorders,* ed. Fred E. Harris and Tom Wicker (New York, 1988), 12; Marcus Jones, *Black Migration in the United States with an Emphasis on Selected Cities* (Saratoga, Calif., 1980); Daniel M. Johnson and Rex R. Campbell, *Black Migration in America: A Social Demographic History* (Durham, N.C., 1981).

19. For more on the First Great Migration, see Peter Gottlieb, *Making Their Own Way: Southern Blacks' Migration to Pittsburgh, 1916–1930* (Chicago, 1989); James Grossman, *Land of Hope: Chicago, Black Southerners, and the Great Migration* (Chicago, 1989); Florette Henri, *Black Migration: Movement North, 1900–1920* (Garden City, N.Y., 1975); Richard Thomas, *Life for Us Is What We Make It: Building a Black Community in Detroit, 1915–1945* (Bloomington, Ind., 1992).

20. Harris and Wicker, 12.

21. Nicholas Lemann, *The Promised Land: The Great Migration and How It Changed America* (New York, 1991), 5.

22. Ibid., 287.

23. Harris and Wicker, 240.

24. Ibid., 239.

25. Neil McMillen, *Dark Journey: Black Mississippians in the Age of Jim Crow* (Urbana, Ill., 1990), 155.

26. For the history of the first wave of southern blacks to the Motor City, see Thomas, *Life for Us Is What We Make It.*

27. Ford traditionally used the black churches, the NAACP, and the Detroit Urban League as "hiring halls" in the black community, which added to his popularity among African Americans. See Njeru Wa Murage, "Organizational History of the Detroit Urban League, 1916–1960," Ph.D. diss. (Michigan State University, 1993); August Meier and Elliot Rudwick, *Black Detroit and the Rise of the UAW* (New York, 1979), 9 and 85; Joyce Peterson Shaw, "Black Automobile Workers in Detroit, 1910–1930," *Journal of Negro History* 64, no. 3 (Summer 1979). Shaw points out that in addition to functioning as an employment agency, the Detroit Urban League also "served the interest of the Employers Association (to which all companies belonged) by instructing black workers in acceptable work habits, from proper clothing to suitable docility and anti-unionism" (178).

28. Joseph Darden, Richard Child Hill, June Thomas, and Richard Thomas, *Detroit: Race and Uneven Development* (Philadelphia, 1987), 67.

29. For statistics on the ethnic composition of Detroit in the 1950s, see "The Foreign-Born White Population by Country of Birth: Detroit and Twelve Major Urbanized Areas in 1950," United Community Services Research Department, 1955, Box 2, United Community Services Studies and Reports Collection, the Walter P. Reuther Library of Labor and Urban Affairs, Detroit. Large groups of immigrants also came from Scotland, Hungry, Austria, Asia, Belgium, Yugoslavia, Greece, Czechoslovakia, and Sweden. On these groups, see

John J. Bukowczyk, *And My Children Did Not Know Me: A History of the Polish-Americans* (Bloomington, Ind., 1987), and Steve Babson, *Building the Union: Skilled Workers and Anglo-Gaelic Immigrants in the Rise of the UAW* (New Brunswick, 1991). Historian Peter Friedlander captures the work lives of ethnic Detroiters and illustrates the ways in which ethnic identity existed even while a collective working-class identity was being forged in the auto plants (*The Emergence of a UAW Local* [Pittsburgh, 1975]).

30. Alan Brinkley, *Voices of Protest: Huey Long, Father Coughlin, and the Great Depression* (New York, 1982), and *The End of Reform: New Deal Liberalism in Recession and War* (New York, 1995); Leslie Tentler, *Seasons of Grace: A History of the Catholic Archdiocese of Detroit* (Detroit, 1990); Ed Pintzuk, *Reds, Racial Justice, and Civil Liberties: Michigan Communists during the Cold War* (Minneapolis, 1997).

31. Detroit's most notable right-wing demagogue was Father Charles Coughlin, who gained a large following via his radio broadcasts. Ronald Carpenter, *Father Charles E. Coughlin: Surrogate Spokesman for the Disaffected* (Westport, Conn., 1998).

32. Carl O. Smith and Stephen B. Sarasohn, "Hate Propaganda in Detroit," *Public Opinion Quarterly* (Spring 1946).

33. "The Cobo-Edwards Choice," in *Detroit Perspectives: Crossroads and Turning Points,* ed. Wilma Hendrickson (Detroit, 1991), 458.

34. Smith and Sarasohn, 37

35. "The Cobo-Edwards Choice," in Hendrickson, 458.

36. For a detailed account of these battles, see Martin Halpern, *UAW Politics in the Cold War Era* (Albany, N.Y., 1988).

37. Roger Keeran, "'Everything for Victory,' Communist Influence in the Auto Industry during World War II," *Science and Society Quarterly* (Spring 1979): 8–9.

38. Ibid., 10.

39. Douglas P. Seaton, *Catholics and Radicals: The Association of Catholic Trade Unionists and the American Labor Movement, from Depression to Cold War* (Lewisburg, Pa., 1981); John Barnhard, *Walter Reuther and the Rise of the Autoworkers Union* (Boston, 1983); Nelson Lichtenstein, *The Most Dangerous Man in Detroit: Walter Reuther and the Fate of American Labor* (New York, 1995).

40. For one of the most interesting accounts of how every local union did not alter its radical course after the Reuther ascendancy, see Nelson Lichtenstein, "Life at the Rouge: A Cycle of Workers' Control," in *On the Line: Essays in the History of Auto Work,* ed. Nelson Lichtenstein and Stephen Meyers (Urbana, Ill., 1989)

41. Keeran, 2.

42. Dominic Capeci, *Race Relations in Wartime Detroit: The Sojourner Truth Housing Controversy of 1942* (Philadelphia, 1984), and Dominic Capeci and Martha Wilkerson, *Layered Violence: The Detroit Rioters of 1943* (Jacksonville, Miss., 1991), 146.

43. For statistics on new housing units in Detroit during the 1950s, see "New Detroit Memo: 'Change in Number of Housing Units in Detroit over a 15 Year Period, 1951–1966,'" in the New Detroit Collection, Box 22, the Walter P. Reuther Library of Labor and Urban Affairs, Detroit.

44. Thomas Sugrue, *The Origins of Urban Crisis: Race and Inequality in Postwar Detroit* (Princeton, N.J., 1996).

45. *Detroit Free Press,* 7 January 1993.

46. John Frederick Cohassey, "Down on Hastings Street: A Study of Social and Cultural Changes in a Detroit Community," M.A. thesis (Wayne State University, 1993).

47. "Death from All Causes: The Distribution of Total Deaths in the City of Detroit by Subcommunity and Census Tract: 1950," United Community Services Research Department, 1954, and "Infant Deaths: The Distribution of Infant Deaths in the City of Detroit by Subcommunity and Census Tract: 1950," United Community Services Research Department; Boxes 2 and 3, UCSSRC.

48. "Social Ratings of Community Areas in Detroit (1950): A Classification of the Subcommunities Based on Indices of Economic Development and Community Problems," United Community Services Research Department, 1955, Box 6, UCSSRC.

49. Interview with Bernard O'Dell, in Elaine Latzman Moon, *Untold Tales, Unsung Heroes: An Oral History of Detroit's African American Community, 1918–1967* (Detroit, 1994), 346.

50. Interviews with Charles Digg Sr., Shelton Tappes, and Hodges Mason, in Moon, 53, 108, and 136.

51. June Manning Thomas, *Redevelopment and Race: Planning a Finer City in Postwar Detroit* (Baltimore, 1997), 25.

52. Ibid., 60.

53. "A Brief Analysis of Housing Incidents," 21 February 1955, Part 3, Box 2, Folder 18, Detroit Commission on Community Relations Collection, the Walter P. Reuther Library of Labor and Urban Affairs, Detroit.

54. Miscellaneous notes, Part 3, Box 2, Folder 18, CCRC.

55. Smith and Sarasohn, 36.

56. Ultimately, Mayor Cobo demolished 700 buildings in the Black Bottom. The area was vacant for many years until a nonprofit organization finally erected a new housing development, called Lafayette Park, there. This new housing was rented out at a rate "four to ten times higher than what the original residents of the area had paid." See Steve Babson, *Working Detroit: The Making of a Union Town* (New York, 1984.), 158.

57. Harold Norris, "Dislocation without Relocation," in Hendrickson, 476.

58. Babson, *Working Detroit*, 158.

59. Robert Sinclair and Bryan Thompson, *Metropolitan Detroit: An Anatomy of Social Change* (Cambridge, Mass., 1977), 31.

60. Harris and Wicker, 90.

61. Arthur Kornhauser, *Detroit as the People See It: A Survey of Attitudes in an Industrial City* (Detroit, 1952), 63. This is an invaluable survey of 593 men and women, black and white, between May and August 1951. The group chosen came from a mathematically based representative cross-section of the Detroit population. The majority of interviewees were between the ages of 35 and 44. Eighty-nine percent of the respondents were white, and 11 percent were black. White respondents were questioned by white interviewers, and black respondents were questioned by black interviewers. See Kornhauser's introduction and appendix for survey guidelines and controls.

62. Shaw, 178.

63. *Michigan Chronicle*, 31 August 1946. Regarding how the Chrysler Corporation requested "white workers" from outside of Detroit for its operations at the Chevy Gear and Axle Plant when it contacted the U.S. Employment Service, see "Recruit Outsiders but Ignore Local Workers," *Michigan Chronicle*, 31 August 1946, Series 1, Box 6, Folder 11, CCRC. See also the *Pittsburgh Courier*, 12 April 1947, Series 1, Box 15, Folder 7, CCRC.

64. Keeran, 26.

65. Ibid., 26.

66. Meier and Rudwick, 125–34; Halpern, 33–34, and 212; Philip Foner, *Organized Labor and the Black Worker* (New York, 1981), 265–66, and 280.

67. Kornhauser, 91.

68. Ibid., 91.

69. Scholars are beginning to recognize this fundamental truth. Steven Gregory, for example, escapes the black victim paradigm and takes black struggle, resistance, and politics seriously (*Black Corona: Race and the Politics of Place in an Urban Community* [Princeton, N.J., 1998]).

70. Historian Joe Trotter rightly warns scholars not to contribute to what he calls a "ghetto synthesis" interpretation of urban black communities because doing so "camouflages the

dynamics of class divisions within the black population." This study in no way minimizes the import of class divisions and economic inequity in urban black communities. It merely suggests that white racial hostility, in turn, fueled black racial alliances. See Trotter, "Afro-American Urban History: A Critique of the Literature," in *Black Milwaukee,* ed. Trotter (Chicago, 1985), 275. See also Kenneth Kusmer, *A Ghetto Takes Shape: Black Cleveland, 1870–1930* (Urbana, Ill., 1978).

71. For an invaluable discussion of this concept of "racialized class consciousness," see Robin D. G. Kelley, "'We Are Not What We Seem': Rethinking Black Working-Class Opposition in the Jim Crow South," *Journal of American History* 80 (June 1993): 75–113. Regarding how racial consciousness informs struggles against oppression, see Gregory, *Black Corona,* and Earl Lewis, *In Their Own Interests: Race, Class and Power in 20th. Century Norfolk, Virginia* (Berkeley, Calif., 1991).

72. Manning Thomas, 106–108.

73. Dr. Remus Robinson, "Statement to Board of Education," Box 5, Folder 14, Detroit Public Schools Commission on Community Relations Division Collection, the Walter P. Reuther Library of Labor and Urban Affairs, Detroit.

74. Wilbur C. Rich, *Coleman Young and Detroit Politics: From Social Activist to Power Broker* (Detroit, 1989), 75.

75. See interviews with Arthur Johnson and Clyde Cleveland in *Detroit Lives,* ed. Richard Mast (Philadelphia, 1994), 199 and 202.

76. Kornhauser, 21.

77. Ibid., 122.

78. Ibid., 122.

79. Interview with Arthur Johnson, in Mast, 199.

80. Capeci and Wilkerson, 89.

81. Foremen such as Herbert W. Sundermeyer and Michael Kolops found their way into the DPD after World War II, as did auto plant inspectors Ronald W. Wilson and Allan J. Brady and security officers Joseph Jakubezak and James Lustig. See "Police Force Roster GG," 20 November 1951–31 January 1955, Detroit Police Archives, Detroit Police Department.

82. As historian Rebecca Reed points out in her detailed study of the DPD between 1880 and 1918, Detroit's police officers had come more from the ranks of the skilled working class than the unskilled and thus were homogeneous with regard to ethnicity and race. The low ethnic diversity of the DPD also dates back to this earlier period as well. Between 1910 and 1918, for example, 93 percent of Detroit's police officers were "native-born" when "native-born" Detroiters constituted only 66 percent of the city. See Reed, "Regulating the Regulators: Ideology and Practice in the Policing of Detroit, 1880–1918," Ph.D. diss. (University of Michigan, 1991), 100 and 105.

83. Burton Levy, "Changing the Police System," discussion paper for the Detroit Public Safety Committee of the Charter Revision Commission, Box 3, Charter Revision Commission Papers, Burton Historical Collection, Detroit Public Library.

84. NAACP, Detroit Chapter, "White Police in Black Communities," in Hendrickson, 451.

85. Ibid., 452.

86. Ibid., 452.

87. Ibid., 452–53.

88. Ibid., 456.

89. Foner, 410; Charles Denby, *Indignant Heart: A Black Autoworker's Journal* (Boston, 1978), 174.

90. Foner, 410–11.

91. Rich, 76.

92. Schoolcraft Gardens Association, "History of Schoolcraft Gardens," in Hendrickson, 459.

93. Ibid., 459.

94. Ibid., 461–62n.

95. Ibid., 462.
96. Ibid., 461.
97. Christopher H. Johnson, *Maurice Sugar: Law, Labor, and the Left in Detroit, 1912–1950* (Detroit, 1988).
98. Kornhauser, 102.
99. Ibid., 100.
100. Ibid., 62.
101. Ibid., 84.
102. Regarding postwar migration to the suburbs, see Kenneth Jackson, *Crabgrass Frontier: The Suburbs of the United States* (New York, 1985); Jon Teaford, *City and Suburb: The Political Fragmentation of Metropolitan America* (Baltimore, 1979); Gregory Weiher, *Fractured Metropolis: Political Fragmentation and Metropolitan Segregation* (Albany, N.Y., 1991); Robert Fishman, *Bourgeois Utopias* (New York, 1987); Margaret Marsh, *Suburban Lives* (New Brunswick, N.J., 1990); Michael Ebner, *Creating Chicago's North Shore: A Suburban History* (Chicago, 1988), Michael Ebner, "Re-Reading Suburban America: Population Decentralization, 1810–1980," *American Quarterly* 37, no. 1 (1985); Sharon Zukin, "The Hollow Center: United States Cities in the Global Era," in *America at Century's End,* ed. Alan Wolfield (Berkeley, Calif., 1991); Thomas Sugrue, "Crabgrass-roots Politics: Race, Rights, and the Reaction against Liberalism in the Urban North, 1940–1960," *Journal of American History* 82, no. 2 (September 1995): 551; Frederick Wirt, Benjamin Walter, Francine Rabinowitz, and Deborah Hensler, *On the City's Rim: Politics and Policy in Suburbia* (Lexington, Mass., 1972).
103. Thomas Sugrue, in the *Detroit Free Press,* 1 June 1997.
104. Ibid., 2.
105. Kornhauser, 38.

Chapter 2

1. "To Fulfill These Rights—in the Area of Police-Community Relations and Effective Law Enforcement," remarks by Police Commissioner Ray Girardin before the Dexter Boulevard Redevelopment, Inc., 28 July 1966, Box 10, Ray Girardin Papers, Burton Historical Collection, Detroit Public Library.
2. Kenneth Cockrel to Dr. Clemens Fitzgerald, p.10. Memo, May 9,1971. Box 5, Ron Glotta Collection, the Walter P. Reuther Library of Labor and Urban Affairs, Detroit.
3. James Johnson Jr., interview with attorney, 8 May 1971, Box 5, RGC.
4. *Detroit Free Press,* 9 November 1961.
5. *Detroit Free Press,* 5 November 1961.
6. *Detroit News,* 8 November 1961.
7. Ibid.
8. *Detroit Free Press,* 7 November 1961.
9. *Michigan Chronicle,* 4 November 1961.
10. *Detroit News,* 8 November 1961; *Detroit Free Press,* 8 November 1961.
11. *Detroit News,* 8 November 1961.
12. Ibid.
13. "TAP Projects Index," memo, Box 6, Folder 24, United Community Services Planning Department Collection, the Walter Reuther Library of Labor and Urban Affairs, Detroit.
14. "Project Head Start: Questions and Answer Fact Sheet," Series 1, Part 2, Box 26, Folder 1, NAACP Collection, the Walter P. Reuther Library of Labor and Urban Affairs, Detroit.
15. "Program Index TAP," 30 June 1966, Series 2, Box 2, Folder 12, Commission on Community Relations Collections, the Walter P. Reuther Library of Labor and Urban Affairs, Detroit.
16. "EOA Proposals and TAP Report," Box 45, UCSPDC.

17. "Progress Report of the Western Community Action Center, TAP," 1 November 1965, Series 7, Part 1, Box 30, NAACP Collection, Walter P. Reuther Library of Labor and Urban Affairs, Detroit.

18. "Available Programs and Services," flyer, 14 January 1965, Box 243, Folder 8, Jerome P. Cavanagh Collection, the Walter P. Reuther Library of Labor and Urban Affairs, Detroit.

19. "TAP Projects Index," UCSPDC.

20. "Project Summaries June, 1966," City of Detroit Mayor's Committee Total Action against Poverty, Box 6, Folder 24, UCSPDC.

21. Regarding how OEO funds were distributed from 1 December 1964 to 31 August 1965, see "Total Action against Poverty Policy Advisory Committee," meeting notes, 15 February 1965, Series 5, Box 243, Folder 8, JPCC.

22. "The Detroit Low-Income Family," Detroit Urban League Report, April 1966, Series 1, Part 2, Box 13, Folder 17, NAACP Collection.

23. Ibid., 33.

24. Ibid., 11.

25. "Detroit Urban League in Action," newsletter, December 1967, Series 1, Part 2, Box 13, Folder 18, NAACP Collection.

26. See Series 1, Part 2, Box 26, Folder 21, NAACP Collection.

27. "Operation Bootstrap: A Project Designed by Region 9 Building Chairman, Detroit Public School System," Series 1 Part 2, Box 23, Folder 31, NAACP Collection.

28. "Economic Opportunity Act of 1964. Community Action Program Proposals," TAP, City of Detroit, 1964, Box 45, UCSPDC.

29. "Detroit Metropolitan Area Employment and Income by Age, Sex, Color, and Residence," Detroit Commission on Community Relations, May 1963, Series 1, Part 2, Box 10, Folder 5, NAACP Collection.

30. Ibid.

31. Albert J. Mayer and Thomas F. Hoult, "Race and Residence in Detroit," in Leonard Gordon, ed. *A City in Racial Crisis: The Pre- and Post-1967 Riot* (Dubuque, Iowa, 1971), 5.

32. Marc Belding Anderson, "Racial Discrimination in Detroit: A Spatial Analysis of Racism," M.A. thesis (Wayne State University, 1969), Table 3, p. 82.

33. Ibid., Map 21: "Relief Case Loads by Tract, 1965," p. 134.

34. Mayor Jerome Cavanagh, "Message to the Open Occupancy Conference, 1963," and Richard V. Marks, "Message to the Open Occupancy Conference, 1963," both in Gordon, ed., *A City in Racial Crisis*, 30, 32.

35. Erwin Canham, chair, Task Force on Economic Growth and Opportunity of the Chamber of Commerce of the United States, Washington, D.C., to Jerome Cavanagh, 27 January 1965, Series 5, Box, 243, Folder 7, JPCC.

36. Morton Engleberg to Robert Toohey, 13 February 1965, Series 5, Box 243, Folder 7, JPCC.

37. "The American Crisis: A Liberal Looks at the Ashes of Dead Dreams and Issues a Manifesto for Survival," *Detroit Free Press Magazine,* 6 August 1967, Part 1, Box 30, NAACP Collection.

38. B. J. Widick, *Detroit: City of Race and Class Violence* (Chicago, 1972), 155.

39. Joseph Darden, Richard Child Hill, June Thomas, and Richard Thomas, *Detroit: Race and Uneven Development* (Philadelphia, 1987), 203.

40. NAACP Complaint Form: Mr. and Mrs. Herbert Wilson, 17 June 1966, Series 3, Part 2, Box 31, Folder 3, NAACP Collection.

41. NAACP Complaint Form: Mrs. Thomasyne Faulkner, 1 April 1966, Series 3, Part 2, Box 31, folder 6, NAACP Collection.

42. Mr. Ulmer to Mr. Patterson, 13 May 1963, Series 5, Part 1, Box 22, NAACP Collection.

43. "Police-Community Relations: Case Review and Present Status 1964 (November–December)" (p. 4), Series 3, Box 2, Folder 35, CCRC.

44. Miscellaneous notes, Series 3, Box 2, Folder 18, CCRC.

45. "Cross-section Survey of the Model Neighborhood," for the Model Neighborhood Citizens Planning Conference, 18–20 September 1968, Box 14, City of Detroit City Planning Commission Collection, Burton Historical Collection, Detroit Public Library.

46. Richard V. Marks, secretary/executive director, CCCR, memo, 14 June 1966, and Housing Committee, CCCR, memo, Series 1, Part 2, Box 10, Folder 8, NAACP Collection.

47. "Detroit Program for an Integrated School System," 5 October 1964, Box 5, Folder 14, Detroit Public Schools Commission on Community Relations Collection, the Walter P. Reuther Library of Labor and Urban Affairs, Detroit.

48. Whereas 8 Detroit schools were all black in February 1962, by October 1965, 10 schools were all black. Despite the fact that black students comprised 54.8 percent of the Detroit school body of 294,822 children in 1965, by that year, 30 inner-city schools had no black kids. It angered city blacks further that very little improvement had been made in integrating the teaching or administrative staff of the Detroit Public School System. In 1961, of the 10,516-person instructional staff, 78.1 percent were white and 21.6 percent were black. In 1965, however, that staff had increased to 11,157, and still 70.2 percent were white while only 29.5 percent were black. As for school administrators, in 1961, 19 out of 293 assistant principals were black, but by 1965, still only 19 out of 295 assistant principals and 13 out of 244 principals were African-American. At the high school level, the degree of segregation that continued to exist by 1965 was particularly dramatic. For more on this, see "Racial Distribution of Students and Contract Personnel in the Detroit Public Schools" and "Racial Composition of Detroit Public High Schools in 1965," December 1965, Series 1, Box 6, PSCCRDC.

49. Joyce Peterson Shaw, "Black Automobile Workers in Detroit, 1910–1930," *Journal of Negro History* 64, no. 3 (Summer 1979): 177; Philip Foner, *Organized Labor and the Black Worker: 1619–1981* (New York, 1981), 221.

50. "Percent Distribution of Family Heads by Their Occupation, by Race Detroit, 1969," Research Division, City Planning Commission, 18 April 1972, Box 15, City of Detroit City Planning Commission Collection.

51. "Employment Conditions in the Model Neighborhood, 1970," Social Planning Division, Detroit Planning Commission, 21 July 1970, Box 14, City of Detroit City Planning Commission Collection.

52. Michael Lipsey and David Olson, *Commission Politics: The Processing of Racial Crisis in America* (New Brunswick, New Jersey, 1977), 348.

53. "Employment Conditions in the Model Neighborhood, 1970," 18.

54. "Who's on Welfare?," Charter Revision Commission, 11 June 1971, Box 3, Charter Revision Commission Collection, Burton Historical Collection, Detroit Public Library.

55. "Public Assistance in Metropolitan Detroit," booklet, August 1964, United Community Services Metro Detroit, Box 16, Folder 29, UCSPDC.

56. "Turnaround in the Seventies," booklet, Detroit Police Department and Michigan Office of Criminal Justice Programs, 1973, Part 3, Box 69, Folder 2, CCRC.

57. Mrs. Jessie Wallace to Robert Tindal, 30 September 1966, Part 2, Box 5, Folder 21, NAACP Collection.

58. Burton Levy, "Changing the Police System," 8. Discussion paper for the Public Safety Committee of the Charter Revision Commission. Box 3, Charter Revision Commission Collection.

59. As quoted in William Serrin, "God Help Our City," *Atlantic Monthly,* March 1969, 115.

60. There is a substantial body of literature on the police in the United States. Regarding how the police feel about race relations, as well as how to historicize police brutality, see Mark Baker, *Cops: Their Own Lives in Their Own Words* (New York, 1985); D. Yarmey, *Understanding Police and Police Work: Psychological Issues* (New York, 1990); Marvin Dulaney, *Black Police in America* (Bloomington, Ind., 1996); Gordon Misner and Lee Brown, *The Police and Society: An Environment for Collaboration and Confrontation* (Englewood Cliffs, N.J., 1981); Jerome Skolnick and James Fyfe, *Above the Law: Police and the Excessive Use of Force* (New York, 1993); Leonard Ruchelman, ed., *Who Rules*

the Police? (New York, 1973); Ronald Kahn, "Urban Reform and Police Accountability in New York City, 1950–1974," in *Urban Problems and Public Police,* ed. Robert Lineberry and Louis Masotti (Lexington, Mass., 1975).

61. "How Detroit Police View Treatment of Negroes," survey in the *Detroit Free Press,* Box 3, Folder 1, Dan Georgakas Collection, the Walter P. Reuther Library of Labor and Urban Affairs, Detroit.

62. The arrest figures of the DPD attest to the fact that officers did not view blacks in the same way as they did whites. See: The Detroit Police Department, "Statistical Annual Reports," 1964, 1965, 1967, 1975, Detroit Police Department Museum and Archives Unit. See also "Total Crime and Prosecution Arrests—Twenty-Five Year Comparison," Detroit Police Department, Museum and Archives Unit.

63. "NAACP Proposals for Effective Law Enforcement and Crime Prevention," statement of Robert Tindal, executive secretary; Bruce Miller, chairman of the Legal Redress Committee, Part 2, Box 24, Folder 3, NAACP Collection.

64. McGowan to Bush, memo, 26 January 1967, Part 3, Box 69, Folder 19, CCRC.

65. "Shooting Investigated by the Inkster and Romulus Branch NAACP," 23 August 1963, Series 5, Part 1, Box 22, NAACP Collection.

66. "Background Statement on Police-Community Relations," the City of Detroit Commission on Community Relations, Box 3, Folder 3, CCRC.

67. The Cotillion Club to Mayor Cavanagh, 22 January 1965, Part 2, Box 24, Folder 3, NAACP Collection.

68. "Police Injury Cases," report, 19 February 1964, Box 3, Folder 1, DGC.

69. Ray Girardin, "The Police and the Community," speech, 17 January 1964, Box 10, Ray Girardin Papers. Burton Historical Collection, Detroit Public Library.

70. Richard V. Marks, "Memo for Commission Information and Action," Box 4, Folder 18, DGC.

71. Ibid.

72. Leigins S. Moore to Rev. Charles Williams, 19 February 1965, Part 2, Box 5, Folder 20, NAACP Collection.

73. Thomas Green Jr., M.D., to Jerome Cavanagh, 22 November 1965, Part 2, Box 5, Folder 20, NAACP Collection.

74. Moore to Rev. Williams, NAACP Collection.

75. Mattie Barrow to Mayor Cavanagh, 16 January 1965, Series 5, Box 217, Folder 7, JPCC.

76. Editorial on WJBK, 30 April 1965, Series 1, Part 2, NAACP Collection.

77. James Geschwender, *Class, Race, and Worker Insurgency: The League of Revolutionary Black Workers* (New York, 1977), 72.

78. A. Rahrig to Mayor Cavanagh, 1965, Series 5, Box 217, Folder 7, JPCC.

79. George Gerhold to Mayor Cavanagh, 7 January 1965, Series 5, Box 217, Folder 7, JPCC.

80. Mrs. E. Vick to Mayor Cavanagh, 6 January 1965, Series 5, Box 217, Folder 8, JPCC.

81. "A Policeman's Wife" to Mayor Cavanagh, 11 January 1965, Series 5, Box 217, Folder 9, JPCC.

82. Ms. Elma French to Mayor Cavanagh, 6 January 196,. Series 5, Box 217, Folder 8, JPCC.

83. Pauline Ford to Mayor Cavanagh, 5 January 1965, Series 5, Box 217, Folder 8, JPCC.

84. Anonymous to Mayor Cavanagh, received in mayor's office 4 February 1965, Series 5, Box 225, Folder 4, JPCC. For more hostile correspondence, see W. Ingersoll to Honorable Mayor's Committee, 6 January 1964, Series 5, Box 225, Folder 4, JPCC.

85. Irving Bluestone to Walter Reuther, 5 June 1967, Box 429, Folder 1, Walter P. Reuther Collection, the Walter P. Reuther Library of Labor and Urban Affairs, Detroit.

86. Cavanagh did, however, rename his Total Action against Poverty program Human Resource Development in 1967, so that "negative comparisons between the agencies clients could be avoided by eliminating the word 'poverty' from the agencies name." See "Mayor's Committee for Human Resources Development," newsletter, March–April 1967, Box 6, Folder 24, UCSPDC.

87. "Report on Investigations of Law Enforcement Claims against the Detroit Police Department" (p. 24), June 1966, Series 1, Part 2, Box 19, Folder 19, CCRC.
88. Ibid.
89. Richard Marks of the CCR, for example, wrote to a local pastor in 1964 that the DPD was recruiting men to fill one hundred vacancies on the force, "recognizing their responsibility to give equal opportunity to all." He told this pastor, "We trust you will communicate the opportunity to the members of your congregation and to others whom you feel may qualify." See Richard Marks to "Dear Pastor," 9 March 1964, Part 3, Box 68, Folder 19, CCRC.
90. CCR to Girardin, memo, 16 September 1964, Series 3, Box 2, Folder 34, CCRC.
91. Criminal Investigation Division to Commission Ray Girardin, DPD memo, 1 October 1964, Part 3, Box 68, CCRC.
92. Richard Marks to Commission Sub-Committee on Police-Community Relations, Ray Girardin, and Robert Tindal, memo, 8 December 1964, Series 3, Box 2, Folder 24, CCRC.
93. Citizens Complaint Bureau, internal memo, Part 2, Box 24, Folder 6, NAACP Collection.
94. Girardin to Wadsworth, memo regarding Joseph et al., 13 January 1965, Series 1, Part 2, Box 4, Folder 22, NAACP Collection.
95. Girardin to Wadsworth, memo regarding Dowdell, 13 January 1965, Series 1, Part 2, Box 4, Folder 22, NAACP Collection.
96. Girardin to Wadsworth, memo regarding the Smiths, 13 January 1964, Series 1, Part 2, Box 4, Folder 22, NAACP Collection.
97. Girardin to Wadsworth, memo, 2 February 1965. For more correspondence from Police Commissioner Girardin during this time period, see Boxes 3 and 4, Ray Girardin Papers.
98. Citizens Complaint Bureau, internal memo.
99. "Interim Report to the Public Safety Commission of the Detroit Charter Revision Commission," Maurice Kelman and David Hood, law professors, Wayne State University, Box 3, Charter Revision Commission Collection.
100. "Citizen Complaint Statistics, 1960–1975," the Detroit Police Department. Museum and Archives Unit.
101. "The Negro Community and City Hall," speech, Dr. Albert Wheeler, 16 January 1967, Series 1, Part 2, Box 19, Folder 21, NAACP Collection.
102. "Background Statement on Police-Community Relations," CCRC.
103. Ibid.
104. For more on this, see Suzanne Smith, *Dancing in the Streets* (Cambridge, Mass., 2000).
105. "The Negro Community and City Hall," NAACP Collection.
106. "Report on Investigations of Law Enforcement Claims," CCRC.
107. H. B. Sissel, Consultant, U.S. Department of Commerce, Community Relations Service, Washington, D.C., to Mr. Anthony Ripley, mayor's office, 24 September 1965, Part 3, Box 67, Folder 23, CCRC.
108. Stanley Webb to Richard Marks, 26 January 1965, Series 3, Box 3, Folder 2, CCRC.
109. Ibid.
110. *Michigan Chronicle,* 4 November 1961.
111. Francis Kornegay to Jerome Cavanagh, 15 April 1965, Series 1, Part 2, Box 3, Folder 16, NAACP Collection.
112. "Eyewitness Account of the Origins of the Riot—Detroit, July, 1967," Rene Freeman (staff director of the West Community Organization), 3 August 1967, circulated by James Campbell of the Detroit Industrial Mission, Box 8, Folder 3, CCRC.
113. Ibid.
114. Albert Bergesen, "Race Riots in 1967: An Analysis of Police Violence in Detroit and Newark," *Journal of Black Studies* (March 1992).
115. Andrew J. Glass and Jesse W. Lewis Jr., "Segment of American Society Turns to Open Insurrection," *Washington Post,* 30 July 1967; quoted in Ann K. Johnson, *Urban Ghetto Riots, 1965–1968: A Comparison of Soviet and American Press Coverage* (Boulder, Colo., 1996), 76.

116. "A Fireman Dies: Negro Is Beaten," *Washington Post*, 26 July 1967; quoted in Johnson, 77.
117. For the most detailed and comprehensive narrative account of Detroit's civic rebellion, see Sidney Fine, *Violence in the Model City: The Cavanagh Administration, Race Relations, and the Detroit Riot of 1967* (Ann Arbor, Mich., 1989), passim.

Chapter 3

1. Eugene Martin, president Local Union 805, UAW, to TULC, 30 July 1963, Box 38, Folder 29, UAW Fair Practices Collection, the Walter P. Reuther Library of Labor and Urban Affairs, Detroit.
2. Kim Moody, *An Injury to All: The Decline of American Unionism* (London: Verso, 1988), 74.
3. Robert Battle III, "United We Won Another Battle," *The Vanguard*, February 1966; in the TULC Vertical File: The 1960s, the Walter P. Reuther Library of Labor and Urban Affairs, Detroit.
4. Horace Sheffield, "Labor Must Erase Last Vestiges of Race Bias," *Michigan Chronicle*, 22 April 1961.
5. *Michigan Chronicle*, 12 March 1960.
6. *Michigan Chronicle*, 14 November 1959.
7. *New University Thought*, (September–October 1963), 1.
8. "Youth and Education Center," TULC brochure, TULC Vertical File: The 1960s.
9. *Michigan Chronicle*, 28 May 1960.
10. Robert Battle III, press release on behalf of the TULC, Wednesday, 24 August 1960, TULC Vertical File: The 1960s.
11. "Trade Union Leadership Council: Experiment in Community Action," interview with Battle and Sheffield, *New University Thought* (September–October 1963).
12. Ibid., 5.
13. Horrace Sheffield in *The Vanguard*, June 1962.
14. Nelson Lichtenstein, "Walter Reuther and the Rise of Labor Liberalism," in *Labor Leaders in America*, ed. Melvyn Dubofsky and Warren Van Tine (Chicago, 1987), 300.
15. According to its constitution, the TULC was "a non-partisan and non-profit organization devoted to the struggles of Negro people, and other oppressed peoples, for first-class citizenship, full freedom, and unrestricted equality in every aspect of the political, economic, and social life of America." See "Constitution of the Trade Union Leadership Council, Inc., Box 3, Folder 19, Ernest Dillard Collection, the Walter P. Reuther Library of Labor and Urban Affairs, Detroit.
16. Executive Board TULC, Inc., to Bill Beckham, 5 July 1959, Part 2, Box 12, Folder 16, Jewish Labor Committee Collection, the Walter P. Reuther Library of Labor and Urban Affairs, Detroit.
17. Ibid.
18. Ibid.
19. Alex Roche, COPE director Local 223, to members Local 223, Series 1, Box 12, Wayne County AFL-CIO Office of the President and Vice President Collection, the Walter P. Reuther Library of Labor and Urban Affairs, Detroit.
20. Joseph Turiani, "The Trade Union Leadership Council and the 1961 Detroit Mayoral Election," unpublished paper (Department of History, Wayne State University), 23.
21. Al Barbour, Wayne County AFL-CIO, to Roy Reuther, 1 November 1961, Series 1, Box 12, OPVPC.
22. *New University Thought*.
23. Horace Sheffield, as quoted in *Michigan Chronicle*, 22 April 1961.
24. Ernest Dillard, "Report of the Public Relations Committee for the Past Two Years," Box 3, Folder 30, EDC.

25. Al Barbour to Horrace Sheffield, 23 October 1961, Box 12, OPVPC.
26. Ibid.
27. Ibid.
28. *Detroit News*, 16 August 1966.
29. For an interesting discussion of the historical relationship between Jews and African-American social movements, see Jack Salzman and Cornel West, eds., *Struggles in the Promised Land: A History of Black-Jewish Relations in the United States* (New York, 1997).
30. Jack Casper to Irwin Small, 14 January 1966, Part 2, Box 12, Folder 16, JLCC.
31. Ibid.
32. Ibid.
33. "TULC Campaign Breaks Race Obstacle in UAW," *The Vanguard*, June 1962.
34. Alphons Steinmetz (president of the Sophie Wright Settlement Community Council and Affiliated Block Clubs) to Walter P. Reuther, 17 January 1965, Box 4, Folder 3, Walter P. Reuther Collection, Walter P. Reuther Library of Labor and Urban Affairs, Detroit.
35. Irving Bluestone to Brendan Sexton, 17 May 1965, Box 378, Folder 6, WPRC.
36. Walter Reuther to Brendan Sexton, 11 May 1965, Box 378, Folder 6, WPRC.
37. See Kevin Boyle, *The UAW in the Heyday of American Liberalism, 1945–1968* (Ithaca, N.Y., 1989).
38. Walter Reuther to Jerome Cavanagh, 26 January 1966, Box 428, Folder 11, WPRC.
39. Mel Ravitz to Jerome Cavanagh, 7 August 1964, Series 2, Box 30, OPVPC.
40. *Detroit News*, 15 October 1953.
41. Irving Bluestone to Walter Reuther, 5 June 1967, "Petition to Remove Cavanagh and UAW Statement on the Matter," Box 499, Folder 1, WPRC. See also a slightly different draft submitted for consideration by Millie Jefferies.
42. Jerome Cavanagh to Walter Reuther, 9 June 1967, Box 429, Folder 1, WPRC.
43. Irving Bluestone to Stephen Shulman, 19 September 1966, Box 378, Folder 6, WPRC.
44. Walter Reuther to Mrs. Medger Evers and Mr. Roy Wilkins, executive secretary NAACP, telegram, Box 54, Folder 41, UAWFPC.
45. Eugene Martin, president Local Union 835, to TULC, Inc., Executive Board, 30 July 1963, Box 38, Folder 29, UAWFPC.
46. Reuther received this award on 17 November 1964.
47. Statement prepared for Mr. Hugh Murphy, Administrator Bureau of Apprenticeship Training, U.S. Department of Labor for Presentation, 4 November 1965, in Lansing, Michigan, Box 54, Folder 42, UAWFPC.
48. Ethel Schlacht to Walter Reuther, 17 April 1966, Box 54, Folder 43, UAWFPC.
49. Wallace H. Brown to Walter Reuther, 27 June 1966, Box 54, Folder 43, UAWFPC.
50. Thomas Brooks, "Workers White and Black: DRUM Beats in Detroit," *Dissent* (January–February 1970); and Horace Harris, graduate student in international relations, and Deanna Utlefe, graduate student in economics, "Dodge Revolutionary Movement (DRUM): A Study through Interviews," unpublished paper (p. 7), 15 September 1969, Box 1, Folder 10, Enid Eckstein Collection, the Walter P. Reuther Library of Labor and Urban Affairs, Detroit.
51. Brooks, "Workers White and Black," 2.
52. As Steve Jefferys points out, Chrysler's "failure to use its considerable profits to borrow or to invest in new plants created a situation where front-line supervisors found themselves forced to use aging machinery at even higher capacities" Steve Jeffreys, *Management and Managed: Fifty Years of Crisis at Chrysler* (Cambridge, 1986), 108.
53. Grievance 3886 of Charles Stein, Badge 9171–2537, 9 September 1960, Box 8, Folder 2, UAW Local 7 Collection, the Walter P. Reuther Library of Labor and Urban Affairs, Detroit.
54. Grievance 3989 of W. Eichrecht, Badge 9150–6488, 13 October 1960, Box 8, Folder 1, UAW Local 7 Collection.

55. Meeting minutes union and management, Grievance 4516, Box 8, Folder 9, UAW Local 7 Collection. See also Grievance 4366, Department 9174, 28 November 1962, Box 8, Folder 8, UAW Local 7 Collection.

56. Grievance 4372, 19 December 1962, Box 8, Folder 8, UAW Local 7 Collection.

57. Ibid.

58. Stamping Group, Eight Mile Road plant, minutes of meeting between Labor Relations Supervisor and Plant Shop Committee, Regional Meeting 28, 24 July 1962, regarding Grievance EM-124, Dept. 3361, 24 May 1962, Box 68, Folder 32, UAW Local 212 Collection, the Walter P. Reuther Library of Labor and Urban Affairs, Detroit.

59. Stamping Group, Eight Mile Road plant, minutes of meeting between Labor Relations Supervisor and Plant Shop Committee, Regional Meeting 33, 13 August 1963, regarding Grievance EM-226, Dept. 9750, 18 July 1963, Employee E. Cherry, Box 69, Folder 4, UAW Local 212 Collection.

60. Stamping Group, Eight Mile Road plant, minutes of meeting between Labor Relations Supervisor and Plant Shop Committee, Regional Meeting 35, 11 September 1962, regarding Grievance EM-148, Dept. 9890, 13 June 1962, Box 68, Folder 32, UAW Local 212 Collection.

61. Report on Shop Committee Grievances to Plant Manager, 11 January 1963, regarding Grievance 4370, 12 December 1962, Box 8, Folder 10, UAW Local 7 Collection.

62. Grievance 4277, employees F. Kranak, Badge 2745, J. Kosik, Badge 5388, and F. Purczynski, 7 March 1962, Box 8, Folder 8, UAW Local 7 Collection.

63. Grievance 4276, C. England, B. Susylo, O. Pearson, and R. Webster, 7 March 1962, Box 8, Folder 8, UAW Local 7 Collection.

64. Charles R. Walker, Robert H. Guest, and Arthur N. Turner, *The Foreman on the Assembly Line* (Cambridge, Mass., 1956), 97.

65. "'The Man in the Middle': A Social History of Automobile Industry Foremen," in *On the Line: Essays in the History of Auto Work,* ed. Nelson Lichtenstein and Stephen Meyers (Urbana, Ill., 1989).

66. Ibid.

67. Walker et. al., 17 and 40.

68. Jefferys, 54.

69. Robert David Leiter, *The Foreman in Industrial Relations,* Studies of History, Economics, and Public Law, Columbia University, 542 (New York, 1948), 17.

70. Ibid., 84–85.

71. Leiter, 89; and see Lichtenstein, "'The Man in the Middle.'"

72. Lichtenstein, "'The Man in the Middle.'"

73. Jefferys, 154.

74. Ibid., 157.

75. Jefferson Avenue assembly plant meeting, minutes, 10 November 1964, Grievance 4716, 13 October 1964, employee H. Lewis, Box 12, Folder 14, UAW Local 7 Collection.

76. NAACP Complaint Form: Mr. James Lee Cowans, 1 June 1966, Series 3, Part 2, Box 31, Folder 11, NAACP Collection. Walter P. Reuther Library of Labor and Urban Affairs, Detroit. NAACP Complaint Form: Mr. Robert Washington, 30, August 1966, Series 3, Part 2, Box 31, Folder 12, NAACP Collection.

77. Jefferson assembly plant meeting minutes, Labor Relations Supervisor and Plant Shop Committee, 9 June 1964, regarding Grievance 4643, Box 12, Folder 12, UAW Local 7 Collection.

78. Ibid.

79. Jefferson assembly plant meeting minutes, 10 November 1964, regarding Grievance 4722, Box 12, Folder 14, UAW Local 7 Collection.

80. Jefferson assembly plant meeting minutes, 15 December 1964, regarding Grievance 4763, Box 12, Folder 14, UAW Local 7 Collection.

81. "Report of Grievance and Adjustment," regarding Grievance AD-1180, Dept. 3200, 27 December 1965, Box 72, Folder 12, UAW Local 3 Collection, Walter P. Reuther Library of Labor and Urban Affairs, Detroit.
82. Ibid.
83. Jefferson Avenue assembly plant meeting minutes, 1 December 1964, regarding Grievance 4760, Box 12, Folder 14, UAW Local 7 Collection.
84. Jefferson Avenue assembly plant meeting minutes, 3 November 1964, regarding Grievance 4709, Box 12, Folder 14, UAW Local 7 Collection.
85. The *BULLETIN* (newspaper of the NCFDA), April 1960, Box 47, Folder 8, Arthur Hughes Collection, the Walter P. Reuther Library of Labor and Urban Affairs, Detroit.
86. See the NCFDA leaflet "The Shameful Mess" and the leaflet "What Our UAW Needs," Box 47, Folder 8, AHC.
87. NCFDA leaflet "Chrysler 7 Women All Out Belle Isle Picnic," Box 47, Folder 8, AHC.
88. Anonymous report, Wednesday, 27 July 1960, regarding 1960 NCFDA "Rank and File" women's picnic, Box 47, Folder 8, AHC.
89. Ibid.
90. Ibid.
91. Report, "A. H.," 27 July 1960, Box 47, Folder 8, AHC.
92. Jefferson assembly plant meeting minutes, Labor Relations Supervisor with the Plant Shop Committee, 2 January 1964, regarding Grievance 4561, Box 12, Folder 11, UAW Local 7 Collection.
93. See "Strike Notices Sent since 1958 Summarized Yearly, Numerically by Local," Box 21, Folder 4, AHC.
94. Stamping Group, Eight Mile Road plant, minutes of meeting between Labor Relations Supervisor and Plant Shop Committee, Regional Meeting 38, 2 October 1962, Grievance EM-188, Dept. 3505, 4 September 1962, Box 68, Folder 32, UAW Local 212 Collection.
95. Stamping Group, Eight Mile Road plant, minutes of meeting between Labor Relations Supervisor and Plant Shop Committee, Regional Meeting 31, 14 August 1962, regarding grievance of 3 May 1962, and Regional Meeting 34, 4 September 1962, regarding Grievance EM-134, 1 June 1962, Box 68, Folder 32, UAW Local 212 Collection.
96. For some of the most valuable information on the use of the grievance procedure within the UAW, see Robert Asher and Ronald Edsforth, eds., *Autowork* (Albany, N.Y., 1995).
97. "Notes on Comments Made on Opening Day, Thursday July 2, 1964 at Noon Break of Contract Negotiations," Series 4, Part 2, Box 20, Folder 6, AHC.
98. Chrysler Corporation, Press Information Services, press statement, 9 September 1964, Series 4, Part 2, Box 20, Folder 6, AHC.
99. Letter from the Executive Board of the TULC reprinted in the *Detroit Free Press,* 10 July 1963, Series 4, Part 2, Box 20, Folder 7, AHC.
100. Ibid.
101. Jefferson Avenue assembly plant meeting minutes, 10 November 1964, Grievance 4720, Box 12, Folder 14, UAW Local 7 Collection.
102. Letter from worker Harold Echols to "whom it may concern," 12 December 1964, Box 63, Folder 77, UAW Local 212 Collection.
103. Ibid.
104. William J. Porter to Executive Board Members UAW Local 212, 25 January 1965, Box 63, Folder 77, UAW Local 212 Collection.
105. Ibid.
106. NAACP Complaint Forms, Series 3, Part 2, Box 31, Folder 16, NAACP Collection.
107. Fair Practices Case A-88-67, Michigan Civil Rights Commission Case 3915-EM, *William E. Mims v. International Union UAW*, regarding 30 November 1966 discharge, Box 17, Folder 47, UAW Local 3 Collection.

108. Michigan Civil Rights Commission Case 3183-EM, "Notice of Disposition," Box 17, Folder 47, UAW Local 3 Collection.

109. Ibid.

110. Chrysler Corporation, Huber Avenue foundry meeting minutes, 15 June 1967, Meeting 8, Grievance HA 69–124, Dept. 9400, Shift 3, 15 March 1967, Box 78, Folder 10, UAW Local 3 Collection.

111. Ibid.

112. See information in Box 47, Folder 6, AHC.

113. Harris and Utlefe, "Dodge Revolutionary Movement (DRUM)," 6.

114. See numerous company charges of excessive employee absenteeism in Box 12, UAW Local 3 Collection.

115. "Special Meeting" minutes, Jefferson Avenue assembly plant union and management, 8 May 1964, Box 12, Folder 12, UAW Local 3 Collection.

116. "Answers from the Plant Committee (First Step) Hamtramck Complex," regarding Grievance AF 212– 200, 28 March 1967, Box 78, Folder 7, UAW Local 3 Collection.

117. Grievance A63–126, Dept. 3330, Shift 3, 16 March 1967, Box 78, Folder 10, UAW Local 3 Collection.

118. Dodge UAW Local 3 UAW-AFL-CIO meeting between local officers and management, 28 July 1967, regarding Grievance AF191–158, Dept. 9150, 7 April 1967, Box 77, Folder 2, UAW Local 3 Collection.

119. Hamtramck assembly plant, meeting minutes of Plant Manager's designated representatives with the officers of Local Union 3, 8 September 1966, Box 77, Folder 21, UAW Local 3 Collection.

120. Grievance AE 571–525, Dept. 9150, 7 June 1966, Box 77, Folder 2, UAW Local 3 Collection.

121. "Answers from the Plant Committee (First Step)–Hamtramck Complex 1967," regarding Grievance AF 146–136, 28 February 1967, Box 78, Folder 7, UAW Local 3 Collection.

122. Grievance 4347, Dept. 9160, 18 October 1962, Box 8, Folder 8, UAW Local 7 Collection.

123. Ibid.

124. Appeal Board of the Chrysler Corporation and International Union, United Autoworkers Aerospace, Agricultural Impalement Workers of America, Case 4059–63:5, June 1963, Box 63, Folder 50, UAW Local 212 Collection.

125. Ibid.

126. Grievance AE 197–194, Dept. 9150, 24 February 1966, Box 77, Folder 2, UAW Local 3 Collection.

127. Dodge UAW Local 3 UAW-AFL-CIO Plant Committee Grievance Report, regarding Grievance AE160–164, Dept. 3200, Box 72, Folder 12, UAW Local 3 Collection.

128. See Grievance AF 145–135, 28 February 1967, R.. Philson, Box 78, Folder 7, UAW Local 3 Collection.

129. Dodge UAW Local 3 UAW-AFL-CIO Plant Committee Grievance Report, regarding Grievance AE 262–259, Dept. 3200, Box 72, Folder 12, UAW Local 3 Collection.

130. Steve Pasica, president, to Mr. R. Kobus, plant manager, Dodge Main plant, 1 November 1963, Box12, Folder 21, UAW Local 3 Collection.

131. Jefferson Avenue assembly plant meeting minutes, 10 November 1964, Grievance 4716, regarding worker H. Lewis, 13 October 1964, Box 12, Folder 14, UAW Local 7 Collection.

Chapter 4

1. Interview with Detroiter Dick Lobenthal, in Detroit Lives, ed. Robert H. Mast (Philadelphia, 1994), 280.

2. James Johnson Jr., interview with attorney, 8 May 1971, Box 7, Ronald Glotta Collection, the Walter P. Reuther Library of Labor and Urban Affairs, Detroit.

3. Testimony of Maggie Taylor (p. 3), Box 5, RGC.
4. Rene Freeman (staff director of the West Community Organization), "Eyewitness Account of the Origins of the Riot—Detroit, July, 1967," 3 August 1967, Box 8, Folder 3, Commission on Community Relations Collections, the Walter P. Reuther Library of Labor and Urban Affairs, Detroit.
5. See the valuable survey responses in Joel D. Aberbach and Jack L. Walker, *Race in the City: Political Trust and Public Policy in the New Urban System* (Boston, 1973), 100.
6. Jerome Cavanagh to David Booth, research coordinator, University of Massachusetts Amherst, 6 February 1968, Series 8, Box 425, Folder 6, Jerome P. Cavanagh Collection, the Walter P. Reuther Library of Labor and Urban Affairs, Detroit.
7. "Black Polish Conference Final Evaluation Report," 7 May 1973, Box 154, New Detroit Collection, the Walter P. Reuther Library of Labor and Urban Affairs, Detroit.
8. Ibid.
9. Mel Ravitz, Common Council president, "The Sociology of the Block Club," September 1962, Box 13, folder 6, Charter Revision Commission Collection, Burton Historical Collection, Detroit Public Library.
10. Interview with Eleanor Josaitis, in Mast, 42.
11. Ibid., 42.
12. Michael Lipsey and David Olson, *Commission Politics: The Processing of Racial Crisis in America* (New Brunswick, New Jersey, 1977), 348.
13. "Power Struggle among Black Militants," *Detroit Scope Magazine*, 11 May 1968; reprinted in Leonard Gordon, ed., *City in Racial Crisis: The Pre- and Post-1967 Riot* (Dubuque, Iowa, 1971), 111 and 112.
14. "Progress Report of the New Detroit Committee," April 1968, 22, Metropolitan Fund, Inc., Suite 1515, 211 W. Fort St., Detroit, Michigan.
15. Ibid., 30.
16. Ibid., 39.
17. Ibid., 103 and 132–33.
18. Lonnie Saunders to Richard V. Marks, memo regarding account of Ralph Williams, New Bethel Church janitor and Trustee Board member, 6:00 p.m., 30 March 1969, Part 3, Box 67, Folder 10, CCRC.
19. Lonnie Saunders to Richard V. Marks, memo regarding accounts of Miss Keyes and Miss Huey, late afternoon, 30 March 1969, Part 3, Box 67, Folder 10, CCRC.
20. Account of Ralph Williams, New Bethel Church janitor and Trustee Board member, continued, Box 67, Folder 10, CCRC.
21. Ibid.
22. Ibid.
23. Lonnie Saunders to Richard V. Marks, memo regarding interview with attorney Milton Henry, vice president of the Republic of New Africa, on 8 April 1969, Part 3, Box 67, Folder 10, CCRC. Also "Statement of Commissioner J. Spreen," 3:00 a.m., Sunday, 30 March 1969, Part 3, Box 67, Folder 10, CCRC.
24. George Crockett was a fascinating character in the Motor City. By the 1960s, he had come to work closely with the city's liberal administration; indeed, he was considered to be part and parcel of that "liberal establishment" by black nationalists and white conservatives alike. But Crockett actually had a far more radical history than many of his liberal colleagues on the bench or in City Hall. He had been one of the key defense attorneys in the infamous Smith Act trials of the 1940s, actually serving time in prison for contempt of court. He also served as counsel for accused Communists during the House Un-American Committee investigations of the 1950s, and he was a prominent figure in the Detroit civil rights movement from the moment it began.
25. "Progress Report of the New Detroit Committee," 28.
26. "Statement by Judge George C. Crockett," 3 April 1969, Box 36, Kenneth Cockrel and Sheila Murphy Collection, the Walter P. Reuther Library of Labor and Urban Affairs, Detroit.

27. "Progress Report of the New Detroit Committee," 29.
28. Richard Marks to Walter P. Reuther, 18 April 1969, Box 429, Folder 5, Walter P. Reuther Collection, the Walter P. Reuther Library of Labor and Urban Affairs, Detroit.
29. Ibid.
30. Ibid.
31. "A Committee to Honor Judge Crockett in Support of Law and Justice," Box 36, CMC.
32. James Ralph, *Northern Protests: Martin Luther King, Jr., Chicago, and the Civil Rights Movement* (Cambridge, Mass., 1993), passim.
33. "Poor People's Campaign, Supportive Committee Meeting," minutes, 11 May 1968, Box 9, CMC.
34. Statement of witness, Sam J. Dennis, field representative, Community Relations Service/U.S. Department of Justice, 3 June 1969, Part 3, Box 67, Folder 10, CCRC.
35. Statement of witness, Philip H. Mason, field representative, Community Relations Service/U.S. Department of Justice, 11 June 1969, Part 3, Box 67, Folder 10, CCRC.
36. "Statement of Protest and Demand for Action," from Detroit coordinating office Southern Christian Leadership Conference, to Jerome P. Cavanagh, Ray Girardin, Lawrence Gubow, Citizens Complaint Bureau, Michigan Civil Rights Commission, Box 9, CMC.
37. "Ad Hoc Action Group Citizens of Detroit," leaflet, Box 9, CMC.
38. See 13 May 1968 case materials, in Box 26, CMC.
39. "Detroit Branch NAACP Position on Unrest in the Detroit Public School System," 16 October 1969, Box 67, NDC.
40. See statement to UNICOM from Daniel Toomer, 22 September 196,. Box 26, CMC, and memo, Cooley High incidents, New Detroit Committee, 2 October 1969, Box 57, NDC.
41. J. Terry, Speaker Bureau, to William T. Patrick, memo regarding meeting on student unrest in the New Detroit Conference Room, 24 September 1969, Box 57, NDC.
42. Interviews with students at Cooley High School by Laura Jackson, 14 October 1969, Box 57, Folder 38, NDC. For additional accounts, see Cynthia Hill statement to UNICOM, 2 September 1969; Glynda Farrior statement to UNICOM, 21 September 1969; Daniel Toomer statement to UNICOM, 29 September 1969, Box 26, CMC.
43. *South End,* 12 March 1969.
44. *Detroit News,* 5 September 1969.
45. "Spotlight," transcript, Radio-TV Reports, Inc., 28 September 1969, Station WXYZ-TV, Box 30, Folder 27, Richard Austin Collection, the Walter P. Reuther Library of Labor and Urban Affairs, Detroit.
46. *Detroit News,* 5 September 1969.
47. Beck's campaign newsletter, *The Broom,* August 1969, which was "dedicated to the promotion of the laws of GOD and MAN"; see also *Southwest Journal,* 28 October 1965, Mary Beck Biography File, Burton Historical Collection, Detroit Public Library.
48. "The Austin Program to Fight Crime," pamphlet, Box 30, Folder 4, RAC.
49. B. J. Widick, *Detroit: City of Race and Class Violence* (Chicago, 1972), 207.
50. "*WHITE* Tax-Paying Honky" to Richard Austin, 30 September 1969, Box 30, Folder 12, RAC.
51. Joseph Darden, Richard Child Hill, June Thomas, and Richard Thomas, *Detroit: Race and Uneven Development.* (Philadelphia, 1987), 209.
52. *Detroit Free Press,* 5 November 1969.
53. *Detroit News,* 4 November 1969.
54. *Detroit Free Press,* 17 August 1969.
55. "Power Struggle among Black Militants."
56. Police-Community Relations Committee and staff CCR to CCR, memo, 2 October 1971, Box 3, Dan Georgakas Collection, the Walter P. Reuther Library of Labor and Urban Affairs, Detroit.
57. Ibid.
58. Ibid.; and "From the Ground Up, Detroit Under S.T.R.E.S.S.," Box 3, Folder 5, DGC.

59. Ibid.
60. James Geschwender, *Class, Race, and Worker Insurgency: The League of Revolutionary Black Workers* (New York, 1977), 171–72.
61. Ibid., 88
62. Interview Ron Lockett, in Mast, 92.
63. For an overview of the politics of black nationalism, which held particular appeal to these young African Americans in Detroit, see William Van Deburg, ed., *Modern Black Nationalism: From Marcus Garvey to Louis Farrakhan* (New York, 1997). See also Manning Marable, *Black Nationalism in the Seventies: Through the Prism of Race and Class* (Dayton, Ohio, 1980).
64. Dan Georgakas and Marvin Surkin, *Detroit: I Do Mind Dying* (New York, 1975), 16.
65. Ibid., 16.
66. John Hersey (with intro by Thomas Sugrue), *The Algiers Motel Incident* (Baltimore, MD, 1998).
67. See *Inner City Voice*, 22 June 1967; June 1969; October 1967; 15 December 1967; 16 November 1967; February 1970; 16 March–1 April 1970; June 1970; 15 April 1970. All in the Detroit Revolutionary Union Movements Newspaper Collection (DRUM News Collection), the Walter P. Reuther Library of Labor and Urban Affairs, Detroit.
68. *Inner City Voice*, November 1969.
69. This movie, which mostly covered black radical activism in the auto plants, had an international audience. In fact, Italian workers invited the movie's producers to Italy and showcased the film in Turin and Milan. For more on the international, and specifically Italian, connections with the black nationalist Left in Detroit, see Georgakas and Surkin, *Detroit: I do Mind Dying*. Updated Edition (Cambridge: South End Press, 1998).
70. Interview Marian Kramer, in Mast, 103.
71. "Wayne and the Inner City: The Survey of Urban Concern," booklet, October 1968, Office of the President, Wayne State University, Wayne State University Brochures, Pamphlets, Reports 1965–69 Vertical Files, the Walter P. Reuther Library of Labor and Urban Affairs, Detroit.
72. *South End*, 26 September 1969; see bound volumes of the *South End*, the Walter P. Reuther Library of Labor and Urban Affairs, Detroit.
73. Ibid.
74. For use of such language, see these issues, among others, of *South End*: 22 October 1968; 24 October 1968; 28 October 1968; and 4 November 1968.
75. Jon Jeter, "A Coat of Pride," in *Detroit Free Press*, Special Reprint, "The Riot—Unending Effects," August 1992.
76. For a still excellent overview of the black church well before the 1960s, see Carter G. Woodson, *A History of the Negro Church in America* (Washington, D.C., 1921). See also C. Eric Lincoln and Lawrence Mamiya, *The Black Church in the African American Experience* (Durham, N.C., 1990), and Hans Baer and Merril Singer, *African American Religion in the Twentieth Century: Varieties of Accommodation and Protest* (Knoxville, Tenn., 1992).
77. For a wonderful account of how political radicalism was reflected and furthered by theologians in Detroit, see Angela Dillard, "From the Reverend Charles Hill to the Reverend Albert B. Cleage, Jr.: Change and Continuity in the Patterns of Civil Rights Mobilizations in Detroit," Ph.D. diss. (University of Michigan, 1995).
78. Vincent Harding, "The Religion of Black Power," in *The Religion Situation*, ed. Donald Cutler (Boston, 1968), 22–30.
79. Albert Cleage, *The Black Messiah* (New York, 1969).
80. Ibid., 66.
81. Harry Cook and Joyce Walker-Tyson, "Politics and the Pulpit: A Tradition," *Detroit Free Press,* "The Riot—Unending Effects,"August 1992, 58.
82. Cleage, *Black Messiah,* 35.

83. Ibid., 45.
84. Ibid., 19.
85. Ibid.
86. Everett Baggerly to Lynne Townsend, chairman of the Education Committee, memo regarding meeting with teachers from Cooley High School relative to student unrest, 10 October 1969. Box 57, NDC.
87. Ibid.
88. "Declaration of Black Teachers," 27 April 1968, adopted at the Black Ministers-Teachers Conference, Detroit, Box 86, American Federation of Teachers President's Collection, the Walter P. Reuther Library of Labor and Urban Affairs, Detroit.
89. Everett Baggerly to all task force leaders, memo regarding student unrest, 23 September 1969, Box 57, NDC.
90. "Causes of Unrest," Box 86, AFTPC.
91. "Desegregation Chronology," Series 1, Box 7, Folder 9, Detroit Public Schools Commission on Community Relations Collection, the Walter P. Reuther Library of Labor and Urban Affairs, Detroit.
92. "PASCC: Parents and Students for Community Control," leaflet, Box 18, CMC.
93. *Inner City Voice,* July 1970.
94. "Progress Report: June–December 1970," PASCC, Box 4, Folder 20, DGC.
95. Ibid.
96. Ibid.
97. Ibid.
98. Ibid.
99. Geschwender, 150.
100. "Osborn High Black Student Voice," *Black Student United Front* 1, no. 2. Series 2, Box 8, Folder 12, PSCCRC. *Soul on Ice* by Eldridge Cleaver, *Black Rage* by William Grier, and *The Rich and The Super-Rich* by Ferdinand Lundberg.
101. "Osborn's 12 Black Student Demands," Series 2, Box 8, Folder 14, PSCCRC.
102. "Northeastern Senior High School Ad Hoc Committee," Series 2, Box 8, Folder 14, PSCCRC.
103. "Northern High: We Demand, BSUF," Series 2, Box 8, Folder 14, PSCCRC.
104. "Press Statement: Detroit Branch NAACP," 22 April 1966, Series 1, Part 2, Box 12, Folder 7, NAACP Collection, the Walter P. Reuther Library of Labor and Urban Affairs, Detroit.
105. "Central High: Black Student Voice, BSUF," Series 2, Box 8, Folder 14, PSCCRC.
106. See "the Black Manifesto," in Baer and Singer, *African American Religion in the Twentieth Century,* 191–202.
107. The most famous of these intellectuals are James H. Cone and C. Eric Lincoln. See, James H. Cone, *Black Theology and Black Power* (New York, 1969), and C. Eric Lincoln, *Sounds of the Struggle: Persons and Perspectives in Civil Rights* (New York, 1968.)
108. *Detroit News,* 17 November 1970.
109. *Detroit News,* 16 November 1970.
110. Ibid., 16.
111. In their newsletter "Support the Children's Free Breakfast Program," the Panthers pointed out that during the summer they had served 350 kids lunches every day out of two of their centers, and they announced that "there will be four centers open [in the fall] to serve the free breakfast for school children. All of the youth of the community of Detroit will be fed a balanced hot breakfast before they go to school" (*Detroit News,* 17 November 1970; and the National Committee to Combat Fascism, "Support the Children's Free Breakfast Program," newsletter, Series 2, Box 8, Folder 14, PSCCRC).
112. Kramer, in Mast, 103.

113. Amy Carrol, Shawn Gilbert, Ellen Schweitzer, and Tim Sabota, "STRESS Fractures" (p. 20), senior research paper written for Dr. Charles Bright (Residential College, University of Michigan, 1995).

114. "STRESS Fractures," 28.

115. See the interviews with Jim Jacobs, Frank Joyce, Pat Fry, and Sheila Murphy Cockrel; all in Mast, 274, 276, 320, and 180.

116. Mast, 257.

117. Interview Jim Jacobs, in Mast, 273.

118. Interview Rich Feldman, in Mast, 266,

119. Interview Dave Riddle, in Mast, 325.

120. "Revolutionary in Legal Sheepskin," interview with Kenneth Cockrel, *Detroit News Sunday Magazine,* 14 October 1973.

121. *Michigan Chronicle,* 11 February 1965.

122. "Some Comments Regarding the West Central Organization as it Relates to University City #2," memo, March 1966, in the Wayne State University Urban Renewal Vertical Files, the Walter P. Reuther Library of Labor and Urban Affairs, Detroit.

123. "STRESS Fractures," 22.

124. Richard Marks to CCR, memo, 16 April 1969, Box 429, Folder 5, WPRC.

125. Press release: Guardians of Michigan, 9 March 1972, Box 16, CMC. See also Guardians of Michigan to Police Commissioner John Nichols, telegram, Part 3, Box 69, Folder 10, CCRC.

126. "The Boundary Plan for School Decentralization in Detroit," Series 1, Box 7, Folder 23, PSCCRC.

127. Amy Rose Dinges, "Theory and Practice: The Busing Controversy in the Detroit Public Schools, 1970–1977," unpublished research paper (Residential College, University of Michigan, 1997).

128. Ibid.

129. Ibid.

130. Charlie Walker, "The April 7th Integration, Decentralization Plan," unpublished paper (Residential College, University of Michigan, 1997), 12, 13, 22, and 23. See also Jeffery Mirel, *The Rise and Fall of an Urban School System* (Ann Arbor, Mich., 1993).

131. Interview with Herman Ferguson and Arthur Harris, 4 February 1970, Box 26, CMC; "White Youth Stand up and Be Counted," leaflet, Youth Corps KKK, Box 7, CMC.

132. Widick, *Detroit: City of Race and Class Violence,* 189.

133. *South End,* 1 November 1968.

134. Aberbach and Walker, *Race in the City,* 108.

135. Ibid., 108.

136. Ibid., 95.

137. *Detroit Free Press,* 19 February 1969. See also *South End* clippings in Vertical Files, the Walter P. Reuther Library of Labor and Urban Affairs, Detroit.

138. Jack Mondin to *Detroit Free Press,*. 1 July 1969, Box 26, CMC.

139. Joel Thurtell, "Inside the Red Squad," *Detroit Free Press Magazine,* 4 November 1990. According to the *Detroit Free Press,* the Red Squad kept tabs on city and labor movement radicals from 1950 to 1974, when its legality was challenged in the courts (*Detroit Free Press,* 21 December 1980).

140. *Detroit Free Press,* 27 September 1971.

141. "STRESS Fractures," 31.

142. Ibid., 32.

143. Ibid., 32.

144. Ibid., 33.

145. Letters to the editor, *Detroit News,* 20 April 1972.

146. Statement by Mayor Roman S. Gribbs, 17 March 1972, Part 3, Box 68, CCRC.

147. For further information on how this famous desegregation case unfolded, see *Bradley v. Milliken,* 433 F.2d 897 (6ᵗʰ Cir., 1970); *Bradley v. Milliken,* 338 F. Supp. 582 (E.D. Mich., 1971); *Bradley v. Milliken,* 345 F. Supp. 914 (E.D. Mich., 1972); *Bradley v. Milliken,* 484 F.2d 215 (6ᵗʰ Cir., 1973); *Milliken v. Bradley,* 418 U.S. 717 (1974). For secondary literature on this famous case, see Mirel, *The Rise and Fall;* Paul R. Diamond, *Beyond Busing: Inside the Challenge to Urban Segregation* (Ann Arbor, Mich., 1985); Eleanor P. Wolf, *Trial and Error: The Detroit School Desegregation Case* (Detroit, 1981); and William Grant, "The Detroit School Case: An Historical Overview," *Wayne Law Review* 21, no. 3 (March 1975).

148. Official Proceedings of the Board of Governors, Wayne State University, 13 February 1969, Vertical File: *The South End.*

149. Official Proceedings of the Board of Governors, Wayne State University, 20 January 1969, 1572, Vertical File: *The South End.* Although John Watson maintained that the *South End* was not anti-Semitic under his editorship, the paper did read that "it is roughly estimated that one third of the power at Wayne, Governors, Deans, and so forth, is Jewish. But the Jews must give up their hold on their portion of the power at Wayne along with other suburban whites" (*South End,* 20 January 1969). While such rhetoric clearly alienated Jewish students at WSU, Arab students came out in support of the paper's editors (*South End,* 21 February 1969).

150. Official Proceedings of the Board of Governors, Wayne State University, 9 February 1973, 2253, Vertical File: *The South End.*

151. Official Proceedings of the Board of Governors, Wayne State University, 10 July 1969. See also Information Services, Wayne State University to Paul J. Pentacost, memo, 9 February 1973, Vertical File: *The South End.*

152. Official Proceedings of the Board of Governors, Wayne State University, 13 February 1969, Vertical File: *The South End.*

Chapter 5

1. *Michigan Chronicle,* 2 March 1969.
2. "Chrysler Corporation Application for Employment," James Johnson Jr., Box 5, Ronald Glotta Collection, Walter P. Reuther Library of Labor and Urban Affairs, Detroit.
3. James Johnson Jr., interview with attorney, 8 May 1971, Box 5, RGC.
4. Testimony of Clarence Horton and Bernard Oweisny, *James Johnson Jr. v. Chrysler Corporation,* State of Michigan, Bureau of Workman's Compensation, John Conley, hearing referee, 22 and 24 November 1971, Box 7, RGC.
5. Testimony of Don Thomas (p. 49), Box 5, RGC.
6. "Chrysler Corporation Employee Medical Records," James Johnson Jr., Box 5, RGC.
7. Trial testimony of Don Thomas (p. 47), Box 5, RGC.
8. "Continuation of Decision" (p. 7), decision of hearing referee John Conley, *Johnson v. Chrysler,* 28 February 1973, Box 3, RGC.
9. "Employment Conditions in the Model Neighborhood, 1970," Social Planning Division, the Detroit City Planning Commission, 21 July 1970, Box 14, City of Detroit City Planning Commission Collection, Burton Historical Collection, Detroit Public Library.
10. James Geschwender, *Class, Race, and Worker Insurgency: The League of Revolutionary Black Workers* (New York, 1977), 74.
11. *Detroit Free Press,* 23 May 1971.
12. William Serrin, *The Company and the Union: The Civilized Relationship of General Motors Corporation and the United Automobile Workers, revised edition*(New York, 1974), 151.
13. Douglas Fraser to Walter P. Reuther, 19 December 1969, Box 51, Folder 4, Walter P. Reuther Collection, the Walter P. Reuther Library of Labor and Urban Affairs, Detroit.
14. *JARUM* 1, no. 1, in the Detroit Revolutionary Union Movements Newspaper Collection (DRUM News Collection), the Walter P. Reuther Library of Labor and Urban Affairs, Detroit.

15. *DRUM* 1, no. 1, Box 41, Folder 26, UAW Local 3 Collection, the Walter P. Reuther Library of Labor and Urban Affairs, Detroit.
16. Philip Foner, *Organized Labor and the Black Worker* (New York, 1981), 374.
17. *New York Times,* 1 October 1968; quoted in Foner, 416.
18. Grievances to this effect can be found in Box 3, Folder 6, DRUM Collection.
19. UAW Grievance 5428, submitted to third-step arbitration, 16 June 1970, Box 3, Folder 13, Dan Georgakas Collection, the Walter P. Reuther Library of Labor and Urban Affairs, Detroit.
20. UAW Grievance 70–482, submitted to third-step arbitration, 16 June 1970, Box 3, Folder 12, DGC.
21. Al and Helen Thompson, parents of Gary Thompson, interview with author, 11 April 1991.
22. Ibid.
23. Case 5428–70:480, Chrysler Corporation, 30 November 1971, Box 3, Folder 27, DRUM Collection.
24. Harry T. Englebrecht, plant manager, Eldon Avenue axle plant, to Eldon Avenue axle employees, 4 June 1970, Box 3, Folder 27, DRUM collection.
25. Interview with Pete Kelly, in *Detroit Lives,* ed. Robert H. Mast (Philadelphia, 1994), 219.
26. *United Justice Train* 1, no. 6, Box 73, Folder 5, UAW Region 1B Collection, the Walter P. Reuther Library of Labor and Urban Affairs, Detroit.
27. *United Justice Train,* memo, 26 December 1972, Box 73, Folder 5, UAW Region 1B Collection. See also undated note, United Justice Caucus, 26 December 1972, and UNC letter to Leonard Woodcock, Douglas Fraser, William Gilbert, and Ken Morris, 30 May 1972, Box 73, Folder 5, UAW Region 1B Collection.
28. Geschwender, *Class, Race, and Worker Insurgency,* 199.
29. Interview with Kelly, in Mast, *Detroit Lives,* 219.
30. See *United Justice Train* 1, no. 6 (December 1972); *United Justice Train* 1, no. 6 (July 1972); United Justice Caucus to Mr. Flowers, recording secretary of Local 7, 31 August 1972, Box 73, Folder 5, UAW Region 1B Collection.
31. Proceedings of the Twenty-third Constitutional Convention, International Union, United Automobile, Aerospace, and Agricultural Implement Workers of America–UAW (pp. 252–52), the Walter P. Reuther Library of Labor and Urban Affairs, Detroit.
32. Ibid., 328.
33. Interview with General Baker, in Mast, *Detroit Lives,* 305–308.
34. William Gilbert, president of Dodge Main plant's Local 3, said that in 1970 "production is up 63 percent over 1949–1953, when there were 14,500 people in the plant. Now we've got 6,500." In the Dodge Main plant specifically, "the line was edged up from 49 units to 58 units an hour"; quoted in Thomas R. Brooks, "Workers, White and Black, DRUM Beats in Detroit," *Dissent* (January–February 1970): 4 and 5; Box 44, UAW Region 1 Collection. Reuther Library. Detroit.
35. "Open Letter to Chrysler Corporation," General Baker, 29 May 1969, Box 44, UAW Region 1 Collection.
36. Geschwender, *Class, Race, and Worker Insurgency,* 145.
37. *Inner City Voice,* 15 July 1970, DRUM Collection.
38. Geschwender, *Class, Race, and Worker Insurgency,* 92.
39. *DRUM* 1, no. 16, Box 41, Folder 26, UAW Local 3 Collection.
40. *DRUM,* vol. 1, nos. 5 and 8; quoted in unpublished paper, Horace Harris, graduate student in international relations, and Deanna Utlefe, graduate student in economics, "Dodge Revolutionary Movement (DRUM): A Study through Interviews" (p. 5), 15 September 1969, Box 1, Folder 10, Enid Eckstein Collection, the Walter P. Reuther Library of Labor and Urban Affairs, Detroit.
41. See "Guide to the Collection," DGC.
42. Brooks, "Workers, White and Black," 5.
43. *CHRY-RUM* 1, no. 1 (November 1970), Kenneth Cockrel and Sheila Murphy Collection, the Walter P. Reuther Library of Labor and Urban Affairs, Detroit.

44. *Inner City Voice* 2, no. 7. (15 July 1970), in the DRUM Collection.
45. For another interesting account of the rise of black dissidents within the UAW during the 1950s and 1960s and the UAW's response to such insurgencies, see Thomas Cornelius Casanova, "Black Workers at the Point of Production: Shopfloor Radicalism and Wildcat Strikes in Detroit Auto, 1955–1976," Ph.D. diss. (University of Notre-Dame, 1993), passim.
46. DRUM Constitution, Box 41, Folder 24, UAW Local 3 Collection.
47. *ELRUM,* July 1970, DRUM Collection.
48. B. J. Widick, *Detroit: City of Race and Class Violence* (Chicago, 1972), 226.
49. *ELRUM,* 1970, DRUM Collection.
50. *DRUM* 1, no. 4, Box 41, UAW Local 3 Collection.
51. *DRUM* 1, Box 41, Folder 26, UAW Local 3 Collection.
52. *DRUM* 2, no. 1, Box 41, Folder 28, UAW Local 3 Collection.
53. Geschwender, *Class, Race, and Worker Insurgency,* 84.
54. "Here's Where We're Coming From" (p. 2), the League of Revolutionary Black Workers, Box 4, DGC.
55. Harris and Utlefe, "Dodge Revolutionary Movement (DRUM)," 11.
56. The quotes are from the "League of Revolutionary Black Workers Constitution," Box 4, Series 1, DGC.
57. *ELRUM* 1, no. 2 (29 November 1968), Box 45, UAW Region 1 Collection.
58. See *ELRUM* 1, no. 2 (29 November 1969), and *ELRUM* 1, no. 9, Box 45, UAW Region 1 Collection.
59. Harris and Utlefe, "Dodge Revolutionary Movement (DRUM)," 19.
60. Geschwender, *Class, Race, and Worker Insurgency,* 94.
61. *ELRUM,* May 1970, DRUM Collection..
62. *ELRUM* 7, Box 41, Folder 28, UAW Local 3 Collection.
63. *ELRUM,* 1970, DRUM Collection.
64. Helen Thompson interview.
65. Ibid.
66. Devon Anne Perez, "The Dodge Revolutionary Union Movement: Rhetoric Defined, Actions Solidified, Opposition Destroyed" (p. 37), unpublished senior honors thesis (Department of History, University of Michigan, 1996); *Chrysler Corporation v. General G. Baker et al.,* 1161, Circuit Court for Wayne County, 16 July 1968, Box 4, DRUM Collection.
67. Harris and Utlefe, "Dodge Revolutionary Movement (DRUM)," 20.
68. Testimony of Clarence Horton, p. 13, Box 5, RGC.
69. Quoted in Geschwender, *Class, Race, and Worker Insurgency,* 147.
70. "Black Workers Protest UAW Racism: March on Cobo Hall," the League of Revolutionary Black Workers, Box 41, Folder 25, UAW Local 3 Collection.
71. See *Detroit Free Press,* 19 August 1973, regarding the growth of left-wing organizations within Detroit's auto plants.
72. Interview with General Baker, quoted in Harris and Utlefe, "Dodge Revolutionary Movement (DRUM)," 10.
73. Even those whites committed to turning their political attention to the plants could not always agree about how best to do this. Some argued that radicals should agitate from within existing reform caucuses, while others advocated pursuing an explicitly "dual union" strategy. For an example of such debates, see International Socialists, internal discussion document, production work, Box 1, Folder 3, EEC.
74. Interview with Rich Feldman, in Mast, *Detroit Lives,* 265.
75. For an explanation of the principle of "Class Struggle Unionism" and "how to use it and win," see International Socialists brochure, "Fighting to Win! Class Struggle Unionism" (Detroit, 1975), Box 1, Folder 3, EEC.
76. Interview with Pete Camarata, in Mast, *Detroit Lives,* 330.
77. Interview with Gene Cunningham, in Mast, *Detroit Lives,* 314.
78. Baker, quoted in Mast, *Detroit Lives,* 309.

79. Interview Mike Hamlin, in Mast, *Detroit Lives,* 87.

80. *JARUM* 1, no. 1, DRUM Newspaper Collection. See the letters-to-the-editor section of *Detroit Free Press,* 13 March 1973, for an example of how whites viewed the murders committed by Johnson. DRUM News Collection.

81. *DRUM* 2, no. 4, Box 41, UAW Local 3 Collection.

82. "Unite and Fight," DRUM leaflet, Box 45, UAW Region 1 Collection.

83. Leaflet, Local 809, August 1971, National Youth Alliance, Centerline, Michigan, Box 16, Folder 11, Ken Morris Collection, the Walter P. Reuther Library of Labor and Urban Affairs, Detroit.

84. "D.U.M.B." 1, no. 1, Box 41, Folder 28, UAW Local 3 Collection; "M.A.P.U.M.B.," 16 September 1969, Box 1, Folder 42, UAW Region 1 Collection.

85. John Taylor, interview with Dan Georgakas, 25 August 1972, Box 3, Folder 17, DGC.

86. Jordan Sims, Eddie Barksdale, and Carla Cooke, interview with Dan Georgakas, 19 August 1972, Box 3, Folder 18, DGC.

87. Brooks, "Workers, White and Black," 8.

88. United National Caucus, booklet, Box 47, Folder 12, Arthur Hughes Collection, the Walter P. Reuther Library of Labor and Urban Affairs, Detroit.

89. *United Justice Train* 1, no. 6 (January 1973). Box 73, Folder 5. UAW Region 1B Collection.

90. Walter Dorosh, president of Local 600, to Walter Reuther, 16 January 1969, Box 45, UAW Region 1 Collection.

91. Ibid.

92. Ron March, quoted in the League documentary *Finally Got the News* (Black Star Productions, 1970).

93. *United Justice Train* 1, no. 6 (December 1972), Box 73, Folder 5, UAW Region 1B Collection.

94. According to Jefferys, there were far more wildcats in the 1950s than in the 1960s (there were 289 between 1955 and 1959 alone). Note, however, that the unauthorized strikes of the 1960s were not remarkable for their frequency; they were remarkable for their *substance.* Indeed, the issues behind the wildcats were often much different from what they had been in the 1950s. See Steve Jefferys, *Management and Managed: Fifty Years of Crisis at Chrysler* (Cambridge, 1986), 7.

95. "Protection Department of the Chrysler Corporation," July–August 1968, Box 3, Folder 4, DRUM Collection; H. G. Phipps, staff investigator, to W. T. Diehl, memo, 1968, Box 3, DRUM Collection; Perez, "The Dodge Revolutionary Union Movement," 40–41.

96. *DRUM* 1, no. 15, Box 41, UAW Local 3 Collection.

97. *DRUM* 1, no. 16, Box 41, UAW Local 3 Collection.

98. *Inner City Voice,* 22 January 1968, and *Inner City Voice,* no. 8 (June 1968), in the DRUM Collection.

99. DRUM rally leaflet, Series 9, Part 2, Box 47, Folder 1, AHC.

100. Interview with Mike Hamlin, 30 August 1969; quoted in Harris and Utlefe, "Dodge Revolutionary Movement (DRUM)," 5.

101. Don Rand to Irving Bluestone, 13 November 1969, Box 74, WPRC.

102. Letter from Jacob Przybylo, in file with collection of ELRUM literature, Series 9, Part 2, Box 47, Folder 3, AHC.

103. *United Justice Train* 1, no. 5 (October 1972); *Community News,* 2 August 1972, Box 73, Folder 5, UAW Region 1B Collection.

104. Dorosh to Reuther, 16 January 1969, Box 45, UAW Region 1 Collection.

105. Bill Beckham to Walter Reuther, 13 February 1969, Box 74, Folder 4, WPRC.

106. Shelton Tappes did not like the style of the RUMs, but he well understood why they were mobilizing. As he wrote, "the failings of the past in these highly volatile areas [can't be] explained away; they cannot be accused away, nor will they leave unless a direct effort

is made to get at the root of these situations." Tappes had been the first black chairman of UAW Local 600's foundry unit and served as a member of the committee that had negotiated the first UAW contract with Ford. He knew discrimination firsthand, and that was why he joined the TULC in the 1950s. Shelton Tappes to William Oliver, 28 March 1969, Series 9, Part 2, Box 47, Folder 1, AHC. See also interview with Tappes, in Elaine Latzman Moon, *Untold Tales, Unsung Heroes: An Oral History of Detroit's African American Community, 1918–1967* (Detroit, 1994), 108.

107. Beckham to Reuther, 13 February 1969, Box 74, Folder 4, WPRC.
108. Ibid.
109. Frank Menedez to George Merrelli, memo regarding Forge and Wooten Altercation at Hamtramck assembly plant, Box 44, UAW Region 1 Collection.
110. Irving Bluestone to Walter Reuther, September 1968, Box 74, WPRC.
111. Interview with George Merrelli, 27 August 1969, in Harris and Utlefe, "Dodge Revolutionary Movement (DRUM)," 13.
112. Douglas Fraser to Nelson Edwards and Marcellius Ivory (copy to George Merrelli and Ed Liska), 4 October 1968, Box 44, UAW Region 1 Collection.
113. "Minutes," special meeting of the IEB, 15 July 1968, Box 16, UAW International Executive Board Collection, the Walter P. Reuther Library of Labor and Urban Affairs, Detroit.
114. Ibid.
115. See Box 16, Folder 11, Ken Morris Collection. See also the folder "Local 3 DRUM Activities 1968," Box 44, UAW Region 1 Collection.
116. Bluestone to Reuther, 2 July 1968, Box 74, WPRC.
117. George Merrelli to Douglas Fraser, memo, 11 October 1968, Box 44, UAW Region 1 Collection; Douglas Fraser to Emil Mazey, Ken Morris, Pat Caruso, and E. Bruce, Box 1, Folder 42, UAW Region 1B Collection.
118. George Merrelli to Ed Liska, president Local 3, 11 October 1960, Box 41, Folder 29, UAW Local 3 Collection.
119. William Gerbe to George Merrelli, 27 January 1969, Box 45, UAW Region 1 Collection.
120. Miscellaneous notes in "Local 3 DRUM Activities Folder," Box 44, UAW Region 1 Collection.
121. Frank Menendez to George Merrelli, memo regarding Forge and Wooten Altercation.
122. Bill Beckham to Victor Reuther (brother of Walter), 22 April 1971, Box 15, Folder 6, Leonard Woodcock Collection, the Walter P. Reuther Library of Labor and Urban Affairs.
123. Harris and Utlefe, "Dodge Revolutionary Movement (DRUM)," 14.
124. Ibid.
125. Leadership Local 961 to all Local 961 members, Box 45, UAW Region 1 Collection.
126. "All Members of the UAW 3," open letter from the International UAW and Douglas Fraser, IEB member, member-at-large, and director of Chrysler Department; George Merrelli, director of Region 1; Ed Liska, president of Local 3; Chas E. Brooks, vice president of Local 3; William Szelepski, treasurer of Local 3; Joseph Gordon, recording secretary of Local 3; Frank Czarny, financial secretary of Local 3, Box 44, UAW Region 1 Collection.
127. John M. Hyatt, Atlanta Area Office, to Leonard Woodcock, letter with a leaflet enclosed from a RUM called GMRUM at a General Motors assembly plant, Box 15, folder 6, LWC.
128. "Voice of the Plantation," *GMRUM*. 2, no. 5, Atlanta, Georgia, Box 33, Shelton Tappes Collection, the Walter P. Reuther Library of Labor and Urban Affairs, Detroit.
129. Quoted in Geschwender, *Class, Race, and Worker Insurgency,* 114.
130. "All Members of the UAW 3," Box 44, UAW Region 1 Collection.
131. Ibid.
132. "A Confused UAW Member" to Region 1, Box 45, UAW Region 1 Collection.
133. *Inner City Voice* 2, no. 6, in the DRUM Collection.
134. *Michigan Chronicle,* 29 March 1969.
135. Chrysler Corporation to James Johnson, June 1970. Box 5, Letter 12, RGC.

136. Testimony of Bernard Owiesny. State of Michigan Workman's Compensation Appeal Board. 28 June 1979. Box 3, RGC.
137. Attorney notes, 18 October 1971, Box 5, RGC.
138. "Continuation of Decision" (p. 8), Box 3, RGC.
139. "Continuation of Decision" (p. 14), Box 3, RGC.
140. Testimony of James Johnson Jr., 22 and 24 November 1971, Box 7, RGC. James Johnson, Jr. v. Chrysler Corporation, State of Michigan, Bureau of Workman's Compensation, Hearing Referee John Conley.
141. "Supervisors Report," 15 July 1970, Chrysler Corporation, Box 5, RGC.
142. Testimony of Clarence Horton (p. 11), Box 5, RGC.
143. "Continuation of Decision" (p. 14), Box 3, RGC.
144. Testimony of Clarence Horton (p. 1), Box 5, RGC.
145. Ibid., 10.
146. Trial summary (p. 30), Box 5, RGC. It was the foremen in Detroit's plants who were known as the "white shirts."
147. Trial summary, prosecution's opening remarks, 30 April 1971, Box 5, RGC.
148. Ibid.
149. Testimony of Melvin Cooper's supervisor (p. 34), Box 5, RGC.
150. Testimony of Ed Lacey, 5 May 1971, Box 5, RGC.
151. *Inner City Voice,* 15 July 1970, DRUM Collection.
152. *ELRUM,* July 1970, DRUM Collection.
153. *Michigan Chronicle,* 25 July 1975.
154. Ibid.
155. *The Metro,* July 1970, Box 3, RGC.
156. For an example of this, see the letters-to-the-editor section of the *Detroit Free Press,* 13 March 1973.

Chapter 6

1. Jerome Cavanagh, "Mayor's Recommendations before Governor Kerner's Commission in Washington, D.C.," 15 August 1967, Series 3, Box 2, Folder 19, Commission on Community Relations Collections, the Walter P. Reuther Library of Labor and Urban Affairs, Detroit.
2. "Police Report," Officer Gerald Raycraft, Badge 3608, and "Police Report," Officer Francis Decrease, Badge 926, regarding arrest of Hibbitt and Hall, State of Michigan, in the Recorder's Court of the City of Detroit, *The People of the State of Michigan v. Raphael Viera,* Case A-152598, and *The People of the State of Michigan v. Clarence Fuller,* Case A-15297, Boxes 10 and 26, Kenneth Cockrel and Sheila Murphy Collection, the Walter P. Reuther Library of Labor and Urban Affairs, Detroit.
3. "Revolutionary in Legal Sheepskin," *Detroit News Sunday Magazine,* 14 October 1973.
4. Affidavit, Douglas Glazier, reporter for the *Detroit News,* and affidavit, Michael J. O'Neill, radio station WKNR, Box 16, CMC; *Detroit News,* 7 June 1969.
5. *Joseph E. Maher, Judge, the Recorder's Court v. Kenneth V. Cockrel,* R.C. A-152599, Box 16, CMC.
6. *DRUM* 2, no. 16, Box 41, Folder 27, UAW Local 3 Collection, the Walter P. Reuther Library of Labor and Urban Affairs, Detroit.
7. Opening Statement, of attorney Harry Philo presenting before Wayne County Circuit Court Judge Joseph A. Sullivan in "Contempt Proceedings of Kenneth Verne Cockrel." As reproduced in *Trial Magazine* (November 1980).
8. Ibid., 13.
9. "Memorandum of Authorities in Support of Motion to Dismiss," *Maher v. Cockrel,* Box 16, CMC.
10. Justin Ravitz to author. Letter. 27 April 2001.

11. Ibid., 2.

12. "Preparation for May 26, the Hearing—Evidence, Witnesses, Tactics," defense team notes, Box 16, CMC.

13. At times during the trial, the New Bethel shooter had been described as a short black man, "about 5'5"," with a green uniform and a white belt. At other times, however, he was described as "six feet one; he was very thin, one hundred and ah, hundred and fifty-five pounds." Clearly, such contradictory accounts helped the defense. See witness interview, Kelly Zanders, 21 February 1970, by Justin Ravitz, and taped telephone witness interview, Gerald McKinney, 17 November 1969, by Justin Ravitz. Box 10 CMC. See also the summary of testimony of Richard Ivy in *People v. Hibbitt*, 12 December 1969, Box 10, CMC.

14. *Black Consciousness* 2, no. 2, Box 2, CMC.

15. State of Michigan in the Recorders Court for the City of Detroit, *The People of the State of Michigan v. Raphael Viera*, Case A-152598, testimony of David Brown Jr. (pp. 146–47), 2 July 1969, Box 10, CMC. Also see *Inner City Voice* Vol. 2, #6 (June, 1970). Detroit Revolutionary Union Movements News Collection, the Walter P. Reuther Library of Labor and Urban Affairs, Detroit.

16. Ravitz to author.

17. See *Detroit Free Press*, 27 March 1970, and *Detroit News*, 27 March 1970.

18. As a result of the contempt charges filed by Recorder's Court Judge Maher against Cockrel, the entire Recorder's Court bench disqualified itself from the New Bethel trials. New Bethel Two was tried before Judge Gilmore, a Wayne County Circuit Court judge sitting in Recorder's Court. Ravitz to author.

19. "Joint Motion to Quash Jury Panel and for Other Relief and Affidavit Thereon," 26 March 1970, Box 26, CMC.

20. *Detroit Free Press*, 12 April 1970.

21. *Michigan Chronicle*, 4 April 1970.

22. *Detroit Free Press*, 12 April 1970.

23. Ravitz to author.

24. *Detroit Free Press*, 17 June 1970.

25. "Order." State of Michigan in the Recorder's Court of the City of Detroit, Honorable Robert E. DeMascio, 31 March 1970. Box 26, CMC.

26. Richard Marks to commission, memo regarding information and action, Box 4, Folder 18, Dan Georgakas Collection, the Walter P. Reuther Library of Labor and Urban Affairs, Detroit.

27. Ibid.

28. *Detroit Free Press*, 29 April 1971.

29. These autoworkers' wives included Mary McCary, a former maid in Alabama who was born in 1905 and married to a Chrysler retiree; Joyce Lockett, a nurse's aide born in 1936 who was married to an employee at the Ford Rouge plant; Ruth Locust, a hospital worker born in 1942 who was married to an assembly worker at Chrysler's Jefferson plant; Mary Wallace, a housewife born in 1925 and originally from Alabama, who was married to an operating engineer from Local 324; and Madeline Tabock, an ex-autoworker who was born in 1917 and was married to a research engineer at Ford. The other jurors included Tina Christiniois, a nurse born in 1942; Margaret Barone, a housewife born in 1920; Nemiah May, an autoworker born in 1914; Jesse Williams, an autoworker born in 1906; Edward March, an autoworker born in 1923; Sharon Woodward, a telephone operator born in 1947; Andrew Green, a truck driver born in 1910; Cyril McCough Jr., a Ford employee born in 1931; and Thelma Haugabook, a secretary. See trial notes, Box 5, Ronald Glotta Collection, the Walter P. Reuther Library of Labor and Urban Affairs, Detroit.

30. Even though Judge Colombo was considered to be "a villain to many liberals for having once sentenced a marijuana defendant to nine years," he was receptive to Cockrel and Ravitz's suggestion that the Johnson murders be put in a broader social context. As he

said, "I used to work on the line in an auto plant during the summers; that's a lot of what persuaded me to go to law school. I hated the men who wore white shirts and always knew how to do your job better than you." As quoted in *Time Magazine*, 7 June 1971.

31. "Opening Remarks of Prosecutor Galligan," Box 5, RGC. Murder chronology based on witness testimony, *Detroit Free Press*, 16 July 1970.

32. "Opening remarks of Kenneth Cockrel," Box 5, RGC.

33. Ibid.

34. Ibid.

35. Ibid.

36. The not guilty by reason of insanity defense has its origins in English Law during the reign of Henry III. It came into usage in the United States in 1868, but the legal definition of "insanity" changed over time with various case law (see *Durham v. United States*, 1954; *Brawner v. United States*, 1972; *Carter v. General Motors*, 1960; and *McQuillen v. United States*, 1974). By 1967, this kind of defense was used in only 2 percent of all criminal jury trials, but when that defense was used by African Americans (and particularly when that defendant's insanity was linked with social deprivation), the cases were extremely controversial. By the 1980s, such controversial insanity defenses were labeled the "excuse" or "black rage" defense. See Richard Allen, Elyce Foster, and Jesse Rubin, *Readings in Law and Psychiatry* (Baltimore, 1968), and Alan Dershowitz, *The Abuse Excuse and Other Stories of Cop-Outs, Sob Stories, and Evasions of Responsibility* (Boston, 1994).

37. Testimony of Edna Hudson and James Johnson Jr. (passim), Box 5, RGC.

38. *Michigan Chronicle*, 22 May 1971.

39. Ibid.

40. Ibid.

41. Trial summary (p. 17), Box 5, RGC.

42. Testimony of Maggie Foster Taylor (pp. 3–5), Box 3, RGC.

43. In 1970, "chronic undifferentiated schizophrenia" was classified as a schizophrenia that is "not easily defined," but if accompanied by "marked paranoid features," it was known to manifest itself as "prosecutory or grandiose delusions and hallucinations" and "sometimes excessive religiosity. [The sufferer] ascribes to others [the] characteristics [he or she] cannot accept in [his or her] self." See Allen, Foster, and Rubin, *Readings in Law and Psychiatry*, 51.

44. Clemens Fitzgerald to Kenneth Cockrel, 15 February 1971, Box 5, RGC.

45. Trial summary (p. 5), Box 5, RGC.

46. Fitzgerald used both the term "schizophrenic reaction, chronic undifferentiated with marked paranoid features" and "schizoid personality" to describe Johnson's condition at various points in the trial. "Schizoid personality" applied to one disabled by "shyness, oversensitivity, seclusiveness, avoidance of close or complete relationships"; this individual "reacts to disturbing experiences and conflicts with detachment." See Allen, Foster and Rubin, *Readings in Law and Psychiatry*, 54.

47. Clemens Fitzgerald to Kenneth Cockrel.

48. *Detroit Free Press*, 19 May 1971.

49. See psychological exams of Johnson by psychologists Dr. William Bowen, 21 July 1970; L. L. Mackenzie, 10 October 1970; and Barbara Stewart, Ph.D., to Judge Richard Dunn, 21 July 1970, Box 3, RGC.

50. *Michigan Chronicle*, 22 May 1971, Box 2, CMC.

51. *Detroit Free Press*, 6 May 1971.

52. Testimony of Clarence Horton (p. 12), Box 5, RGC.

53. Testimony of James Johnson Jr. (p. 3), Box 5, RGC.

54. Ibid., 3, 4, and 8.

55. *Detroit News*, 1 May 1971.

56. Dr. Mackenzie exam.

57. Fitzgerald to Cockrel.

58. Testimony of James Johnson Jr. (pp. 9 and 10), Box 5, RGC.

59. "Continuation of Decision," decision of hearing referee John Conley (p. 2), Box 3, RGC.
60. Testimony of James Johnson Jr. before Workman's Compensation Appeal Board (p. 3). Box 3, RGC.
61. Testimony of Clarence Horton (p. 12), Box 5, RGC.
62. Ibid., 11.
63. Testimony of Ellsworth J. Rhodes (p. 21), Box 5, RGC.
64. Testimony of James Johnson Jr. (p. 8), Box 5, RGC.
65. Trial summary of Cockrel's opening remarks to the jury, Box 5, RGC.
66. *Michigan Chronicle,* 22 May 1971.
67. Ibid.
68. On the day of the murders, the outside temperature was 86 degrees, as compared with the 52-degree weather on the day of the jury's tour.
69. *Time Magazine,* 7 June 1971, 39.
70. Ibid.
71. *Detroit Free Press,* 29 May 1971.
72. Trial summary of Cockrel's closing remarks (p. 54), Box 5, RGC.
73. *Michigan Chronicle,* 29 May 1971.
74. *Time Magazine,* 7 June 1971, 39.
75. Ibid.
76. Ibid.
77. *Michigan Chronicle,* 29 May 1971.
78. Roy and Joy Johnson to Kenneth Verne Cockrel, 27 May 1971, Box 16, CMC.
79. *Michigan Chronicle,* 29 May 1971.
80. *Detroit Free Press,* 18 December 1971.
81. See case complaint and list of all litigants in Box 11, CMC.
82. Case complaint (p. 21), Box 11, CMC.
83. Details of the Manning murder are noteworthy when assessing Detroit's STRESS operation. See case complaint (p. 17), Box 11, CMC.
84. *United Justice Train* 1, no. 2 (July 1972); *United Justice Train* 1, no. 1 (June 1972), Box 73, Folder 5, UAW Region 1B Collection, the Walter P. Reuther Library of Labor and Urban Affairs, Detroit.
85. See: State of Michigan in the Court for The county of Wayne. *Labor Defense Coalition, et al. v. Roman Gribbs, et. al.* Civil Action no. 204539R. 4, May 1972. Box 11, CMC.
86. Press release, Labor Defense Coalition, 7 June 1972, Box 16, CMC.
87. Field Division Staff to CCR, memo regarding "Changes in the Detroit Police Department's STRESS Program," 17 March 1972, Part 3, Box 66, Folder 34, CCRC.
88. "New Criteria for STRESS Program," statement by Mayor Roman S. Gribbs, 17 March 1972, Part 3, Box 68, Folder 19, CCRC.
89. *Community Reporter,* 20 April–3 May 1972, Part 3, Box 68, Folder 19, CCRC.
90. "Strength to Families under STRESS," leaflet, Box 2, CMC.
91. Interview with Hayward Brown, *South End,* 9 May 1973, Part 3, Box 67, Folder 13, CCRC; "Statement of Hayward Brown, Age 18, to Sergeant Fitzpatrick and Inspector Clifton Casey," 12 January 1973, Box 11, CMC.
92. Ibid.
93. Interview with Brown, *South End* 8, June 1973. Vol.8 #4 Part 3, Box 67, Folder 14 CCRC (p. 2). According to two bills of sale located by the DPD, John Percy Boyd had purchased $189.65 worth of weaponry at Wessel Gun Service, Inc., on 16 November 1972 and $208.35 worth of weapons at another Detroit arms store. See sales receipts found by DPD, Box 11, CMC.
94. "Police Request Warrant," Box 11, CMC.
95. Testimony of Billy Price, 1 May 1973 (pp. 38–39), State of Michigan in the Recorder's Court for the City of Detroit, *The People of the State of Michigan v. Hayward Brown,* Case 72–09659, Box 11, CMC.

96. Statement of Hayward Brown to Fitzpatrick and Clifton. Part 3, Box 67, Folder 13, CCRC.

97. Amy Carroll, Shawn Gilbert, Ellen Schweitzer, and Tim Sabota, "STRESS Fractures" (p. 42), senior research paper (Residential College, University of Michigan, 1995).

98. Rachel Paster, "'A Hero Ain't Nothing but a Man': The Trials of Hayward Brown and the Resulting Police Controversy in Detroit, 1972–1973" (p. 6), unpublished senior seminar paper (Residential College, University of Michigan, 1996).

99. "STRESS Fractures," 44.

100. Testimony of Robert Dooley, 23 January 1973, Box 11, CMC. p. 19.

101. Howard Kohn, "Detroit's Supercops: Terror in the Streets," *Ramparts* (December 1973): 41.

102. Teletypes, 3 February 1973, Box 11, CMC.

103. "Fugitive Apprehension Notes," Box 11, CMC.

104. On 23 February 1973, Atlanta police killed John Boyd, along with his half-brother Owen Winfield. Three days later, Bethune was killed with a bullet from his own gun on the roof of a dormitory at Morris Brown College in Atlanta (see *Detroit News,* 24 February 1973). There was much controversy surrounding these deaths. Regarding the Boyd shooting, coroners found non–police issue ammunition in his body that no one could explain. Regarding Bethune, officers claimed that he shot at them first from the roof of the dorm, but later tests showed otherwise. Evidence seems to suggest that while Bethune took aim at officers with his .357 magnum, Officer Walker shot at him first, hitting Bethune in the upper shoulder. Moments later, Bethune's .357 went off, firing its one bullet directly into his own head. While the incident was written up as a suicide, the coroner stated that it was odd that the gun would not have been directly against Bethune's head if it were a suicide. Instead, he suggested, the impact of Walker's shot to Bethune's shoulder undoubtedly caused Bethune's hand to fly up and discharge a shot to his own head accidentally. The coroner also noted that "there was no needle marks on the arms . . . nor was there any trace of narcotics in their blood." *Michigan Chronicle,* 10 March 1973; "STRESS Fractures," 75.

105. For a full account of the meeting at Ford Auditorium, see CCR Field Division to Police-Community Relations Commission, memo regarding Common Council, 11 January 1973, Hearing on Charges of Police Department Violations of Citizens Rights, 1 February 1973, Part 3, Box 69, Folder 10, CCRC; Commissioner Nichols's remarks to Common Council, STRESS Hearings, Ford Auditorium, 11 January 1973, Part 3, Box 69, Folder 10, CCRC.

106. Testimony of Richard Grapp (pp. 56 and 57), 1 May 1973, Box 11, CMC.

107. Testimony of Robert Rosenow, quoted in Brian Dunn, "Hayward Brown and the Trials of 1973," unpublished senior seminar paper (Residential College, University of Michigan, 1996).

108. See testimony of Grapp (pp. 33–35) and testimony of Rosenow (pp. 25–27 and 58–59), Box 11, CMC. See also testimony of Eugene Fuller (pp. 13 and 40–41) in the pretrial examination, 17 January 1973. Box 11, CMC.

109. Testimony of Richard Rosenow (p. 16) and Eugene Fuller (p. 74), pretrial examination. Box 11, CMC. See also testimony of Eugene Fuller (p. 37), 1 May 1973. Box 11, CMC.

110. Cockrel's objection (pp. 2–4 and 19), 23 January 1973. Box 11 CMC. *The State of Michigan v. Hayward Brown, Defendant.* Recorders Court File #72-10249.

111. "STRESS Fractures," 52.

112. Rachel Cardone, "The Tool of Justice" (p. 13), unpublished senior seminar paper (Residential College, University of Michigan, 1996).

113. Transcript of *The Lou Gordon Show,* 24 June 1973, Box 11, CMC.

114. *Detroit Free Press,* 7 July 1973.

115. Ibid.

116. *Detroit Free Press,* 10 July 1973.

117. *Detroit News,* 8 July 1973.

118. Ibid.

119. Ibid.

120. Margaret Borys, "Towards Our Own Courts . . . and Beyond," Box 4, Folder 21, DGC, the Walter P. Reuther Library of Labor and Urban Affairs, Detroit.

121. Ibid.

122. Ibid.

123. Letters to the editor, *Detroit News,* 20 April 1972.

124. "Interview with the Honorable George Crockett," *Ebony,* August 1969; quoted in Gregory Parker, "Judge George Crockett: Radical under the Robe" (p. 13), unpublished senior seminar paper (Residential College, University of Michigan, 1996).

125. *Detroit News,* 10 June 1973.

126. Letters to the editor, *Detroit News,* 16 July 1973.

127. *Detroit Free Press,* 16 December 1971.

128. *Tuebor,* January 1973 and February 1973. Both quoted in John Bauman III, "Superfly Suits and Blue Suits with Silver Badges: STRESS, the Election of Coleman Young, and the Reform of the Police Department" (p. 49), unpublished senior honors thesis (Department of History, University of Michigan, 1998).

129. *Michigan Chronicle,* 5 July 1969.

130. *Inner City Voice* 2, no. 7 (15 July 1970), in the DRUM Collection.

131. Ibid. In fact, as African American columnist Bill Black stated, "At no time did I condone what James Johnson did. . . . I abhor violence" (*Michigan Chronicle,* March 1973).

132. Parker, "Judge George Crockett: Radical under the Robe," 14.

133. Ken Cockrel, "Speech at the Repression Conference," January 1970, Box 26, CMC.

134. Draft of editorial on the New Bethel verdicts, Box 10, CMC.

135. Borys, "Towards Our Own Courts."

136. "Detroit under STRESS," 36.

137. Jerome Cavanagh, "Mayors Recommendations before Governor Kerner's Commission in Washington, D.C."

138. Borys, "Towards Our Own Courts."

139. Ibid.

140. *Detroit News Magazine,* 14 October 1973.

Chapter 7

1. Thomas Brooks, "Workers White and Black: DRUM Beats in Detroit," *Dissent,* January–February 1970, 8.

2. Horace Harris, graduate student in international relations, and Deanna Utlefe, graduate student in economics, "Dodge Revolutionary Movement (DRUM): A Study through Interviews," unpublished paper, 15 September 1969, Box 1, Folder 10, Enid Eckstein Collection, the Walter P. Reuther Library of Labor and Urban Affairs, Detroit.

3. James Geschwender, *Class, Race, and Worker Insurgency: The League of Revolutionary Black Workers* (New York, 1977), 103–104.

4. Irving Bluestone to Walter Reuther, memo, Series 6, Subseries B, Box 229, Walter P. Reuther Collection, the Walter P. Reuther Library of Labor and Urban Affairs, Detroit.

5. *DRUM* 2, no. 24, Box 41, UAW Local 3 Collection, the Walter P. Reuther Library of Labor and Urban Affairs, Detroit.

6. Geschwender, *Class, Race, and Worker Insurgency,* 107.

7. "Special Trustee Election Tally," 3 October 1968 runoff, Box 17, Folder 8, UAW Local 3 Collection.

8. "Victory, Victory," DRUM leaflet, October 1968, Box 41, UAW Local 3 Collection.

9. Interview with General Baker, 9 August 1969, in Harris and Utlefe, "Dodge Revolutionary Movement (DRUM)," 17.

10. Devon Anne Perez, "The Dodge Revolutionary Union Movement: Rhetoric Defined, Actions Solidified, Opposition Destroyed" (p. 43), senior honors thesis (Department of History, University of Michigan, 1996); notes of meeting held 1 October 1968 at Dodge

Main plant, UAW Local 3, with the mayor, chief of police, and sergeant of police, Hamtramck Police Department, Box 47, Folder 17, UAW Local 3 Collection.

11. George Merrelli to Ed Liska, copy of the *South End* with comments on the election attached, 11 October 1968, Box 41, Folder 29, UAW Local 3 Collection.

12. Interview with General Baker, 9 August 1969, in Harris and Utlefe, "Dodge Revolutionary Movement (DRUM)," 18.

13. *DRUM* 1, no. 15, Box 41, UAW Local 3 Collection.

14. UAW International Executive Board to All Members, 10 March 1969, Box 45, UAW Region I Collection, the Walter P. Reuther Library of Labor and Urban Affairs, Detroit.

15. "Andy Hardy for Vice President Local 3," leaflet, Box 41, Folder 25, UAW Local 3 Collection.

16. Brooks, "Workers White and Black," 10.

17. *DRUM* 2, no. 1, Detroit Revolutionary Union Movements News Collection, the Walter P. Reuther Library of Labor and Urban Affairs, Detroit.

18. *DRUM* 2, no. 10. See also caricature drawn of Andy Hardy as part of the cartoon duo Amos and Andy, *DRUM* 2, no. 27, Box 41, Folders 28 and 27, UAW Local 3 Collection.

19. "Open Letter to Local 3 Membership: Ron March Speaks," Box 41, Folder 25, UAW Local 3 Collection.

20. Lee Cain (former executive board member and former chairman Dodge Local 3 Anti-Discrimination Committee) to members, leaflet, Box 41, Folder 25, UAW Local 3 Collection.

21. *Michigan Chronicle*, 9 May 1969.

22. *DRUM* 1, no. 15, Box 44, UAW Local 3 Collection.

23. Ibid.

24. Don Jackson, Ron March, et al., to President Ed Liska, 30 April 1969, Box 41, UAW Local 3 Collection.

25. *Finally got The News*. Black Star Productions. 1971. Film and Video Collection. The Walter P. Reuther Library of Labor and Urban Affairs, Detroit.

26. See "Election Special," *Inner City Voice* 2, no. 3 (16 March–1 April 1970), DRUM News Collection.

27. Interview with Mike Hamlin, in Robert H. Mast, ed., *Detroit Lives* (Philadelphia, 1994), 228.

28. *DRUM* 2, no. 3, Box 41, UAW Local 3 Collection.

29. See the UAW's Official Election Count, Box 229, WPRC.

30. Michael Adelman to the secretary of labor, U.S. Department of Labor, 16 July 1970, Subseries 2-A, Box 4, Folder 34, DRUM Collection.

31. *DRUM* 3, no. 5, Box 41, Folder 28, UAW Region 1 Collection; Perez, "The Dodge Revolutionary Union Movement," 54–55.

32. Box 4, Folder 34, DRUM Collection.

33. Ken Simmons, secretary, Credentials Committee UAW, to Aaron Pitts, telegram, 17 April 1970, Box 4, Folder 34, DRUM Collection.

34. "Local Officers and Delegates, Election Day: Wed. March 18, 1970 4:45am-6:00pm," teletype, Series 6, Subseries B, Box 229, Folder 8, WPRC.

35. Frank Menendez to George Merrelli, memo regarding brief of election held at Local 3 on 18 and 19 March, 24 March 1970, Box 44, UAW Region 1 Collection.

36. See "Election Notes," Series 6, Subseries B, Box 229, Folder 8, WPRC.

37. Ibid.

38. Ed Liska to Walter P. Reuther, telegram, Series 6, Subseries B, Box 229, Folder 7, WPRC.

39. John Watson, quoted in Dan Georgakas and Marvin Surkin, *Detroit: I Do Mind Dying* (New York, 1975), 50.

40. Ibid.

41. During this election on 21 April 1969, ELRUM had run its candidate, Fred Holsey, for the position of trustee; James Edwards for a position as steward; and Alonzo Chandler for a job as union "guide." See *South End* 27, no. 121 (14 May 1969), Series 9, Part 2, Box

47, Folder 3, Arthur Hughes Collection, the Walter P. Reuther Library of Labor and Urban Affairs, Detroit.

42. "Jordon U. Sims for President," parody leaflet, Series 9, Part 2, Box 47, Folder 3, AHC.

43. DRUM Questionnaire, Local 961, Box 45, UAW Region 1 Collection.

44. Leadership Local 961 to Local 961 members, Box 3, Folder 12, Dan Georgakas Collection, the Walter P. Reuther Library of Labor and Urban Affairs, Detroit.

45. Ibid.

46. Ibid.

47. "Jordan Sims Your Man for President," pamphlet. Box 4, Folder 14, DRUM Collection.

48. "Jordan U. Sims for President," Box 47, Folder 3, AHC.

49. *Detroit Free Press,* 23 May 1971.

50. Ibid.

51. Geschwender, *Class, Race, and Worker Insurgency,* 201.

52. *Michigan Chronicle,* 22 March 1969.

53. Steve Babson, *Working Detroit: The Making of a Union Town* (New York, 1984), 174.

54. John Taylor, interview with Dan Georgakas, 25 August 1972, Box 3, Folder 17, DGC.

55. *ELRUM* 1, no. 9, Box 45, UAW Region 1 Collection.

56. *ELRUM,* 3 April 1968, DRUM Collection.

57. Taylor, interview with Dan Georgakas, Box 3, Folder 17, DGC.

58. Member of the Employees Committee on Human Equality to ELRUM, Box 1, Folder 16, DRUM Collection.

59. Taylor, interview with Dan Georgakas, Box 3, Folder 17, DGC.

60. Ibid.

61. *DRUM* 1, no.5, Box 41, Folder 26, UAW Local 3 Collection.

62. Ibid.

63. Ibid.

64. Jordan Sims, Eddie Barksdale, and Carla Cooke, interview with Dan Georgakas, August 19, 1972. Box 3, Folder 18, DGC.

65. Member of the Employees Committee on Human Equality to ELRUM, Box 1, Folder 16, DRUM Collection.

66. Taylor, interview with Dan Georgakas, Box 3, Folder 17, DGC.

67. Ibid.

68. Quoted in Harris and Utlefe, "Dodge Revolutionary Movement (DRUM)," 17.

69. *DRUM* 1, no. 6, Box 41, Folder 26, UAW Local 3 Collection.

70. *DRUM* 1, no. 7, Box 41, Folder 26, UAW Local 3 Collection.

71. See *DRUM* 1, no. 7, Box 41, UAW Local 3 Collection. For more on black manhood, see Lawson Bush, "Am I a Man? A Literature Review Engaging the Sociohistorical Dynamics of Black Manhood in the United States," *Western Journal of Black Studies* 23, no. 1 (Spring 1999): 49–57; Michael Kimmel, *Manhood in America: A Cultural History* (New York, 1995); Gail Jardine and Nathan McCall, "To Be Black, Male, and Conscious: Race, Rage, and Manhood in America," *American Quarterly* 48, no. 2 (June 1996); Bruce Dorsey, "History of Manhood in America," *Radical History Review* 64 (1996); Robert Stapes, *Black Masculinity: The Black Males' Role in American Society* (San Francisco, 1982); Daniel Black, *Dismantling Black Manhood: An Historical and Literary Analysis of the Legacy of Slavery* (New York, 1997).

72. "Negro Lovers," DRUM newsletter, Box 41, Folder 28, UAW Local 3 Collection.

73. See the biography of Black Panther Assata Shakur, *Assata: An Autobiography* (Chicago, 1987).

74. Miriam Kramer, former DRUM member, *Village Voice,* 26 March 1991, 27.

75. Interview with Marian Kramer, in Mast, *Detroit Lives,* 103–104.

76. Interview with John Watson, in Georgakas and Surkin, *Detroit: I Do Mind Dying,* Updated Edition. (Cambridge: 1988) 224–25.

77. Notes on "Committee Assignments," Box 1, Folder 31, DRUM Collection.

78. As quoted in Geschwender, *Class, Race, and Worker Insurgency,* 160.

79. "Negro Lovers," DRUM newsletter, Box 41, Folder 28, UAW Local 3 Collection.

80. *DRUM* 2, no. 22, Box 41, Folder 27, UAW Local 3 Collection.

81. Interview with Edna Hewell Watson, in Mast, *Detroit Lives,* 225.

82. Cockerel, Hamlin, and Watson, "The Three Way Split," position paper (pp. 13–25), Box 4, Folder 11, DGC.

83. "Rationale for Revolutionary Leadership Dictatorship of the Proletariat," League position paper, 2 January 1971, Box 1, Folder 25, DRUM Collection.

84. Interview with General Baker, in Mast, *Detroit Lives,* 310.

85. "The Split in the League of Revolutionary Black Workers: Three Lines and Three Headquarters," position paper, Box 1, Folder 19, DRUM Collection.

86. Ibid., 20.

87. Ibid., 16.

88. Ibid., 18.

89. Ibid., 28.

90. "Code of Conduct," League of Revolutionary Black Workers, 1971 document, Box 4, Folder 11, DGC.

91. "Confidential Communication for Internal Use Only," League of Revolutionary Black Workers Executive Board, 29 March 1971, Box 18, Kenneth Cockrel and Sheila Murphy Collection, the Walter P. Reuther Library of Labor and Urban Affairs, Detroit.

92. Steve Jefferys, *Management and Managed: Fifty Years of Crisis at Chrysler* (Cambridge, 1986), 166.

93. Ibid., 152.

94. Box 3, Folders 6 and 9, DRUM Collection.

95. "Preliminary Results of the First Annual Survey of Occupational Injuries and Illnesses," Bureau of Labor Statistics, report, 21 January 1974, Box 5, Folder 11, DGC.

96. *Detroit Free Press,* 15 August 1973.

97. *The Washington Report,* 20 April 1970, and 23 March 1970, Box 3, Folder 2, DRUM Collection.

98. *Frederick Holsey v. Chrysler Corporation,* the State of Michigan, Civil Rights Commission, Case 5980-EM, Decision of Philip Colista, November 1971, Ronald Glotta Collection, the Walter P. Reuther Library of Labor and Urban Affairs, Detroit.

99. Georgakas and Surkin, *Detroit: I Do Mind Dying,* (New York: 1975) 102.

100. Ibid.

101. Geschwender, *Class, Race, and Worker Insurgency,* 101.

102. Notes from attorney, Ron Glotta, RGC.

103. Ibid.

104. See "Section One: Automobiles," Rachel Scott, *Muscle and Blood* (New York, 1974).

105. Ibid., 125.

106. Quoted in ibid., 125–26.

107. See Local 7 membership meeting minutes, Sunday, 25 June 1972, in bound volumes: "Membership / Leadership Meetings," 25 March 1962–23 April 1978, Box 14, UAW Local 7 Collection.

108. Telegram to U.S. Department of Labor, Occupational Safety and Health Administration inspectors, 9 August 1973, Box 87, UAW Region 1 Collection.

109. United Justice Caucus to Mr. Flowers, recording secretary of Local 7, 31 August 1972, Box 73, Folder 5, UAW Region 1B Collection.

110. Nathaniel Williams, Mack plant Local 212, to Leonard Woodcock, 7 August 1973, Box 157, Folder 8, Leonard Woodcock Collection, the Walter P. Reuther Library of Labor and Urban Affairs, Detroit.

111. Beulah Wallace, Local 933, to Leonard Woodcock, 21 August 1973, Box 157, Folder 9, LWC.

112. In *Carter v. GM* (361 Mich. 577, 106 N.W. 2nd 105, 1960) The Bureau of Workman's Compensation awarded benefits to James Carter, a machine operator, for psychosis.

Donald Loria argued that Carter's psychosis was a result of the emotional pressure of his job. On 24 October 1956, Carter had a breakdown that led to his filing for compensation. This was an extremely significant case because prior to it, one could only be eligible for workman's compensation if one had a physical disability.

113. Dr. Gorden Forrer to R. G. Moir, Workman's Compensation, 9 September 1971, Box 3, RGC.
114. Ibid.
115. Ibid.
116. "Continuation of Decision," 28 February 1973, *James Johnson Jr. v. Chrysler Corporation*, State of Michigan Bureau of Workman's Compensation, attachment, decision of Hearing Referee John Conley, Box 16, CMC.
117. "Continuation of Decision," Box 16, CMC. Also in Box 3, RGC.
118. Ibid., 14.
119. Ibid., 1–2 and 25.
120. *Detroit Free Press,* 26 April 1971.
121. *Detroit Free Press,* 6 March 1973.
122. Glotta, Adleman, and Dinges, press release, 6 March 1973, Box 3, RGC.
123. *Detroit Free Press,* 6 March 1973.
124. Ibid.
125. *Wall Street Journal,* March 1973, Box 3, RGC.
126. *Detroit News,* 8 March 1973.
127. Editorial, *Detroit Free Press,* 13 March 1973, Box 5, Folder 23, DRUM Collection.
128. Ibid.
129. Suburban newspaper clipping found for 17 March 1973, in Box 2, Folder 23, DRUM Collection.
130. B. J. Widick, *Detroit: City of Race and Class Violence* (Chicago, 1972), 223.
131. Undated notes, Box 5, Folder 23, DRUM Collection.
132. Elroy Richardson, president; James R. Franklin, recording secretary, UAW Local 961; and Walter Waller, Region 1 representative International UAW, article, *The Criterion,* 12 August 1970.
133. *The Metro* (July 1970), Box 3, RGC.
134. Unidentified notes from persons working on the Johnson case, Box 5, Folder 23, DRUM Collection.
135. Motor City Labor League leaflet, Box 3, RGC.
136. Jordan Sims, John Taylor, and Fred Holsey to Leonard Woodcock, 12 March 1973, Box 3, RGC.
137. Jordan Sims, John Taylor, and Frederick Holsey, letter to the editor, *Detroit Free Press,* 15 March 1973, Box 3, RGC.
138. John Taylor to Homer Jolly, representative International UAW, Chrysler, 16 March 1973, Box 3, RGC; John Taylor, news release, Box 3, RGC.
139. Heather Thompson, "Autoworkers, Dissent, and the UAW," in *Autowork,* ed. Robert Asher and Ronald Edsforth (Albany, N.Y., 1995); Emma Rothschild, *Paradise Lost: The Decline of the Auto Auto-Industrial Age* (New York: 1973); Stanley Aronowitz, *False Promises: The Shaping of American Working Class Consciousness* (New York: 1973); and Barbara Garson, *All the Live Long Day: The Meaning and Demeaning Routine of Work* (New York: 1977).
140. "Walk Outs: Unauthorized Strike Must Stop!!!," Local 7 worker leaflet, from the personal archives of autoworker Neal Chacker.
141. As Douglas Fraser, vice-president of the UAW put it, the union should "take issues away from them, not allow issues to arise upon which they can exploit the situation [because] unless you do they are going to grow and grow." As quoted in William Serrin, *The Company and the Union: The Civilized Relationship of General Motors Corporation and the United Automobile Workers,* (New York, 1974), 321.
142. *United Justice Train* 1, no. 2. (July 1972), Box 73, Folder 5, UAW Region 1B Collection.

143. *United Justice Train* 1, no. 6 (January 1973), Box 73, Folder 5, UAW Region 1B Collection.

144. International Socialists, UNC discussion document, Box 2, Folder 4, EEC.

145. *JARUM* 2, no. 8 (13 December 1974), Box 73, Folder 7, UAW Region 1B Collection.

146. *JARUM* 2, no. 1 (14 August 1974), Box 73, Folder 7, UAW Region 1B Collection.

147. This distinction between the "old" and "new" RUM movements is more rhetorical than real. After 1973, there was no significant RUM activity in the plants, but original RUM activists—now in other, oftentimes more broad-based groups—thought of themselves as part of a "new" RUM movement nevertheless. See *DTRUM* 1, Box 7, RGC.

148. *JARUM* 3, no. 2 (27 May 1975), Box 73, Folder 7, UAW Region 1B Collection.

149. International Socialists, UNC discussion document, Box 2, Folder 4, EEC.

150. United Justice Caucus Leaflet. (February 1973). Box 73, Folder 5, UAW Region 1B Collection.

151. Events at UNC conference on racism, as reported in the *Fifth Estate,* 1972, Box 2, Folder 28, DRUM Collection.

152. "Special Edition," *United National Caucus* (January 1973), Box 47, Folder 12, AHC.

153. "Attention Autoworkers," UNC leaflet, Box 47, Folder 12, AHC.

154. Minutes, Local 7 membership meeting, 25 March 1973, in bound volumes, "Membership / Leadership Meetings," 25 March 1962–23 April 1978, Box 14, UAW Local 7 Collection.

155. United Justice Caucus leaflet, February 1972, Box 73, Folder 5, UAW Region 1B Collection.

156. *United National Caucus* (August 1973); quoted in Geschwender, *Class, Race, and Worker Insurgency,* 202.

157. Emil Mazey to Ken Morris, 15 August 1972, Box 73, Folder 5, UAW Region 1B Collection.

158. George Merrelli to Doug Fraser, 23 October 1973, Box 47, Folder 12, AHC.

159. Walter Wallers to George Merrelli, 24 August 1973, Box 87, Folder 14, UAW Region 1 Collection.

160. Interview with Roger Robinson, in Mast, *Detroit Lives,* 197.

161. *United National Caucus* 4, no. 1 (March–April 1973), Box 11, Folder 7, UAW Public Relations Department, Simon Alpert Collection, the Walter P. Reuther Library of Labor and Urban Affairs, Detroit.

162. Willie F. Pride to UNC. Printed in *United Justice Train,* vol. 1, no. 4. (September 1972). Box 73, Folder 5, UAW Region 1B Collection.

163. It was particularly ironic that Frank McKinnon, who had successfully defeated Sims in the 1971 election and enjoyed much support from the UAW's top brass, was prosecuted by the U.S. government in 1974 for alleged financial improprieties. He was cited for his "false entries in the books and records of Local 961 between June 1. 1971 and June 30, 1972." See notes regarding *United States v. Francis D. McKinnon,* 26 February 1974, Box 4, Folder 20, DRUM Collection.

164. Georgakas and Surkin, *Detroit: I Do Mind Dying,* (New York: 1975) 103.

165. Jordan Sims, "Going for Broke," in *Rank and File: Personal Histories by Working Class Organizers,* ed. Staughton and Alice Lynd (Princeton, N.J., 1973), 263.

166. Georgakas and Surkin, *Detroit: I Do Mind Dying,* 230.

167. Geschwender, *Class, Race, and Worker Insurgency,* 191.

168. Transcript, interview with Isaac Shorter and Larry Carter, *The Lou Gordon Show,* Box 73, Folder 12, UAW Region 1B Collection.

169. Ibid. See also Isaac Shorter and Larry Carter, interview in *Workers' Power* (August 1973), Labadie Collection, University of Michigan, Ann Arbor.

170. Transcript, interview with Isaac Shorter and Larry Carter, *The Lou Gordon Show.*

171. Leaflet, *United Justice Caucus* (February 1973), Box 73, Folder 5, UAW Region 1B Collection.

172. *Detroit News,* 24 July 1973.

173. Isaac Shorter and Larry Carter, interview in *Black Voice* 3 (September 1973).

174. Shorter and Carter, interview in *Workers' Power.*

175. "Victory at Jefferson," leaflet by UNJ-Jefferson, Jordan, Strike Back-Dodge Main, Mack Safety Watchdog-Mack, UNC. From the personal archives of autoworker Neal Chacker.

176. Isaac Shorter and Larry Carter, interview, in *The Journey;* quoted in Geschwender, *Class, Race, and Worker Insurgency,* 192–93.

177. "As Our Readers See It: Chrysler Hijacking: Anarchy or Justice?," *Detroit Free Press,* 4 August 1973.

178. *Detroit News,* 8 August 1973.

179. See case materials *Scott, et al., v. Chrysler Corporation, et al.,* and deposition of Jerome Scott, Box 4, RGC.

180. UAW's chronology of plant upheaval at Jefferson forge and Mack, 15 September 1973, Box 73, Folder 14, UAW Region 1B Collection.

181. Order granting an injunction in *Chrysler Corporation v. Fredrick McAlister, et al.* before Judge Cornelia G. Kennedy in the U.S. District Court for the Eastern District of Michigan, Southern Division. Box 87, UAW Region 1 Collection.

182. *Scott, et al., v. Chrysler Corporation, et al.,* deposition of Leon Klea, 19 September 1977, Box 4, RGC.

183. *Detroit News,* 8 August 1973.

184. Ibid.

185. *Detroit News,* 9 August 1973.

186. Handwritten and mimeographed leaflet signed by "Fifteen Forge workers," Box 87, UAW Region 1 Collection.

187. *Detroit News,* 10 August 1973.

188. Geschwender, *Class, Race, and Worker Insurgency,* 191.

189. *Detroit News,* 11 August 1973.

190. "Vote Strike Friday" Leaflet United Forge Workers. From the personal archives of autoworker Neal Chacker.

191. Forge leaflet, signed by Fraser, Merrelli, and Klea, Box 87, Folder 14, UAW Region 1 Collection.

192. See handwritten account in Box 87, Folder 14, UAW Region 1 Collection.

193. Telegram to the U.S. Department of Labor, Occupational Safety and Health Administration inspectors, 8 August 1973, Box 87, Folder 14, UAW Region 1 Collection.

194. Ibid.

195. Leaflet to Forge Workers, signed by Fraser, Merrelli, and Klea. UAW Region 1 Collection.

196. *Detroit News,* 11 August 1973; *Detroit Free Press,* 12 August 1973.

197. *Detroit Free Press,* 11 August 1973.

198. *Detroit Free Press,* 13 August 1973.

199. *Detroit Free Press,* 14 August 1973.

200. Ibid.

201. Geschwender, *Class, Race, and Worker Insurgency,* 176.

Chapter 8

1. Interview with Roger Robinson, in Robert H. Mast, ed., *Detroit Lives* (Philadelphia, 1994), 195.

2. Interview with Arthur Johnson, in ibid., 199.

3. Steve Jefferys, *Management and Managed: Fifty Years of Crisis at Chrysler* (Cambridge, 1986), 35.

4. Johnson was institutionalized at the CFP between June and September 1971, and then again between February and November 1973. He was institutionalized at Ionia from September 1971 to November 1972 and from November 1974 to March 1975. He was institutionalized at Ypsilanti State Hospital from November 1972 until February 1973.

5. North Detroit Coalition, notice, Box 2, Folder 4, Kenneth Cockrel and Sheila Murphy Collection, the Walter P. Reuther Library of Labor and Urban Affairs, Detroit.

6. "Draft Cockrel for Mayor Committee," press release, 8 June 1972, Box 2, Folder 4, CMC.

7. Mrs. Hoskins to Kenneth Cockrel, 1 January 1973, Box 2, Folder 4, CMC.

8. Statement of the Black Workers Congress, Box 1, Dan Georgakas Collection, the Walter P. Reuther Library of Labor and Urban Affairs, Detroit.

9. Justin Ravitz to Ken Cockrel and Sheila Murphy, Box 18, CMC.

10. Wilbur C. Rich, *Coleman Young and Detroit Politics: From Social Activist to Power Broker,* (Detroit: 1989), 71; Joseph Darden, Richard Child Hill, June Thomas, and Richard Thomas, *Detroit: Race and Uneven Development* (Philadelphia: 1987), 213.

11. See interview with Young in the *Detroit News*, August 15, 1973 and FBI memo printed in the *Detroit News* January 27, 1985. In the Young Biographical File, the Walter P. Reuther Library of Labor and Urban Affairs, Detroit.

12. *Detroit News*, November 8, 1968.

13. *Detroit Free Press*, September 22, 1968.

14. Radio and TV Reports, Inc., April 14, 1972, WWJ-TV, News 4, Box 3, Charter Revision Commission Collection. Burton Historical Collection. Detroit Public Library, Detroit.

15. *Detroit News*, October 8, 1973.

16. Many candidates entered this race, including black judge Edward Bell, white sociology professor John Mogk, and white Breakthrough leader Donald Lobsinger.

17. *Detroit News*, 19 August 1973.

18. Ibid.

19. Ibid.

20. Rich, *Coleman Young,* 102. See also *Detroit Free Press*, 13 September 1973.

21. *Detroit News*, 16 August 1973.

22. *Detroit News*, 14 October 1973.

23. *Detroit Free Press*, 13 September 1973.

24. *Detroit News*, 11 July 1973.

25. Ibid.

26. *Detroit News*, 20 October 1973.

27. John Nichols, quoted in *Detroit News*, 21 August 1973.

28. Ibid.

29. For more information on how the DPD altered crime statistics, see the report by Gerhard Long, William Deane Smith, David O. Porter, Delores Weber, and L. L. Loukopoulus, "The Detroit Police Department—a Research Report on Previous Studies; Criminal Statistics; and Police Technology, Productivity, and Competence," May 1970, Box 37, CMC. This exhaustive report includes 74 pages of text, 60 pages of graphs and tables, and a 43-page appendix. See also Loukopoulus, "The Detroit Police Department" and "The Detroit Police Department—Statistical Section," May 1970, Charter Revision Commission Collection, Burton Historical Collection, Detroit Public Library. This independent study was conducted by a fact-finding team at Wayne State University and its Urban Studies Department. Regarding the phenomenon of police manipulating crime statistics elsewhere (in some cases downward, where politically expedient), see Stephen C. Brooks and Robert Lineberry, "Politicians and Urban Policy Change: The Case of Crime and City Politics," in *Urban Policy Analysis*, ed. Terry Clark (Beverly Hills, Calif., 1982); David Seidman and Michael Couzens, "Getting the Crime Rate Down: Political Process and Crime Reporting," *Law and Society Review* 8 (1984).

30. *Detroit News*, 24 October 1973.

31. Desmond Brandy, elections specialist for the city of Detroit, to author, 14 November 1990.

32. Detroit Election Commission, "Official Canvas of Votes, 1953–1978," Vertical Files, Sociology and Economics Department, Detroit Public Library. In 1973, there were 820,243 registered voters, and 456,675 came to the polls.

33. *New York Times*, 6 January 1974.
34. Interview with Gene Cunningham, in Mast, *Detroit Lives*, 315.
35. *New York Times*, 6 January 1974.
36. Ibid.
37. *Detroit News*, 7 November 1973.
38. *Detroit News*, 9 August 1973.
39. Jack Weinberg, "Detroit Auto Uprising: 1973," pamphlet, 1974, author's copy.
40. James Geschwender, *Class, Race and Worker Insurgency: The League of Revolutionary Black Workers* (New York, 1977), 195.
41. *Detroit Free Press*, August 15,1973.
42. "WAM Uses Struggle as Publicity Stunt," *Workers' Power, Special: Auto Revolt 1973*, the Labadie Collection, University of Michigan, Ann Arbor.
43. *Detroit Free Press*, 15 August 1973.
44. *Detroit News*, 16 August 1973.
45. *Detroit Free Press*, 16 August 1973.
46. "Mack Safety Protest," leaflet, the personal archives of autoworker Neal Chacker.
47. Ibid.
48. Ibid.
49. E. J. Morgan to Bluestone, Bannon, and Fraser, 12 June 1973, Box 158, Folder 8, Leonard Woodcock Collection, the Walter P. Reuther Library of Labor and Urban Affairs, Detroit.
50. *UNC* 5 (August 1973); quoted in Geschwender, *Class, Race and Worker Insurgency*, 202.
51. For a glimpse of what was going on inside the plant, see "Night in Captive Auto Plant: Unlikely Place for a Drama," *Detroit Free Press*, 16 August 1973, and "Workers Holdout Quietly," *Detroit Free Press*, 15 August 1973.
52. "Rebels Ousted at Chrysler," *Detroit Free Press*, 15 August 1973.
53. *Detroit News*, 15 August 1973.
54. *Detroit News*, 16 August 1973.
55. Ibid.
56. "UAW Muscle Opens Plant," *Detroit Free Press*, 17 August 1973.
57. *Black Voice* 3 (September 1973).
58. *The Fifth Estate*, 1–14 September 1973.
59. *Detroit News*, 18 August 1973.
60. Ibid.
61. "Proceedings of Special Session IEB/UAW," 5 September 1972, Box 19, UAW International Executive Board Collection, the Walter P. Reuther Library of Labor and Urban Affairs, Detroit.
62. UAW leaflet signed by Doug Fraser, Ken Morris, Hank Ghant, Joe Zappa, Bill Marshall, and Steve Despot, Box 87, Folder 14, UAW Region 1 Collection, the Walter P. Reuther Library of Labor and Urban Affairs, Detroit.
63. "I Take My Stand: Coleman A. Young for Common Council," campaign brochure, YBF.
64. See State of MI Public Act no. 370.
65. "I Take My Stand."
66. Rich, *Coleman Young and Detroit Politics*, 209.
67. These cases received much attention because fourteen-year-old Smith had stolen a purse when he was killed by police, Denice Grant was the nineteenth person killed by STRESS officers, and fifteen-year-old Moorer, a student at Webber Junior High School, was shot in the back as he jumped over a fence after being chased by the police allegedly for having stolen a car. See "Case Draft #565: Glen D. Smith, October 4, 1973"; "Case Draft #173: Anthony Moorer, December 13, 1973"; and "Case Draft #562: Jewel Denice Gant, October 2, 1973," Part 3, Box 69, Folder 2, Commission on Community Relations Collections, the Walter P. Reuther Library of Labor and Urban Affairs, Detroit.

68. News release, Detroit Police Department, Mayor Young and Chief Phillip Tannian, 11 April 1974, Part 3, Box 69–1, CCRC.

69. Mayor's Office press release, 13 February 1974, Box 11, CMC.

70. Booklet, "A Turn Around in the Seventies," Detroit Police Department and Michigan Office of Criminal Justice Programs, 1973, Part 3, Box 68, Folder 19, CCRC; WJR editorial by Denise Lewis of the Detroit Commission on Community Relations, Part 3, Box 68, Folder 19, CCRC.

71. B. J. Widick, *Detroit: City of Race and Class Violence* (Chicago, 1972), 24.

72. *Detroit Free Press*, 5 December 1997.

73. No matter how many hard times befell Detroit, residents still stood by Young and his liberal agenda in election after election. Note the voter returns from the mayoral elections of 1977, 1981, 1985, and 1989. Figures courtesy of the Department of Sociology and Economics, Detroit Public Library.

1977	Young: 164,626	Browne: 63,626
1981	Young: 176,710	Koslowski: 91,245
1985	Young: 141,551	Barrow: 90,907
1989	Young: 138,312	Barrow: 107,073

74. Rich, *Coleman Young and Detroit Politics*, 266.

75. Bill McGraw, "Questions of Rank, Tank Promotions: Fire Department Puts Integration to Work, but not without Conflict," *Detroit Free Press*, 20 December 1994.

76. Darden et al., *Detroit: Race and Uneven Development*, 76.

77. John Bauman, "Super Fly Suits and Blue Suits with Silver Badges: STRESS, the Election of Coleman Young, and the Reform of the Detroit Police Department" (p. 59), senior honors thesis (Department of History, University of Michigan, 1998).

78. *Tuebor* (May 1973); quoted in Bauman, "Super Fly Suits and Blue Suits with Silver Badges," 49.

79. Bauman, "Super Fly Suits and Blue Suits with Silver Badges," 61.

80. Regarding how white suburbanites came to feel about Detroit and the politics of Great Society liberalism, the work of David Riddle is vital. See his "HUD and the Open Housing Controversy of 1970 in Warren, Michigan," *Michigan Historical Review* 24, no. 2 (Fall 1998), and "The Rise of the 'Reagan Democrats' in Warren, Michigan: 1964–1984," Ph.D. diss. (Wayne State University, 1998).

81. City of Detroit Department of Heath Data Book: 1969, 1973, 1976, City of Detroit Municipal Library. Detroit City County Building.

82. *Detroit Free Press*, 22 January 1985.

83. "Summary Characteristics for Government Units and Standard Metropolitan Statistical Areas—Michigan," U.S. Department of Commerce, Bureau of the Census, 1970, 1990.

84. *Detroit Free Press*, 28 April 1994.

85. As quoted in Z'ev Chafets, "The Tragedy of Detroit," *New York Times Magazine*, 29 July 1990, 167. See also Carlito H. Young, "Constant Struggle: Coleman Young's Perspective on American Society and Detroit's Politics," *The Black Scholar* 27, no.2. (Summer 1997).

86. Mike Soules, "White Detroit and the 1973 Election." Unpublished paper. Residential College. university of Michigan. July 1997. 17–18.

87. June Manning Thomas, *Redevelopment and Race: Planning a Finer City in Postwar Detroit* (Baltimore, 1997), 83.

88. Bryan Thompson and Robert Sinclair, *Metropolitan Detroit: An Anatomy of Social Change* (Cambridge, Mass., 1977), 14.

89. Darden et al., *Detroit: Race and Uneven Development,* 109, 138, and 96.
90. Thompson and Sinclair, *Metropolitan Detroit,* 54.
91. Darden et al., *Detroit: Race and Uneven Development,* 101.
92. Ibid., 70.
93. Ibid., 100.
94. Rich, *Coleman Young and Detroit Politics,* 112.
95. Sheldon Friedman and Leon Potok, "Detroit and the Auto Industry: An Historical Overview," UAW Research Department, International UAW, December 1981.
96. "Mayor's Press Release," Coleman Young, 10 April 1975, Box 38, CMC.
97. Darden et al., *Detroit: Race and Uneven Development,* 217.
98. Interview with Martin Glaberman, in Mast, *Detroit Lives* 163.
99. Mel Ravitz, quoted in "The Riot—Unending Effects," *Detroit Free Press,* Special Reprint, August 1992.
100. Mel Ravitz, "Economic Development: Salvation or Suicide," *Social Policy* 19 (Fall 1988): 19.
101. Ibid.
102. Ibid.
103. *New York Times,* 22 January 1975.
104. For an examination of how white hostility to black mayors compromised the viability of inner cities other than Detroit, see Jack White, "The Limits of Black Power," *Time Magazine,* 11 May 1992.
105. Thomas, *Redevelopment,* 2.
106. Friedman and Potok, "Detroit and the Auto Industry."
107. Chafets, "The Tragedy of Detroit," 51.
108. *Detroit Free Press,* 19 February 1994.
109. Interview with Arthur Johnson, in Mast, *Detroit Lives,* 200.
110. Interview with Morris Gleicher, in Mast, *Detroit Lives,* 188.
111. Interview with Moira Kennedy, in Mast, *Detroit Lives,* 139–40.
112. Interview with Mary Sue Shottenfels, in Mast, *Detroit Lives,* 142–43.
113. "An Evening with . . . Coleman A. Young," pamphlet, Detroit Chapter of the National Negro Labor Coalition, 13 August 1994, YBF.
114. Interview with Kenneth V. Cockrel, *Socialist Review* (January–February 1980).
115. By December 1974, Police Chief Bannon was forced to investigate an accusation of police involvement in the drug trade that had been levied by a Ronnie David McCullough and then given to Police Commissioner John Nichols on 11 April 1973. This official complain alleged that STRESS officers Worobec, Fuller, and Dooley ("who would be with Worobec and Fuller but would always stay in the car") and an identified black male officer would pick drug money up at the Sunny Wilson Hotel, 1616 Leslie, Apt. 12, and 1620 Fullerton, Apts. 3 and 4. See Detroit Police Department interoffice memo, 27 December 1974, Box 11, CMC.
116. *Detroit Free Press,* 6 June 1975; *Detroit News,* 7 December 1976.
117. "Chrysler Pleased," UNC leaflet, Box 47, Folder 12, AHC.
118. "Rally, 11–7–73 at 10:00am," UNC leaflet, Box 47, Folder 12, Arthur Hughes Collection, the Walter P. Reuther Library of Labor and Urban Affairs, Detroit.
119. As evidence that the union was determined not to let such dissent emerge again, in 1974, when a JARUM leaflet surfaced at UAW Local 212, it was reported to Regional Director Ken Morris that Local 212 leader Tony Calo's suggestion for dealing with the leaflet's authors was "we should kick the shit out of those guys." See letter from "Bob" to "Ken," 8 March 1974, with copy of *JARUM* (1, no. 3) attached, Box 73, Folder 7, UAW Region 1B Collection, the Walter P. Reuther Library of labor and Urban Affairs, Detroit.
120. "Disposition of Grievance: Karl Williams—1270–0919, W. M. Ector, Sr. Labor Relations Supervisor, Detroit Plant," 17 August, 1973, Box 2, Ronald Glotta Collection, the Walter P. Reuther Library of Labor and Urban Affairs, Detroit.

121. Ibid.
122. "Disposition of Grievance: Thomas Stepanski—0360–4097, W. M. Ector, Sr. Labor Relations Supervisor, Detroit Forge Plant," 17 August 1973, Box 2, RGC.
123. Grievances filed 14 and 23 August 1973; "Statement on Behalf of Chrysler Corporation: Appeal Board Cases 6887, 6889, 6898," Box 2, RGC.
124. Decision by Gabriel Alexander, impartial chairman, 30 August 1974, Appeal Board of the Chrysler Corporation and the International Union, United Automobile, Aerospace, and Agricultural Implement Workers of America, Cases 6887, 6889, 6898—1974:5, Box 2, RGC.
125. Statement on behalf of Chrysler Corporation Appeal Board, Cases 6887, 6889, 6898. In both RGC, Box 2, and DRUM Collection, Box 5, Folder 2.
126. Decision by Gabriel N. Alexander, impartial chairman. Box 2, RGC.
127. For transcripts of the depositions in Case 75–066–303–CZ, see Box 4, RGC. For more information on the rising number of lawsuits filed by workers against their unions in this period, see R. Dinges, "Ruzicka vs. GM: An Unlikely Hero of the Trade Union Movement—the Individual Employee in a Section 301 Case Who Has Been the Victim of Union Negligence," *Wayne Law Review* 24 (September 1978): 5.
128. John Taylor to Riley, Dinges, Davis, Anderson, Glotta, and Middletown, 15 September 1974, Box 5, Folder 2, DRUM Collection.
129. Deposition of Dennis Baliki, 15 December 1977, Box 4, RGC.
130. Ibid., 20–21.
131. Ibid., 22.
132. Ibid., 23.
133. Ibid., 24–25.
134. Ibid., 26.
135. Ibid., 73.
136. Kim Moody, *An Injury to All: The Decline of Business Unionism* (New York, 1988).
137. Ibid.
138. Ibid.
139. Ibid.
140. Steve Babson, "Restructuring the Workplace: Postfordism or the Return of the Foreman?," in *Autowork*, ed. Robert Asher and Ronald Edsforth (Albany, N.Y., 1995), 231, and Lynn Bachelor, "Regime Maintenance, Solution Sets, and Urban Economic Development," *Urban Affairs Quarterly* 29, no.4. (June 1994): 598.
141. Jefferys, *Management and Managed,* 212 and 40.
142. Press release, UAW, 15 August 1978, Box 11, Folder 3, UAW Public Relations Collection, Simon Alpert Collection, the Walter P. Reuther Library of Labor and Urban Affairs, Detroit.
143. Notes, Box 11, Folder 3, SAC.
144. Jerry Dale to public relations staff, memo regarding latest layoff figures for 17 December 1979; Jerry Dale to public relations staff, memo regarding latest layoff figures for 8 February 1980, Box 11, Folder 1, SAC.
145. Jerry Dale to public relations staff, memo regarding latest layoff figures for 25 April 1980; Jerry Dale to public relations staff, memo regarding latest layoff figures for 2 May 1980, Box 11, Folder 1, SAC.
146. Jerry Dale to public relations staff, memo regarding latest layoff figures for 16 May 1980, Box 11, Folder 1, SAC.
147. Babson, "Restructuring," 231.

Conclusion

1. Dan Georgakas and Marvin Surkin, *Detroit: I Do Mind Dying*, Updated Edition. (Cambridge: 1998).

2. June Manning Thomas, *Redevelopment and Race: Planning a Finer City in Postwar Detroit* (Baltimore, 1997), 175.

3. B. J. Widick, *Detroit: City of Race and Class Violence* (Chicago, 1972), 253.

4. Thomas, *Redevelopment and Race,* 171.

5. Thomas, *Redevelopment and Race,* 203–04.

6. Regarding New York City, for example, Jim Sleeper has maintained that it was the power wielded by "white-left and black activists and their liberal apologists" that eventually "broke the spine of New York's civic culture." And, as Fred Seigel has written, under the leadership of liberals in the early 1970s, "the great causes of thirty years ago . . . degenerated into a series of squalid shakedowns." Specifically, it was cities run by black liberals, according to Siegel, such as Detroit and Washington, D.C., that created the most shameful regimes of personal excess and corruption, fiscal mismanagement, and social chaos. Seigel maintains for example that the longer that black mayor Marion Barry ruled D.C., the further that city atrophied, because the black middle class abused power by doing such things as weakening the police department with budget cuts and collapsing standards and creating a center of crime and racial entitlement that sent law-abiding citizens scurrying for the affluent suburbs. Indeed, for Siegel, D.C. is the example par excellence of what happened when liberal plans to aid the poor and adjust racial imbalances became administered by incompetent but threatening black politician hacks. See Jim Sleeper, *The Closest of Strangers: Liberalism and the Politics of Race in New York* (New York, 1990), 102 and 103, and Fred Siegel, *The Future Once Happened Here: New York, D.C., L.A., and the Fate of America's Big Cities* (New York, 1998), 235 and 61.

7. Thomas, *Redevelopment and Race,* 150.

8. Interview with Herb Boyd, in Georgakas and Surkin, *Detroit: I Do Mind Dying.* Updated Edition. (Cambridge: South End Press, 1998), 219.

9. Boyd, in *Detroit: I Do Mind Dying,* 221.

10. Ibid., 220.

11. Interview with Edna Ewell Watson, in Georgakas and Surkin, *Detroit: I Do Mind Dying.* Updated Edition. (Cambridge: 1998), 222.

12. Thomas Brooks, "Workers White and Black: DRUM Beats in Detroit," *Dissent* (January–February 1970): 10.

13. Ibid., 6.

14. Widick, 225.

15. Brooks, 7.

16. Interview with Sheila Murphy Cockrel, in Georgakas and Surkin, *Detroit: I Do Mind Dying,* 211.

17. Interview with George Crockett, in Robert Mast, ed., *Detroit Lives* (Philadelphia, 1994), 169.

18. For a history of TDU, see Dan LaBotz, *Rank and File Rebellion* (New York, 1990).

19. For more on worker dissent after the 1970s, see Kim Moody, *An Injury to All: The Decline of Business Unionism* (New York, 1988).

Epilogue

1. *Michigan Chronicle,* 29 May 1971.

2. Dr. Ames Robey, "Not Guilty by Reason of Insanity Evaluation," 19 December 1972, Box 7, Ronald Glotta Collection, the Walter P. Reuther Library of Labor and Urban Affairs, Detroit.

3. Dr. Lynn Blunt, "Report," 1 September 1971, Box 7, RGC.

4. Dr. Lynn Blunt, "Report," and Dr. Ames Robey, "Psychiatric Evaluation," Box 7, RGC.

5. Robey, "Not Guilty by Reason of Insanity Evaluation."

6. Robey, "Psychiatric Evaluation" and "Not Guilty by Reason of Insanity Evaluation."

7. James Johnson Jr., personal affidavit, 19 August 1971, letter to sister Marva Johnson from Johnson, 31 August 1971, Box 3, RGC.

8. Ibid.

9. Ibid.

10. Robey, "Psychiatric Evaluation."

11. Blunt, "Report."

12. Ibid., 4.

13. Dr. Santiago Caberto, "Exam," 8 December 1971, Box 7, RGC.

14. Howard Simpson Jr., "Notes," Box 7, RGC.

15. Dr. Gordon Forrer to R. G. Moir, 9 September 1971, Box 3, RGC.

16. Caberto, "Initial Psychiatric Evaluation," 14 November 1973, Box 3, RGC.

17. Jalal Ahmed, M.D., "Progress Report," 15 November 1973, Box 3, RGC.

18. James Johnson Jr., *Plaintiff-Appellee v. Chrysler Corporation*, Defendant-Appellant, State of Michigan, Workman's Compensation Appeal Board, "Brief in Support of Motion to Take Additional Testimony," August 1974, Box 7, RGC.

19. Johnson, Brief on Appeal of Defendant-Appellant (p. 62), 29 August 1974, Box 5, RGC.

20. Ibid., 45.

21. Johnson, Affidavit of Dr. Ames Robey, February 1975, Box 5, RGC.

22. Ibid.

23. James Johnson Jr. to the Workmen's Compensation Appeal Board, 19 August 1975, Box 3, RGC.

24. James Johnson Jr., letter, 15 April 1975, Box 3, RGC.

25. Trial transcript (pp. 275–76), March 1976, Box 3, RGC.

26. Ron Glotta to Eugene Labelle, letter regarding investigation, 2 September 1979, Box 3, RGC.

27. *Detroit Free Press,* 3 July 1976.

28. Ibid.

29. *Detroit Free Press,* 3 July 1979.

Index

Page numbers in italics refer to photographs.